The Word:
Cover to Cover in 100 days

Translated by Haena Lee

A third-generation Christian, Haena Lee received her bachelor's degree from Grove City College, a Christian liberal arts college in Grove City, Pennsylvania. She attended the Graduate School of Translation and Interpretation at Ewha Womans University in Seoul, Korea.

The Word: Cover to Cover in 100 Days

1st edition is printed in August 25, 2021
Published by Kyujang Publishing Company
Edited and Designed by Kyujang Publishing Company
Phone : +822-578-0003
Email : kyujang0691@gmail.com
HomePage : www.kyujang.com
Address: 20, Maeheon-ro 16-gil, Seocho-gu, Seoul 06770, Republic of Korea

Originally published in Korean under the title
말씀관통 100일 통독 (which means The Word: Cover to Cover in 100 Days)

ISBN 979-11-6504-233-2 03230

The Word:

Cover to Cover in 100 Days

Hong SungGun

Translated by Haena Lee

NCMN NATIONS-CHANGER MOVEMENT & NETWORK · KYUJANG

Now Is the Time for the Word of God to Flourish

Renewed Like the Eagle

August 2011 was a year of many changes. As I did every year, I spent one week in fasted prayer seeking the face of the Lord. It was a special time for me. When I asked the Lord what it was that I should strive for in the new year at the end of December 2010, He replied, 'You must be renewed.' He also told me the areas in which I must renew myself.

'You, the ministries and organizations that have been currently entrusted to you, and the church must all be renewed. But above all, you must first renew yourself.'

I responded with an "Amen!" and resolved to spend my time first renewing myself. Coincidentally, it was around that time I received a video about an eagle in an email. That video helped me determine the specifics of how I would renew myself. This is the story of the eagle.

"The eagle has the longest life span of all birds, and like

humans, it can live up to 70 years. But in order to live to such an age, the eagle must first make a fateful decision at around 40. At this period of its life, the eagle's long beak becomes bent and grows into its neck; its sharp talons are no longer able to grab prey as they harden in their long and bent form. The eagle's once majestic feathers become too heavy and thick for its muscles and make it difficult for the eagle to fly.

It is at this time the eagle must decide whether to simply wait for its eventual demise and die within a year or seek a different path. If it chooses the latter it will fly to a mountain top and there, build and sit on a nest on the edge of a cliff for 150 days, neither eating nor flying. Doing so will help it live for another 30 years. During this time, the eagle continually bashes its beak against rocks until it completely plucks it out. When its beak has fallen off, the eagle waits motionless in its nest for days, sometimes even weeks, until a new beak grows in its place.

As soon as its new beak has grown, the eagle begins to pluck the inwardly bent claws off its feet one by one. The claws of an eagle act as a buffer for its nerves, meaning that it is excruciatingly painful for the eagle to remove its talons. No matter how much it bleeds and scars while pulling its claws out with its beak, the eagle must not eat until it has plucked out the very last of its talons. The eagle then sits once more in its nest for a long time until its new claws have grown back in.

Lastly, the eagle plucks at its old heavy feathers one at a time with its new beak and claws. Then, the eagle once again sits motionless in its nest until new lighter and stronger feathers have grown back in. After having persevered for a very lonely 150 days of fighting for its life on the edge of a high cliff in solitude, the eagle waits for a warm air current to rise over the land. This is because the eagle could crash into a cliff trying to fly with wing muscles that have atrophied after a long period of inactivity. So, it is by using this warm air current to gradually rise into the skies and rebuild its muscle strength that the eagle is able to once again soar high and ultimately extend its life for another 30 years."

After watching this video, I decided to take the time to remain before the Lord. If the eagle took 150 days to renew itself, I decided that I would take 180 days to do so. But towards the end of June that year, I found my wings unchanged. Moreover, after six months, they even felt heavier than before. I grew anxious. Being renewed was not a matter of time. I learned that while my own determination is important, it is only when the Lord renews me that I can actually become renewed.

I decided to spend time and stay in the presence of the Lord, no matter how long it took. And in order to do so, I decided to lay down everything that was on my plate at the time. So, in July, I gave up all the ministries of which I had been in charge.

All Revolutions Start with the Word

At the end of August, I spent a week at a prayer center engaging in fasted prayer. During that time, the Lord told me, 'I will renew you.' This was a time of hope. Only after I had laid everything down and come into the presence of the Lord, seeking His will and His will only, did the Lord tell me to begin a new ministry.

That was the beginning of "NCMN (Nations-Changer Movement & Network)." Its aim is to establish the Kingdom of God by kickstarting a revolution that is found upon the Word of God in every realm of society: from politics (including law and the military), the economy, education, mass media, festivals (including the arts, entertainment, and sports), religion, science and technology (including medicine) to the family. Because the central force to lead such a revolution is in the church, the Korean local church is aiding in building this new ministry.

The Lord showed me exactly where to start as I began preparing for this ministry. It was in the realms of 'the Bible,' 'leadership,' and 'finances' that He wanted me to start. I decided to set aside a year as the preparation period for the 'Shema Bible School,' a school designed to provide a biblical foundation, the 'Changer Leadership School,' a school to enact leadership and change, and the 'King's Finances School,' a school central to all these efforts.

During the International YWAM Leadership Conference in Mexico in December 2011, the Lord spoke to me and said, 'You have been renewed.' Although there were no palpable signs of change, I received His words with faith. Since then I have undergone the progress of having my beak, talons, and wings all renewed.

I initiated the three ministries of NCMN beginning in the

fall of 2012. I first founded the Shema Bible School and the Changer Leadership School and structured a 40 to 50-hour curriculum for each. Then, in July 2013, I founded the King's Finances School.

The first class of the Shema Bible School started as a 6-week course in the winter of 2011. In the winter of 2012, the second class opened as a 7-week course. In 2013, the course was extended to 9 weeks and the third class of the Shema Bible School began in September of that year. This book was published as part of that process.

The revolution of a country should not be built upon the ideas, methods, or strategies of man but must be founded solely upon the Bible, the Word of God. This is because changes within a country all take place as part of God's plan. In Genesis Chapter 1 Verses 26 through 28, God gives a commandment to those created in His image. This commandment is also called the 'cultural mandate' (It echoes Jesus' 'Greatest Commandment' in Matthew Chapter 28 Verses 18 through 20). The "culture" here is the "culture that reflects the character of God through His principles and by His power."

God's principle is written in the Bible alone. The Bible is the textbook of all things. The Word of God is a plumb rule: a plumb line is that attached to a board to ascertain the level of alignment. God created the world with His Word, and with His Word, He holds the world. So in order to partake in God's wondrous works, the Bible, the Word of God, must first flourish in us. This is because the building of righteous leadership and financial principles begins through the Bible.

The principles to set each realm of society upright are within the Bible. The Book of Deuteronomy can be considered the guidelines that established God's Kingdom in the land of Canaan, which had previously been promised to Israel. And at its core, there is only the Word of God. 'Shema' is the central message. Shema has the meaning of "hear" as in "Hear, O Israel" written in Deuteronomy 6:4-9. It means that we need to hear the Word of God and make it our plumb rule for everything.

Now is the time for God's Word to flourish. Now is the time to make the Word of God the standard in both our personal lives and in all areas of society. That is where we will begin to see a revival. Let us hear the Word of the Lord! I sincerely hope that you are encouraged through this book, *The Word: Cover to Cover in 100days.*

Shema! I love you.

A fellow lover of the Word,
Hong SungGun

C O N T E N T S

GENESIS בראשית

ת [a] בָּרָא אֱלֹהִים אֵת הַשָּׁמַיִם וְאֵת הָאָ

וְחֹשֶׁךְ עַל־פְּנֵי תְהוֹם וְרוּחַ אֱלֹהִים מְ

אֱלֹהִים יְהִי אוֹר וַיְהִי־אוֹר׃ 4 וַיַּרְ

וַיַּבְדֵּל אֱלֹהִים בֵּין הָאוֹר וּבֵין הַחֹ

וֹם וְלַחֹשֶׁךְ קָרָא לָיְלָה וַיְהִי־עֶרֶב

יֹּאמֶר אֱלֹהִים יְהִי רָקִיעַ בְּתוֹךְ הַמָּ

7 וַיַּעַשׂ אֱלֹהִים אֶת־הָרָקִיעַ וַיַּבְדֵּל

בֵּין הַמַּיִם אֲשֶׁר מֵעַל לָרָקִיעַ [a] וַיְהִי

שָׁמָיִם וַיְהִי־עֶרֶב וַיְהִי־בֹקֶר יוֹם

יִקָּווּ הַמַּיִם מִתַּחַת הַשָּׁמַיִם אֶל־מָקוֹ

׃ 10 וַיִּקְרָא אֱלֹהִים ׀ לַיַּבָּשָׁה אֶרֶץ

אֱלֹהִים כִּי־טוֹב׃ 11 וַיֹּאמֶר אֱלֹהִים

THE OLD TESTAMENT

The Pentateuch

The five books of Genesis, Exodus, Leviticus, Numbers, and Deuteronomy are referred to as the Pentateuch. These five books record the preparation process to use all nations as a channel for His blessings beginning with the creation of the world, choosing Abraham to realize His masterplan for all the earth, and then raising Abraham's descendants to become a nation who then become His people. We also find the Great High Priest, Jesus, in the Pentateuch.

The keyword in Genesis is "toledoth (meaning generations, genesis)." 'God's image' means living in close relationship with God and in a way that exerts influence on the world. The toledoth does an excellent job of showing who it is that is able to live in such a manner.

The keywords of Exodus are "royal priesthood." God leads His people out of the land of Egypt and first prepares them in Mount Sinai so that they may live as "a royal priesthood, a holy nation" in the land of Canaan. The Ten Commandments and the Tabernacle are both good representations of this.

The keywords of Leviticus are "be holy." God here

wants His people to live holy lives set apart from Canaanite culture and, by doing so, to influence all nations. Leviticus can be considered a "supplementary text to Exodus" which records the preparation of His people in Mount Sinai.

The keyword in Numbers is "wilderness." It records the journey that began in Mount Sinai until the people arrived in the plains of Moab across from the land of Canaan. The actions of the people in the wilderness were marked by disobedience, grumbling, and refusal. As a result, the people wandered in the wilderness for 40 years until the generation of Egypt perished and the generation of the wilderness arose.

The keyword in Deuteronomy is "shema (hear)." It is Moses' last message from the plains of Moab as they conclude wandering through the wilderness for 40 years, poised to enter Canaan. Here, the people hear how they enter into the land of Canaan and establish a Christian nation.

GENESIS

TOLEDOTH (GENERATION)

The Hebrew name of the Book of Genesis, Bereshit, is taken directly from the first words of Genesis Chapter 1 Verse 1, "in the beginning." However, as with the Septuagint, the book later took on the name Genesis ('generation' in English), the Greek translation of the keyword of Genesis, "toledoth." Genesis means 'the beginning or generation' of something, or 'genealogy' or 'birth.' That is why the first book of the Bible is now called "Genesis."

Understanding Genesis

Genesis is broadly divided into two sections. From Chapter 1 through Chapter 11, God, the Creator of the universe, makes man, places him in that universe, and makes him rule over the world. The core content of this section comprises events such as the Garden of Eden and man's sin, Noah's flood, and the Tower of Babel. Many struggle to comprehend the meaning of these chapters. Rather than understanding them as historical events, they consider these instead to be legends, symbolic, or as fantastical writings from a prescientific era. They also tend to consider historical accounts or real events, those which take place after Chapter 12, as the beginning of Israel.

However, Genesis does not separate Chapters 1 through 11 and Chapter 12 to the end as completely different sections of the book. Chapter 12 does not introduce Abraham as a historical figure that suddenly emerged out of nowhere. The Bible begins its genealogical account not with Abraham but with Terah in Chapter 11 (Gen. 11:27-32) in order to show that the events of Chapter 1 through 11 and those of Chapter 12 to the end are not separated into two distinct sections and that these events take place as part of a single historical thread that continues through time and space. Psalms Chapter 136 treats the events which take place in between Chapters 1 through 11 and those after as historical facts that have occurred on the same historical continuum.

We must begin with the understanding that the accounts of Genesis Chapter 1 through 11 provide amazing historical value and insight if we are to truly understand these chapters. They are the most important part in the Bible. It is only with such an understanding that we will be able to understand and interpret these times in which we live today.

The Book of the Beginning

Genesis is the "book of the beginning." It explains how everything in this world first began with God's creation. As stated in Hebrews Chapter 11 Verse 3, "By faith we understand that the universe was created by the word of

God," Genesis accounts for the beginning of light, plants, animals, mankind, and all things. Specifically, Genesis tells the story of the beginning of mankind until Chapter 11 and then tells the story of the beginning of the Hebrew nation from Chapter 12.

Chapter 1 is the beginning of man and woman; Chapter 3, of sin; Chapter 4, of the family and of the city of Enoch, which was named after Enoch, the son of Cain. Chapter 10 explains how the three sons of Noah lived apart while referencing the names of the 70 nations. Chapter 11 describes the events at the Tower of Babel and tells the story of how the languages of this world came to be. Chapter 12 explains the beginnings and formation of the Hebrew nation. It explains how the nation first began with Abraham, and then continued on with Isaac and Jacob, ultimately forming the Hebrew nation and the 12 tribes of Israel.

The Book of Separation

We can also call this book "the book of separation." Chapter 1 tells us that God separated light from dark and made the expanse; He separated the waters that were under and above it. Chapter 3 explains man's separation from God. In Chapter 10, it is recorded that the earth was divided. This refers to the division of the two brothers, Peleg and Joktan, who are the sons of Eber and the descendants of Shem. They went their separate ways into the east and the west respectively. This event is especially noteworthy in that is also recorded in 1 Chronicles 1:19.

Also, the languages are divided and all the people are scattered by language and region due to the Tower of Babel in Chapter 11. Then, beginning in Chapter 13, we are told of the separation between Abraham and Lot, Isaac and Ishmael, and Jacob and Esau.

Toledoth

The word toledoth plays an important role when speaking of the structure of the book of Genesis. Toledoth refers to the "beginning or generation" or "origin or genealogy" of something. To put the structure of this book in very simple terms, we can separate it into the event-centric chapters of 1 through 11 and the people-centric chapters of 12 through 50. Creation and the fall, the flood and Babel; Abraham and Isaac, Jacob and Joseph: these four events and people are at the center of it all. However, consideration of Genesis in a toledoth (genealogy)-centric manner is required for a more accurate and detailed look at the book. Genesis is separated into ten toledoths.

The first four chapters explain how the heavens and the earth began through toledoth recorded in Chapter 2 Verse 4; Chapter 5 Verse 1 through Chapter 6 Verse 8 detail Adam's genealogy; Chapter 6 Verse 9 through Chapter 9 account for Noah's family tree; Chapter 11 Verse 1 through Chapter 10 Verse 9 provide the family trees of Shem, Ham, and Japheth, the sons of Noah; then Chapter 10 Verses 10 through 26 once again highlight Shem's family tree to show us the areas that are of interest to God. Moving on, Chapter 11 Verse

27 through Chapter 25 Verse 11 show Terah's genealogy, explaining how the beginning of Abraham started with Terah. Chapter 25 Verses 12 through 18 explain Ishmael's family tree; Chapter 25 Verses 19 through 35, Isaac's; all of Chapter 36, Esau's; and Chapters 37 through 50 account for Jacob's family tree.

Looking at the amount of page space given to each of the family trees, we can gain an understanding of what God considers to be important as well as what He considers to be of lesser importance. For instance, Shem's family was emphasized over the other sons of Noah, Isaac's over Ishmael's, and Jacob's over Esau's.

The God of Abraham, Isaac, and Jacob

In Genesis, God is introduced as the "God of Abraham, Isaac, and Jacob" from time to time. These three people help us see the God of the Trinity. Through Abraham, we see God the Father; through Isaac, we see Jesus Christ, God the Son; and through Jacob, we get a glimpse of God the Holy Spirit. These three people also help us understand the role of each. Abraham shows us God the Father's vision and pioneering; Isaac shows us Jesus Christ the Son's sacrifice, obedience, and communion with God; Jacob shows us how God the Holy Spirit guides and refines us.

Abraham's Faith

Genesis shows us the many different dimensions of Abraham's growth in faith. Abraham begins his journey of faith when he obeys God's words and goes to the land of Canaan. But there are also periods of disobedience in Abraham's life where he turns away from his faith.

In Chapter 12, Abraham flees to Egypt to escape his circumstances when famine strikes the land of Canaan. His actions have a very negative impact on his life. When Abraham and Lot separate in Chapter 13, Abraham correctly chooses the land to live in from God's point of view. However, in Chapter 16, he could not wait because he was impatient with the word of God's promise. As a result, he took the maid Hagar based on his wife Sarah's opinion, causing serious difficulties and discord in his family.

But overall, God said that Abraham was a man of faith, and he regarded this as the greatest righteousness in his life. Through Abraham, we can learn the consequences of acting according to our faith and the consequences of acting based on our circumstances and our own thoughts.

The God of Promises

In Genesis, we see the way in which God makes covenants and fulfills them through people. We see His covenant with Abraham (Ch. 12,13,15,17,22), his son Isaac (Ch. 26), his son Jacob (Ch. 28), and how He fulfills this covenant with the 12 sons of Jacob (Exodus Ch.3,19).

God's covenant is threefold. First, it is a covenant about land. God tells Abraham that He will give the land of Canaan to him as an inheritance. Second, God promises descendants. And third, He promises to bless all the nations through

Abraham's offspring.

God makes this covenant with Abraham, then not with Ishmael but with Isaac, not with Esau but with Jacob. Then, He continues the covenant with the twelve sons of Jacob. In Exodus 19:5-6, God makes a covenant with the entire nation of Israel with the words, "You shall be to me a kingdom of priests and a holy nation."

The same covenant is continued with the church of the New Testament. He tells us in Acts 1:8, "But you will receive power when the Holy Spirit has come upon you, and you will be my witnesses in Jerusalem and in all Judea and Samaria, and to the end of the earth." And in Matthew 28:19, He says, "Go therefore and make disciples of all nations."

God is faithful and keeps His promises. He is an Almighty God. The covenant He made with Abraham, Isaac, and Jacob was fulfilled after 570 years. Just as it is written in Hebrews 6:11-12, "And we desire each one of you to show the same earnestness to have the full assurance of hope until the end, so that you may not be sluggish, but imitators of those who through faith and patience inherit the promises," the path to fulfilling God's promises is through diligence, faith, and patience.

Genesis calls on us to be participants in God's covenant. God is only interested in two things: first, in blessing us, and second, in blessing nations through us. God wants us to heed His covenant and to give ourselves to Him.

Outline

Chapers 1-4	The history of the heavens and the earth
Chapers 5-6:8	Adam's genealogy
Chapers 6:9-9	Noah's family tree
Chapers 10-11:9	Shem, Ham, and Japheth's family tree
Chaper 11:10-26	Shem's family tree
Chapers 11:27-25:11	Terah (Abraham)'s family tree
Chaper 25:12-18	Ishmael's family tree
Chapers 25:19-35	Isaac's family tree
Chaper 36	Esau (Edom)'s family tree
Chapers 37-50	Jacob's family tree

Voice Outline

GENESIS

100-Day Bible Reading Plan

		CHECK
Day 1	Genesis 1-10	
Day 2	Genesis 11-20	
Day 3	Genesis 21-30	
Day 4	Genesis 31-40	
Day 5	Genesis 41-50	

EXODUS

A KINGDOM OF PRIESTS AND A HOLY NATION

Exodus reveals God's purpose to lead Israel to the Promised Land so that it can become a great nation and a kingdom of priests that blesses all the nations as promised to Abraham, Isaac, and Jacob in Genesis. It also shows how God calls people to work with and through Him for this purpose.

God Calls Moses

God called Moses. Moses' calling was to save the people of Israel, lead them, and settle them in the Promised Land. Moses, however, knowing the difficulty of the task at hand, was afraid.

In the 430 years that Jacob and the 70 members of his family spent in Egypt after entering it, their descendants' numbers proliferated to between two to three-and-a-half million, growing into a great nation. They had been forced to live as slaves in a foreign land for over 300 years. Moses' task was to deliver these people from what was the most powerful nation on earth at the time, cut through the desert, settle in the Promised Land of Canaan, and establish a new nation.

Let us take a moment to picture the Israelites as they passed through the desert. They were a poverty-stricken people, unable to meet the most basic needs of life on their own. They were without medical facilities, schools, roads, or proper sanitary facilities. Furthermore, they were completely lacking in any legislative processes, economic and currency systems, and welfare and ethical labor policies. They possessed no scientific, agricultural, or industrial technologies; they neither had a military nor any territory of their own. They were an enormous nation with no sovereignty or religious system. Simply, they were the greatest refugee nation on earth. They were surrounded by danger: an unforgiving environment, hunger, thirst, fear, and uncertainty.

It was under these circumstances that God called on Moses to do His work. Despite the vast number of challenges that lay ahead, Moses had to deliver the people from Egypt, cross the treacherous desert, evict the militarily strong nations of Canaan, and settle and establish a nation in those lands. This was a truly overwhelming mandate for Moses.

There is one thing God taught Moses beforehand to help him handle this task. He taught Moses how to trust that God will do all that is necessary, to rely on Him instead of relying on his own strength and knowledge. It was to teach Moses of God's greatness and that these circumstances are nothing before God.

What God demanded from Moses was not 'ability,' it was 'loyalty.' Moses trusted God and obeyed Him.

The Passover

Moses performs nine marvels before the eyes of Pharaoh, the ruler of Egypt. Turning water to blood, the infestations of frogs, lice, and flies, the pestilence of livestock, boils, hails, locusts, and darkness. These signs should have been enough to soften Pharaoh's heart. Yet Pharaoh's heart hardened even more.

The Passover was the decisive event that caused Pharaoh to surrender, enabling the people of Israel to leave Egypt. During the Passover, only those houses marked with a lamb's blood above their doorposts and lintel were spared; those that were not lost their firstborn, man or animal, regardless of the social standing of the residents. Pharaoh's firstborn was no exception. This was the event that led to the Israelites' Exodus from Egypt.

It is written, "Knowing that you were ransomed from the futile ways inherited from your forefathers, not with perishable things such as silver or gold, but with the precious blood of Christ, like that of a lamb without blemish or spot" (1 Pet. 1:18-19), "In him we have redemption through his blood, the forgiveness of our trespasses, according to the riches of his grace" (Eph. 1:7), and "Therefore, brothers, since we have confidence to enter the holy places by the blood of Jesus… let us draw near [to God] with a true heart" (Heb. 10:19,22).

Salvation comes only through the blood of Jesus Christ. Just as the Israelites received their freedom from slavery in Egypt with the blood of the lamb during the Passover…

The Ten Commandments

God leads the people of Israel to the land of Canaan through Moses. But before bringing all His plans to completion, God makes them stay at the foot of Mt. Sinai in the wilderness for almost a year and begins the preparations to establish His Kingdom. He then gives them the Ten Commandments. He first laid down the laws on how the Israelites should conduct themselves before God as well as the laws that should be followed as they interact with each other.

He also ordered the construction and completion of the tabernacle. This signifies the centrality that God should have in our lives. It is also why God prepared the Israelites at the foothills of Mount Sinai and taught them the importance of worship and living a God-centric life before they were able to continue in their journey. There, He taught them how to organize themselves and effectively manage a military, treat disease, establish laws on sanitation, and the rules of leadership in order to prepare them for the nation the Israelites would establish upon entry into the land of Canaan.

Giving the land of Canaan to the Israelites as their inheritance was not God's sole purpose in bringing them out of Egypt. His greater purpose was to make Israel a nation that serves Him, glorifies Him, and shines His glory upon all the nations. "Now therefore, if you will indeed obey my voice and keep my covenant, you shall be my treasured possession among all peoples, for all the earth is mine and you shall be to me a kingdom of priests and a holy nation" (Ex. 19:5-6).

The same applies to us who are living in the era of the New Testament. "But you are a chosen race, a royal priesthood, a holy nation, a people for his own possession, that you may proclaim the excellencies of him who called you out of darkness into his marvelous light" (1 Pet. 2:9).

While staying at the foothills of Mount Sinai, Moses climbed it three times over a period of nearly nine months and spent time preparing the Ten Commandments and statutes, God's covenant with the people, God's law, the tabernacle, and the rules for priests. The book of Exodus concludes with the Israelites completing their preparations to establish a God-fearing nation in the land of Canaan beyond the desert as well as the completion and dedication of the tabernacle.

The Tabernacle

The tabernacle has a truly fascinating construction process. In Hebrews 8:5, we are told, "They serve a copy and shadow of the heavenly things. For when Moses was about to erect the tent, he was instructed by God, saying, 'See that you make everything according to the pattern that was shown you on the mountain.'" In other words, the construction of the tabernacle was not based on Moses' own thoughts, his learnings, or decisions through meetings.

Moses saw the actual tabernacle on Mount Sinai. The tabernacle he built in the desert was an exact copy of what God had shown to him on the mountain. That is why we are told that the tabernacle was a 'copy and shadow' (Heb. 8:5;

9:23-24). The tabernacle was a copy of the heavenly things just as a model home serves as an accurate representation before purchasing a new home. Moses saw the actual pattern of the tabernacle. This was also the case for Noah when he was building the ark. It is written, "By faith Noah, being warned of God of things not seen as yet, moved with fear, prepared an ark" (Heb. 11:7). Here, the phrase 'moved with fear,' means 'to move as God instructed' and is the same word that is used about Joseph in Matthew 2:22, "being warned of God in a dream, he turned aside into the parts of Galilee" (Matt. 2:22).

Exodus Chapters 39 and 40 describe the completion phase of the construction of the tabernacle. In Chapter 39, the phrase, "As the Lord commanded Moses," is repeated a total of ten times (39:1, 5, 7, 21, 26, 29, 31, 32, 42, 43). Then, in Chapter 40, the same phrase appears another 7 times (40:19, 21, 23, 25, 27, 29, 32). After seeing the completed tabernacle, Moses says, "They had done it as the Lord had commanded" and blesses the people (Ex. 39:43). Moses supervised the construction to ensure the tabernacle was built in accordance with what God had shown to him, just as an architect would check to see if construction was completed according to the architectural plans.

In the end, we are told, "Thus did Moses: according to all that the Lord commanded him, so did he" (Ex. 40:16). Then, the cloud of God covered the tabernacle. Here, the cloud of God represents God's presence.

The most important task for us is not to have many ideas or solutions; rather, it is to go before the presence of the Lord and listen. Then, it is to obey His words exactly. Therein lie God's blessings and anointing. Therein lie His presence and glory.

Outline

Chapter 1	Israel under oppression
Chapters 2-14	Exodus God calls Moses, Moses and Pharaoh, Ten Plagues, the Passover, Exodus, Crossing of the Red Sea
Chapters 15-18	The Journey to Mount Sinai The Song of Moses and Miriam, Manna and quail, Water from the Rock, Battle with Amalek, Leadership
Chapters 19-24	Law given to Moses at Sinai Proclamation of the Law, the Ten Commandments, Social laws
Chapters 25-40	Rules for the Tabernacle and Priests Instructions about the tabernacle, instructions about the priesthood, the golden calf incident, the completion of the Tabernacle

Voice Outline

EXODUS

100-Day Bible Reading Plan

		CHECK
Day 6	Exodus 1-10	
Day 7	Exodus 11-20	
Day 8	Exodus 21-30	
Day 9	Exodus 31-40	

LEVITICUS

YOU SHALL THEREFORE BE HOLY, FOR I AM HOLY

We can consider Leviticus the 'Hebrews of the Old Testament.' Conversely, you also often hear Hebrews being referred to as the 'Leviticus of the New Testament.' Just as Hebrews is filled with images of Jesus Christ as the Great High Priest, Leviticus contains a vast array of representations of the beauty of Jesus Christ. Leviticus and Hebrews have much in common. They speak of the holiness of God, how He, in His holiness, compels us to lead holy lives, and lay down ways in which we can come before Him.

The phrase, "You shall be holy, for I the LORD your God am holy," (Lev. 19:2) is critical in the book of Leviticus. The word 'holy' appears 90 times and the word 'consecrate' appears 17 times. Nouns, verbs, and adjectives related to the word 'holy' appear a total of 261 times. Furthermore, the words 'separate' and 'redeem' appear 200 times. The word 'atonement' appears 36 times. The Book of Leviticus focuses heavily on ways to come before God and remain in His presence.

The Way to Come Before Our Holy God

Leviticus presents five types of offerings when explaining ways to come before God. These are the burnt offering, the meal offering, the peace offering for thanksgiving, the sin offering for the forgiving of sins, and the trespass offering. A requirement and constant for all these was the offering of either a lamb or a calf.

When someone brought a lamb or calf to the Holy Place, the priest would kill it and bring the blood to the altar. God would see this and forgive that person of their sins and consider them then 'holy.' After making our offerings, God opens ways for us to come before him. These offerings symbolize Jesus Christ, the Lamb of God, who was to come and die for all our sins. Nothing but the blood of Jesus Christ can cleanse us from our sins and make it possible for us to come before God.

However, something to be grateful for is God's generosity toward the poor. God allowed those who did not have the means to offer a calf or lamb to bring a dove as an offering instead. And for those who could not afford even a dove, God allowed them to offer fine flour instead. Such is the generosity of our God who allows us to come before Him according to our means.

Christianity is not a religion of strict nomism. Neither is it about focusing on religious formalities and rituals. Our living God wants us to come before Him with love. Leviticus tells us that God forgives our sins because He loves us and that He deeply wants us to come before Him and remain in His presence.

Chapters 1 through 7 discuss the five kinds of offerings and Chapters 8 through 10 tell us about the priests. These chapters tell us about the priesthood's service and ministry as well as its attire. A priest is someone who brings offerings before God on behalf of others. They also proclaim and teach God's Word so that all of God's people may hear and take action.

The Way to Remain in the Presence of God

The first half of the book (Chapter 1-10) presents the way to come before God and the latter half (Chapter 11-27) presents the way to remain in the presence of our holy God.

Chapters 11 through 15 explain what it is to live a cleansed life. We are told what we can and cannot eat, from animals of the land to the fish of the sea. These chapters reveal the path we must take to lead holy lives. Some verses explain how a new mother becomes clean after giving birth. Leviticus lays down the path to living a wholly clean and holy life, explaining how to be cleansed of skin diseases or leprosy as well as mildew in homes and on clothing.

Chapter 16 speaks of the 'Day of Atonement,' which is the one day a year the priest enters the Most Holy Place. This chapter represents how Jesus, with His death on the cross of Calvary, gave His life as a ransom so that we may come before God. Chapters 17 through 22 then once again reiterate how we can live a cleansed life.

Beginning with Chapter 23, the book goes on to talk about

the seven 'feasts.' We are told how to live free and joyous lives reflecting on, celebrating, and being thankful for the saving grace that God has extended to us through each year.

In particular, the three largest feasts the Feast of Unleavened Bread, Pentecost, and Tabernacles were a time when all male Israelites would make a pilgrimage to the Temple to worship God and take joy in their salvation. The Feast of Unleavened Bread is the season to serve our God, who has given us our amazing salvation, with great joy. At the heart of this Feast lies one of the single most important events of the Exodus: the Passover. The Feast of Pentecost represents the descent of the Holy Spirit and a season to live by the power of the Holy Spirit. In other words, it signifies "the great spiritual harvest" of all nations. The Feast of Tabernacles is also called the Feast of the Tent. It is a season to commemorate the days of wandering in the desert and reflect upon how to live a life of the tent on this earth while loving the eternal Kingdom of God and living the life of a martyr at the same time.

These feasts are all feasts that tell us how to rejoice, take joy, and remember God's salvation while living on this earth. The Feast of the First fruits, or the Feast of Weeks, is a day on which the first fruits of the barley harvest are offered to God, the day on which the first fruits of the resurrection are guaranteed. The Feast of Trumpet, the first day of every seventh month, is a day of rest and a day to declare the Lord's Second Coming. The tenth day of the seventh month is the Day of Atonement. It is the day in which the high priest enters the Most Holy Place once a year. It is a symbol for us to remember that Jesus Christ redeemed us by dying on the cross.

The final part of Leviticus speaks of the weekly Sabbath, the Sabbatical year which is taken every seven years, and the Jubilee which is the fiftieth year at the end of seven cycles of Sabbatical years. These three time markers are there to remind us of the true freedom and rest God has provided us within Jesus Christ and to enable us to rejoice in the knowledge of this fact.

Generosity toward the Poor

More than any other book of the Bible, Leviticus delves deep into the heart that God has for the poor. God allows the poor to give doves or fine flour as offerings instead of a lamb or calf (Lev. 14:21,22); He mandates that grapes and grains should not be harvested bare so as to leave some for the poor (Lev. 19:10; 23:22); He tells us that we must not let a poor man leave with empty hands (Lev. 25:35). He also allows vowers who are too poor to pay the valuation pay according to what he can afford (Lev. 27:8); He mandates that when a brother becomes poor and sells part of his property, his next of kin shall redeem what his brother has sold (Lev. 25:25) and that if a brother becomes poor and sells himself to his brother, he shall not be made to serve his brother as a slave (Lev. 25:39). He also provides us freedom during our Sabbatical years.

God as a Person Who Speaks

The different laws of offerings, rules on priests, and seasons are not Moses' own ideas. Moses is not someone who drew up a religion or specific laws about offerings based on the education he received from school. Leviticus begins with the God who speaks. God is a person who speaks. Moses was merely a man who listened when God spoke and obeyed exactly as He said.

Chapter 1 Verse 1 of Leviticus begins with these amazing words, "The Lord called Moses and spoke to him." The same phrase is repeated 36 times, including the first verse. When God calls Moses in Exodus 3, God calls Moses' name. He tells Moses exactly what he is supposed to do. This was the relationship Moses had with God. It was not a vague belief in the existence of God where Moses performed religious acts based on his own experience, thoughts, and ideas. The relationship Moses had with God was one in which Moses listened to God's voice and heard the exact words spoken by God who is a person who speaks.

We see the same description in Numbers Chapter 1 Verse 1, "The Lord spoke to Moses." This phrase appears a total of 60 times in the book. Moses' relationship with God serves to present a clear depiction of how we must live and serve the Lord.

Outline

Chapters 1-10	The way to come before our holy God
Chapters 1-7	Laws of offerings
	The burnt offering, meal offering, peace offering, sin offering, and trespass offering
Chapters 8-10	Rules for priests
	Dedication, ministry
Chapters 11-27	The way to remain before our holy God
Chapters 11-15,17-22	Cleanliness laws
Chapter 16	The Day of Atonement
Chapters 23-24	The Seven Feasts
Chapter 25	The Sabbatical year and Jubilee year
Chapters 26-27	Vows

Voice Outline

LEVITICUS

100-Day Bible Reading Plan

		CHECK
Day 10	Leviticus 1-10	
Day 11	Leviticus 11-16	
Day 12	Leviticus 17-27	

NUMBERS

THE WILDERNESS EXPERIENCE

The Book of Numbers records the path the Israelites took in their journey from Mount Sinai to their arrival at the Promised Land. It outlines the routes they took as well as the events that took place during that time. In short, we could call the book of Numbers, 'the wilderness experience' of the Israelites.

Journey through the Wilderness

The Israelites set out from Rameses in Egypt on the fifteenth day of the first month, the day after the Passover (Exo. 12:37; Num. 33:3), reached the Red Sea past Succoth (Exo 14), crossed the Red Sea, and passed through Marah, Elim, and the wilderness of Sin (Exo. 15:22-18:27), and finally arrived at the wilderness of Sinai. That was on the third new moon (Exo. 19:1-2). We can see that they arrived in Mount Sinai about a month and a half after they left Rameses.

After arriving at Mount Sinai, the people of Israel remained there for 11 months and 19 days (Exo. 19:1-Num. 10:11). Then, they took an 11-day journey to Hazeroth (Num. 11:34-35; Deut.

1:2) from where they moved on to the wilderness of Paran at Kadesh. There, Moses sent twelve spies to scout the land of Canaan (Num. 13-14; Deut. 2:7,14).

The people of Israel, who believed the words of the ten faithless spies and cried, wept, and grumbled against God, left Kadesh-barnea and wandered around Edom and Moab for 38 years until everyone 20 years old and upward had died. Thus it is the second generation of Israelites born in the wilderness that was able to make it to the plains of Moab across from the River Jordan. The journey the Israelites took was along a v-shaped path: from Rameses in Egypt across the Red Sea to Mount Sinai, where they remained a while, then to Kadesh-barnea and unto the plains of Moab.

Chapter 1 Verse 1 to Chapter 10 Verse 11 covers the process of the Israelites preparing to march to Canaan from Mount Sinai. Then, Chapter 10 Verse 12 to Chapter 36 Verse 13 records the process of about 38 years of wandering in the wilderness from Mount Sinai to the plains of Moab, opposite Canaan. Although the distance from Sinai to the Promised Land was not that great, the journey unfortunately took 40 years. The reasons for this are well documented in Chapters 13 and 14.

When the Israelites passed through Hazeroth and arrived in Kadesh-barnea in the wilderness of Baran from Mount Sinai, they decided to remain there and send twelve spies to scout the lands that they would be going into beforehand. After spending 40 days spying, the spies returned with a branch with a single cluster of grapes to report back about the land. The lands were so fertile the branch had to be carried by two adult males. When the people of Israel saw the enormous cluster of grapes and heard the spies' first report, they were enthralled and overjoyed.

It is written, "They (spies) came to Moses and Aaron and to all the congregation of the people of Israel in the wilderness of Paran, at Kadesh. They brought back word to them and to all the congregation, and showed them the fruit of the land. And they told him, "We came to the land to which you sent us. It flows with milk and honey, and this is its fruit" (Num. 13:26-27).

However, ten out of the twelve men claim that the people of Israel will never be able to go into those lands. They said, "The people who dwell in the land are strong, and the cities are fortified and very large. And besides, we saw the descendants of Anak there" (Num. 13:28).

They cite three reasons why it is an impossible task. First, the giant race of the descendants of Anak lived in those lands. In other words, they said the difference in their sizes put them at a physical disadvantage. Second, the people of the land had a military armed with powerful weapons, putting the Israelites at an absolute disadvantage militarily. Third, the cities that the Israelites would have to conquer were very large and strong; they said these circumstances made it impossible for the Israelites to enter those lands. Archaeologists say that the fallen walls of Jericho were wide enough for two trains to pass through side by side. Such was the size and strength of the cities in the land of Canaan.

Caleb and Joshua

Upon hearing the words of the ten spies, all the people of Israel cried and grumbled about Moses. They began saying that all of them would end up dying in the desert. Seeing the people's reactions, Caleb told them boldly, "Let us go up at once and occupy it, for we are well able to overcome it" (Num. 13:30). But no one that heard believed him. Instead, they tried to stone him.

It was in that very moment that God appeared among them to judge who was right and who was wrong. God says that the words of Caleb are true and that those of the ten spies are false.

Why were that Caleb's words right? After all, Caleb too admitted that the descendants of Anak were just as strong as the ten spies had said. He was with them and saw their military and all their weapons; he also witnessed firsthand how strong and mighty those cities were. Caleb was not in denial of these facts. Nevertheless, Caleb was still able to say that they could conquer those lands because he believed in God's promise.

He believed in the promise that God had made to Abraham, Isaac, and Jacob: that He would give them the land of Canaan as an eternal inheritance. No matter how bleak or difficult the circumstances, Caleb believed that God would carry out His words in His power.

These are the words of Pastor Billy Graham, "When our God is small, the world looks big; but when our God is big, the world looks small."

To the ten spies, the world seemed enormous. But Caleb looked at God who was much greater.

God told the ten spies and all the Israelites who believed in their words and despaired and grumbled that they would all die in the wilderness as they said and believed. He told them that only the next generation would step into those lands. God tells them they will have to spend a year in the wilderness for each of the forty days the spies spent spying on the Promised Land. But He promises that Caleb and Joshua, who continued to have faith in the promise, will live and enter the Promised Land as they believed.

The Significance of Numbers

The Israelites' attitude in the wilderness serves as an example for us today, as stated in 1 Corinthians 10:1-13. Initially, they received the promise, came out of Egypt, and in God's grace witnessed and experienced God's amazing work. And yet most of them still perished in the wilderness.

"Do not be idolaters as some of them were...We must not indulge in sexual immorality... We must not put Christ to the test... Nor grumble, as some of them did and were destroyed by the Destroyer. Now these things happened to them as an example, but they were written down for our instruction, on whom the end of the ages has come" (1 Cor. 10:7-11).

The Israelites' main wrongdoing was to 'grumble.' They complained and moaned because of food (Num. 1), water (Num. 20), and the journey (Num. 21). God hears their words and judges them harshly. Another one was to 'rebel.' Aaron and Miriam rebelled against Moses (Num.12); the people of Israel rebelled against Moses and Aaron because of the descendants of Anak (Num. 14); and the most serious of these rebellions was when Korah, Dathan, and Abiram gathered 250 chiefs and rose up to rebel against Moses and Aaron (Num. 16). However, the Israelites' greatest wrongdoing was 'faithlessness' (Num. 13-14). It was their faithlessness that caused them to die in the wilderness without having set foot in the Promised Land (Heb.3:7-4:11).

However, what we must never forget is that despite everything else God extended His forgiveness, compassion, and patience to them. We must also remember the roles of Moses and Aaron who understood God's heart and prayed on behalf of the people as their leaders.

"Therefore he said he would destroy them—had not Moses, his chosen one, stood in the breach before him, to turn away his wrath from destroying them" (Psa. 106:23).

A Journey of Principle

In Chapter 1, we see there was a census on the entire population of Israel before they left Mount Sinai. Then, we see another census taking place in Chapter 26. Why might they have conducted two censuses? This is because the first one was a census of the generation that left Egypt while the second one, some forty years later, was of the new generation after the previous generation had died off. So, the population counted in the census of Chapter 1 was of the older generation out of Egypt and the population counted in the census of Chapter 26 was of the new generation born in the wilderness.

The Book of Numbers describes the progression of events, from how the generation out of Egypt died in the wilderness to how the new generation that was born in the wilderness arrived. Their story shows what it means to live on this earth as a believer in God.

'Will we live in reaction to our circumstances, or will we live by relying on God's words of promise?'

God commands us to influence the world and establish the Kingdom of God. But the world which we must influence is so potent that we often find ourselves being influenced by it. Many Christians speak of how difficult it is to influence the world. That is the reality we face as Christians every day. But we must not react as the ten spies did but respond as Caleb did. God wishes for us to influence the world. We need to have Caleb's heart.

The Tabernacle

The Book of Numbers also shows the principles that must be followed during a journey through the wilderness. At the center of every march, is the Tabernacle. The Tabernacle represents God's presence. It is the place where the Ark of the Covenant containing the words of God is kept. A cloud covered the Tabernacle and when it moved, the Tabernacle moved with it. The cloud is a representation of the guidance of the Holy Spirit and the Word.

In the center, there were the Levites who served the

Tabernacle. The twelve tribes of Israel marched around the Tabernacle in groups of three tribes, each group surrounding the north, east, south, and west sides of the Tabernacle. The tribe at the forefront of the procession was the tribe of Judah, which means 'praise' (Gen. 29:35). In Psalms 68:4, it is written, "Sing to God, sing praises to his name; lift up a song to him who rides through the deserts; his name is the Lord; exult before him!"

This verse depicts how God opened up a path in front of the Israelites and guided them as they marched through the desert singing His praises. Singing praises opens up a path in the wilderness. The image of the Israelites marching through the desert should be an image in our lives today. The Holy Spirit and the Word of God guide us. And as the tribe of Judah led the journey across the wilderness, our lives should be led by praise and worship. If we are able to do this, God will surely lead us with the Holy Spirit.

Outline

Chapters 1-10:10	**Preparation for the journey** The first census, encampment layout, the Levites, the Nazirite, the offerings of the tribal leaders, the first Passover
Chapters 10:11-12	**From Mount Sinai to the Kadesh-barnea in the wilderness of Paran** Beginning the journey, Kibroth-hattaavah and the graves of greed, Aaron and Miriam
Chapters 13-20	**Wandering in the desert** The spies and the report, Korah's conspiracy, Aaron's flowering staff, Moses strikes the stone twice, The death of Aaron
Chapters 21-36	**From Kadesh to the plains on Moab by the River Jordan** Victory at Hormah, fiery serpents, Balaam, Phinehas, the second census, Joshua as successor, the inheritance of the two tribes and the half-tribe, city of refuge

Voice Outline

NUMBERS

100-Day Bible Reading Plan

		CHECK
Day 13	Numbers 1-10	
Day 14	Numbers 11-20	
Day 15	Numbers 21-36	

DEUTERONOMY

GUIDELINE FOR THE ESTABLISHMENT OF A CHRISTIAN NATION

The Book of Deuteronomy can be considered the end of the Book of Numbers. After wandering for forty years, the people of Israel only had the River Jordan to cross before they could finally enter the land of Canaan. Deuteronomy is an account of the words spoken by God through Moses when they were on the other side of the River Jordan on the plains of Moab.

The events of the book took place over the course of two months, consisting of the month God spoke before Moses' death and the one month of mourning following his death. Moses was faithful until death. The Scriptures our Lord quoted when He was tested by Satan were all from the Book of Deuteronomy (Matt. 4:4,7,10).

Preparing to Enter Canaan

Before the generation from Egypt died and the next generation born in the wilderness could enter the land of Canaan, God needed to speak to them through Moses one last time. There was something He wished to reiterate to them.

The book of Deuteronomy is filled with information about "the preparations necessary to enter the land of Canaan, and how the Israelites must conduct themselves in the future."

With the exception of the death of Moses, the contents of Exodus, Leviticus, and Numbers are largely repetitive. It is for this reason that the phrase "The Lord said to Moses," is not repeated in the book of Deuteronomy as in the previous books. Deuteronomy repeatedly explains and elaborates certain issues, and underlines that the Israelites must act in accordance with God's words in Canaan.

The Book of Deuteronomy can be divided into three sections. The first section reflects upon the forty years of wandering in the desert, going over how God worked and how the people responded. The second section looks at how we must live going forward as well as the work that we must do. And finally, the third section is on how we must live once we enter Canaan in the future. In summary, Chapters 1-4 look back on the past 40 years; Chapters 5-26 arm us for today; Chapters 27-34 prepare us for what is coming.

The Second Law

Unlike the first generation there at Mount Sinai, the second generation needed to hear the words of God that were spoken on the mountain. That is why the book refers to the Ten Commandments again. The name 'Deuteronomy' literally means the "second law." In other words, the Book of Deuteronomy is a reiteration of God's commandment.

The phrases "the Lord your God," and "serve the Lord

your God," are repeated a total of 282 times in Deuteronomy (hereon, all repetition numbers are based on original texts). It shows that God is at the center of everything. It is also why the word "heart" appears 46 times, telling us to guard our hearts and serve with our hearts. References to fearing the Lord appear 11 times, references to purging the evil 9 times, and we see specific references teaching the next generation with an emphasis on education a total of 6 times. The Book of Deuteronomy also repeatedly reminds its readers to remember the past works of God a total of 15 times. When the events and circumstances facing us are overwhelming, we gain renewed strength by remembering all the things that God has done in the past. This is why the Book of Deuteronomy is filled with the word "remember."

One peculiarity to note, however, is that the book uses the present tense to describe the works God has done in the past. This is not a peculiarity but a declaration of the faith that God's works are not merely events of the past but that He does and will continue to work in the same way.

The Kingdom of God

The book also explains how to establish the Kingdom of God once in the land of Canaan. These are instructions on how we, in all areas of our lives, should live in accordance with God's will with the fundamental identity of a "Christian." The focus here is not partaking in but changing the culture of the world and establishing the Kingdom of God. That is why the words "Go in and take possession of the land that the

Lord swore to your fathers," are repeated a total of 72 times. And in Chapter 6:1-3, we are told, "Therefore, when you enter the land and possess it, keep my commands."

Chapter 6 Verses 4-9 can be considered the central passage in the Book of Deuteronomy. In Verse 4, it is written, "Hear, O Israel." The Hebrew word used for 'hear' is 'shema.' This is not telling us to simply hear God's words but to regard them as the plumb rule for our actions in all areas of our lives and live accordingly.

These words instruct us to build a Christian nation based on God's principles and values when we enter and seize the land of Canaan which is infested with worldly standards and values. God's words on government organization (Deut. 1:9-18), economic and financial relations (Deut. 15:1-10), and healthcare and sanitation (Deut. 23:9-14) reveal specific directions on how the Israelites should build a nation.

Leaders, in particular, were expected to transcribe the book with their own hands and read the book for the duration of their entire lives (Deut. 17-19). After crossing the River Jordan, the Israelites were given the mandate to record the book on large stones (Deut. 27:2-8). And every seven years, during the Feast of Tabernacles, priests were required to read these words before the entire congregation of Israel (Deut. 31:9-13).

Moses' First Sermon: A Reflection on the Past 40 Years (Chapters 1-4)

Moses delivered this sermon when all the preparations to enter Canaan from the plains of Moab across the Jordan River had been completed. His sermon is not about the strategy or tactics to be employed during the war. Rather, the focus was on the events of the past 40 years as they passed through the wilderness. Who God is, what God's principles are, and what there is to learn from their experiences in the wilderness were the questions that Moses felt were important to address. This was because it was the answer to these questions that would serve as the bedrock of the nation once in the Promised Land.

However, the Israelites were swayed by their circumstances and disbelief, responding with faithlessness and dissatisfaction despite God's promise of Canaan. The consequences of their disbelief were severe. Even with a clear promise, disbelief prevents them from seizing the Promised Land (Chapter 1).

The lands conquered through war on the eastern side of the River Jordan comprise the inheritance of two and a half tribes (the tribe of Reuben, the tribe of Gad, and half of the tribe of Manasseh; half of the territory allotted to the tribe of Manasseh fell on the east and half fell on the west of the River Jordan). The Israelites were able to defeat the strong and magnificent nations of these fertile lands not because they were powerful, but only because God gave them victory. This fact, that war belongs to God, becomes ever more evident when the Israelites cross the River Jordan to seize the land of Canaan (Chapters 2-3). We see Moses exhorting the people to obey God and His commands with the heart of a father instructing his children (Chapter 4).

Moses' Second Sermon: A Review of the Law (Chapters 5-26)

1. Moral Laws

Moses proclaims the Ten Commandments once again. However, the underlying motivation to heed these commandments should be love, not fear. The Ten Commandments further emphasize God's love for our salvation and life. In particular, the fifth commandment to honor one's parents includes the words "so that you may live long in the land the Lord your God has given you," as it is the key to receiving God's blessing and success (Chapter 5).

Similar to Chapter 4, Chapter 6 advises the Israelites to live a life of obedience in Canaan. Above all, this chapter serves to show them that we can build a strong nation by carving the Word of God in our hearts and obeying them. Chapter 7 strongly urges us the people to completely reject idol worship even after having entered the land of Canaan. If Chapter 6 says to "love God with all our hearts," Chapter 7 tells us to, "vigorously abhor sin." Chapter 8 'warns' the Israelites, telling them to take the learnings of the 40 years in the wilderness with them as they enter into the land of Canaan.

Chapters 9 and 10 remind the Israelites not to forget that when they enter into the land of Canaan and defeat the Canaanites, it will not be achieved by their power but only because God gave them victory. These chapters emphasize the need for the Israelites to fear, love, and serve God in the knowledge of the fact that they as a people have nothing to show for themselves in terms of power, wisdom, or righteousness. Obedience will bring the Israelites blessing whereas disobedience will only bring curses upon them (Chapter 11).

2. Ceremonial Laws

Chapter 12 reiterates how the Israelites should obey. The second commandment introduces a jealous God. This chapter explains how one must act before God. In particular, Chapter 13 speaks of the perils of idol worship.

Chapter 14 speaks about tithing and relief, or the work of taking care of the poor. Forgiving debt and setting slaves free (Chapter 15), three important feasts that must be observed (Chapter 16), and the ministries of priests and Levites (Chapters 17-18) are also addressed.

3. Civil Laws

While the previous chapters were on how the Israelites should conduct themselves before God, chapters hereon speak about how people should act in their relationships (Chapter 19). Chapter 20 speaks of laws regarding warfare and Chapters 21-26 talk about holiness in relationships as well as living a righteous life.

Moses' Third Sermon: Blessings and Curses of Future (Chapters 27-28)

Previous sermons outlined how the Israelites must act before God and toward people. In other words, they explained what is good and bad, and what it is that the law requires. This particular sermon, however, explains the means with which one can abide by those commandments. This sermon is a proclamation of God's words, blessings and curses, the unfolding of those words as we respond with a resounding "Amen," our responsibilities and obligations, as well as the consequences of all these.

Moses' Fourth Sermon: The Agreement in Moab (Chapters 29-30)

Settling the Accounts of Moses' Life and Ministry (Chapters 31-34)

The School of Wilderness

God commands us to remember how He walked us through the wilderness, all our experiences of life in the wilderness, and His guiding hand through all of those moments. The wilderness is a miserable place. It provides no direction; it gives no stability. It is impossible to find proper food, water, or even other people. The wilderness is not a place in which you can have a social life (Deut. 8:1-2). But there is a reason why God made the Israelites walk through such a gruesome place. There is something that God wishes to know and something which we must know. We can only learn that which we must know in the school of wilderness. There is no better place to teach us humility and to test us than the path of the wilderness (Deut. 8:2-3).

What God wishes to know is whether, even under such dire circumstances, we can serve God and God only with joy in our hearts and whether we can proclaim that our contentment comes only from God. God also wants to know whether or not we are able to live by the words, "Man shall not live by bread alone, but by every word that comes from the mouth of God" (Matt. 4:4).

Like this, the wilderness reveals the innermost corners of our hearts. Our time in the wilderness is a time to find contentment in God, fear Him, and obey His commands. If you find yourself in the wilderness at this very moment, know that now is the time to experience God.

Outline

Chapters 1-4	A review of the history God's works in the wilderness
Chapters 5-26	A summary of the law God's expectations from His people
Chapters 5-11	Moral laws
Chapters 12-18	Ceremonial laws
Chapters 19-26	Civil laws
Chapters 27-34	Signing of an agreement God's works to be done in Canaan, the Promised Land

Voice Outline

DEUTERONOMY

100-Day Bible Reading Plan

		CHECK
Day 16	Deuteronomy 1-11	
Day 17	Deuteronomy 12-26	
Day 18	Deuteronomy 27-34	

The Historical Books

Twelve books of the Old Testament, from Joshua to Esther, are grouped under the heading "the Historical Books." These are the books that record the history of Israel: from the crossing of the River Jordan, through the conquering and settlement in the land of Canaan, to their destruction by the Assyrians and Babylonians. In these books, we see the King who is Jesus Christ, the rule and providence of God who is the master of history, and the wonderful mercy of our God.

The Historical Books can be divided into three sections.

The Books of Joshua, Judges, and Ruth are mainly about the period during which the Israelites conquer Canaan under the leadership of Joshua to the period of the judges when judges serve as leaders.

First and Second Samuel, First and Second Kings, and First and Second Chronicles mainly cover the approximately 500-year period of Kings that began with Saul and David's succession.

The Books of Ezra, Nehemiah, and Esther cover the Babylonian Exile and Israel's restoration through their return from captivity.

JOSHUA

THE CONQUEST AND DIVISION OF CANAAN

The Book of Joshua explains the process of Joshua leading the Israelites across the River Jordan to conquer the Promised Land of Canaan and the distribution of the land among the twelve tribes of Israel. This book also reveals to us a faithful God who keeps His promises. As promised long ago to Abraham, Isaac, and Jacob, God gives the Promised Land to the Israelites. Throughout the book, God repeatedly reminds the Israelites that it was not due to their own righteousness or faithfulness that they were given the land but because He promised it, and that it was given to them because of the wickedness of the Canaanites living in that land.

In Joshua, the words "possess" and "possession" are repeated 22 times. The words "inherit" and "inheritance" appear a total of 63 times. The book's main focus is on how to possess and inherit the land that was promised by God.

Conquering Canaan

The Canaanites, the Amorites, the Philistine, the Hittites, the Hivites, the Jebusites, and the Perizzites inhabited Canaan at the time. They comprised thirty-one small kingdoms, each with its own king. God tells the Israelites to conquer and possess these lands. God tells Joshua and His army not only to drive out the nations but to drive out everyone and everything, including children and livestock. God's greatest concern was that the Israelites live as a holy people and that the Kingdom of God be established in those lands. And the greatest barrier to achieving the required holiness was Canaanite culture.

At the time, Canaan was very much a part of the fabric of a highly developed Mesopotamian civilization. The culture of Nimrod, humanistic ideals, and a culture of disregard and rebellion against God were rampant throughout these lands. There was Baal, a male deity of agriculture and affluence, and Asherah, a female deity who oversaw childbirth; they were the two main idols worshipped in Canaan.

In the process of worshiping these gods, the people had fallen morally, socially, ideologically, and spiritually. God wanted to make this earth anew. He wanted the Israelites to inherit and occupy those lands to establish a holy nation through which He could bless all the nations. Conquering the land of Canaan was not a matter that could be solved through compromise or integration, it was a matter of 'conquer or be conquered.'

God promised the Israelites that He would give the land of Canaan to them as an inheritance. But God's promise did not mean that the nations living in that land would surrender and welcome them with wide open arms when they entered. Joshua had to seize the Promised Land through warfare.

It was a long and drawn-out war that required a lot of sacrifices. The choice was to 'seize or be seized'; the war was a matter of life and death. Though they may have had God's promise, it did not mean that conquering the Promised Land was going to be easy. It took the 'spirit of Caleb' to conquer and the 'spirit of Joshua' to settle in those lands.

The same applies today. When we rely on God's commands and promises and do our best in all aspects of our lives, we can influence the world and advance toward establishing the Kingdom of God.

The Spirit of Caleb

The Book of Joshua places great importance on the 'spirit of Caleb' during the process of conquering the Promised Land (Josh. 14:6-15). Caleb was one of the men who gave a different testimony of faith than that of the ten spies. God sees him and promises to let him enter Canaan. God also tells Caleb that he will inherit the land. When Caleb turned 85, he asks the then leader, Joshua, to seize the land that God had promised them 45 years ago (Josh. 14:12).

The land Caleb received from God is called "Kiryat Arba." It takes its name from a man named Arba. Arba was the strongest warrior among all the descendants of Anak. Caleb was determined to take the land that belonged to Anak's strongest warrior as his inheritance. After he conquered the land, Caleb changed its name to "Hebron."

What we can learn from Caleb is that faith does not react to circumstances but instead only responds in accordance with God's words and promises. Another takeaway is Caleb's pioneering spirit, the boldness to enter and cultivate the most challenging, barren lands, with a foundation in the Word of God.

Kiryat Arba lies in front of us now. Today's culture is full of humanistic worldly pleasures that do not recognize God. This is the challenge we must tackle: how can we seize and establish a God-centered culture in these lands? What we need is the faith and pioneering spirit of Caleb.

The Spirit of Joshua

As Joshua addresses the people of Israel with his last message, he challenges them, "If it is evil in your eyes to serve the Lord, choose this day whom you will serve, whether the gods your fathers served in the region beyond the River, or the gods of the Amorites in whose land you dwell. But as for me and my house, we will serve the Lord" (Josh. 24:15).

Joshua resolves to serve God only. We too must choose whom we will serve every day and for the duration of our lives. God tells us to make the choice 'this day.' We must make the choice every day to either serve God or Baal; we must decide between whether to serve God or Asherah. Baal, as the 'deity of material things,' causes us to serve money as our master. Asherah, who is the 'deity of pleasure,' causes us to live according to our bodily greed and pleasure.

Just as in the times of Joshua, we are surrounded by countless temples and wooden poles for Baal and Asherah today. These have slyly seeped into our societies and cultures. The culture of Baal and Asherah is hidden in everything we see and hear. This is why we must make the choice to serve only God every day of our lives just as Joshua did. We must live in accordance with God's will and ensure that God's Kingdom is established in all areas of our lives.

The Book of Joshua reveals the secret behind just how Joshua was able to conquer and settle in Canaan. The secret is the Word of God and only the Word of God. There is no other secret. God tells Joshua what he needs to do to conquer Canaan, "This Book of the Law shall not depart from your mouth, but you shall meditate on it day and night, so that you may be careful to do according to all that is written in it. For then you will make your way prosperous, and then you will have good success" (Josh. 1:8).

God also reveals to us how Joshua was able to settle and establish the Kingdom of God in Canaan: "So Joshua made a covenant with the people that day, and put in place statutes and rules for them at Shechem. And Joshua wrote these words in the Book of the Law of God. And he took a large stone and set it up there under the terebinth that was by the sanctuary of the Lord. And Joshua said to all the people, 'Behold, this stone shall be a witness against us, for it has heard all the words of the Lord that he spoke to us. Therefore it shall be a witness against you, lest you deal falsely with your God'" (Josh. 24:25-27).

As it is written, the Book of Joshua started with and ended with the Word of God.

Conquest and Settlement

Chapters 1-5 record the preparation process as the Israelites prepare to conquer the land of Canaan. Both Joshua and the Israelites needed time to prepare before they entered the land. So, Joshua sent two spies across the Jordan to scout Jericho prior to their attack. And when these two men found themselves facing imminent danger, Rahab the prostitute protected them. Then finally, they cross the River Jordan and set camp in Gilgal where they perform circumcision and observe the Passover.

Chapter 6-12 record the conquests of Canaan. It begins with the conquest of Jericho and the Israelites continue to successfully expand into the north and south. The Israelites offer all of Jericho, their first conquest, to God. This serves as a guarantee for their future conquests just as paying tithes would guarantee God's blessings. Though Achan sins during this time, the Israelite thoroughly addresses his sin.

Chapter 12 lists the names of the 31 kings that the Israelites defeated.

Chapters 13-22 explain how the conquered lands were divided among the twelve tribes. Chapter 13 lists the lands east of the Jordan that had already been conquered before the Israelites crossed the river, under the leadership of Moses. These lands east of the river were given to the half tribe of Manasseh and the tribes of Reuben and Gad.

Chapters 14-19 list the lands west of the Jordan that were conquered seized under Joshua's leadership. These lands were divided among the half tribe of Manasseh and the remaining nine tribes. The tribe of Levi, however, did not receive an allocation of land but were scattered in 48 cities throughout the land of the twelve tribes to serve as priests.

Chapters 20-22 record the founding process of a community of faith. These chapters list the three cities of refuge on each side of the River Jordan. We can also find a list of the 48 cities given to the Levites. After the conquest was over, only the two tribes that had already settled east of the river returned back to their cities.

Chapters 23-24 are the account of Joshua's final sermons and teachings about serving God. These chapters mention the secret to establishing a Christian nation in the conquered lands.

Outline

Chapters 1-5	Preparations for the conquest of Canaan
Chapters 6-12	The conquest of Canaan
Chapter 13	Settlement in the east of the Jordan The tribes of Reuben, Gad, and the half tribe of Manasseh
Chapters 14-19	Settlement in the west of the Jordan Nine and a half tribes
Chapters 20-22	Founding of a community of faith
Chapters 23-24	The terms of settlement

Voice Outline

JOSHUA

100-Day Bible Reading Plan

		CHECK
Day 19	Joshua 1-12	
Day 20	Joshua 13-24	

JUDGES

A REPEATING PATTERN OF FAITH

The Book of Judges records the story of how the people of Israel who settled in Canaan continued their lives. The title of the book 'Judges,' refers to the word in its literal sense. Moses and Joshua are often referred to as the 'first judges' and the judges from Samuel through Eli are often called the 'last judges.' This period between the death of Moses and Saul's ascension to the throne which marks the beginning of the period of Kings is called the 'period of the judges.'

Judges deals with the history of the community of Israel under the judges' leadership after Joshua's death and beyond, from Othniel through Samson. As we can see from reading the words, "In those days there was no king in Israel. Everyone did what was right in his own eyes" (Judg. 17:6, 18:1, 19:1, 21:25). These are repeated several times between Judges Chapter 17-21, and the Book of Judges reveals the Israelites' pattern of living according to the Word of God when a judge was alive but soon reverting back to doing as they saw fit after the death of a judge.

The Judges

Othniel, the nephew of Caleb from the tribe of Judah served as a judge for 40 years; the left-handed Ehud from the tribe of Benjamin and Shamgar who killed 600 Philistines with an ox goad for 80 years; the prophetess Deborah from the tribe of Ephraim and Barak from the tribe of Naphtali for 40 years; the fearless warrior Gideon from the tribe of Manasseh for 40 years; Gideon's son Abimelech for three years; Tola from the tribe of Issachar for 23 years, Jair from the tribe of Gilead (descendants of the tribe of Manasseh) for 22 years; the great warrior Jephthah from the tribe of Gilead for six years, Ibzan from the tribe of Bethlehem (tribe of Judah) for seven years; Elon from the tribe of Zebulun for ten years, the Abdon from Pirathon (territory belonging to the tribe of Ephraim) for eight years; and Samson from the tribe of Dan served as a judge for twenty years.

The Book of Judges covers the 299 years during which 14 judges (Balak and Abimelech are excluded sometimes) ruled over Israel. Three of these judges were from the tribe of Manasseh, two from the tribe of Ephraim, and the tribes of Benjamin, Issachar, Zebulun, Naphtali, and Dan each put forth one judge. All the judges are from eight tribes. Eli and Samuel were from the tribe of Levi. The tribes of Reuben, Simeon, Gad, and Asher did not produce any judges. Nevertheless, we can safely say that judges were not solely from a single or specific tribe.

Judges were not characterized by their educational background or appearance. They did not rely on their own experiences, power, or knowledge but instead consistently served the Lord with the Spirit of God, the Holy Spirit, and performed their duties. In Judges 3:10, it is written "The Spirit of the Lord was upon him (Othniel)." And in Judges 13:25, 14:19, and 15:14, we read the words, "Then the Spirit of the Lord rushed upon him (Samson)." The source of Samson's power was neither his hair nor his muscles. As written in Judges 16:20, "But he did not know that the Lord had left him," the source of Samson's strength was the power of the Holy Spirit.

In the days of the judges, Israel was under constant attack. They were oppressed by Cushan-rishathaim king of Mesopotamia for eight years, by Eglon king of Moab for 18 years, by Jabin king of Canaan for twenty years, by Midian for seven years, by the Ammonites and Philistines for 18 years, and for 40 years by the Philistines. Israel had to bear great suffering under these nations (tribes) which afflicted them for a total of 111 years.

A Repeating Pattern

Chapter 2 Verse 6 to Chapter 16 of the book covering the works of the 14 judges make up the core content of the book. In these chapters, we see a reoccurring pattern. When the Israelites are with a judge, they serve God; however, once the judge dies, they abandon God and sin again. When that happens, God hands the Israelites to their enemies and they undergo great suffering until they turn away from their sin. It is only when they are faced with such suffering that the Israelites go before the Lord, repent, and ask for His deliverance from their enemies. Then God hears their prayers, forgives them, and sends them a judge to rescue them from their oppressors.

The same pattern repeats as a fixed cycle: "the death of a judge → Israel's sin → afflicted by enemies → crying out in repentance → God sends a judge to deliver them." This cycle repeats a total of six times after Joshua's death during the period of the 14 judges.

Appendix

Chapters 17-21 are like an appendix attached to the book. These chapters contain two stories that are useful for explaining the period of the judges. Chapters 17-18 talk about idol worship and Chapters 19-21 provide a brief idea of just how severe moral corruption was at the time. Strangely enough, both stories are about the Levites.

This part of the book clearly displays the Levites' dereliction of duty. Their duty as the priest tribe was to make sure that the people led a temple-oriented, God-oriented, and Word-oriented life. However, because they did not fulfill their duties, events which put the entire Israelites in jeopardy occurred.

The first of the two stories is a story of a Levite who lived in Micah's house. As compensation for his priestly services for the family, the Levite was guaranteed ten pieces of silver, a suit of clothing, and food. However, the Levite accepts a better offer as the priest of a whole tribe rather than just a house, steals the idol that Micah made, and becomes the priest of the tribe of Dan. This story can be summed up as one about a Levite who worshipped idols and lived in pursuit of money and honor.

The second story is about the wife of a Levite who was violated by a Benjaminite mob and left dead. This incident causes war to break out between the tribe of Benjamin and the other tribes, killing all but 600 Benjaminite men. The tribe of Benjamin, almost wiped out by the war, is saved from near extinction by the thoughtfulness of the other tribes. This story plainly reveals the immorality of Israel.

The Book of Judges, including this appendix, clearly lays down the consequences of living a life that is not dictated by the Word of God.

Passing the Baton

Judges Chapter 2:7-10 records a historic turning point: "And the people served the Lord all the days of Joshua, and all the days of the elders who outlived Joshua, who had seen all the great work that the Lord had done for Israel. And Joshua··· died··· And they buried him··· And all that generation also were gathered to their fathers. And there arose another generation after them who did not know the Lord or the work that he had done for Israel."

These verses reveal the third generation. The first generation is the generation of Joshua; the second generation is the generation of the elders; and the third generation is a generation that is unknown, a generation X. What the first and second generation have in common is that they both knew who the Lord is and had all witnessed the great works that the Lord had done for the people of Israel. However, the third generation did not know the Lord and did not know the work that He had done for Israel.

The generation of Joshua and the elders served God well. They knew who God was and knew of God's principles and laws. As people who had experienced the wonders of God's work, they lived according to the will of God. Unlike them, the third generation had neither the knowledge nor experience of God, nor did they know how to serve Him. They had no understanding of God's will, and even if they did, they had no intention of living according to His will. As a result, they abandoned the Lord and lived in sin.

When a new generation rises that knows God, God walks with and works through that generation. He uses that generation as a nation that influences the nations around it. But a generation without the knowledge of God lives in sin and apart from the will of the Lord. Rather than provide influence, they are influenced by the world and are bound and afflicted by their enemies. This principle is well illustrated by the reoccurring pattern in the period of Judges in Chapter 2:11-16.

In the women's 400-meter relay at the 2008 Beijing Olympics, the Jamaican team was everyone's favorite to win the race. The team led until the third runner, but due to an unexpected mistake made when making the final baton pass, the team was not able to take the title. The Book of Judges tells us how to successfully pass the baton on to the next generations.

The first generation of Joshua did a good job at passing the baton on to the second generation of elders. However, the generation of elders failed to pass the baton to the third generation. This resulted in tremendous chaos and suffering for the entire nation which is recorded in Chapters 17-21.

What exactly is this baton that we must pass on to the next generation? Is it money? Or perhaps property or real estate? Judges tells us that the baton is the knowledge of God and His principles, and an experience of God's wondrous works. And the Word of God lies at the core of this important work. It is when we live a life centered on the Word and when the Word is active that we can know and experience God. The baton that we must pass on to the next generation is "the Word of God" and "the faith to obey the Word."

First, God blesses us and helps us prosper when we diligently ponder upon these words and apply them in our lives. Then, He will bless all the nations through us. Individuals and nations are only strong when they stand on the Word of God. We must make sure to pass on the baton of the Word to the next generation.

Outline

Chapters 1-2:5	Settling in Canaan Nations conquered and nations not conquered, The consequences
Chapters 2:6-16	A repeating cycle Judge's death and sin → captured by the enemy → crying in repentance → rise of a judge and delivery
Chapters 17-21	Two stories representing the period of the judges Appendix
Chapters 17-18	Idol worship Ten pieces of silver and a suit of clothing
Chapters 19-21	Immorality and civil war The Levite and his concubine

Voice Outline

JUDGES

100-Day Bible Reading Plan

		CHECK
Day 21	Judges 1-11	☐
Day 22	Judges 12-21	☐

RUTH

THE RIGHT CHOICE LEADS TO ETERNITY

As can be understood with the first words of Chapter 1 Verse 1, the Book of Ruth tells the story of a family that lived during the time of the judges: "In the days when the judges ruled." Even when looking at the book as a part of the entire Bible, Ruth is not an account of history. Nevertheless, the message God sends us through this book goes beyond the events that occur within a single family. The Book of Ruth gives us a glimpse of the bright side of the period of the judges. Although the beginning of the book feels like the continuation of the Book of Judges, beginning with sorrow and abandonment, the book ends with God's care, restoration, and blessing.

Moreover, the Book of Ruth allows us to look beyond the blessing of God's restoration to something much greater. The book explains how Ruth, a Moabite woman who was outside God's promises, became the great-grandmother of King David. The book shows the glorious life of a forsaken being who was able to partake in carrying out God's will through God's wondrous love. The book shows the importance of making the right choice; the blessings of the right choice we make do not remain simply within our generation, but are passed on to the next and the next generation. They continue all the way to eternal life.

The Book of Ruth is one of the two books of the Bible that are named after a woman along with the Book of Esther.

Choosing Eternity

Ruth Chapter 1 Verse 1 begins in sorrow. When a famine strikes Bethlehem, a family has to leave their hometown and take refuge in the foreign land of Moab. "Bethlehem" means house of bread. It is almost as though the famine and the consequent loss of abundance, joy, and life that should be enjoyed is a representation of the period of the judges. There was no bread left to eat in the house of bread.

Naomi, a Bethlehemite in Judah, lived in Moab with her husband Elimelech and her two sons. She had a glimpse of happiness when her two sons married and brought home two daughters-in-law. But the ten years of happiness quickly vanished with the death of her husband and two sons. Although they left famine-stricken Bethlehem, Naomi and her family were not able to find abundance anywhere. They fled to Moab to escape the famine only to face yet another famine there. Under such circumstances, Naomi decides to go back home and there tells her two daughters-in-law to go their own way. One of the daughters-in-law, Orpah, parts ways with Naomi but her other daughter-in-law, Ruth, chooses to follow Naomi back to Judah.

In Ruth 1:16, we find Ruth's amazing confession. "Where you go I will go, and where you lodge I will lodge. Your people shall be my people, and your God my God."

Ruth's determination and choice have a significant impact on her life. At a glance, it may seem like a foolish decision. After all, this is a young widow saying that she will give up the opportunity to start a new life and instead follow her mother-in-law. However, with this single decision, Ruth became an ancestor in the Davidic line and was ultimately listed in the genealogy that brought Jesus Christ to this earth despite being a Moabite woman. A choice made in an instant can determine eternity. The Book of Ruth shows how the correct decision, like that which Ruth makes, can guarantee our lives for all eternity.

This incident also serves to show that honoring one's mother and father is the secret to a blessed and prosperous life, just as the Lord promised. Ephesians 6:1-3 says, "Children, obey your parents in the Lord, for this is right. 'Honor your father and mother' (this is the first commandment with a promise), that it may go well with you and that you may live long in the land."

The fifth commandment is there wholly for our own benefit. God has already provided us with the secret to a good, successful, and prosperous life. The secret is quite simple. Nothing is easier than honoring one's parents and obeying the Lord. The fifth commandment of the Ten Commandments is entirely for us. God has already given us the secret to a good, successful, and prosperous life. It is plain and simple. Honoring our parents and obeying the Lord is easier than anything else. This goes beyond simple moral and ethical rules. The Book of Ruth encourages us with specific examples.

In Chapter 2 Verse 3, we read that Ruth "happened to come to the part of the field belonging to Boaz." This was an important incident that led Ruth to meet Boaz. Here, the words "happened to" are written from a human perspective, but from God's point of view, it was out of "necessity" and His divine providence. This was God's way of blessing Ruth's love for her mother-in-law and her correct choice. God allowed her to meet a godly man named Boaz, brought her in as one of His people, and used her as an important tool to accomplish His will.

We are faced with choices on a daily basis. We must learn to choose what is eternal. We must learn to see beyond the temporary in the visible world and choose the eternal in the world unseen. The Lord will do wonderful things through us when we make our choices according to His will and obey and serve Him to the best of our abilities.

Redemption

The process Boaz undergoes with the elders of the city when he wants to receive Ruth as his wife shows the process of redemption as presented in the Bible. God made it possible for a person (slave) or property that was sold to another person to be bought back by a close relative of the seller so that the person or property could be returned to their ancestors. This process of recovery on behalf of someone else is called 'redemption.' Those who are allowed to redeem must be close relatives, competent and motivated, and must have nothing that may be redeemed by others.

Boaz was a man who was qualified to redeem others. He welcomed Ruth as his wife and sought to redeem the family of Naomi's husband, Elimelech. Priority to redeem is given to the closest relative. Although there was another relative who was closer to Elimelech than Boaz, that redeemer waived his right to redeem and transferred it to Boaz. Today, we would mark a transaction to waive our rights with a seal or signature, but in those days, such a transaction was confirmed by taking off one's sandals and giving them to the other party (Moses taking off his sandals in front of the Lord also means that Moses waived all his rights and transferred them to the Lord).

By doing this, Boaz redeemed Ruth and her status. Ruth, with the status of a Moabite woman, had never been allowed to partake in the assembly of the Lord. But with her marriage to Boaz, she not only became a member of God's people, she also became a holy channel through which God's will would be fulfilled. Through Boaz, Ruth underwent a tremendous change of status. We find Jesus Christ in Boaz. And we see ourselves in Ruth.

Jesus Christ is our Redeemer. Jesus redeemed us who were originally slaves, as free men and women. And as Redeemer, He gave His own life. We have been redeemed from darkness to light, from death to life, from slavery to freedom, from slaves of sin to children of God, as children of righteousness. God not only redeemed us through Jesus Christ, but He also allowed us to partake in establishing the Kingdom of God.

Ruth's Confession

"Do not urge me to leave you or to return from following you. For where you go I will go, and where you lodge I will lodge. Your people shall be my people, and your God my God. Where you die I will die, and there will I be buried. May the Lord do so to me and more also if anything but death parts me from you" (Ruth 1:16-17).

Ruth's confession is not only the confession of a disciple of Jesus Christ; it is also the confession of a Christian who has become the bride of Christ with Jesus as her husband. Jesus said, "Foxes have holes, and birds of the air have nests, but the Son of Man has nowhere to lay his head," (Luk. 9:58) and "Whoever does not bear his own cross and come after me cannot be my disciple… So therefore, any one of you who does not renounce all that he has cannot be my disciple" (Luk. 14:27,33). These verses tell us that there is a price to pay if we are to follow the Lord.

Ruth was fully determined to pay that price. She gave up everything in order to follow Naomi.

Before we commit to living as a disciple, before we decide to live as the bride of Christ, we must fully weigh the consequences. With ulterior motives, we may just end up giving up in the middle when the time comes for us to pay the price.

Naomi's Confession

"She said to them, 'Do not call me Naomi (pleasant); call me Mara (bitter), for the Almighty has dealt very bitterly with me. I went away full, and the Lord has brought me back empty. Why call me Naomi, when the Lord has testified against me and the Almighty has brought calamity upon me?'" (Ruth 1:20-21)

As the words coming out of her mouth suggest, Naomi was fully aware that God is almighty. She twice professes that God is the Almighty.

"Humble yourselves, therefore, under the mighty hand of God so that at the proper time he may exalt you" (1 Pet. 5:6). Naomi leaves her life entirely in the hands of God. She did not try to exalt herself; she neither complained nor grumbled and she did not wallow in self-pity. She humbled herself before the Lord and obeyed him completely. "For when they are humbled you say, 'It is because of pride' (Job 22:29).

Like Peter and Job, Naomi knew what to profess in times of suffering. She knew that she must humble herself in the mighty hands of God and entrust herself to Him wholly. In the end, God in His might raises Naomi and restores her.

"Then the women said to Naomi, 'Blessed be the Lord, who has not left you this day without a redeemer'" (Ruth 4:14).

I hope that you too are able to refrain from dwelling on your suffering, sadness, and self-pity and look up to the Lord Almighty. Entrust yourselves to Him wholly.

Outline

Chapter 1	Ruth chooses to follow Naomi
Chapter 2	Ruth follows Naomi back to Israel and serves her mother-in-law
Chapter 3	Naomi plans for Ruth's future and Ruth obeys
Chapter 4	Ruth's choice and the fruits of her love and dedication

Voice Outline

RUTH

100-Day Bible Reading Plan

		CHECK
Day 23	Ruth 1-1 Samuel 7	

1 AND 2 SAMUEL

LEADERSHIP SCHOOL

If one groups Genesis, Exodus, Leviticus, Numbers, and Deuteronomy as the 'Pentateuch,' Joshua, Judges, Ruth, and First and Second Samuel can be seen as another group. First Samuel is the book that lays the foundation for King David in the period of kings. David is so central to the Book of First Samuel that it would be safe to call it the "Book of First David." So, if you want to get to know David, all you need to do is read 1 and 2 Samuel. First and Second Samuel are originally one book so it is important to look at the contents of both books as a whole.

The two books can be divided over six periods.

1. Days of Samuel
2. Days of Saul
3. Emergence of David
4. Early days of King David's rule
5. Middle of King David's rule
6. End of King David's rule

Samuel the Prophet and Judge

First Samuel Chapters 1-8 tells the story of Samuel's life. He served God and the people as a prophet and the last judge. He was the son that Hannah had conceived through her prayers. And just as she had vowed, Samuel grew up in the temple assisting priests as soon as he had been weaned. Samuel began serving God at a time of spiritual confusion when God's words were rare.

He began serving the Lord during a time when the people did not seek His face or have a hunger for His Word. But surprisingly, God came to find Samuel. In Samuel, God saw hope.

From a very young age, Samuel hears the voice of the Lord and his relationship with Him grows (1 Sam. 3). Samuel's first ministry when he reaches adulthood is the "Mizpeh Revival Movement" (1 Sam. 7). He routinely travels around the nation, focusing on Bethel, Gilgal, and Mizpeh, as the nation's spiritual leader.

The days of Samuel were a transitional phase between the period of the judges and the period of kings. First Samuel Chapter 8 covers the story of the Israelites' request for a king and God's granting of their request. Chapter 12 is Samuel's last sermon and in his sermon, Samuel sets an example of how a leader should handle money. "Whose ox have I taken?… Or whom have I defrauded? Whom have I oppressed? Or from whose hand have I taken a bribe to blind my eyes with it?" (1 Sam. 12:3).

He also sets an example as a leader teaching prayer and the

Word. "Moreover, as for me, far be it from me that I should sin against the Lord by ceasing to pray for you, and I will instruct you in the good and the right way" (1 Sam. 12:23).

And he speaks these last words with the heart of a father. "Only fear the Lord and serve him faithfully with all your heart. For consider what great things he has done for you" (1 Sam. 12:24).

Israel's First King, Saul

First Samuel Chapters 9-15 introduce Saul, the first king of the period of kings. These chapters explain the process from how Saul became king to his eventual fall. As king, Saul makes three big mistakes that determine his future.

The first mistake was that he did not defend his territory and was impatient. He did not wait for the priest. Instead, he offered the sacrifices the priest was supposed to make by himself. Saul's mistake was the sin of "pride" (1 Sam. 13). Impatience and an inability to wait are dangerous traits whose roots stem from pride. Because of this, Samuel prophesies to Saul that "his kingdom" will not last long.

"And Samuel said to Saul, 'You have done foolishly. You have not kept the command of the Lord your God, with which he commanded you. For then the Lord would have established your kingdom over Israel forever. But now your kingdom shall not continue. The Lord has sought out a man after his own heart, and the Lord has commanded him to be prince over his people, because you have not kept what the Lord commanded you'" (1 Sam.13:13-14).

Saul's second mistake is "disobedience" (1 Sam. 15). God told Saul to destroy all the people and property of Amalek. However, instead of killing King Amalek, he captured him and kept the best sheep and the cows, destroying only the worthless and insignificant (1 Sam. 15:8-9). Saul's obedience was only partial. Obedience must be complete. Because of this, God tells Saul that He will "reject his kingship."

"And Samuel said, 'Has the Lord as great delight in burnt offerings and sacrifices, as in obeying the voice of the Lord? Behold, to obey is better than sacrifice, and to listen than the fat of rams. For rebellion is as the sin of divination, and presumption is as iniquity and idolatry. Because you have rejected the word of the Lord, he has also rejected you from being king'" (1 Sam. 15:22-23).

Saul's third mistake was to seek out a woman as a medium to ask for help during hardship. This was, in other words, an act of idolatry. This was the mistake that cost Saul his life.

"Then Samuel said to Saul, 'Because you did not obey the voice of the Lord and did not carry out his fierce wrath against Amalek, therefore the Lord has done this thing to you this day. Moreover, the Lord will give Israel also with you into the hand of the Philistines, and tomorrow you and your sons shall be with me. The Lord will give the army of Israel also into the hand of the Philistines'" (1 Sam. 28:18-19).

Studying Saul's fall can help us learn how to exercise leadership the right way. That is, by learning to wait on Lord.

"For thus said the Lord God, the Holy One of Israel, 'In

returning and rest you shall be saved; in quietness and in trust shall be your strength.' ... Therefore the Lord waits to be gracious to you, and therefore he exalts himself to show mercy to you. For the Lord is a God of justice; blessed are all those who wait for him" (Isa. 30:15,18).

When we are backed in to a corner, due to impatience and haste, it is easy to handle them by our own wisdom and methods as Saul did. However, we must learn to wait on God. We must also learn to obey Him completely. When we are practicing obedience, we must obey immediately, fully, and with joy. Even Jesus had to learn to obey. "Although he was a son, he learned obedience through what he suffered. And being made perfect, he became the source of eternal salvation to all who obey him" (Heb. 5:8-9).

Obedience is something we must all learn. Obedience does not come naturally. We must learn to turn only to God for help. "Put not your trust in princes, in a son of man, in whom there is no salvation... Blessed is he whose help is the God of Jacob, whose hope is in the Lord his God" (Psa. 146:3,5).

Though Saul's beginning was good, it did not last.

Trainee at the King's Training School, David

David finally emerges in 1 Samuel Chapters 16-31. In these chapters, we see God anointing David on behalf of Saul. Afterward, David defeats the giant Goliath and rises from a shepherd boy to national hero. This raises the jealousy of King Saul and David starts living in the wilderness to escape from Saul's persecution. However, God uses Saul as a tool in a leadership course to train David as a king.

The cave of Adullam is the center of David's life in the wilderness. All those who were troubled by, indebted to, and held grievances against Saul came to David. David became their leader and received training to become their spiritual shepherd and leader.

By looking at David, we learn how to prepare to be a leader and exercise leadership. He teaches us how to respond correctly in the face of crisis, how to interact with authority, and how to accept those around us and train them to be warriors.

David in the Early Days of His Rule

Second Samuel Chapters 1-4, records David becoming king after the deaths of Saul and Jonathan. David does not engage in political retaliation. Rather, he finds the dead bodies of Saul and Jonathan and arranges a funeral for them. He begins as the king of only two tribes. As a result, David has to continue fighting Saul's son, Ishbosheth even after he has taken the throne. As he fights, David grows stronger and stronger, while the house of Saul becomes weaker and weaker. (2 Sam. 3:1).

Abner, the commander-in-chief of his army, betrays Ishbosheth and joins David. Although he is welcomed by David, he is killed by David's followers. David laments the death of Abner, for whom the entire nation mourns. David also holds a funeral for his greatest adversary Ishbosheth after his death.

David in the Middle of His Rule

Second Samuel Chapters 5-19 shows David in the middle of his rule as king. After Ishbosheth dies, the elders of all the tribes of Israel come to David and anoint and seat him as king. At last, David becomes king of all Israel seven years and six months after becoming king of Judah.

David is anointed three times in the process of becoming king. He is initially anointed in Bethlehem by Samuel (1 Sam. 16:13), after which he is driven into the wilderness by Saul. The second anointing is when he is recognized by the two tribes of Judah and Benjamin as their king (2 Sam. 2:4). He then reigns in Hebron for seven years and six months. And finally, elders from every tribe of Israel anoint David, making him king over all of Israel.

For each time he was anointed, David's ministry became deeper, broader, and more powerful. His authority and influence also increased. His anointing became an opportunity for God to entrust him with His work and give him sufficient strength to carry out that work through the Holy Spirit.

David longed for God's Word, sought God's presence, and loved God with all his heart. Before he was king, he was a worshiper before God (2 Sam. 6). Through the prophet Nathan, God promised that David's throne would be strong and be preserved forever (2 Sam. 7). He also provided David with victory wherever and with whomever he fought (2 Sam. 8:6,14). Before every decision, David stood in front of the Lord and sought His will.

David sinned against the Lord with his servant Uriah's wife Bathsheba, but he repented with all his heart when he was confronted by the Prophet Nathan. Seeing that David had truly repented, God forgave him and as a gift allowed Bathsheba to bear him a son, Solomon (2 Sam. 11,12). After that, the most unfortunate event in the house of David takes place. One of David's sons, Absalom organizes a revolt against his father. David, however, does not fight back and flees Jerusalem and only returns after the death of his son (2 Sam. 13-19).

Before God uses His people, He puts them through a "training program." David took courses in subjects such as obedience, being broken, prayer and worship, and proper leadership in the "School of God." And after he became king, he learned humility, patience, obedience, and honesty as he worked through his own limitations. David did not become king the moment Samuel anointed him. He faced many tribulations for a long time afterward. Even when he finally became king, he was not fully king; only two of the twelve tribes of Israel recognized him as their king. It was not until much later that he was recognized as king over all of Israel.

David made no attempts to become king of his own accord. Neither did he ever try to remain as king. He never laid claim to the throne. He acted with the fear of God and within his limits; he submitted to God's authority, and committed himself to God's sovereign governance.

He adhered to the words, "Humble yourselves, therefore, under the mighty hand of God so that at the proper time he may exalt you" (1 Pet. 5:6).

David in the Last Days of His Rule

Second Samuel Chapters 20-24 record David's last days as king. Chapter 21 lists the names of Philistine giants killed by David's warriors, and Chapter 23 lists the names of David's warriors. The praises of Chapter 22 are placed in between Chapters 21 and 23 to show that all of David's victories came not from his own power, but by the power of God.

David does not try to show off his own greatness but only tries to reveal the greatness of God. He showed us that he is not a 'great man of God,' but a 'man of the great God.'

One of the biggest mistakes he made at the end was ordering the Joab, the commander-in-chief, to survey the population of Israel and Judah. God penalizes him for this act. So, are censuses biblical or unbiblical If you look at what happened to David, it would be difficult to argue that it is biblical. However, in Luke's Gospel in the New Testament, we read about the counting of the ninety-nine sheep that were not lost because of a single sheep that was lost (Luke 15). Therefore, a census may or may not be God's will.

It is in accordance with God's will to count numbers with the heart of a shepherd searching for a lost sheep. However, it is not God's will to conduct a census with the intention of flaunting one's own righteousness and authority, as if to say as David had done, "Look at how successful, how powerful I am!"

The Babylonian king Nebuchadnezzar faced similarly

tremendous trials when he held such intentions in his heart. He was stripped of all his power and might. God only restored him after Nebuchadnezzar realized that all his power and might came from the Lord alone (Dan. 4). God opposes the proud but is gracious to the humble (1 Pet. 5:5; James 4:6).

First and Second Samuel account the stories of three kings: Saul, David, and David's son Absalom who rebelled against him. As these stories unfold, we read about the relationship David had with Saul, an authority figure who was unrightfully trying to harm David. These books also reveal how David responded to his son Absalom who rebelled, betrayed, and slandered him.

Reading these two books, we can draw lessons on true leadership. The relationships between Saul and David, and David and Absalom offer a good course on leadership where we learn about leadership that stems from brokenness, humility, waiting on God, submission to authority, and the proper use of authority.

Outline

1 Samuel	
Chapters 1-8	Samuel the prophet and judge
Chapters 9-15	King Saul
Chapters 16-31	David as a candidate for the throne

2 Samuel	
Chapters 1-4	The early days of David's rule
Chapters 5-19	The middle of David's rule
Chapters 20-24	The last days of David's rule

Voice Outline

1 AND 2 SAMUEL

100-Day Bible Reading Plan

		CHECK
Day 23	Ruth 1-1 Samuel 7	
Day 24	1 Samuel 8-15	
Day 25	1 Samuel 16-31	
Day 26	2 Samuel 1-10	
Day 27	2 Samuel 11-20	
Day 28	2 Samuel 21-1 Kings 2	

1 AND 2 KINGS

CONFLICT, DIVISION, AND DESTRUCTION OF THE KINGDOM

The Hebrew Bible does not separate the books of First and Second Kings. First and Second Samuel are a prelude to First and Second Kings. If 1 and 2 Samuel cover Saul's reign and the beginnings of the House of David, 1 and 2 Kings cover David's son, Solomon and the division of the kingdom, the history of the two kingdoms from the destruction of the Kingdom of Israel by Assyria, to the destruction of the Kingdom of Judah by Babylon and up to the Babylonian exile.

But we can expand these stories beyond the two kingdoms as stories about the Kingdom of God. We can look beyond the stories of kings and see our Lord Jesus Christ, the only king. If Genesis taught us the principles of ruling a 'family,' 1 and 2 Kings teach us the principles of ruling a 'nation.'

The Books of 1 and 2 Kings are like sweet potato vines: when you tug on one, the twelve prophetic books (excluding the books of Esther and Daniel from the exile period, the books of Haggai, Zechariah, and Malachi from the return to Zion period) from the era all come out connected to each other. First and Second

Kings record events centered on the Northern Kingdom of Israel. First Kings, in particular, tells the stories of the kings Solomon, Rehoboam, and Ahab.

Of the 22 chapters in 1 Kings, 20 chapters are centered on these characters. The remaining two chapters briefly introduce the kings of the Kingdoms of Judah and Israel. After the destruction of the Northern Kingdom of Israel in 1 King 17, the latter chapters and 2 Kings record only the history of the Southern Kingdom of Judah up to its destruction by Babylon and the consequent exile.

When we take the books of 1 and 2 Kings as a whole and look at Israel's history within that context, we can segment the books into an introduction, discourse, and conclusion.

Prelude: the Division into the Southern Kingdom and the Northern Kingdom

Chapters 1-15 of 1 Kings record the division of Israel into the Southern Kingdom of Judah and the Northern Kingdom of Israel. This part can also be divided into two. Chapters 1-11 describe the process of Solomon becoming king after David, his wisdom and devotion to God, his building of a temple as well as his own palace. Solomon got off to an outstanding start. He obeyed God and lived in accordance with His will. However, after marrying foreign women for political ends, he began worshipping their idols, leading Israel to sin and corruption. He was a king who started spectacularly well but ended in failure, very much like King Saul.

First Kings Chapters 12-15 record how the country was divided into the Northern and Southern Kingdom after the death of Solomon during the reign of his son Rehoboam. Solomon, rather than Rehoboam, is to blame for the division, the greatest cause being Solomon's worship of idols. Rehoboam's rejection of the requests for help made by the people who had suffered while building the temples and royal palaces can also be considered a cause.

After the division, the majority of the tribes of Israel decided not to follow the House of David any longer and founded the "Northern Kingdom of Israel" with Jeroboam as its king. Ultimately, the ten tribes, excluding the two tribes loyal to Rehoboam, form the Kingdom of Israel with Jeroboam as the founder.

However, Jeroboam commits a serious sin in an attempt to strengthen the country. Because the Northern Israelites went to the temple in Jerusalem to worship God, he proposes an alternative offer that prevents them from going to Jerusalem. First, he restricts places of worship to locations within Northern Jerusalem and bans entry into Jerusalem. Then, he makes two golden calves and places them in two locations, one in a place called Dan, in the northernmost end of the country, and one in Bethel, by the southern Judean border. And instead of burning incense according to the Lord's direction, he burns it at the times he pleases.

Jeroboam's sin stemmed from his fear of the people. He was afraid that people would leave him and flock to Judah. God tells us that Jeroboam's decision is a serious sin. It is a great sin to have people worship idols other than God, to have anyone other than the Levites, the people who were chosen by God, serve God, and to set arbitrary dates for feasts other than the ones set by God. Jeroboam's sin became the starting point of the entire nation's spiral into sin.

That is why whenever we talk about the sins of the kings of Northern Israel, we say, "They followed in the footsteps of Jeroboam's sins." All then kings of the Northern Kingdom of Israel, including Baasha (1 Kings 15:34), Shimri (1 Kings 16:19), Omri (1 Kings 16:26), Ahab (1 Kings 16:31), Ahaziah (1 Kings 22:52), Jehoahaz (2 Kings 13:2), Joash (2 Kings 13:11), Menahem (2 Kings 15:18), Pekahiah (2 Kings 15:24), and Pekah (2 Kings 15:28), exercised wrong leadership under the influence of Jeroboam's sin. Their sins were the cause of the destruction of Northern Israel (2 Kings 17:21-23).

Discourse: Conflict between the Northern and Southern Kingdoms

First Kings 16 to Second Kings 15:12 is a part of the discourse of the narrative, covering the emergence of King Ahab and his evil deeds through to the time of Elijah. This part also records Elijah's wonderful ministry, Elisha's (Elijah's protégé) rebuke against the kings of Northern Israel and their sins, and the wonderful works of God performed through Elisha.

King Ahab took Jezebel, a Gentile woman from Tyre and Sidon, as his wife. He also had the people serve Baal, which she had brought with her. "And Ahab the son of Omri did evil in the sight of the Lord, more than all who were before him. And as if it had been a light thing for him to walk in the sins of Jeroboam the son of Nebat, he took for his wife Jezebel the daughter of Ethbaal king of the Sidonians, and went and served Baal and worshiped him. He erected an altar for Baal in the house of Baal, which he built in Samaria. And Ahab made an Asherah. Ahab did more to provoke the Lord, the God of Israel, to anger than all the kings of Israel who were before him" (1 Kings 16:30-33).

Ahab was the evilest of kings. He earns this title not just for his own sins but for driving the entire nation into sin. He angered God. And despite God's numerous warnings, Ahab did not turn from his sins. Eventually, God raised Jehu to judge Ahab and his descendants, bringing the House of Ahab to destruction. This established the new Jehu dynasty in Northern Israel, replacing Ahab and the Omri dynasty. However, the Northern Kingdom of Israel was destroyed by Assyria during the time of King Hosea regardless.

Assyria exiles the Israelites to neighboring countries, and moves Gentiles to live in Northern Israel. The Israelites who remained in Northern Israel lose their integrity by marrying the Gentiles. These people later come to be known as the "Samaritans" and are treated as Gentiles by the Jews.

The Two Great Prophets: Elijah and Elisha

The ministries of Elijah and his disciple Elisha were centered on Northern Israel. Elijah's ministry is well documented in First Kings Chapter 17 through 2 Kings

Chapter 2. Elijah's counterpart in his ministry was King Ahab. The most notable event in Elijah's ministry is his prophecy during the time of King Ahab that it would not rain for three years, and his prayer that brought rain again.

Other notable stories include God using a crow and the poor widow Zarebda to provide for Elijah's needs. We also read about Elijah saving the dead son of the poor widow. We read about Elijah's face-off with 850 men by himself. Elijah challenges 850 of Baal and Asherah's false prophets on Mount Carmel and gains total victory with the power of God. Elijah was a man of God who never died but was instead lifted into heaven.

Despite all this, Elijah had a fatal weakness: fear. In spite of his victory on Mount Carmel, he flees to Mount Horeb when Jezebel continues to threaten him. The great danger of being fearful remains to this day. God is harsh in His judgment of fear. This is because fear can only be the result of one's unbelief.

Proverbs 29:25 states, "The fear of man lays a snare, but whoever trusts in the Lord is safe." When Elijah was unable to handle his fears properly, the Lord tells him to "Pack up your bags." From that point on, Elijah's main ministry became to train his disciple Elisha. He calls Elisha his protégé and nurtures him.

By responding to Elijah's call, Elisha displayed tremendous obedience and dedication. Elisha was a wealthy man who owned a lot of land. When Elijah calls him, he was plowing his land but immediately dropped everything and obeyed upon receiving Elijah's call. So he burned his plows, killed his oxen, boiled the flesh, and gave them to his neighbors as a farewell gesture. He burned all the bridges to negate the possibility of return. He gave up all that he had in order to respond to Elijah's call.

But his ministry did not begin immediately. He first served and trained with Elijah for ten years (1 Kings 19:19-21). Elisha's ministry began after Elijah's ascension. As Elijah is ascending into heaven, Elisha asks of him, "Please let there be a double portion of your spirit on me" (2 Kings 2:9), and his ministry, in fact, doubles Elijah's ministry.

Elisha's miracles include filling all the empty vessels of a poor widow with a single jar of oil, raising a Shunammite woman's son from the dead, purifying a large pot of gourd stew during a famine, feeding 100 men with 20 loaves of barley and a bag of corn (2 Kings 4), curing Naaman, the commander of Aram's army, of his leprosy (2 Kings 5), recovering the lost ax head, blocking the attack route of the Aramean army and triumph in war (2 Kings 6), and stabilizing the economy by controlling inflation (2 King 7).

Elisha was particularly used for settling economic challenges. He also devoted a lot of time to training disciples just as Elijah did. His place of ministry was centered on Gilgal, Bethel, Jericho, and Jordan

Conclusion: the Destruction of the Northern and Southern Kingdoms

Second Kings 15:13 to the final Chapter 25 make up the

conclusion of the Book of Kings. If the introduction dealt with the division of a single kingdom into two kingdoms, the conclusion deals with the survival of only one of the two kingdoms. The discourse records the events that took place in the two divided kingdoms. To explain this numerically, the introduction is 'from one kingdom to two kingdoms', and the conclusion is 'from two kingdoms to one kingdom.'

Even after the fall of Northern Israel, the Southern Kingdom continues on for another 136 years. Later, even the Southern Kingdom of Judah is driven into crisis by the continued Assyrian attacks. However, King Hezekiah defeats Assyria with God's help through the Prophet Isaiah. Assyria continues to decline after that until it is completely destroyed.

Taking advantage of Assyria's decline, Babylon, a small city-state at the time, conquers Assyria and rises as a great empire. Babylon attacks Judah three times, taking many captives each time. Later, Babylon conquers Jerusalem, plundering the temple and completely wiping out the Kingdom of Judah.

When evaluating the kings of Northern Israel, God focuses on whether or not they walked in the sins of Jeroboam. Of the 19 kings of the Northern Kingdom, ten were under the influence of Jeroboam. However, when evaluating the kings of Southern Judah, God's concern is whether they walked the path of David. Seven of the 20 kings of the Southern Kingdom (Asa, Jehoshaphat, Joash, Uzziah, Jotham, Hezekiah, and Josiah) followed in the footsteps of King David.

In particular, five of these kings (Asa, Jehoshaphat, Joash, Hezekiah, and Josiah) were reformers. They demolished the Gentile altars, broke idols, took down statues of Asherah, and rebuilt the altar. They sought God and listened to His Word. The revival of the Word was at the center of their reforms.

However, there are two rather unconventional kings among the kings of Judah: Jehoram and Ahaziah. Jehoram son of Jehoshaphat walked in the ways of the kings of Israel (2 Kings 8:16-19) because his wife was Ahab's daughter, Athaliah. Jehoram's son Ahaziah also walked in the sins of Ahab because of the influence of his mother, Athaliah (2 Kings 8:27). When Ahaziah died, his mother Athaliah tried to annihilate all of Jehoram's descendants, but Joash, Ahaziah's son, was able to escape death with the help of his aunt Jehosheba and went on to live in hiding.

Jehoshaphat was one of the reformer kings who followed in the footsteps of his father Asa in the way of David. However, he makes the fatal mistake of marrying his son to Ahab's daughter to reconcile with King Ahab of Northern Israel. That is why his son Jehoram and his grandson Ahaziah walked in the shameful ways of Ahab. This almost leads to someone who is not of the House of David, Athaliah from the lineage of Ahab and Jezebel, taking the throne in Judah. But God, who is faithful to his promises, protected Judah from destruction for the sake of David (2 Kings 8:19).

These are the characteristics of the kings of Judah in the House of David. David is godly; Solomon is wise; Rehoboam is simple; Abijah is courageous; Asa is honest; Jehoshaphat is religious; Jehoram is wicked; Ahaziah blasphemes God; Joash restores the House of David from crisis; Amaziah is imprudent; Uzziah is powerful; Jotham is peace-loving; Ahaz is an idolater; Hezekiah is a reformer; Manasseh is a repenter; Amon is of ambiguous character; Josiah has a tender heart; and Jehoahaz, Jehoiakim, Jehoiachin, and Zedekiah are all kings who, in their wickedness, quickly brought themselves and the kingdom into ruin.

The kings who walked in the way of David generally had enduring reigns, while those who did evil did not reign for long. The same principle applies to the Northern Kingdom of Israel. During the reigns of 19 kings over a 208-year period and before the destruction of the Kingdom of Israel by the Assyrians, the kingdom experiences seven coups. South Judah lasted for 344 years and the reigns of 20 kings until it was destroyed by Babylon. A coup overthrew the House of David once but God brought the throne back to David's line. The Israeli dynasty that began with Saul and lasted for nearly 500 years was ultimately destroyed by the Assyrian and Babylonian empires.

Outline

1 Kings Chapters 1-15	Introduction: the division of the Northern and Southern Kingdoms
Chapters 1-11	Solomon
Chapters 12-15	The division of the kingdom
1 Kings Chapter 16- 2 Kings Chapter 15:12	Discourse: Conflict between the Northern and Southern Kingdoms
1 Kings Chapter 16- 2 Kings Chapter 8	King Ahab of the House of Omri
2 Kings Chapters 9-15:12	The House of Jehu
2 Kings Chapters 15:13-25	Conclusion: the destruction of the Northern and Southern Kingdoms
Chapters 15:13-17	The fall of the Northern Kingdom of Israel
Chapters 18-25	The fall of the Southern Kingdom of Judah

Voice Outline

1 AND 2 KINGS

100-Day Bible Reading Plan

		CHECK
Day 28	2 Samuel 21-1 Kings 2	
Day 29	1 Kings 3-11	
Day 30	1 Kings 12-22	
Day 31	2 Kings 1-8	
Day 32	2 Kings 9-17	
Day 33	2 Kings 18-25	

1 AND 2 CHRONICLES

A TEMPLE-CENTERED PEOPLE WHO SERVE THE LORD

At first glance, we might wonder why God chose to record Israel's history again in 1 and 2 Chronicles when 1 and 2 Kings could have served that purpose. But with a more detailed look at these books, we realize that God communicates His will to us by placing the focus on different aspects.

The Books of Kings alternates between two nations: Israel in the north and Judah in the south. They also explain how the nations are connected. However, the Books of Chronicles only focuses on Judah, the Southern Kingdom. Second Samuel and First Chronicles are records of the same person from two different perspectives. Both deal with King David's reign; however, the Book of Samuel emphasizes war and conquest from a political perspective while the Book of Chronicles emphasizes temple-centered worship. Second Samuel tells the story of Bathseba whereas First Chronicles does not mention her.

The Books of Kings and the Book of Second Chronicles also provide two different perspectives on the same period. Both cover the period between Solomon's era and the Babylonian Exile but the Books of Kings approach it from a prophetic viewpoint and Second Chronicles approaches it from a priestly viewpoint. If the Books of Kings mainly address the issues around continued human sin and failure, the Book of Second Chronicles focuses on God's temple of worship and His compassion and faithfulness.

The beginning of 1 Chronicles also differs from the beginning of the Books of Kings. First Kings begins with King Solomon whereas First Chronicles starts at the very beginning with Adam. As such, we can consider the books of 1 Chronicles, 2 Chronicles, Ezra, Nehemiah as a historical bundle. These four books make up the "Abridged version of Israel's History" that summarizes the entire history of Israel, starting with Genesis.

The Books of 1 and 2 Chronicles are characterized by their re-examination of Israeli history from the perspective of the Kingdom of God. Through 1 and 2 Chronicles, God tells us that the Kingdom of God continues through what remains, even if a stump is all that remains.

Even as the kingdom continues to deteriorate, God speaks of 'hope.' Through the Books of 1 and 2 Chronicles, God sheds light on how He was with the Israelites even in their exile, how he spoke among them, and the process of how he ultimately brought them back from exile and rebuilt the nation. The end of 2 Chronicles and the first part of Ezra overlap, implying that the books of 2 Chronicles, Ezra, and Nehemiah are continuous parts of a whole. This shows us that though the Kingdom of Israel may have perished, the Kingdom of God shall never perish or decline.

Structure

1. Family Tree

First Chronicles Chapters 1-9 record the genealogy from Adam to David. It arranges Israel's history in order, beginning with Genesis. From Adam to Noah, from Noah to Shem, from Shem to Eber's two sons Peleg and Joktan, from Peleg to Abraham, and from Abraham to Jacob's twelve sons who form the 12 tribes of Israel, these chapters quickly summarize the genealogy leading up to David. It is evident that this genealogy was recorded with a specific purpose. Rather than simply summarizing the history of Israel, the purpose was to record David's genealogy to point toward "Jesus, the coming Messiah."

It is generally assumed that the Books of Chronicles were written by Ezra. He wished to make the Israelites who had returned from captivity take a second look at the history of Israel. This is because Ezra wanted them to be people who overcame the period of darkness between the Old and New Testaments and meet the Messiah of the New Testament.

Matthew Chapter 1 Verse 1 starts with the words, "The book of the genealogy of Jesus Christ, the son of David, the son of Abraham." From these words, we understand that the Book of Chronicles is the "bridge to the New Testament". By placing David center stage and as the main character, the Books of Chronicles direct our gaze directly to the coming King. Unlike the Book of Kings, the Book of Chronicles explains temple customs for the same purpose. The Books of Chronicles explain the activities and organization of the Levites who serve in the temple as well as the offerings made to God. These books also emphasize the preparation for the temple's construction, the construction and completion of the temple, and worship in the temple of God.

2. David's Reign

First Chronicles Chapters 10-29 record how David served God and behaved as king. The reason Saul's death is mentioned before David is that his death opened the way for David to become king. It was God's plan for David to become king (1 Chron. 11:1-3). The reason why David's conquest of Jebus after he becomes king is mentioned first is that those lands came to be known as Jerusalem, or at times, as the 'City of David' or 'Zion.' This is to make us look to the Messiah who will come to Zion and reign over the land.

Although the book lists the names of the warriors who helped David establish the kingdom, it first makes it known that their victory was not because of them but rather because of the Lord of Armies. This is attested to by the words 1 Chronicles 11:9, "And David became greater and greater, for the Lord of hosts was with him" (11:9), which comes before the names of the warriors.

The book also covers how David moved the Ark of the

Covenant, prepared for the building of the temple, recorded the offices of the Levites and priests, directed the persons responsible for the temple's choir, gate, and treasuries, and commanded the construction of the temple.

David prepares Zion (1 Chron. 11), moves the Ark of the Covenant (1 Chron. 15-16), prepares the Levites (1 Chron. 23), the priesthood (1 Chron. 24), the choir (1 Chron. 25), and the temple priests (1 Chron. 26) and gives Solomon the blueprint for the temple along with the instruction to start building (1 Chron. 28). He prepares the material for the construction of the temple (1 Chron. 29). This is achieved not by David alone, but with the people also joyfully partaking and contributing to the construction. They are not oppressed or coerced into giving, but give generously what they have prepared in advance.

3. Solomon's Reign

Second Chronicles Chapters 1-9 detail Solomon's reign as king and specifically the temple-building process. Solomon, who succeeded his father King David as king of Israel, was gifted with special wisdom and knowledge by God (2 Chron. 1). In Chapter 2, Solomon decides to build the temple and selects those who will work with him. In Chapter 3, he begins the construction of the temple on Mount Moriah. Chapter 4 lists the furnishings in the temple, and we finally read about the completion of the temple after which the Ark of the Covenant is placed in the Most Holy Place.

Just as clouds and the glory of God settled on Mount Sinai

after Moses finished the construction of the tabernacle, the temple completed by Solomon was also filled with the glory of God (2 Chron. 5). How glorious and beautiful it must have been that the priests were unable to stand and minister in the presence of God's glory!

Standing in the finished temple, Solomon blessed the whole congregation of Israel and lifted his hands to God in prayer (2 Chron. 6), "Now, my God, I pray, let Your eyes be open and let Your ears be attentive to the prayer made in this place" (2 Chron. 6:40). When Solomon had finished praying, fire came down from heaven and consumed the burnt offering and the sacrifices. All the children of Israel bowed their faces before the glory of the Lord and worshiped and praised Him.

They held a feast for the temple's dedication for seven days and God made them an amazing promise, "When I shut up heaven and there is no rain, or command the locusts to devour the land, or send pestilence among My people, if My people who are called by My name will humble themselves, and pray and seek My face, and turn from their wicked ways, then I will hear from heaven, and will forgive their sin and heal their land" (2 Chron. 7:13-14).

4. The Reigns of the Kings of Judah

The fourth section of the Books of Chronicles, which is from 2 Chronicles Chapters 10-36, records the history of Judean kings. The Book of 2 Chronicles begins with the construction of the temple and ends with its destruction. Though it begins with the temple being filled with the glory of God, it ends with His glory departing from the temple.

The clear distinction here can be found in the distinction between the fear of God and evil deeds. The history of the kings of Judah shows that the deeds of God-fearing kings are followed by God's blessings and prosperity and that the deeds of evil kings are followed by pain and suffering.

This is also the reason God chooses to speak strictly to the Southern kingdom of Judah even though the Northern Kingdom of Israel continues to exist during this time. The history of kings shows how important it is to live as loyal servants of God. God wants to bless all kings and wish them goes well, but it is up to them. They made their own choice and determined the futures of both them and the nation.

What happens during the reigns of kings who follow Solomon's peaceful reign is the result of their choices. Rehoboam abandoned God's Word, did not seek Him, and did evil (2 Chron. 10-12). And although Abijah's reign lasted a short three years, his reliance on God allowed him to defeat Jeroboam's army (2 Chron. 13). Asa ruled 41 years, becoming the first reformer of the Southern Kingdom of Judah. Because he sought God, God gave peace to Judah. But in his later years, he stopped relying on God and died from sickness as a result (2 Chron. 14-16).

Jehoshaphat was the most David-like king. Just as David did, he sought God with all his heart. The Word of God lay at the core of every reform he pursued (2 Chron. 17:7-9). God's Word is like a plumb rule by which we set the standards in our lives. God's Word shows us what needs to be torn down and what needs to be rebuilt. God gave peace to Judah in all areas (2 Chron. 17). The one regrettable thing about Jehoshaphat is that his marriage with the House of Ahab became a snare which eventually entrapped him (2 Chron. 18-19).

The Book of 2 Chronicles depicts a beautiful and thrilling scene where Jehoshaphat triumphs over the army of Aram. The key to Jehoshaphat's victory can be found in praising God (2 Chron. 20). However, the wicked and ungodly reign of Jehoshaphat's son and grandchild, Jehoram and Ahaziah, puts the nation in turmoil. They went far beyond not following in the ways of David, instead following the ways of Ahab. This was the direct result of having one of Ahab's daughters as their wife and mother (2 Chron. 21-22). This highlights the importance of a woman's influence in a household.

King Joash and King Amaziah of Judah did not seek the face of God with all their hearts. So Joash suffered defeat under the Aramites and Amaziah under the Northern Kingdom of Israel (2 Chron. 24-25). Uzziah had the longest reign of 52 years. As long as he sought God, God prospered him. However, when he mistakenly tried to take credit for his success as the result of his own strength, he grew arrogant and sinned. As a result, he became leprous and had to live in isolation, cut off from the Temple of God (2 Chron. 26). Although Jotham sought the face of God, he unfortunately did not enter the Temple of God (2 Chron. 27). Ahaz, on the other hand, walked in the ways of the kings of Israel and engaged in idol worship. As a result, he faced tribulation on all fronts (2 Chron. 28).

Hezekiah was the leader of a powerful revival. He cleansed the temple, restored worship, and observed the Passover. At the center of his revival was the restoration of God's Word and tithing. It was during the days of Hezekiah that God Himself struck the Assyrian army, which had caused the destruction of the Northern Kingdom of Israel and thrust the nation into its period of decline. And although Hezekiah became arrogant near the end of his reign, he repented and God allowed him to prosper for the remainder of his life (2 Chron. 29-32). He is then succeeded by his son Manasseh and grandson Amon who do evil in the eyes of the Lord (2 Chron. 33).

Josiah was the king who led the revival during the final days of the Kingdom of Judah. Once again, the restoration of the Word of God lay at the center of that revival. He cleansed the temple and observed the Passover (2 Chron. 34-35). However, his sons Jehoahaz, Jehoiakim, Jehoiachin, and Zedekiah all did evil in the eyes of the Lord and drove the nation into ruin until it was ultimately destroyed by Babylon (2 Chron. 36).

Four Periods of the Southern Kingdom of Judah

The history of the Southern Kingdom of Judah from Rehoboam's reign after Solomon to its destruction can be divided into four periods.

The first is the period of conflict between the Northern and Southern Kingdoms. After Rehoboam, the Southern and Northern Kingdoms clashed continuously and the war went on.

The second is the period of reconciliation between the Northern and Southern Kingdoms. During the reign of Judah's fourth king Jehoshaphat, his son Jehoram marries Athaliah, the daughter of King Ahab of the Northern Kingdom of Israel reconciling the two kingdoms for a period.

The third is the period of suffering under Assyria. Starting with Hezekiah's father, King Ahaz, and through the reigns of Hezekiah, Manasseh, and Amon, the Kingdom of Judah was constantly plagued by Assyria for four generations. However, God delivers and protects Judah from the hands of Assyria during King Hezekiah's time.

Assyria was a robust nation that had existed for 600 years. It was the war that Assyria fought with King Hezekiah that enabled Babylon, an emerging nation, to defeat Assyria. Isaiah, who served as the prophet during King Hezekiah's time, warns the king not to rely on Assyria but to rely only on God. At first, Hezekiah does not heed Isaiah's warnings and relies on Assyria in the north and Egypt in the south, only to eventually find himself pestered by both kingdoms.

However, near the end of his reign, the king requests help from Isaiah and prays earnestly to God. And God, who hears Hezekiah's prayers, answers him and delivers him for the hands of the Assyrian King. More than 180,000 soldiers of the Assyrian army were killed at once. Historians sometimes attribute this event to the Black Death or a very serious epidemic.

Ultimately, Sennacherib, king of Assyria who harassed

the kingdom of Judah, returns to his own country where he is killed by his own son. After Sennacherib's death, the Assyrian Kingdom enters a period of rapid decline until it is destroyed by Babylon.

The fourth is the period of suffering and ultimate destruction under Babylon. From King Josiah to the last King Zedekiah, the Kingdom of Judah is constantly plagued by Babylon. The Israelites are taken as captives into Babylon in a total of three waves. During those times, it was the Prophet Jeremiah that prophesied that the Israelites would be exiled to Babylon. He also prophesied that God would surely bring them back to Jerusalem. And just as Jeremiah had prophesied, the people of Israel returned, rebuilt the temple, and renewed their nation after 70 years in captivity.

Outline

1 Chronicles	
Chapters 1-9	Family tree
Chapters 1-3	From Adam to David
Chapters 4-8	The lineage of each tribe
Chapter 9	Those who returned from captivity
Chapters 10-29	David's reign
Chapter 10	Saul
Chapters 11-21	The Ark of the Covenant and the covenant
Chapters 22-29	Preparation for the temple's construction
2 Chronicles	
Chapters 1-9	Solomon's reign
Chapter 1	Solomon's inauguration
Chapters 2-7	Completion of the temple
Chapters 8-9	Solomon's glory
Chapters 10-36	The reigns of the kings of Judah
Chapters 10-13	The division of the kingdom
Chapters 14-35	Five kings who are the reformers
Chapter 36	After the fall of Judah

Voice Outline

1 AND 2 CHRONICLES

100-Day Bible Reading Plan

		CHECK
Day 34	1 Chronicles 1-10	
Day 35	1 Chronicles 11-20	
Day 36	1 Chronicles 21-29	
Day 37	2 Chronicles 1-10	
Day 38	2 Chronicles 11-20	
Day 39	2 Chronicles 21-28	
Day 40	2 Chronicles 29-36	

EZRA

THE RECONSTRUCTION OF THE TEMPLE AND REVIVAL MOVEMENT

The Book of Ezra paints a picture of a completely changed Israel. Through the books of Samuel, Kings, and Chronicles, we saw the Israelites during the kingdom period. We read about how the kings ruled and even witnessed the destructions of the Kingdoms of Israel and Judah in the final chapters of 2 Kings and 2 Chronicles. These chapters portray despair, giving us a sense that it is all over now. However, Chapter 36 of the Book of 2 Chronicles ends with the Israelites' return to Jerusalem after a long period of captivity in Babylon.

Their return is as though we are witnessing Ezekiel's vision of the dry bones coming back to life. Israel is freed from its yoke of captivity and now wears its new cloak of freedom. What has changed is that we no longer have stories of their kings; the Israelites have been stripped of the crown on their heads. However, the prophets remain by their side, even through captivity. They join the captives in their return to Jerusalem and lead the restoration of the temple and the city.

Reconstruction and Restoration

The Book of Ezra consists of two main storylines. The first is a record of the first Babylonian captives returning and rebuilding the temple from its ruins. This return is also referred to as the "second Exodus." The second is a record of the second wave of returnees to Jerusalem, which takes place 80 years after the first return, 60 years after the construction of the Temple of Zerubbabel. It tells the story of how the returnees came back and restored their lives around the Temple to live a life that befits the people of God.

The Works of the First Returnees

Just as God declared through the Prophet Jeremiah, we see the people of Israel return from their exile in Babylon after 70 years in Ezra Chapters 1-6. The powerful Babylonian Empire perishes and is replaced by the Persian Empire. The Persian Empire was centered in what is now Iran, and the Babylonian Empire was centered in what is Iraq today.

Babylon can be considered the single most powerful empire in history. It was a remarkable state in many ways, including politics, economy, culture, art, astrology, and medicine. Surprisingly, however, the Babylonian Empire, an empire that would seemingly last a very long time, perished in less than 100 years. In its place, a new empire arose: Persia. Cyrus, the founder and first king of the empire, in the first year of his rule, orders the return of the people of Israel and says:

"The Lord, the God of heaven, has given me all the

kingdoms of the earth, and he has charged me to build him a house at Jerusalem, which is in Judah. Whoever is among you of all his people, may his God be with him, and let him go up to Jerusalem, which is in Judah, and rebuild the house of the Lord, the God of Israel he is the God who is in Jerusalem" (Ezra 1:2-3).

Cyrus knew who the sovereign Lord was. He also knew his own calling. God had spoken through the Prophet Isaiah about him around 150 years before Cyrus was even born (Isa. 45:1-3). Cyrus also provided all the necessary materials for the temple's construction and had the Israelites go back with all the treasures that had previously been taken from the temple in Jerusalem (Ezra 1:5-11).

Just as He had told the people through Jeremiah, God forgave all their sins and restored them. God is faithful, compassionate, and gracious. For the sake of His Master Plan, He builds up and destroys nations; he raises and takes down kings. God is the master of history.

In 536 B.C., Zerubbabel the governor and Yeshua the priest return to Jerusalem with 49,897 captives and begin rebuilding the destroyed temple. At that time, the Gentiles who lived in the land of Judah also request to help rebuild the temple. They were the people who were moved into the Northern Kingdom of Israel instead of deporting the Israelites to various parts of Assyria after Assyria defeated Israel in war. However, the Israelites reject their request to help with the construction.

After their offer was rejected, the Gentiles begin to

interfere with the construction of the temple. They even block construction plans by bribing officials. They also sent representations opposing the rebuilding of the Temple of Jerusalem (Ezra 4:7-16) to King Cyrus' successor Ahasuerus (Ezra 4:6-7, also called "Cambyses"). Then, Ahasuerus issues a decree ordering work on the temple to cease (Ezra 4:17-22).

Confronted with this opposition, the construction of the temple was stopped after the foundations were laid. And after 16 years of interruption, construction begins again with the encouragement of the prophets Haggai and Zechariah. When people realize construction has resumed, they send a letter to King Darius of Persia, who succeeded King Ahasuerus, and ask him to order the suspension of the work. Those who sent the letter this time were much more sensible than those who had asked before. Thus, they asked King Darius to confirm whether King Cyrus had in fact allowed the rebuilding of the temple (Ezra 5:6-17). Upon receiving the letter, King Darius finds Cyrus' decree in the archives and issues a decree allowing the reconstruction of the temple rather than suspending it (Ezra 6:1-12).

Finally, four years after resuming construction and twenty years after the return of captives, the temple is completed. The temple is dedicated and the Israelites begin observing the Passover. Although it took 70 years from the destruction of Solomon's temple, the Temple was finally rebuilt by Zerubbabel.

Works of the Second Returnees

Although Chapter 7 might seem like the continuation of Chapter 6, there is a long gap of 60 years between the first and second parts of the book, which goes from Chapters 7 to Chapter 10. In 458 B.C., when Artaxerxes was king of Persia, 1,754 Israelites return in the second wave of returnees under Ezra's guidance, about 60 years after the completion of the temple. The time gap between the 1st and 2nd returns is as much as 78 years.

After seeing the situation in Jerusalem upon his return, Ezra resolves to reform the nation. This was because although the first returnees built a temple and lived a temple-centered life, their spiritual life and passion were in gradual decline. Zerubbabel and Yeshua were already dead, and most of the first returnees had passed away. The majority of those living there were second and third generations who had not experienced exile in Babylon. They were the generation who had not even heard of Haggai and Zechariah. God wished for them to regain their spiritual passion through Ezra.

Ezra the priest was the 16th direct descendant of Aaron. He was a scholar of the Bible familiar with the Word and a priest of Aaron's 16th generation. He was a scholar of the Bible with knowledge of the Word. In his decree, Artaxerxes specifically points to Ezra and commands him to work for the restoration of Jerusalem and to supply him with everything necessary for the work (Ezra 7:11-26). It is indicated in Artaxerxes' decree that he was familiar with Ezra as a Biblical scholar. Artaxerxes also knew that Ezra's job was to bring revival to the land with the Word.

God's wisdom and insight are truly amazing. When Persia, the Empire that had destroyed Babylon, was founded, He made Cyrus the first king build the temple in Jerusalem through Zerubbabel and Yeshua and used all of Persia for the construction. Moreover, He uses Artaxerxes to start a revival in Jerusalem through Ezra about 80 years later, once again making use of the Persian Empire.

We must trust in God. God is the master of history and always accomplishes His work. He calls men, uses kings, and moves nations to accomplish His will. We must know what God is doing now and participate in it. We must understand what God will do in the future and proactively prepare for it. We must also know how to read the times.

As it is written in 1 Chronicles 12:32, "Of Issachar, men who had an understanding of the times, to know what Israel ought to do, 200 chiefs, and all their kinsmen under their command," we must have the insight to see through the times. We need to ask God for this. God, at any point in history, has never halted His work.

Restoration of the Word

Ezra's ministry was focused on the restoration of God's Word. The building of the temple did not mean that his work was complete; he needed to restore the Word so that the people could live God-centric lives after the completion of the temple.

Ezra was determined to study, obey, and teach God's Word

(Ezra 7:10). One thing we must learn from Ezra's actions is that he did not study the Word and then simply teach it right away. He first started out by applying the Word to his own life. The purpose of studying and training the Word is not to increase knowledge, but to experience Jesus Christ. It is to be obedient to the Word. It is when these things first occur within us that we can preach and teach the Word to others. This is the correct attitude to have toward God's Word.

First, we must study and know the Word, apply the Word to our own lives, and then share the Word that we have experienced with others. At that time, we experience the power of the Word of God and the changes it creates in people. Ezra was such a man; he first studied the Word and put it into practice to restore the nation. And by preaching the Word to all of Israel, he strove to strengthen the nation through a revival of the Word.

Spiritual Reform Movement

Ezra Chapters 1-6 are about the first return of the Israeli captives from Babylon and the rebuilding of the temple during a time in which Ezra was not yet in existence. The second wave of returnees did not come back until about 80 years after the first wave. Ezra records the earlier history in Chapters 1-6 and returns with the second wave to restore the nation.

What we need in our lives today is a spiritual revival. We need to live a life that is centered on God. I wish for us to serve with passion and influence the world. But to do this, the first and most important step is to restore the Word of God within us. It is only when we begin to study the Word, obey the Word, and build on the Word in all areas of our lives that we, as individuals, families, and nations can become healthy, and the Church can energize the world.

Outline

Chapters 1-2	The first return of captives
Chapters 3-6	Reconstruction of the temple and restoration of worship
Chapters 7-8	The second return of captives
Chapters 9-10	Restoration of the word and spiritual revival

Voice Outline

EZRA

100-Day Bible Reading Plan

		CHECK
Day 41	Ezra 1-10	

NEHEMIAH

REBUILDING THE WALLS OF JERUSALEM

In the original Hebrew text, Ezra and Nehemiah are one book, giving credibility to many scholars who point to Ezra as the author of both books. In the Septuagint, the Ezra is titled '1 Ezra,' and Nehemiah is titled '2 Ezra.' Thirteen years after Ezra returns from captivity and initiates the revival of the Word, Nehemiah is appointed governor of Jerusalem.

As a scholar and priest, Ezra is a spiritual leader; Nehemiah, as governor, is a political leader. If Ezra worked hard to restore the Word, Nehemiah worked hard to rebuild the walls of Jerusalem. These two are representative figures who worked hard to restore a nation.

Rebuilding the City Walls

Although Ezra's return and the Word-centered reform brought about a great revival, the people of Jerusalem continued to live in anxiety. They had rebuilt the temple and experienced a revival of the Word but still had not rebuilt the walls around Jerusalem. With its walls broken down and its gates destroyed by fire, Jerusalem was under frequent attack from its enemies. It was not until about 100 years after the first return which took place under Zerubbabel's guidance that the people of Jerusalem felt the need to rebuild the city walls.

Nehemiah was heartbroken to find out that the returnees were still anxious despite having rebuilt the temple and being in the midst of a revival of the Word. So, he fasted and prayed. He asked God for an opportunity to go to Jerusalem to rebuild the broken walls and gates (Neh. 1).

Nehemiah lived in the palace in Susa the citadel of Persia and was cupbearer to Artaxerxes (Neh. 1:1,11). During those days, a cupbearer held significant influence as someone who had the trust of the king. Artaxerxes was the God-fearing king who issued the decree that allowed Ezra to work hard for the restoration of Jerusalem.

One day, the king sees the worried look on Nehemiah's face and asks why. Nehemiah tells the king about the conditions in Jerusalem and asks if he can go there to build a wall. He asks the king for three things: a deadline, a decree, and timber to build the city walls. Artaxerxes allows Nehemiah to go to Jerusalem in the capacity of governor to rebuild the walls and gates, and he issues a decree to help him in his work.

It was the seventh year of Artaxerxes the king that Ezra went up to Jerusalem (Ezra 7:7-8), and it was 13 years after that, in the twentieth year of Artaxerxes the king (Neh. 2:1), that Nehemiah arrived in Jerusalem. This shows us that Ezra and Nehemiah worked together for Jerusalem's revival.

Starting to Rebuild the City Walls

Nehemiah leads a small crowd to Jerusalem. This is called the third wave of returnees. At the time of the first wave, Zerubbabel led the construction of the Jerusalem Temple; in the second wave, Ezra led a revival of the Word. In the third wave, Nehemiah leads the reconstruction of the city walls of Jerusalem.

Through the ministries of the three waves of returnees, we can get a sense of how we can restore things in our personal lives, our church, and our social communities. The construction of Zerubbabel's temple is the restoration of a God-centered life. It is the restoration of intimacy with God. Ezra's restoration of the Word points to the restoration of a Word-driven restoration in individuals, church communities, and all areas of society.

Even though our personal lives and relationship with God may be restored, what continues to negatively impact our lives is that the change of character may not take place at the same pace. The process of rebuilding the walls shows the process through which our character is molded into God's character and all realms of society are completely rebuilt in alignment with God's character.

In other words, we must build upon God's justice in the realm of politics, God's honesty in the realm of economics, God's wisdom in the realm of education, God's truth in the realm of the mass media, God's holiness in the realm of festivals, such as arts, sports, and entertainment, God's compassion and godliness in the realm of the church, God's creatorship in the realm of science and technology, and God's loving character in the realm of our homes.

God works to restore individual lives and the church community through these waves of returns from captivity. And through His church, God impacts society so that it may be built on the right foundations.

Nehemiah Chapter 3 records the construction of walls and gates. The Chapter also records the details of who did what in the construction of the walls and gates, as well as provides a list of those who participated in the construction. Their profession and area of origin are also recorded.

The list included a number of priests, merchants of gold and perfumery, businessmen, and high-ranking people such as provincial governors and military leaders. People from all walks of life participated in the construction. They did not fund the construction with debt but participated with what they had to the best of their abilities. Some contributed little and some contributed much. Moreover, the participants were not from a single region but different regions, all participating equally.

The participants' names are indicated, including information about whose son and grandson they are. This was to prevent confusion between participants with the same name. Here, we see that God remembers everyone's hard work, whether it is big or small, and records it all in His book.

The Book of Nehemiah depicts the process of the reconstruction of Jerusalem wall. Nehemiah completes the construction while building the walls on the one hand and defending against disrupters on the other.

Disrupters of the Construction

Nehemiah Chapters 4-6 describe how Nehemiah dealt with those disrupting the construction of the city walls. Although the Gentiles interfered with the wall's reconstruction, Nehemiah continued to rebuild the walls unceasingly despite the obstacles. "From that day on, half of my servants worked on construction, and half held the spears, shields, bows, and coats of mail. And the leaders stood behind the whole house of Judah, who were building on the wall. Those who carried burdens were loaded in such a way that each labored on the work with one hand and held his weapon with the other. And each of the builders had his sword strapped at his side while he built. The man who sounded the trumpet was beside me" (Neh. 4:16-18).

These disruptors also spread rumors. They made up lies, slandered Nehemiah, and bribed officials to interfere. They stirred fear in the hearts of those who worked with Nehemiah and weakened their hands in an attempt to stop the construction (Neh. 6:1-14). Nehemiah hardened his determination, pressed on, and prayed to God continuously. "But now, O God, strengthen my hands" (Neh. 6:9).

Even false prophets joined the disrupters. "Remember Tobiah and Sanballat, O my God, according to these things that they did, and also the prophetess Noadiah and the rest of the prophets who wanted to make me afraid" (Neh. 6:14).

However, Nehemiah did not delay, hesitate, or become discouraged in doing the work that God had assigned him and saw it through to the end. While working on the construction, he set up watchmen to get rid of the disrupters. If we face hindrances as we try to carry out God's will, we must relentlessly work to do the will of God and ask God for His help as we continue to engage in spiritual warfare and intercessory prayer. We must diligently work to complete the task ahead while being awake, praying, and not falling prey to despair.

Another obstruction to the building of the walls came from the inside. The poor appealed to the governor Nehemiah about their plight. During those times, there was a famine which meant that those who borrowed money had to pay a very steep rate of interest: 12 percent per year (Neh. 5:7,11). They also had to provide their land or home as collateral (Neh. 5:3-4). Some were even sold as slaves (5:5). These were the circumstances that slowed the construction of the walls.

Thus, Nehemiah proceeded to investigate the truth. Ezra and Nehemiah held a convention for this, and they all came together to stand before the Lord. They commanded that people stop taking interest and to instead return any interest already received as well as the land or homes that had been taken as collateral. The creditors obeyed Nehemiah and Ezra's command and the debtors praised God.

During the 12 years that Nehemiah served as governor, he not once received any remuneration for his service. He limited himself to what was given by the Persian palace and did not ask for what he could rightfully demand from the people to relieve them of this heavy burden (Nem. 5:14-15).

Nehemiah and Ezra, Leaders of the Revival

Nehemiah Chapters 8-13 record Ezra and Nehemiah's joint ministry to reform the nation and to continue the revival movement. After the completion of the wall, Ezra and Nehemiah lead the revival movement through a joint ministry. They built a strong nation, calling people to repent, renewing worship, and reorganizing all the works of those who serve God.

As Ezra and Nehemiah united to establish the kingdom of God, their leadership creates a synergic effect. Nehemiah may not have had the eloquence of a seasoned scholar like Ezra, but as a politician, he was skilled at carrying out tasks dynamically and actively. Nehemiah's enthusiasm and Ezra's spirituality became the driving force behind the nation.

Ezra and Nehemiah held a meeting in the square in front of the Water Gate during the Feast of the Trumpets. Ezra preaches the Word of God from a pulpit built especially for that purpose. Fourteen ministers, including the six partner preachers of the Word he set on his right and the seven on his left, minister to the people. The people gather voluntarily and listen to the Word for six hours, from six o'clock in the morning until noon (Neh. 8:1-12). They hear the Word and are moved; they respond by obeying the Word of God. This meeting continued for eight days. Everyone set up tents in the square and celebrate the Feast of Booths for an entire week. Ezra preached the Word from day one to the end (Neh. 8:13-18).

On the 24th of that month, all the children of Israel gathered and fasted for 12 hours from 6 a.m. to 6 p.m., sharing the Word and praying. They listened to the Word of God from 6 am to 9 am, prayed from 9 am to noon, listened to the Word again until 3 pm, then prayed again until 6 pm (Neh. 9:3). Listening to the Word, they confessed their sins and, bowing before the Lord, spent their day in worship.

Nehemiah 9:5-38 is the wonderful prayer they professed before the Lord on that day. They confessed their sins by relying on God's mercy and sought God's forgiveness and restoration.

"You are a God ready to forgive, gracious and merciful, slow to anger and abounding in steadfast love, and did not forsake them" (Neh. 9:17). In their confession, the people speak of this mercy five times (Neh.9:17,19,27,28,31).

The result of the repentance movement is to obey and act according to the Word of God at the individual, ecclesial and social community levels. The people obeyed the Word immediately, completely, and joyfully. And they promised to live a life of holiness with God. In particular, they decided to forgive all debts (Neh. 10:31). The later chapters also mention tithing several times, reiterating its importance (Neh. 10:37-39, 12:44, 13:5,12).

Outline

Chapters 1-2	Nehemiah's preparations for the reconstruction of the temple Understanding the situation and making plans
Chapters 3-7	Nehemiah's completion of the wall Resolving disruptions within and without, completion of construction
Chapters 8-10	Nehemiah leads the revival with Ezra
Chapters 11-13	The completion of the revival and its participants Leading the revival and solving internal and external disruptions

Voice Outline

NEHEMIAH

100-Day Bible Reading Plan

		CHECK
Day 42	Nehemiah 1-13	

ESTHER

A DRIVING FORCE OF A BLESSING IN DISGUISE

Through the books of Ezra and Nehemiah, we see how God cared for His people and brought them back home to Jerusalem from exile. We also read about the great work that God did through them. However, not all the Jews had returned yet. There were still many living scattered in foreign lands. The Book of Esther shows how God's special care did not only remain with those who returned to the land of Judah, but also with the Jews dispersed throughout Gentile lands.

It is not clear who wrote the book of Esther, but by many measures, it was most likely written by Mordecai since he was in a position to know the events of that time in the greatest detail. The Book of Esther also provides the basis for how the scattered Jews came to celebrate Purim. This book urges and encourages all the scattered Jews to stand firm in their lands as the people of God.

Conspiracy and the Great Upset

The Book of Esther tells the story of Haman the Amalekite

in his plot to destroy the Jews. However, God's providence leads to a remarkable and unexpected turn of events. The conspiracy to exterminate the Jews is upended and instead comes back to bite the conspirators, like a boomerang. So the Jews, who were on the verge of being exterminated, find themselves instead in a position to exterminate the conspirators.

The Book of Esther describes the unfolding of events in detail, showing how God intervened and worked in each of those events. Overall, the book itself quite interesting; it is best read in one sitting for a better understanding. Even in the most difficult and painful of times, God gives His people faith and hope, encourages them, and inspires them. Just as the Book of Exodus describes the Israelites' dramatic exit out of Egypt, the Book of Esther describes the great upset how God protects the Israelites in His amazing ways.

Substitution

Esther Chapters 1-2 tell the process of Esther becoming queen. She is a descendant of the Jews driven to exile in Babylon. After she was orphaned at a young age, her cousin Mordecai raised her as his own daughter. She was beautiful in her appearance, and she respected Mordecai.

Esther became queen of the Persian Empire by the providence of God. The Bible details her path through which she became queen. This part is very important as it is her position that provides her the key to solve all problems later when Haman's conspiracy puts all the Jews in crisis.

By making Esther queen, God allows us to see His plan of salvation unveiled through her.

Utter Chaos

Esther Chapter 3 is about Haman's tricks. Haman, an Amalekite, devises a scheme to destroy all the Jews. He is a descendant of Agag. Agag was the title used to refer to the ruler of Amalek (Num. 24:7). Haman was likely a member of Amalekite royalty that had been taken as captives.

The king favors Haman and makes him his chief minister to keep him close and requires that all should prostrate themselves before Haman. However, Haman was neither a respectable nor just man. He was arrogant, hot-blooded, and vengeful. Mordecai refused to prostrate himself before Haman as he knew that Haman was an Amalekite.

In Exodus 17, God vows to fight against Amalek from generation to generation. In Deuteronomy 25, as well, God tells the Israelites that they must remember how Amalek interfered with Israel. For these reasons, Mordecai did not bow before Haman.

Angered by Mordecai's refusal, Haman plots to destroy not only Mordecai but all the Jews in Persia. He is entrusted with full authority from the king to exterminate the Jews, and after discussing this with fortune tellers, he chooses the best day to slaughter them all. This was about five years after Esther became queen (Est. 2:16; 3:7). After this, a decree to kill all the Jews is made, sealed, and proclaimed. With this news, all the enemies rejoice, while all the Jews who hear this news fall into deep despair.

For This Very Moment

Chapter 4 records the Jews' great distress and suffering. When Mordecai and many other Jews hear of the news, they mourn and cry out to God. Their sorrow becomes known to Esther. Mordecai writes to Esther, asking her to meet the king and convince him to withdraw his decree.

At the time, it was not only forbidden but also very dangerous to go to the king without being summoned. Nevertheless, Esther decides to go to the king after fasting and praying. Mordecai says to Esther:

"Do not think to yourself that in the king's palace you will escape any more than all the other Jews. For if you keep silent at this time, relief and deliverance will rise for the Jews from another place, but you and your father's house will perish. And who knows whether you have not come to the kingdom for such a time as this?" (Est. 4:13-14).

Mordecai tells Esther that it was for this very moment that she was allowed to become queen. Her purpose was to save God's people and Mordecai tells her to take full advantage of her status and lead the movement to save the Jews. Christians in a high position should discern and know when that "this very moment" is without pride and with humility. It is God who exalts people for His work. Esther responds to Mordecai like this.

"Go, gather all the Jews to be found in Susa, and hold a fast on my behalf, and do not eat or drink for three days, night or day. I and my young women will also fast as you do. Then I will go to the king, though it is against the law, and if I perish, I perish" (Est. 4:16).

Esther's words, "If I perish, I perish," is a confession of Esther's ironclad determination to save the nation and God's people. Esther decides to go to the king after three days of fasting.

Self-Sabotage

Esther Chapters 5-7 show how Haman's plan to kill Mordecai quickly unravels. On the night King Ahasuerus was unable to fall asleep, the king begins reading the diaries of former kings and learns about Mordecai's service in foiling an assassination plot against a former king.

The king calls Haman, who happened to be standing outside and asks him what should be done for such a man of great service. Haman, believing the king was referring to himself, says, "Let him be one of the king's most noble officials, with all paying homage to him." The king accepts Haman's opinion and commands, "Mordecai is such a man, let him be the most honorable man" (Est. 6:6-10).

God's providence for the salvation of His people is truly amazing. On the very night that Haman had erected a 23-meter-high pole in his own courtyard to hang Mordecai, God did not allow the king to sleep. This led him to read the diaries of former kings and consequently the achievements of Mordecai. And when the king finds out about Haman's pole to hang Mordecai, the king uses it to hang Haman instead (Est. 7:9).

The Great Upset

In Chapters 8-10, Mordecai is exalted, in a vastly unexpected turn of events: the Jews destroy their enemy. The king removes the ring he gave to Haman and gives it to Mordecai. He also gives all of Haman's fortunes to Esther and Mordecai. Esther asks the king to lift Haman's evil plot to exterminate the Jews.

Then the king issued a decree to not only overturn the plan to exterminate the Jews, but going as far as to avenge the enemies of the Jews. Two royal decrees regarding the Jews were promulgated at the palace in Susa. The first decree was written on January 13th and ordered the death of all Jews on December 13. The second decree, written on the 23rd of March, orders Jews to destroy those who tried to kill them on the 13th of December.

Haman's chosen day became a despicable day, and for the Jews, the day turned from a day of sorrow to a day of joy and holiness. It was a great upset: the day on which Haman had schemed to exterminate the Jews became the day on which the Jews avenged their dead and instead exterminated their enemies. The Jews celebrate this day as 'Purim' when they were under God's protection but their enemies were slaughtered. Mordecai sends a letter to all the Jews who were in the provinces of Persia: "Keep the fourteenth day of the month Adar and also the fifteenth day of the same, year by year, as the days on which the Jews got relief from their enemies, and as the month that had been turned for them from sorrow into gladness and from mourning into a holiday;

that they should make them days of feasting and gladness, days for sending gifts of food to one another and gifts to the poor" (Est. 9:21-22).

Purim is a day of joy, a day of gift-giving, and a day of salvation for the poor. It is the day of thanksgiving for God's salvation, and the day when those who have been shown mercy show mercy. God always cares for, protects, and guides His people. In Psalms 37:12-13, it is written, "The wicked plots against the righteous and gnashes his teeth at him, but the Lord laughs at the wicked, for he sees that his day is coming."

The Book of Esther clearly reveals to us how God looks after His people, removes their enemies, and exalts them. Through the cross of Jesus Christ, God has exalted from cursed to blessed, from darkness to light, from death to life, and from bondage to freedom.

Outline

Chapters 1-2	Esther becomes the queen of Persia
Chapter 1	Queen Vashti is dethroned
Chapter 2	Esher becomes queen
Chapters 3-5	Haman's plot and Esther's decision
Chapter 3	Haman's plot
Chapter 4	Esther's decision
Chapter 5	Esther's wisdom
Chapters 6-7	Self-sabotage
Chapter 6	Haman's fall and Mordecai's rise
Chapter 7	Haman hanged on his own pole
Chapters 8-10	The great upset - Purim
Chapter 8	Mordecai is exalted
Chapter 9	The origin of Purim
Chapter 10	Epilogue

Voice Outline

ESTHER

100-Day Bible Reading Plan

		CHECK
Day 43	Esther 1-10	

The Poetical Books

The books of Job, Psalms, Proverbs, Ecclesiastes, and the Song of Solomon, categorized as the 'Poetical Books' as a group, are very different from the Law and Historical Books that come before them as well as the Prophetical Books that come after them. The previous books are easy to understand since they contain stories that are clear and straightforward historical facts. However, it is much more difficult to understand the Poetical Books and grasp their meaning, just as it might be for the textbook of an advanced level class. So, we need to focus our minds and hearts if we are to find the hidden treasures within these texts.

They also differ in style and composition. Except for the Book of Ecclesiastes, all are poetry. Even the Book of Ecclesiastes is not in prose, but rather in verse. The Book of Job is a heroic poem, the Book of Psalms a holy song, and the Song of Solomon is often referred to as a lyrical poem.

JOB

THE MEANING OF SUFFERING

The books of Job, Psalms, and Proverbs are connected in their main themes. The Book of Job teaches us what we need to believe about God, and the Book of Psalms teaches us how to worship, dedicate ourselves to, and maintain intimacy with God. The Book of Proverbs specifically teaches us how to manage ourselves in each aspect of our lives.

These three books are listed in chronological order, but it could also be said that they are arranged according to the natural progression of one's faith. This is because when we gain knowledge of God, we can form correct judgments about God, correct our misunderstandings, and learn how to go before God to worship Him. Beyond this, we can learn how to make wise choices in the world as well as the ways to please God. Thus, we can consider the Book of Job our doctrine, the Book of Psalms our hymns and prayers, and the Book of Proverbs our practice.

Also, the Book of Job was written based on actual facts and not fictitious stories. Job was a historical figure whom the Prophet Ezekiel placed alongside Noah and Daniel (Ezek.

14:14). The conversations between God and Satan about Job, those between Job and his friends, as well as those between Job and God are written exactly as they took place.

There are many verses in the Book of Job that are difficult to understand, but grasping the whole story is of great benefit to our lives. By understanding the Book of Job, we gain an understanding of God and His absolute sovereignty and providence. This book also teaches us patience during times of suffering. In particular, Job shows us the image of Jesus who denied himself, suffered on the cross, and ultimately reached glory through suffering.

Structure

The Book of Job is structured into three parts and each of these parts is composed of discussions.

The first discussion takes place in Chapters 1-2 between God and Satan about Job's faith. The second takes place in Chapters 3-37 among Job, his three friends, and Elihu. These chapters present the counterarguments of Job's three friends on his suffering. The third discussion takes place in Chapters 38-42 between God and Job. The Chapters conclude with God's words on Job's faith. By the end of the book, Job gains an accurate understanding of both himself and God.

The first discussion is presented in prose form and the second long discussion is in verse form. The third discussion is again then written in prose.

First Discussion: God and Satan

Chapters 1 and 2 provide the background necessary to understand the entire Book of Job. Despite being in prose, it is structured like a scenario that can be performed directly as a play.

Chapter 1 can be divided into three main scenes.

The first scene in Verses 1-5 introduces Job and his family. These verses explain his wealth, children, fame, and strong faith. The second scene in Verses 6-12 is a conversation between God and Satan before the throne of God. And the third scene in Verses 13-22 again records Job and his family's great suffering.

The first scene describes events that occurred here on earth, the seen world; the second scene describes events that took place in the heavens, the unseen world. The third scene then comes back to earth, the seen world again. Without a full understanding of the events of the second scene, it is not possible to correctly interpret all the suffering Job faces in his life. How could Job, a man so rich, happy, and faithful be subjected to such immense suffering in such a short span of time? If we do not keep God's conversation with Satan in the second scene in mind, it is easy to fall into a false assessment.

When we understand the unseen spiritual world, we can correctly assess, understand, and respond to the events of the seen world. Generally, what happens in the seen world begins in the unseen and then flows into the seen.

The Book of Job presents several different perspectives on Job. Each of the perspectives that Satan, Job's friends, and

God have on Job is described through dialogue.

Satan says this to God about Job: "Does Job fear God for no reason? Have you not put a hedge around him and his house and all that he has, on every side? You have blessed the work of his hands, and his possessions have increased in the land. But stretch out your hand and touch all that he has, and he will curse you to your face" (Job 1:9-11).

But God responds to Satan by saying, "Job's faith is not a result of the blessings I have given him, but because he knows me." Satan argues that Job's faith is dependent on his circumstances but God tells Satan that Job judges his circumstances based on his knowledge of God. God says that Job's faith will not falter no matter the circumstances.

In order to determine who best understands Job's faith, God allows tremendous suffering in Job's home and his works. He suffers through two big hardships, all bringing him tremendous suffering. It is hard to imagine anyone other than Job going through such great misfortune in such a short amount of time.

- First suffering (Chapter 1—all occurring within less than an hour, four times)
  - The people of Sheba kill his servants and rob him of 500 cows and 500 female donkeys.
  - Fire falls from the sky and burns 7,000 of his sheep and servants.
  - Three groups of Chaldeans raid and kill his servants and steal 3,000 camels.

- A big wind blows the roof of his house down, killing all seven of his sons and three of his daughters who were celebrating his birthday.

- Second suffering (Chapter 2)
  - Job is covered in boils from the sole of his foot to the crown of his head. He takes a piece of broken pottery and scrapes himself.

Despite all his suffering, Job still did not lose his faith in or his faithfulness to God. Chapters 1-2 tell us twice that Job did not sin with his lips (Job 1:22; 2:10). In conclusion, God's judgment was correct.

Second Discussion: Job's Friends and Elihu

In Chapters 3-37, three of Job's friends and Elihu come to comfort Job about the tremendous suffering that has been brought down upon him. His friends are at a loss for words when they witness Job's suffering and the state in which he is. A week later, Job cries out in his resentment, "Let the day perish on which I was born" (Job 3:3). Here, we see Job's patience hit rock bottom.

Hearing his words, Job's friends start talking. They judge Job without hesitation: "If you were faithful before God, God would have blessed you. But because you were not, God has given you suffering."

They attack and accuse Job of being a hypocrite, saying that his suffering was caused by his unfaithfulness before

God. Their debate was fierce. The three friends take turns interrogating and attacking Job, and Job continues to defend himself against their attacks. They urge Job to repent. However, Job objects to his friends' accusations and justifies his suffering. He tells them that he is a faithful and righteous person before God and that he does not know the reason for his suffering. Rather than comforting him, the three friends drive Job further into a corner with all their criticism (Job 3-31).

When Job and his three friends are tired from arguing their own positions and become silent, Elihu, who was listening to their discussion, finally opens his mouth. He appears not to be of the same age as Job and his friends. He is much younger, and from the three friends' point of view, he was more like a disciple.

Fed up with the words that are coming out of the three friends' mouths, Elihu violently rebukes them. He tells the three friends that they are judging Job's faith from the wrong perspective. At the same time, he tells Job to live a truly humble life before God. No one, not Job nor his friends, is able to rebut the eloquent words of rebuke that pierce their hearts (Job 32-37).

Third Discussion: God and Job

Chapters 38-42 record the dialogue between God and Job. God tells Job, "Do not try to make excuses for yourself; do not grumble or complain and be still." In short, God tells Job to "Shut your mouth." He also asks him these questions, "Have you? ", "Do you know?", and "Where were you?"

"On what were its (the earth's) bases sunk?" (Job 38:6)

"Have you entered into the springs of the sea?" (Job 38:16)

"Have you comprehended the expanse of the earth?"(Job 38:18)

"Where is the way to the dwelling of light, and where is the place of darkness?"(Job 38:19)

"Have you seen the storehouses of the hail?"(Job 38:22)

"Who has cleft a way for the thunderbolt?"(Job 38:25)

"Who has begotten the drops of dew?"(Job 38:28)

"Do you clothe the horse's neck with a mane?" (Job 39:19)

These questions force Job to admit the extent of his own ignorance and incompetence (Job 38-41).

In the final Chapter 42, Job, after gaining a deeper understanding of God, ends his words with, "I will no longer open my mouth and keep it shut." He confesses and repents his arrogance and responds by living a life of stillness before the Lord.

"I had heard of you by the hearing of the ear, but now my eye sees you; therefore I despise myself, and repent in dust and ashes" (Job 42:5-6).

God heals Job's diseases and restores him with twice as much as he had before.

Outline

Chapters 1-2	Job's suffering
Chapters 3-37	Job's discussions
Chapters 3-14	The flow of the first discussion
Chapters 15-21	The flow of the second discussion
Chapters 22-26	The flow of the third discussion
Chapters 27-31	Job's last defense
Chapters 32-37	Elihu's solution
Chapters 38-42	Job's salvation
Chapters 38-41	God's rebuke
Chapter 42	Job's repentance and restoration

Voice Outline

JOB

100-Day Bible Reading Plan

		CHECK
Day 44	Job 1-10	
Day 45	Job 11-20	
Day 46	Job 21-30	
Day 47	Job 31-42	

PSALMS

PASSION AND LONGING TOWARDS GOD - A CONFESSION OF LOVE

The Book of Psalms is one of the most remarkable and outstanding books of the Old Testament. This book not only contains content about God and the law but also much about Christ and the Law. It is for these reasons that Psalms is also called a 'summary of the Old and New Testaments' or an 'abridged version' of both. More than three-quarters of the Old Testament quotes in the New Testament are from the Book of Psalms.

The Historical Books of the Old Testament draw us toward God. The Book of Job takes us to God's school and teaches us who God is and about His providence. The Book of Psalms, on the other hand, draws us out of the conversations of the politicians, philosophers, and polemicists of the world and brings us before the throne of God. The book then pours out our souls before the Lord, enabling us to worship and stand before Him.

Purpose

The Book of Psalms is a useful book for praise and worship while at the same time abundant in excellent truths that lead us to serve God the right way. Meditating on its words which are like the waters of an overflowing freshwater spring allows us to draw that water with joy. These are words that bring vigilance, encouragement, counsel, comfort, and strength. But above all, they teach us how to come before the Lord to worship and praise Him. They also help us to gain greater intimacy with God. The seven Penitential Psalms (6; 32; 38; 51; 102; 130; 143) also help us restore our faith.

Structure of Psalms

The Book of Psalms is composed of five "books."

Book 1 extends from Psalms 1-41, mostly comprising David's poems. Book 2 goes from Psalms 42-72, composed by David and the "sons of Korah." Book 3 goes from Psalms 73-89 and contains most of the psalms of Asaph. Book 4, whose author is unknown, goes from Psalms 90-106. The final Book 5 from Psalms 107-150 is mostly composed of David's poems.

Out of the 150 psalms in the book, 100 psalms state the name of the author; 73 of those psalms are ascribed to David. Asaph the Levite, who headed the service of Music, authored 12 psalms; 10 of the psalms belong to a few Levite musicians; two belong to Solomon; Heman, a Levite musician during David's reign authored one; Ethan, a musician during David's reign wrote one; and one is ascribed to Moses.

Each of these books ends with a doxology. These are found

in 41:13 in Book 1, 72:18-19 in Book 2, 89:52 in Book 3, 106:48 in Book 4, and the entire Chapter of 150 in Book 5. Book 1-3 end with "Amen, amen," and Book 4 and Book 5 end with "Halleluiah."

The five "books" of Psalms resemble the five books of the Pentateuch. Book 1 has a similar theme to that of Genesis, centering on the creation of mankind. Book 2 is similar to Exodus, focusing on themes such as salvation and redemption. Book 3 follows the themes of Leviticus, referring to themes such as worship and sanctuary life. Book 4 is similar to Leviticus centered on the theme of life as a pilgrim in the wilderness and this world. The last book, Book 5, shares themes with the Book of Deuteronomy, focusing on praise and the Word of God.

- Psalms starting with Halleluiah (111;112)
- Pslams ending with Halleluiah (104; 105; 115; 116; 117)
- Psalms beginning and ending with Halleluiah (106; 113; 135; 146; 147; 148; 149; 150)

God's Image

The Book of Psalms is filled with images of God that explain who He is.

- God who is my **shield**, "But you, O Lord, are a shield about me"—God who protects us from the fiery arrows of our enemies (3:3)
- God who is my **rock**, "The Lord is my rock"—God who is a steadfast and strong foundation (18:2)

- God as **King**, "Give attention to the sound of my cry, my King and my God"—God who is worthy of our worship; God who rules over our entire lives (5:2)
- God who is my **shepherd**, "The Lord is my shepherd; I shall not want"—God who looks over and guides our lives (23:1)
- God as **Judge**, "God is a righteous judge"—God who is the executor of justice and passes sentences when we have been wronged (7:11)
- God who is my **refuge**, "God is our refuge and strength, a very present help in trouble"—God who keeps me safe and protects me through all my troubles (46:1)
- God who is my **fortress**, "For you are my rock and my fortress"—God who keeps us safe from the hands of our enemies (31:3-4)
- God who is my **avenger**, "O Lord, God of vengeance, O God of vengeance, shine forth"—God who avenges our enemies because He does not wish for us to do it ourselves (94:1)
- God as **Creator**, "By the word of the Lord the heavens were made"—God who created everything in existence in this world with His word (33:6,9)
- God who is my **Savior**, "The salvation of the righteous is from the Lord"—God who saves us from trouble and secures our feet when we slip (37:39-40)
- God who is my **Healer**, "O Lord my God, I cried to you for help, and you have healed me"—God who heals all our sicknesses (30:2)

- God who is my **Protector**, "But let all who take refuge in you rejoice; let them ever sing for joy"—God who protects us when we take refuge in Him and not in man (5:11)
- God who is my **Provider**, "He rained down on them manna to eat and gave them the grain of heaven"—God who fills all our needs with plenty (78:24-29)
- God who is my **Redeemer**, "Let the redeemed of the Lord say so, whom he has redeemed from trouble and gathered in from the lands, from the east and from the west, from the north and from the south"—God who redeems us from the claws of the archenemy (107:2,3)

Messiah in the Psalms

The Book of Psalms explains who the Messiah is and explains how the prophecy will be fulfilled in the New Testament.

- 2:7 Jesus the Son of God (Matt. 3:17)
- 8:2 Jesus who is praised by the children (Matt. 21:15-16)
- 8:6 Jesus who is ruler over all things (Heb. 2:8)
- 16:10 Jesus who rose from the dead (Matt. 28:7)
- 22:1 Jesus who is forsaken by God (Matt. 27:46)
  "Eli, Eli, lema sabachthani?"
- 22:7-8 Jesus who is laughed at by the archenemy (Luk. 23:35)
- 22:16 Jesus who is nailed by his hands and feet (John 20:27)
- 22:18 Jesus whose garments were divided by casting lots (Matt. 27:35,36)
- 34:20 Jesus who had not one bone in His body broken (John

19:32-33,36)

- 35:11 Jesus who was falsely accused (Mark. 14:57)
- 35:19 Jesus who is despised without reason (John 15:25)
- 40:7-8 Jesus who takes pleasure in doing the will of God within God's will (Heb. 10:7)
- 41:9 Jesus who is betrayed by His friends (Luk. 22:47-48)
- 45:6 Jesus who is the Eternal King (Heb. 1:8)
- 68:18 Jesus who rose to the heavens (Act. 1:9-11)
- 69:9 Jesus who had zeal for the House of God (John 2:17)
- 69:21 Jesus who was offered wine mixed with gall (Matt. 27:34)
- 109:4 Jesus who prays for his enemies (Luk. 23:34) "Father, forgive them, for they know not what they do."
- 109:8 The office of the enemy is taken by another (Act. 1:20)
- 110:1 Jesus who rules over his enemies (Matt. 22:44)
- 110:4 Jesus who is a priest forever (Heb. 5:6)
- 118:22 Jesus who is the cornerstone of the Temple (Matt. 21:42)
- 118:26 Jesus who comes in the name of the Lord (Matt. 21:9)

Psalm 1 is the introduction of the entire Book of Psalms; Psalm 150 is the conclusion. Both Psalms have an equal number of verses. If Psalm 1 prepares us for worship, Psalm 150 fills us with overwhelming joy and moves us deeply.

Psalm 22 depicts the Messiah's suffering on the cross, Psalm 23 depicts the Shepherd who leads His sheep, and Psalm 24 depicts a Messiah who is mighty in battle. Overall, these psalms describe Jesus Christ as the Shepherd.

- The Good Shepherd (John 10:11)
- The Great Shepherd (Heb. 13:20)

The eight psalms of Psalms 93-100 and the five psalms of Psalms 103-107 are referred to as the "Psalms of Worship."

The five psalms of Psalms 140-144 are the "Psalms of Prayer."

The six psalms of Psalms 145-150 are the "Psalms of Praise."

Psalm 18 is a modified version of 2 Samuel 22 recorded and made suitable for worship.

Psalm 117 is the shortest chapter in the Bible. Psalm 2, 67, and 87 raise passion for missions in our hearts.

Of course, God's heart for all the nations is revealed throughout the Psalms.

Psalm 19, along with Psalm 119, awakens a passion for God's Word in our hearts.

Psalm 119

Unlike the other Psalms, this Psalm can be considered to be a book of its own. It could even be referred to as the "Psalm of Psalms." Psalms 119 can be likened not so much to a chain of linked golden rings but rather a treasure chest full of gold rings. It is not only the longest chapter of the Bible; it is also very unique and exquisite in its structure.

Psalm 119 is divided into 22 stanzas, each corresponding to the 22 letters that make up the Hebrew alphabet. Each stanza is composed of eight verses and each of these eight verses begins with the same Hebrew letter. For example, Verses 1-8 of the first stanza all start with the Hebrew letter, "Aleph," the verses (Verses 9-16) of the second stanza start with "Bet," with all other stanzas following the same pattern. Psalms 119 is composed of 22 such stanzas for every letter of the alphabet with 8 verses each (8×22), adding up to 176 verses in total.

The entirety of Chapter 119 speaks of one thing: the characteristics and power of God's Word. It describes ten characteristics of the Word of God.

1. God's law—drafted by the Lord, our God
2. God's path—God's principles and the rules by which we must abide
3. God's evidence—that have been testified
4. God's commandments—those that have been given to us by God's authority
5. God's rules—given to us by God for us to follow
6. God's Word—given by God who is the Word
7. God's judgment—shaped by God's wisdom
8. God's righteousness—serving as the standard for all areas of our lives for it is holy and righteous
9. God's penal code—determined and confirmed by God
10. God's truth—that is everlasting and unchanging

Outline

Chapters 1-41 (Book 1)	Creation of mankind (resembles Genesis)
Chapters 42-72 (Book 2)	Salvation and redemption (resembles Exodus)
Chapters 73-89 (Book 3)	Worship and the sanctuary (resembles Leviticus)
Chapters 90-106 (Book 4)	The wilderness and wandering (resembles Numbers)
Chapters 107-150 (Book 5)	The Word and worship (resembles Deuteronomy)

Voice Outline

PSALMS

100-Day Bible Reading Plan

		CHECK
Day 48	Psalms 1-20	
Day 49	Psalms 21-40	
Day 50	Psalms 41-60	
Day 51	Psalms 61-80	
Day 52	Psalms 81-100	
Day 53	Psalms 101-120	
Day 54	Psalms 121-150	

PROVERBS

WISDOM FOR LIFE

The author of the Book of Proverbs is the Holy Spirit. However, it was recorded by Solomon after God filled him with the Holy Spirit. Some say that Solomon wrote Song of Solomon in his youth, Proverbs in his mid-years, and Ecclesiastes in his later years. He is assumed to have written Song of Solomon at a young age because he refers to himself as Solomon without the title of king. It is assumed that he wrote the book as a young man filled with the Holy Spirit before he ascended the throne.

It is also assumed that Solomon wrote the Book of Proverbs in his mid-years since he introduces himself as "Solomon, son of David, king of Israel," indicating that he was ruling over all of Israel at the time of his authorship of Proverbs. Scholars attribute the Book of Ecclesiastes to his later years because he introduces himself as the "son of David, king in Jerusalem," coinciding with his later years when his influence over the tribes had diminished and he was sovereign only over Jerusalem.

The Books of Chronicles and Kings tell us that, "many from

countries near and far came to meet Solomon." They also tell us that they came to "witness Solomon's glory and hear his wisdom."

The Book of Proverbs teaches us God's wisdom through each proverb and concise sentences.

These present ideas are not necessarily connected to each other, but are rather individual ideas on their own. They are a clear, easy, and efficient way of instruction that make it easy to understand and remember them.

If the Book of Psalms allows us to go before God in deep fellowship, the Book of Proverbs helps us go into this world and live a righteous life. The Psalms give rise to a fiery, holy passion for God, and the Proverbs make us shine by allowing us to live a life full of wisdom and discernment.

Reading the Psalms benefits our prayers and reading the Proverbs helps us correct our conduct. Therefore, it is desirable to read and meditate on 5 Psalms and 1 chapter of Proverbs a day. By reading through the Books of Psalms and Proverbs with in a month, we will not only grow closer to God, we will also see great improvements in our relationships with others.

***Prologue** (Chapter 1:1-6)*

The Book of Proverbs contains God's amazing principles on ethics, politics, the economy, and mass media. It also provides the wisdom to lead all our relationships correctly as well as the wisdom to know how to properly conduct ourselves. The Book of Proverbs deals with the issues of wisdom and discernment in life.

Chapter 1:1-6 does a good job of explaining the purpose of Proverbs. It tells us who wrote the proverbs and for what purpose, as well as what the results of obedience or disobedience are. "The proverbs of Solomon, son of David, king of Israel: To know wisdom and instruction, to understand words of insight, to receive instruction in wise dealing, in righteousness, justice, and equity; to give prudence to the simple, knowledge and discretion to the youth—Let the wise hear and increase in learning, and the one who understands obtain guidance, to understand a proverb and a saying, the words of the wise and their riddles." (Pro. 1:1-6).

1. Purpose

The Book of Proverbs brings us wisdom and instruction. Wisdom is the ability to apply the knowledge gained in our lives. It is to know what to say and do in life, and to know how to help others. It also enables us to understand words of sagacity, gives the knowledge to distinguish between truth and falsehood, good and evil, allows us to hate sin, and helps us live according to the Word in our lives (1:2). They act as a guide that shows us how to conduct ourselves wisely, fairly, justly, and honestly (1:3).

2. Usage

The Book of Proverbs makes a wise man out of the fool. The book is written in a way that enables anyone to understand it easily and clearly so that they may not lose their way. It gives the youth knowledge and spirit. Youth is a learning period. Youth are impatient, reckless, and often lacking in thought. Through the Book of Proverbs, they can gain knowledge, discipline, and discernment (1:4).

3. Results

The wise will gain greater wisdom as they hear and read the words of Proverbs. Not only does the fool become wise, the wise becomes even wiser. It teaches the reader what God's will is. The discerning man will become more resourceful and understand how to execute God's will (1:5). As the reader goes through the Book of Proverbs, they will gain insight into proverbs, parables, words of the wise, and their subtle pronouncements (1:6).

An Outline of the Book for the Youth (Proverbs Chapter 1:7 through Chapter 9)

Proverbs 1:7 to Proverbs 9 can be considered an outline that paints the picture of the entire Book of Proverbs. These chapters present the two most important principles by which youth must live. The first principle is the fear of God. The fear of God is the foundation of knowledge. Without getting this principle right, it is impossible to know anything. If we wish to gain knowledge that makes us better individuals, we must first and foremost learn to fear God.

The alpha and omega of knowledge is the fear of the Lord. The foolish who do not fear God disregard wisdom and instruction. Those who fear the Lord pay attention to God's Word.

The second principle is respect for one's mother and father. Those who respect their parents listen to their instructions. They engrain the teachings of their parents into their hearts. These principles are to be worn as a graceful garland for their heads and pendants adorning their necks. All Scripture following these chapters in the Book of Proverbs build on the foundation of these two principles.

Chapter 1 Verses 10-18 introduces another important principle which is not to be in the company of the wicked. The wicked are like a trap that brings lives to ruin. These verses tell us not to walk on the same path as them. God tells us strongly, "Do not follow in the path of the wicked; stubbornly reject their ways; do not be in fellowship with them or be in their company."

Verses 19-33 tell us how foolish it is not to heed God's calling. Failing to heed God's words (1:19-33) is just as foolish as it is foolish to listen to the words of the wicked (1:10-18). To be wise is not to pay attention to the voices of the wicked but to pay attention to the voice of God.

The Lord calls us through wisdom. He tells us to hear the Word and abide by it. God pours the Holy Spirit into those who obey and gives them the strength to live (1:23). But those who hear but ignore Him will be faced with disaster and live in fear. Those who listen will be safe and live in peace.

Chapter 2 tells us about the blessings that the Lord gives to those who pay attention to His words and obey them. Seek and search for wisdom and insight as though you are looking for hidden treasures. By doing so, you will learn to fear God and know Him. It is wisdom that will keep the paths of those who obey straight and safe.

Chapter 3 contains one of the most exceptional writings on faith in the Book of Proverbs. The secret to maintaining intimacy with God and living a godly life is to keep God's Word in our hearts. It is to believe in, depend on, and revere God's sovereign providence. If we serve God with our wealth, He will, in turn, bless us with riches.

Proverbs 6:1-5 warns us that guaranteeing someone's debt will entrap us. If you find yourself in such a trap, you must do your utmost to free yourself as soon as possible. Verses 6-11 tell us that diligence is the way to increase wealth.

Chapter 7 tells us that the way for a young man to control his body is through placing the Word of God in his heart (4:20-27; Psalms 119:9).

In Chapter 8, wisdom is personified as a force powered by the dynamic Word of God. In the New Testament, Jesus is the embodiment of this wisdom and he shows us how to act by the Word of God. In particular, Verses 22-30 tell us the origin of wisdom. Wisdom existed in God long before the creation of the world, before anything else ever came into being, and it has been with us since God's creation of the entire universe.

Verses 5-8 and 12-16 speak of the teachings of wisdom. The teachings of wisdom guide all insight and understanding, the good and the truth, hatred of evil, righteousness, knowledge, and good behavior. Verses 18, 19, and 21 speak of the value of wisdom. Wisdom is divine, holy, the source of spiritual life, righteous and moral, and beneficial to those who seek it (Col. 2:2-3).

Verses 17 and 34-35 tell us that wisdom is given to those who fervently seek it and wait for the Lord daily. When we fervently seek the Lord every day, we meet Jesus Christ who is Himself wisdom, and through Him, we gain the insight and understanding that allows us to live righteous lives.

In Chapter 9, we see the invitation of two women. They both throw a feast and invite us, but their intentions and the results they reap are vastly different. "Christ" is depicted as the wise woman and "sin" is depicted as the foolish woman.

Topic 1: Everyday Wisdom (Chapters 10-24)

Chapter 10 is when Proverbs begins in earnest. These chapters are short but have gravitas. Most of them comprise one or two verses that bring clarity to each other. However, the chapters are not related. Thus, it is not necessary to ascribe a title for each chapter or paragraph; instead, they are best read when viewed as individual sentences.

Chapters 10-24 are the first collection of Solomon's Proverbs and address topics such as controlling one's tongue, a wise mouth, how to gain wealth, righteous behavior, managing anger, a sincere life, pride and humility, diligence and laziness, and relief for the poor.

Topic 2: Wisdom for Leaders (Chapters 25-29)

Chapters 25-29 are the second collection of Solomon's

Proverbs. In 1 Kings 4:32, it is written that Solomon wrote 3000 proverbs. As mentioned in 25:1, Chapters 25-29 contain proverbs that were edited by Hezekiah's officials. These chapters were written for kings about the management of a nation. In these verses, we find the secret to leadership that can change a nation. Therefore, it is important to read these verses from the perspective of a leader.

***Epilogue* (Chapters 30-31)**

Chapters 30-31 appear to be somewhat of an appendix to Solomon's proverbs. Regardless, it is abundantly clear that the author was moved by God to write them.

Chapter 30 is unique in its use of numbers. In particular, the number four plays an important role. Verses 11-14 explain the four kinds of evil people, Verses 15-16 about four things that are never satisfied, Verses 18-20 about things that cannot be fathomed, Verses 21-23 about four unbearable things, Verses 24-28 about four things that are small but wise, and Verses 29-33 are about four things that walk with dignity.

Chapter 31 is a lesson a mother gives to her son and daughter. It is about the things to watch out for as a man (Verses 3-9) and the values to uphold and keep as a woman (Verses 10-31).

Outline

Chapter 1:1-6	Prologue
Chapters 1:7-9	An outline of the book for the youth
Chapters 10-24	Topic 1: Everyday wisdom
Chapters 25-29	Topic 2: Wisdom for leaders
Chapters 30- 31	Epilogue

Voice Outline

PROVERBS

100-Day Bible Reading Plan

		CHECK
Day 55	Proverbs 1-10	
Day 56	Proverbs 11-20	
Day 57	Proverbs 21-31	

ECCLESIASTES

THE WORTHLESSNESS OF LIFE

As stated in Ecclesiastes 1:1, "The words of the Preacher, the son of David, king in Jerusalem," the Book of Ecclesiastes was inspired by the Holy Spirit as Solomon looked back on his life in his old age. Although Solomon started off strong, he could not stand straight before God as a result of the foreign women in his life (1 Kings 11:1-13, 33). At the time of his authorship of Ecclesiastes, Solomon's influence on each of the tribes had declined, hence the introduction as "the son of David, king in Jerusalem" and not the "son of David, king of Israel" as in Proverbs 1:1. Ecclesiastes contains teachings derived from the years and wisdom that comes with old age.

The book of Ecclesiastes is a sermon whose title is 'the futility of life under the sun.' The word futility here does not refer to foolish pride, but rather it points to emptiness and the futility of a life without purpose. The keywords of Ecclesiastes are "wisdom" and "wise," which are repeated over 50 times. Other keywords include "vanity," which is recorded 37 times; the phrase, "under the sun," is recorded a total of 31 times.

The Book of Proverbs and the Book of Ecclesiastes each offer a different kind of wisdom. The wisdom of Proverbs speaks of the wisdom of God who is above the sun, and the wisdom of Ecclesiastes speaks of the wisdom of man who is below the sun. Therefore, it can be said that the wisdom of Proverbs leads to godliness whereas the wisdom of Ecclesiastes leads to simple knowledge. Ecclesiastes does more than merely speak of the futility of life however; it humbles us and creates in our hearts a thirst in the search for true happiness. That is why the Preacher ends his sermon with, "Remember also your Creator in the days of your youth... Fear God and keep his commandments, for this is the whole duty of man" (12:1,13).

Ecclesiastes is a sermon of penance. It is of the same character as some of David's penitential psalms. Solomon confesses and repents of his own past mistakes. He confesses that although he wished to be satisfied through the sensual pleasures of this world, those pleasures were more bitter than death and, in the end, were foolish. He takes complete ownership of his own foolishness and utter weakness. But God, in His wondrous grace and compassion, forgives and purifies even this man.

Amazing Wisdom

The Book of Ecclesiastes can be summarized into the simple question: "What does the value of human existence mean?" In Chapters 1-6, man endeavors to obtain true happiness and satisfaction. However, he comes to the conclusion that his efforts are futile and that, in the end, "all is vanity." Ecclesiastes 7:1-11:8 advises on vanity. It speaks of how to conduct oneself correctly in an evil world. These chapters also tell us that the only antidote to be free from all the temptations and sufferings of this world is wisdom, which is why we must attain it. In Ecclesiastes 11:9-12:14, we are told that the greatest wisdom of all is the fear of and obedience to God.

The Preacher tells us that though we pursue wisdom and pleasure to find true happiness and satisfaction, everything under the sun is vanity. But what he speaks of is neither nihilism nor pessimism. Nor is it fatalism of which he speaks.

All is Vanity without God

"Without God, all pleasure (2:1-2), the wisdom and labor of man (2:20-23) is vanity. Purpose (2:26) and human success (4:4) without God is futility. Human greed (4:8), prestige (4:16), and even wealth (5:10-11) without God too is all futility."

These verses tell us that the absence of God is the reason for the vanity of human life. Solomon was in a position to have all he wanted and more. He also observed and tried everything: he tried to do good with the wisdom of man. But he learned that none of those things can bring true happiness to man. He reaches the conclusion that the only true satisfaction that man can attain can only come from a fear of the Lord.

Solomon sought but failed to find happiness in laboratories, libraries, and meeting rooms. He entertained the best scholars in his court and even spent time in the company of vagabonds. He visits fancy restaurants and even trendy bars and clubs. And yet, he still could not be satisfied.

The final stop in his pursuit was before the presence of the Lord. He finds that it is in the presence of the Lord that true happiness lies. It was the same place he had been during his youth. It took him a while, but he found himself in that same place again. And there, he finally found satisfaction. It was also there that he decided to advise the young so that they may not repeat his foolish mistakes and wander.

As a result, the Book of Ecclesiastes is full of the hope that young people will realize what Solomon realized in his later years. In Ecclesiastes 11:9 Solomon says, "Rejoice, O young man, in your youth, and let your heart cheer you in the days of your youth. Walk in the ways of your heart and the sight of your eyes. But know that for all these things God will bring you into judgment." He follows with these words in 12:1-2, "Remember also your Creator in the days of your youth, before the evil days come and the years draw near of which you will say, 'I have no pleasure in them'; before the sun and the light and the moon and the stars are darkened and the clouds return after the rain." And in 12:12, he says, "My son, beware of anything beyond these. Of making many books there is no end, and much study is a weariness of the flesh." Also in 12:13, he says, "The end of the matter; all has been heard. Fear God and keep his commandments, for this is the whole duty of man."

Only when we fear and serve the Lord can we be freed

from the agony and emptiness that comes from the vain things of this world. This is the remedy that Solomon prescribes to us.

True Satisfaction

Ultimately, the older Preacher tells us that only those who fear the Lord, keep His commandments, and obey His Word can have true satisfaction and joy in this world. This is similar to Peter's confession that even though he worked all night, he caught nothing. However, when he obeyed Jesus and lowered his net, he caught so much that the net broke.

No matter how hard you toil, it is in vain if it is before meeting Jesus. Life without Jesus is a life wasted. Only in meeting Jesus is there true satisfaction. In 1960s North America, a hippie movement called "back to nature" gained popularity among young people. They wandered all around in search of true happiness and satisfaction through drugs, sex, and mystical religious experiences. Some of them even visited the deep mountains of the Himalayas, and yet they found nothing.

Then, Jesus came to them. After that, the tremendous "Jesus People Movement" swept across North America, bringing many young people to Jesus Christ. A young lady in that group famously sang this song after meeting the Lord.

Like the woman at the well I was seeking
For things that could not satisfy:
And then I heard my Savior speaking:

Draw from my well that never shall run dry
Fill my cup Lord, I lift it up, Lord!
Come and quench this thirsting of my soul;
Bread of heaven, Feed me till I want no more
Fill my cup, fill it up and make me whole!

There are millions in this world who are craving
The pleasures earthly things afford;
But none can match the wondrous treasure
That I find in Jesus Christ my Lord.
Fill my cup Lord, I lift it up, Lord!
Come and quench this thirsting of my soul;
Bread of heaven, Feed me till I want no more
Fill my cup, fill it up and make me whole!

So, my brother, if the things this world gave you
Leave hungers that won't pass away,
My blessed Lord will come and save you,
If you kneel to Him and humbly pray:
Fill my cup Lord, I lift it up, Lord!
Come and quench this thirsting of my soul;
Bread of heaven, Feed me till I want no more
Fill my cup, fill it up and make me whole!

- Richard E. Blanchard, *Fill My Cup Lord*

This young woman's confession is the Preacher's confession. They both went out searching for answers to happiness, to where true satisfaction comes from, and whether these are attainable. Though they thought their pursuit of pleasure would lead them to these things, their path only led them to despair. And surprisingly, it was in their moment of despair that they began their search for God. The knowledge of their own insignificance and misery did not simply condemn them to despair but instead ignited a deep longing for the truth. Just as we seek water when thirsty and food when hungry, it is in this place of despair that we turn to God.

In this hymn, the chorus is repeated three times. In Ecclesiastes, the chorus is repeated seven times (2:24-26; 3:12-15; 3:22; 5:18-20; 8:15; 9:7-10; 11:7-10). In the chorus, Solomon tells us, "Eat, drink, enjoy, seize, labor, and do good." Then, he tells us, "I thought that there was nothing better under the sun." What really shocks us is the confession he makes at the end of all these ventures. He does not say, "Joy of joy; all is joy," but rather, "Vanity of vanities, all is vanity" (12:8).

This confession leads us to despair. But its purpose is not to make us avoid the world or to remove ourselves from the affairs of this world. It is not the kind of despair that leads to suicide or pleasure. This is because this despair of which Solomon speaks is not the end. His last confession leads us to an even more amazing confession: "Remember also your Creator in the days of your youth" (12:1), and "The end of the matter; all has been heard. Fear God and keep his commandments, for this is the whole duty of man" (12:13).

Jesus Says to the Woman by the Well:

"Everyone who drinks of this water will be thirsty again, but whoever drinks of the water that I will give him will never be thirsty again. The water that I will give him will become in him a spring of water welling up to eternal life" (John 4:13-14).

This woman only found satisfaction after meeting Jesus. "So the woman left her water jar and went away into town and said to the people, 'Come, see a man who told me all that I ever did. Can this be the Christ?' They went out of the town and were coming to him" (John 4:28-30).

The woman told the people in the town: "I met Him and now I am satisfied. The happiness I was searching for is in Him."

True satisfaction and happiness can only be found once we have met Jesus.

Outline

Chapter 1:1-11	Introduction: All is vanity
Chapters 1:12-2	Evidence 1: Evidence through experience
Chapters 3-6	Evidence 2: Evidence through observation
Chapters 7-9	Advice: How to conduct oneself in a wicked world
Chapters 10-11:8	Recommendation: The correct way to use authority and wealth
Chapters 11:9-12	Conclusion: Fear and obey God

Voice Outline

ECCLESIASTES

100-Day Bible Reading Plan

		CHECK
Day 58	Ecclesiastes 1-12	

SONG OF SOLOMON

SONG OF SONGS

The author of this book is Solomon. Song of Solomon 1:1 begins with, "The Song of Songs, which is Solomon's." However, the true author of this book is the Holy Spirit, who used Solomon's hand to write Proverbs, Ecclesiastes, and Song of Songs. Solomon's name is on the cover of the Song of Songs without a title, indicating that he wrote the book before he ascended the throne.

Christ as the Bridegroom and the Church as the Bride

There are three reasons why the Song of Songs was written.

The first of these reasons is that Solomon wanted to express his love for his bride and his love through marriage using beautiful words. In 4:7-10, he writes, "You are altogether beautiful, my love; there is no flaw in you. Come with me from Lebanon, my bride... You have captivated my heart, my sister, my bride... How beautiful is your love, my sister, my bride! How much better is your love than wine."

The second reason is sometimes said to be an expression of God's love for the Israelites. As it is written in Hosea 2:19-20,

"And I will betroth you to me forever… And you shall know the Lord," there are many places in the Bible in which God's love for His people is likened to the love a bridegroom has for his bride.

The third reason is said to express the love between Christ the bridegroom and the Church, His bride. Generally, this third reason is considered to be the main reason that the book was written.

Ephesians 5:32 (a verse on wives and husbands) says, "This mystery is profound, and I am saying that it refers to Christ and the church," using the relationship between a husband and wife to explain Christ being the bridegroom and the Church being His bride. Moreover, 2 Corinthians 11:2 says, "For I feel a divine jealousy for you, since I betrothed you to one husband, to present you as a pure virgin to Christ," and uses the relationship a groom has with his bride to explain the relationship the Church has with Christ. That is why the Song of Songs is said to show the love between Jesus Christ as the bridegroom and the Church as the bride.

Song of Songs

Just like Esther, the word "God" does not appear once in the Book of Song of Solomon. Nevertheless, God's love is revealed abundantly throughout the book. Moreover, it is written in verse rather than prose form and shows us all the different kinds of love. The book records not only love between human beings such as 'Eros,' 'Storge,' and 'Philia,' but also 'Agape,' God's unconditional love that He gives unilaterally.

The Song of Songs stimulates our emotions and evokes passionate desire. Its contents are fun and full of joy, as though we are witnessing an opera stage filled with beautiful, bright scenes on an idyllic backdrop.

The Song of Solomon is the "song of songs." It is an exquisite and passionate love song that Christ, the bridegroom, sings to his bride, the Church. His song is more outstanding than any other song written by man or contained in the Bible. It is said that Solomon composed 1,005 songs (1 Kings 4:32). Although none of his other songs remain, this holy song of love remains to this day and will continue to do so until the bridegroom returns. That is why the Song of Solomon begins with "The Song of Songs, which is Solomon's."

Beautiful Love

The theme of the Song of Solomon can be said to be the beautiful love of the bride and groom. "My beloved" appears 32 times in the book. And the placement of this book, after Ecclesiastes, is very appropriate because through the Book of Ecclesiastes we realize that "everything under the sun is vanity, vanity" and cannot satisfy or make us happy. This leads us to Jesus Christ, in whom we can taste the true satisfaction, joy, and happiness that only comes from being in fellowship with Him.

Deep Adoration

Song of Solomon 1:1-3:5 tells the story of a man and woman who meet for the first time and fall passionately in love, in deep adoration.

For Christians who have received the love of Christ, His love is more precious and valuable than any joy this world has to offer. "For your love is better than wine" (1:2,4; 4:10). His kiss is a token of His love (1:2). Jesus, the bridegroom, is the Rose of Sharon, the most beautiful and fragrant among flowers, and the Church is the bride, the lily of the valley that keeps its wholeness and purity among the thorns (2:1). The love of the bridegroom is expressed as his desire to hear the voice and see the face of the bride. "O my dove, in the clefts of the rock, in the crannies of the cliff, let me see your face, let me hear your voice, for your voice is sweet, and your face is lovely" (2:14).

How happy is the Lord Jesus to have us come before Him to worship and pray! How He adores seeing us just as much as we adore Him!

In 3:6-5:1, a woman accepts an invitation to accompany the bridegroom in glory and unites in love. This paints a picture of the Church, the bride, looking to her bridegroom who is coming in all his glory (3:6-11). These verses show us just how holy is the Church's beauty (4:1-5) and just how beautiful is Jesus the bridegroom's confession of love to his bride (4:7-15)! "You have captivated my heart, my sister, my bride; you have captivated my heart with one glance of your eyes, with one jewel of your necklace" (4:9). He is saying, "You have taken over my heart. With one glance of your pure eyes, you have captivated my heart."

When we eagerly yearn to meet the Lord, the Lord comes to meet us (5:1). "You will seek me and find me, when you seek me with all your heart" (Jer. 29:13). "I love those who love me, and those who seek me diligently find me" (Pro. 8:17).

Song of Solomon 5:2-6:3 describes a temporary parting between lovers and their longing for each other. The Lord loves us with a love that is constant. He knocks on our door, wanting to come inside. But these verses paint a sad story that rebukes us for our spiritual laziness and foolishness despite the love Jesus Christ has for us. Because of our habitual sins, we cannot find the Lord even when we seek Him (5:2-7). However, we must not be discouraged but instead continue to seek the Lord. We must not get caught up in self-condemnation and confess to the Lord:

"Lord, it is my love for You that has healed my disease."

How do we describe our Lord? How do we explain the Jesus Christ that we love to others? Jesus' depiction in Song of Solomon 5:10-16 is the same Christ that the Apostle Paul met on the Island of Patmos (Rev. 1:13-16). He is the Lord of Glory, the One who is untainted, beautiful, pure, and meek, the One whose words are like honey that revitalizes our souls; He is fair, righteous, and bright.

Chapter 6:4-8:14 records the growth of two lovers' love for each other. Finally, we meet the amazing and beautiful Jesus. He forgives our transgressions and meets us again and tells us:

"You are beautiful and lovely. You are my love."

"I am pleased with you. I love you."

"I am always with you."

"I will give you gifts from my abundance."

And we, too, love the Lord. We boast of Him; we rejoice and yearn for Him. We deeply desire to be with Him always. We are joyous and thankful that our love for Him grows each and every day.

Place me like a seal over your heart,
like a seal on your arm.
For love is as strong as death,
its jealousy as enduring as the grave.
Love flashes like fire,
the brightest kind of flame.
Many waters cannot quench love,
nor can rivers drown it.
If a man tried to buy love with all his wealth,
his offer would be utterly scorned.

- Song of Solomon 8:6-7, New Living Translation

A Beautiful Story

We are told a beautiful story about the background of the Book of Song of Solomon. The Song of Solomon begins with his visit to a vineyard in the region of Ephraim, a region known for its vineyards, just before he becomes king.

"The keeper of the vineyard had died, so his wife and two daughters took care of the vineyard. The eldest daughter, a Shulamite woman, was as Cinderella in the eyes of her family. Though she was born naturally beautiful, no one recognized her beauty. Her two half-brothers made her work hard all day, leaving her no time to take care of her appearance. She trimmed grapevines, made trails for fox cubs, and shepherded a herd of sheep. Her face was always sunburned from all the time she spent laboring outside.

Then one day, a tall handsome young man came to the vineyard. It was Solomon in disguise. And the moment he laid eyes on her, he fell in love with her. She assumed him to be a shepherd and asked him about his flock. The young man avoided answering her question and professed his love for her. Then he promised her that he would be back with many gifts for her and left. The eldest daughter saw the young man in her dreams. She missed him, sometimes picturing that he was there with her. Then, finally, the young man returned, dressed as a king, and took her as his wife."

This is the story that is passed down as the background behind the Book of Song of Solomon. This story illustrates the Second Coming of Jesus Christ, who first came to this world as a shepherd and made us his bride, and who will return as a king and take us to the wedding feast of the Lamb.

Outline

Chapters 1-3:5	Falling in love
Chapters 3:6-5:1	Uniting in love
Chapters 5:2-6:3	Testing the power of love
Chapters 6:4-8	The growth of love

Voice Outline

SONG OF SOLOMON

100-Day Bible Reading Plan

		CHECK
Day 59	Song of Solomon 1-8	

The Prophetic Books

The 17 books from Isaiah to Malachi are referred to as the "Prophetic Books." Of these, the five books of Isaiah, Jeremiah, Lamentations, Ezekiel, and Daniel are called the "Major Prophets," and the remaining 12 books from Hosea to Malachi are called the "Minor Prophets."

The Prophetic Books supplement the Historical Books rather than being historical narratives themselves. They record the words of the prophets that God sent to deliver certain messages at specific times.

The purpose of the Prophetic Books is not just to point out sins and declare judgment, but to convict us of our sins and lead us back to serving the Lord. These books also bring comfort, inspiration, and hope to the discouraged and give the weak strength to stand. In these books, we see Jesus Christ as the Prophet. However, to correctly understand the content of the Prophetic Books, we need to consider the conditions of the times in which these books were written.

ISAIAH

GOD'S JUSTICE AND GRACE

The books of Isaiah, Jeremiah, Lamentations of Jeremiah, Ezekiel, and Daniel are called the "Major Prophets," and the remaining books are called the "Minor Prophets." However, this organization is not based on any hierarchy; it is simply based on the larger volumes of the Major Prophets. The prophets who ministered before Isaiah were Hosea, Joel, Amos, and Obadiah. Isaiah came shortly after them. Nevertheless, the Book of Isaiah is at the very beginning of the Prophetic Books due to its size.

Prophet Isaiah

The Book of Isaiah was authored by the Prophet Isaiah. He is mentioned a total of 13 times in Chapters 19 and 20 of 2 Kings. Also, 2 Kings Chapters 18-20 are recorded in the same position with Isaiah Chapters 37-39.

Isaiah was of royal descent. According to Jewish tradition, his father was King Uzziah's younger brother. He lived in the courts of Hezekiah and ministered in the days when the Northern Kingdom of Israel was destroyed by Assyria and only the Southern Kingdom of Judah remained. Isaiah begins his ministry at the end of King Uzziah's reign and serves for 60 years during the reigns of Jotham, Ahaz, and Hezekiah.

According to Jewish tradition, Isaiah was persecuted by Hezekiah's son, the wicked king Manasseh, and was sawed to death. It is possible that the martyrdom by sawing mentioned in Hebrews 11:37 refers to Isaiah. In the Book of Isaiah, Isaiah speaks to Judea and Jerusalem. He also prophesies against the perished Northern Kingdom of Israel and Babylonian Empire and Damascus. He warns not only these nations but several other neighboring nations as well.

The days of Uzziah, Jotham, and Hezekiah were good, albeit on the surface, but the times under King Ahaz were different. He was so wicked that during the 16 years he ruled, he led the entire nation into idolatry. During this time, Isaiah urges the nation to return to God. Otherwise, he prophesies, that they will be cast out of the land. And yet, throughout all this, Isaiah comforts them with God's mercy and grace. He tells them that even though they may have to scatter now, a king named Cyrus will rise and restore them in the distant future.

He speaks of a glorious future by the grace of God and proclaims the coming of the Messiah. He tells them that through the scattered Jews, God's blessings will flow even to the Gentiles.

Uniqueness

The Book of Isaiah makes more prophecies about the

Messiah than any other Prophetical Book. Some refer to Isaiah as the "evangelical prophet," and the Book of Isaiah is sometimes called the "Fifth Gospel."

The theme of the Book of Isaiah is "God's justice and grace." The words "Holy God" are mentioned 25 times, "judgment" 52 times, "comfort" 18 times, and the word "salvation" is mentioned 26 times. In particular, Chapter 53, about the suffering servant, best describes Jesus' work of salvation. This chapter is cited a total of 85 times in the New Testament. If we were to summarize the contents of the Book of Isaiah in a single sentence, it would be, "God is the only Savior and the Most High Ruler."

The Book of Isaiah covers a vast range of topics. It has 66 chapters just like the number of books in the Bible. Not only that, they resemble each other in their characteristics. Isaiah Chapters 1-39 have similar characteristics to those in the Old Testament. These chapters emphasize God's justice and judgment for the sins of Israel, and repentance for sins. Also, Chapters 40-66 have similar characteristics to those in the New Testament. The main themes in these chapters are salvation, hope, forgiveness, and restoration. It could be said that Chapters 1-39 summarize the Old Testament and that Chapters 40-66 summarize the New Testament.

The Book of Isaiah is also an amazing piece of literature that is made up entirely of poetry. It is very beautiful and sophisticated in its style. In literary terms, it is likened to Shakespeare; in theological terms comparisons are drawn to the writings of the Apostle Paul. The Book of Isaiah comprises 66 chapters and 1,292 verses. Again, this is similar to the entire Bible's 66 books and 1,189 chapters. In the New Testament, the Book of Isaiah is cited a total of 472 times.

Important Passages

An important and noteworthy aspect of the Book of Isaiah is the passages that show us God's mercy in dealing with our sins. "Come now, let us reason together, says the Lord: though your sins are like scarlet, they shall be as white as snow; though they are red like crimson, they shall become like wool" (1:18); "I, I am he who blots out your transgressions for my own sake, and I will not remember your sins" (43:25); "I have blotted out your transgressions like a cloud and your sins like mist; return to me, for I have redeemed you" (44:22).

Isaiah also tells us that Jesus Christ will be born by a virgin. "Behold, the virgin shall conceive and bear a son, and shall call his name Immanuel" (7:14); "For to us a child is born, to us a son is given" (9:6).

The Book of Isaiah repeats the words "Fear not." "Fear not, for I am with you; be not dismayed, for I am your God; I will strengthen you, I will help you, I will uphold you with my righteous right hand" (41:10); "Fear not... I am the one who helps you" (41:14); "Fear not" (43:5; 44:8).

Also, God promises us that He will "do a new thing." "Remember not the former things, nor consider the things of old. Behold, I am doing a new thing" (43:18-19).

The Book of Isaiah contains many more confessions of God's abundant love, salvation, and grace in addition to these passages.

Judah and Israel in the Days of the Lord

The first part of Isaiah, Chapters 1-39, is reproof for sin and warning against the coming judgment. The second part, Chapters 40-66, is filled with promises and words of comfort.

Chapters 1-12 are prophecies against Judah and Israel, especially against Jerusalem. The God of justice brings distant nations to enforce his judgment for their sins. However, the God of mercy also promises them the Messiah.

Chapter 1 records Prophet Isaiah's first sermon. Isaiah 1:1 could be considered the title of the book, "The vision of Isaiah concerning Judah and Jerusalem." Verse 2 starts with "Hear, O heavens, and give ear, O earth," as though the book is a notice posted on the temple's public bulletin board so that everyone can read and write it down.

He rebukes the people of God for their sins and tells them that their sins have brought the earth to the brink of destruction. God is greatly discouraged to see His people continue in their ways of life despite Isaiah's warnings. God promises them forgiveness and restoration if they turn from their sins but warns that they will be destroyed if they are stubborn and disobey.

Chapters 2-4 record Isaiah's second sermon. As stated in Isaiah 2:1, these are the words of God on Judah and Jerusalem that Isaiah received from Him. The "latter days" in Verse 2 refer to the day of the Messiah. The "day" here is not a single day but rather a period of time. It is referring to the period during which the Church of Jesus Christ will be established and all the nations will gather there. Although the Gentiles will gather to come before the Lord, Israel will not return to the Lord with its hardened heart, calling judgment upon itself. But the grace of salvation will be given to those who remain in the Lord.

Chapter 5 is God's "bill of indictment" on the sins of His people. God indicts His people of six sins in six sentences that begin with "woe to."

1. Accumulation of wealth through illegal means (5:6-8) — pension manipulation, profiteering, growing one's business at the expense of others' businesses, purchase of land and property for speculative purposes
2. Putting pleasure first (5:10-17) — alcoholism and use of narcotics
3. Not fearing God and sinning (5:18-19) — hypocritical faith
4. Destroying God's standards and ignoring His principles (5:20) — warping truth into lies and romanticizing sin
5. Arrogance and relying on one's own judgment (5:21) — being pompous, arrogant, and boastful
6. Drunkenness (5:22) — indulging in pleasures, parties, etc; being dishonest

God's impartial ruling against them is, "Their wealth will dissipate; their lands will become desolate; they will be captured, isolated, hungry, and humbled." God also calls distant nations to be the "enforcers" of the judgment against Judah's sins.

Chapter 6 covers Isaiah's calling. Isaiah first sees the glory of God and then sees his sinful self. However, he experiences God's forgiveness and pardoning of sins. He also sees God's heart for all nations. To the Lord's words saying "Whom shall I send, and who will go for us?" Isaiah responds, "Here I am! Send me" (6:8).

Chapter 7 is a sermon of counsel and comfort given under special circumstances. God judges Judah's sins, but He still has mercy. The prophecy of the Messiah is a sign of God's mercy. "The virgin shall bear a son, and shall call him Immanuel."

Chapters 8-12 are a series of sermons. They tell a prophecy of how Israel will be destroyed by Assyria and Judah will also suffer under Assyria. At the same time, they prophesize that if the Israelites do not rely on man but on God, God will be their refuge and Assyria will be destroyed. In particular, these chapters foreshadow the coming and reign of the Messiah (Chapters 9,11). In that day, we will sing the song of salvation (Chapter 12). These chapters also talk about the "remnants" who are those who rely on the Lord and wait on the Messiah (10:20-22; 11:11,16).

The Burden of the Nations

Chapters 13-23 contain prophecies of God's judgment against nations. This judgment is based on each nation's treatment of the people of God. It is a judgment on the good and bad done to His people. It is a warning for the likes of Babylon, Moab, Damascus, Egypt, and Tyre. At the time of this prophecy, God's judgment had already been brought upon the powerful nation of Assyria.

Babylon was a small and little-known nation at the time. But God knew that it would become a vast empire. He also knew that the nation would be destroyed. The Lord is a God who opposes the arrogant and shows mercy to the humble. Arrogance was the reason that these nations had the Lord's judgment brought upon them. Humility means to know where God Almighty's place is and to know where man's place as His creation is, and not to overstep. To forget one's place is arrogance and to know one's place is humility.

God set the purpose for all nations. "As I have planned, so shall it be, and as I have purposed, so shall it stand... This is the purpose that is purposed concerning the whole earth, and this is the hand that is stretched out over all the nations. For the Lord of hosts has purposed, and who will annul it? His hand is stretched out, and who will turn it back?" (14:24,26-27).

God's criteria for His judgment are whether the people have forgotten the God of salvation and whether God has remained in their hearts as their solid rock (17:10). The God of justice begins His judgment with His people. Then, He judges the nations surrounding them. Through this process, God wishes for His people to fear Him and for their neighboring nations to return to Him by knowing and fearing Him as ruler over all the earth.

That Day and Foreign Nations

Chapters 24-27 contain Isaiah's new sermons. These sermons have within them a precious promise for the righteous that things will go well for them while giving the wicked a frightening warning that things will not go well for them. These promises and warnings are structured in a way so that they complement each other. These promises and warnings are not for a specific nation but for all nations. Through them, God will be glorified in the east and the coastlands of the sea (24:15). God is a fortress, refuge, shade, and rock to those who wait and depend on him. However, God is a God who judges the arrogant.

A Warning for Jerusalem

Chapters 28-35 are a reproof and warning against the sins of the people, especially against those in Jerusalem. Nevertheless, God promises them that if they turn from their ways and rely on Him, He will deliver them out of their suffering and judge their enemies.

Chapters 28-29 issue a warning as reproof and judgment against Ephraim's arrogance, drunkenness, complacency, and debauchery, and do the same for the arrogant leaders of Jerusalem. Again, God, despite everything, extends His grace and mercy to those who have faith. In Chapters 30-31, He rebukes Judah, who did not depend on God during the attack of King Sennacherib of Assyria, but instead relied on Egypt. But He also tells them that He will defeat the Assyrian Army for them if they rely on Him.

In Chapters 32-33, God tells the people that He will deliver them if Hezekiah relies on Him. These are words of promise that apply to the coming Kingdom of God. Chapter 34 says that nations who oppress the people of God will eventually face utter destruction. Although Chapter 35 does speak of the prosperity of Jerusalem, it speaks beyond that to the beauty that will be bestowed upon the Church once God's Kingdom comes. It speaks of the Church living on the holy path as guided by the Lord.

God as the Master of History

Chapters 36-39 are Isaiah's message as a historian. These chapters reveal how God's prophecies have been fulfilled throughout the course of history. God is the master of history, and history is His story. These chapters are almost identical to 2 Kings 18-19 in terms of content. They speak of how God brings salvation to the humble that rely on God but opposes the arrogant that rely on their own strength.

However, God is wary that their hearts will be filled with arrogance after they experience God's wondrous salvation through Hezekiah. Hezekiah, the king who drove the Assyrians away, one of the most powerful nations of the world at the time, and whose life was extended by God, had risen to superstar status as a result of these events. He becomes especially arrogant when messengers from the rising nation of Babylon come to see him. Unfortunately, this becomes a cause for Judah's captivity in Babylon in the future.

The Prophecy of Blessings

Chapters 40-66 make up the second half of Isaiah's

prophecy. These chapters are different from the previous chapters, both in terms of the purpose and style of their prophecies. The first half is composed of many sermons and Isaiah's name is mentioned several times (2:1; 7:3; 13:1). However, the second half of the book comprises a single discourse and does not mention Isaiah's name once.

The first half talks about God's anger and warnings; the second half talks about His blessings. The first part contains God's words about suffering under Assyrian invasion and salvation thereof, and the second part contains words about captivity under Babylon and the promise of salvation. These words serve as a source of strength and comfort later in Babylonian Exile. Both first and second parts reference the coming and grace of the Messiah but this message is emphasized much more in the second half.

The second half begins with the cries of John the Baptist in the wilderness (40:3) and ends with the new heavens and the new earth (66:22). That is why this second half could be called a summary of the New Testament. In particular, Chapters 40-55 describe a servant who travels to preach the word (42), preaches the Gospel to the ends of the earth (49), displays obedience to his mandate to preach the Gospel through humiliation and suffering (50), accomplishes the work of salvation through suffering, and ultimately achieves victory and glory (52-53). These chapters, also known as the "Servant Songs," are the pinnacle of Old Testament missions.

The Sovereignty of God

Chapters 40-41 describe the proclamation of the Kingdom of God through the ministry of John the Baptist. These chapters contain God's words of comfort for His people (40:1-11). Nowhere is there such a realistic and definite mention of God's glorious image, especially His greatness (40:12-26). Therefore, He says, "Do not be discouraged, have hope, and only look to Me." God knows the foolishness of idolatry and tells us to abandon it and rely only on Him. He wants us to profess, "The Lord is God."

Chapters 42-48 declare the coming of the Messiah and salvation. In particular, God promises to deliver the people from Babylonian oppression and to do new works. He promises the forgiveness of sins. Idols are false and only the Lord our God is the One worthy of praise. God also discloses His plan to use Cyrus to return His people from the Babylonian captivity in the future. Through this, God's eternal might and sovereignty will be revealed.

God alone is the master of history. He will fulfill His promises for those who rely on Him (45). He tells us not to worship Babylonian idols, but to look to Him, to rely on His power, and to serve Him alone (46).

Although Babylon is God's judgment on His people, Babylon cannot escape God's judgment for its undue cruelty and arrogance that oversteps its place (47). Likewise, God will judge the sins of the House of Jacob but will give them salvation for the sake of His name (48).

A Servant of the Lord

The grandiosity of God's scheme revealed through Chapters 49-57: the salvation of the entire world. The servant who appears in Isaiah is a representation of the coming Messiah. His redemption is the redemption that will be undertaken by the Messiah. Furthermore, His Church will be established among the Gentiles (49). Even during the periods of darkness that hide all light, if we listen to, heed, and depend on the Word of God, we will experience God's salvation. Only God is our Comforter (51).

Although Israel wishes for God to "wake up" (51:9) and deliver them, God commands His people to "wake up" (51:17; 52:1). He encourages Israel to stand up on their two feet and experience His salvation.

The three verses at the end of Chapter 52 (52:13-15) share the same theme as the first three verses of Chapter 53 (53:1-3), the humbling and exaltation of Christ. There is no other passage in the Bible that explains Christ's suffering and glory in greater detail and clarity than Chapter 53. It is also full of Christ's unsearchable riches. Therefore, the church of Christ will flourish (54).

Isaiah prophesies that Babylon and Assyria will be on the receiving end of God's judgment as a result of their arrogance, even though they were the executor of God's judgment on His people for their sins. But in the end, God in His mercy will give salvation to His people. Likewise, God wants the churches of the New Testament to find comfort and strength.

Chapter 53 is about Christ, Chapter 54 is about the church of Christ, and Chapter 55 is God's covenant with the Church in Christ. When we come to God, we can receive forgiveness of sins and restoration. Chapter 56 outlines the duty of those who have received God's grace. He wants them to hold tightly to His promises and serve as an intercessor for the nations. Even though God judged them for their idol worship, God will heal and revive them if they turn back to Him (57).

The Lord's Challenge

Chapters 58-66 are the prophetic words about Israel's glorious future. But they also speak of the glory of the Church in the New Testament. God tells us to abandon religious hypocrisy. He tells His people that if they practice fasting and keep the Sabbath, He will not only heal and renew them but also make them healers of the nations (58). Where there is much sin, there will be much grace (59). God will come to deliver his people. And the saved will shine and expand into the ends of the earth (59:19-60:3). Many will come to the Lord.

Chapters 61-62 speak of Israel's restoration, joy, glory, and blessing. These chapters also speak to the New Testament Church. God will hear the earnest prayers and longings of His people and deliver them amidst their tribulations (63-64).

Chapters 65-66 make us look at the promise of the new heaven and the new earth. These chapters are related to the words of Romans 9-11. Gentiles will hear the Gospel and come to the Lord, but the Jews will be abandoned and judged on their unbelief. But the Jews who remain will return to the Lord.

God desires our humanity, not our sacrifices. He desires for us to know Him rather than our offering of burnt sacrifices (Hos. 6:6). He will judge those who oppose His people. Nations will turn to the Lord and His Church will stand forever.

Outline

Chapters 1-35	Prophecy on judgment
Chapters 1-6	The Lord's day and Judah
Chapters 7-12	The Lord's day and Israel
Chapters 13-23	The burden of the nations
Chapters 24-27	The day and foreign nations
Chapters 28-33	The grief brought upon Israel
Chapters 34-35	The restoration of Zion
Chapters 36-39	Historical considerations (Hezekiah)
Chapters 40-66	A prophecy of blessing
Chapters 40-48	God's sovereignty
Chapters 49-57	A servant of the Lord
Chapters 58-66	The Lord's challenge

Voice Outline

ISAIAH

100-Day Bible Reading Plan

		CHECK
Day 60	Isaiah 1-12	
Day 61	Isaiah 13-25	
Day 62	Isaiah 26-38	
Day 63	Isaiah 39-52	
Day 64	Isaiah 53-66	

JEREMIAH

JUDAH'S EXILE AND RETURN

Although Jeremiah ministered long after the time of Isaiah, due to its size, the Book of Jeremiah was placed immediately after the Book of Isaiah and before many prophets who ministered before him. The Book of Jeremiah, which consists of 52 chapters, has many chapters after the Book of Isaiah. This book also holds a high level of importance in that it was quoted directly or indirectly a total of 137 times in the New Testament.

King Josiah and Jeremiah the Prophet

The prophet Jeremiah, as introduced in 1:1-3, comes from a family of priests in the province of Anathoth. Just like his father Hilkiah, he too was to grow up to be a priest in the future. He received God's calling to be a prophet in the 13th year of King Josiah, a king who walked in the way of David during the final years of the Kingdom of Judah.

Josiah was eight years old when he became king; at the age of 16, he began to seek the true God. When he turned 20, he led a national revival movement (2 Chron. 34:1-7). And a year after starting the revival movement, at the age of 21, God called Jeremiah to work alongside Josiah. Jeremiah answers God's calling for him to be a prophet for the nations: "Ah, Lord God! Behold, I do not know how to speak, for I am only a youth" (1:6). His age at the time is assumed to have been around 18 to 20.

Surprisingly, it was this young King Josiah, aged only 21, and Jeremiah, a prophet at a mere 20 years of age, who were at the center of the remarkable revival that occurred in the last days of the Kingdom of Judah. King Josiah displays the leadership needed to lead the direction of the nation, and Prophet Jeremiah does his part to balance the king's leadership with the Word so that they made proceed in accordance with God's ways.

We see a similar arrangement during the Israelites' return from Babylonian Exile and subsequent restoration of the nation between Nehemiah the governor and Ezra the priest and scholar. In God's revivals, those who hold positions of power and have the necessary gifts such as kings, and servants of the Lord who have the necessary gifts such as prophets and priests are used together as a team.

If David is to be considered the central force of the revival movement during the early days of the kingdom, Josiah could be considered the central force behind the revival movement in the last days of the kingdom. Furthermore, if David symbolizes the work of the Holy Spirit in Early Church, Josiah symbolizes the work of the Holy Spirit in the last days of the Church. What the Book of Jeremiah tells us is that it is a young leader who will invigorate and raise the church to lead the revival movement in the last days. Therefore, we must raise young leaders like Josiah and Jeremiah and provide them with the opportunities to exercise their leadership.

Historical Background of the Period

Second Kings 22-25 and 2 Chronicles 34-36 illustrate the historical background of the times during Jeremiah's ministry quite well. Jeremiah begins his ministry approximately 100 years after Isaiah. By Jeremiah's time, the Kingdom of Israel had already been conquered by the Assyrians. And when Assyria began declining in power, God called Jeremiah. Around the same time, Babylon, a small and emerging nation, was in the process of rapid expansion. Egypt also remained a powerful nation to the south of Israel.

When Assyria was weakened, Egypt seized the opportunity and carried out a northward expansion policy. Simultaneously, Babylon conquered Assyria and began to expand its territory. And right in the middle of this vicious fight for hegemony between the two great powers of Babylon and Egypt lay Palestine. The Kingdom of Judah, stuck and unable to take a stance between these two powers, ultimately is brought to destruction by Babylon.

Jeremiah the Weeping Prophet

Jeremiah is the weeping prophet who ministered while witnessing the events of the period. Jeremiah was the prophet of suffering who served during the reigns five kings including King Josiah and his sons Jehoahaz, Jehoiakim, Jehoiachin (also known as Jechoniah, Jeconiah, or Coniah), and Zedekiah. Because he prophesied that it was in the interest of Judah to surrender to Babylon sooner than later, Jeremiah is despised, imprisoned, and beaten for being a "pro-Babylonian traitor" by the Kingdom of Judah.

Jeremiah encountered many tribulations amid such circumstances. However, whenever he tried not to speak His words, he would feel as though there was a burning fire in his heart and could not hold it in (20:7-9). He lived in solitude all his life, obeying God's command that he should not take a wife or have children (16:1-4). He was ostracized by his neighbors and even his own family (12:6). All the people of Jerusalem plotted against him, beat him, and He framed him to the people of Jerusalem, beat him, and put him in the stocks (20:2).

Jeremiah told the people that it was God's will that Judah surrender to Babylon. He also prophesied that their captivity would last 70 years (25:11, 29:10). He told them that God would restore the nation and bring them back from exile after this period and that, as a result, they should settle down in Babylon and wait patiently during their exile. He also told the people about an amazing new covenant God had made with them (31:31-34).

However, the greatest challenge of all for Jeremiah was the false prophets that were active during the same period. These false prophets lied and prophesied according to their hearts in order to gain favor with the king and the people. They demanded that the king not surrender and instead resist Babylon because God would save them from its hands. Among them, Hananiah was the most prominent; he openly belittled, slandered, and attacked the words God had spoken through Jeremiah.

Jeremiah delivers a message to Hananiah from God: "Listen, Hananiah, the Lord has not sent you, and you have made this people trust in a lie. Therefore thus says the Lord: 'Behold, I will remove you from the face of the earth. This year you shall die, because you have uttered rebellion against the Lord'" (28:15-16). Hananiah dies in the seventh month of that year. The prophet's work is only to hear and communicate the Word of God. A prophet must never say what he thinks or chooses just to please others.

Jeremiah witnessed the entire process of the Kingdom of Judah's fall into Babylonian captivity. And although Babylon offers to protect Jeremiah and provide him with a home after Judah has fallen, he refuses. Instead, he chooses to stay with the remaining Jews by whose hands he later suffers martyrdom by stoning.

Nine Imageries for Effective Communication

In order to make them realize their sins, Jeremiah makes use of visual imagery to deliver a message to the Jews that had broken their covenant with God and were engaging in idol worship. Jeremiah conveys the gravity of Judah's sins using nine different visual images.

1. **Almond branch** - God will destroy Judah because of its depravity (1:11-12).
2. **A boiling pot, facing away from the north** - God will raise the Babylonians in the north to punish Judah (1:13-15).
3. **The spoiled loincloth** - udah's arrogance will make it as useless as a spoiled loincloth (13:1-11).
4. **The potter with clay in his hands** - As the sole master of all history, God will do with Judah as the potter breaks down clay if they continue to disobey him (18:1-12).
5. **The broken flask** - Judah will be broken into pieces by the sword of its enemy for its idol worship (19:1-12).
6. **Two baskets of figs** - the basket of good figs signifies the godly, and the basket of bad figs signifies the wicked (24:1-10).
7. **Yoke** - Jeremiah prophesized wearing straps and yoke-bars around his neck that the people will have to put their neck under the yoke of the king of Babylon (27:1-11).
8. **Large stones hidden in the mortar in the pavement at the entrance to Pharaoh's palace** - the large stones represent Babylon's future conquest of Egypt (43:8-13).
9. **The book cast into the midst of the Euphrates** - as the book which contains all the disasters that will strike Babylon sinks into the waters of the Euphrates, so will Babylon (51:59-64).

Surprisingly, although the Babylonian Empire seemed like it would endure for a long time, it did not even last 100 years before it was destroyed by the Medes and Persians. When

Jeremiah prophesied the fall of Babylon, no one believed him or thought it possible. However, just as God had told Jeremiah, Babylon is very quickly erased from history.

God is sovereign over all nations. He used Babylon as a tool to discipline His people, and then, disciplined Babylon for its own arrogance and depravity. God is the King of all kings, and He surely extends His grace and restoration to those who submit to Him.

God's Righteousness, Compassion, and the Weeping Prophet

Chapter 2 contains one of the most vivid and passionate messages of the Prophetic Books in the Bible. Jeremiah vehemently criticizes the Jews for putting idols in places that belong to God. It is said that they had as many idols as the number of cities in Judah.

In Chapters 3-4, God says to Israel who has left Him, "Return, O faithless children" (3:12,14,22; 4:1). He tells Israel to break up its fallow ground, meaning that it must remove the skin of its heart and commit to Him (4:3-4). He tells Israel to wash its heart from evil (4:14). And He promises that He will heal, nurture and treat it with great compassion (3:12-19).

Chapters 5-6 alternate between words of rebuke against sins and words of warning for judgment. God indicts Israel for its sins and reveals that Babylon will invade and take the people of Israel as captives as the consequence for their sins. God's admonishment continues but they do not listen.

Chapters 7-9 seek to humble and awaken the people after

warning them of their sins and the judgment that is to follow. These chapters tell us that the people did not obey His words four times (7:24; 26-28). God wanted them to hear His voice and return to Him but they stiffened their necks and did not look back.

God says with regret, "Even the stork in the heavens knows her times, and the turtledove, swallow, and crane keep the time of their coming, but my people know not the rules of the Lord" (8:7). Jeremiah also grieves for his people, "My joy is gone; grief is upon me; my heart is sick within me" (8:18).

The prophet weeps watching his people remain in sin; he sheds tears as he watches the people unable to receive healing in their shock and sorrow: "Oh that my head were waters, and my eyes a fountain of tears, that I might weep day and night for the slain of the daughter of my people!" (9:1). God wishes for His people to know Him. He tells us there is no greater thing of which to boast (9:23-24).

Chapter 10 warns those who have already been exiled to Babylon not to abide by or be stained by their customs. Those who remain are warned not to be complacent and to live in preparation for the coming disaster.

Chapter 11 is a complaint filed by Jeremiah against the people who deliberately disobeyed the king's orders as though he was a prosecutor.

Chapters 12-13 state God's judgment on Jeremiah's complaint and continue to urge the people to repent and return.

Chapter 14 presents God's words about times of drought

and lays out the severity and cause of the drought. Jeremiah goes before the Lord on behalf of the people and intercedes with tears and a broken heart: "We acknowledge our wickedness, O Lord, and the iniquity of our fathers, for we have sinned against you. Do not spurn us, for your name's sake; do not dishonor your glorious throne; remember and do not break your covenant with us" (14:20-21).

Chapter 15 expresses hope for God's compassion and restoration based on Jeremiah's earnest intercessory prayer in the previous chapter. However, God enforces their sentence and brings the people to destruction. Though God's plan of judgment is firm, His servant Jeremiah promises that God will protect them during this time of tribulation.

Chapters 16-17 detail the magnitude of the disaster that will be brought upon Israel. But, at the same time, God also gives them hope for restoration.

Chapter 18 shows God's principles with which He rules over the nations. Just as a potter shapes and destroys clay as he wishes, God will act righteously and fairly to the nations in accordance with His will.

Chapter 19 continues to maintain a depressive tone. The destruction of Judah and Jerusalem is imminent due to their sins. Although Jeremiah declares God's judgment with the example of the broken flask to bring the people back to God, his efforts are in vain.

In chapter 20, we see the people refusing the repent despite the messages delivered by Jeremiah. Instead, Jeremiah is persecuted by Pashhur the priest.

Chapters 2-20 contain Jeremiah's general prophecies with no indication of the time foretold. Chapters 21-39 are not written in the order in which they were declared, but instead they are marked with a specific time to record when and under what circumstances. The first half reveals Jeremiah's personal situation and emotional state, and much of it consists of his prayers and sighs.

- Jeremiah's intercession (3:22-25; 14:19-22; 16:19-20; 17:12-18)
- Jeremiah's anguish (4:19-22; 8:18-9:2; 18:19-23; 20:7-18)
- Jeremiah's question (12:1-4)

A Message of Judgment

Chapter 21 is a message proclaimed during the reign of King Zedekiah. The chapters that follow are not in chronological order given that they are about Jehoiakim and Jeconiah, all kings that came before Zedekiah. Zedekiah humbly sends a man to Jeremiah to ask the Lord about the future of Jerusalem.

Jeremiah says to the messenger in response, "It is futile to protect the city as it will surely perish according to the Word of God." He tells the messenger that the best way is to surrender to the king of Babylon. He tells him that the most important thing right now is to repent and turn to God.

Chapter 22 is a message proclaimed during the days of Jehoiakim. It contains the prophecy that Shallum (Jehoahaz), who became king after Josiah and was exiled to Egypt, will die in Egypt. It also contains a message of reproof and warning for Jehoiakim who became king after Shallum. It is a message of judgment on Coniah who became king after Jehoiakim and refused to listen to the Word of God.

Chapter 23 is a comprehensive message of rebuke and warning for dignitaries who do not care for the people, for prophets and priests who deliver messages that are not from God, and for people who ignore the Word of God.

Chapter 24 talks about good and bad figs. Good figs are those who have already been taken into captivity and bad figs are those who resisted and will later be taken into captivity. It is a prophecy that there is hope for those who have already been exiled, but disaster will strike those you resisted and were exiled last.

Chapter 25 is a message from the first year of King Nebuchadnezzar. It foretells the destruction of the people of Judah who ignored God's warnings. It also prophesies the return of the Israelites from captivity in 70 years and the destruction of nations surrounding Israel by the hands of Babylon.

Chapter 26 is a message from the reign of Jehoiakim. Jeremiah delivers a warning to the priests, prophets, and people of the temple: "Then I will make this house like Shiloh, and I will make this city a curse for all the nations of the earth" (26:6). Jeremiah is persecuted for this prophecy. Although Jeremiah survives under the protection of dignitaries, another prophet, Uriah, is killed.

In chapters 27-28, Jeremiah urges the nation to surrender to Babylon if they are to save the nation in the days of Jehoiakim. Though he urges them not to listen to false prophets, Hanani the false prophet preaches the exact opposite. Hanani dies within two months of Jeremiah's prophecy that he would die that year.

Chapter 29 is a message to the Jews who have already been taken captive in Babylon. They are told to set long-term plans there because they will only be able to return after 70 years. But Jeremiah encourages and reassures them that God's plan is not a disaster but rather peace and hope for the future. Jeremiah also warns the people to be wary of false prophets in the land of Babylon.

Chapters 30-31 contain a promise of restoration. In particular, Jeremiah 31:31-34 contains an amazing new covenant. In this chapter, a new covenant is proclaimed for His people who are being judged for their failure to keep the covenant made on Mount Sinai.

In Chapters 32-33, Jeremiah is once again imprisoned for delivering the message of destruction. He spends this time in prayer. Jerusalem will fall, but God restores it to its "former self." Jeremiah prophesies the coming of the Messiah. The captives will return.

Chapter 34 is a message for King Zedekiah. He will be exiled to Babylon and live there. King Zedekiah, his dignitaries, and the people broke the covenant they made before God. They released slaves only to enslave them again. That is the reason for the prophecy of their demise.

In Chapter 35, the Israelites are compared to the Rechabites and rebuked for their actions. Jeremiah prophecies that the Rechabites will be blessed. Jeremiah rebukes the people for

Judah for disobeying the Word of God, unlike the Rechabites who upheld their ancestors' teachings. He tells them to feel remorse and turn back from their ways.

In Chapter 36, Jeremiah commands Baruch to write as he dictates the Word of God in the days of Jehoiakim. The Word is then proclaimed to the people in the temple. The Word was heard by Jehoiakim and his dignitaries, but Jehoiakim slashed the words in the scroll with a sword and threw them into a fire to burn them. God tells Jeremiah to take another scroll and to write on it all the former words that were in the first scroll as well as additional words of judgment against Jehoiakim.

Chapters 37-38 are about events that took place just before the destruction of Jerusalem. Zedekiah asks Jeremiah to pray. When Jeremiah, who had been freed at the time, tells the king that the Babylonian army will come and besiege the city, he is once again put back in prison. Zedekiah does a favor for Jeremiah in prison. The king asks him to keep the conversation between them private.

Chapter 39 is the sad story of Jerusalem's fall. The reason Jerusalem's fall is recorded in detail is to show that Jeremiah's prophecies were fulfilled. This chapter also proves the false prophets wrong. Jerusalem falls just as Jeremiah had prophesied, but the Chaldeans treat him well.

After the Fall

Chapters 40-44 detail what happened to the few remaining people who were not taken captive after the fall of Jerusalem.

In Chapter 45, God promises to protect Baruch, a faithful servant. Chapters 46-51 lead us to the place where the 'The Court of the Nations' is held. The judge there is the Lord our God. He says that Israel's neighboring countries will be brought to destruction by Babylon and that Babylon too will be judged.

The first of these prophecies is on Egypt. It is to be conquered by Nebuchadnezzar. Then, prophecies against the Philistines, the destruction of Moab, and the judgment of eight neighboring nations including Ammon, Edom, Damascus, Kedar, Hazor, and Elam follow. The common denominator of their judgment is their "arrogance." Babylon must fulfill its role as the executor of God's universal judgment, but it, too, will be judged for its arrogance and failure to remain in its place.

Chapter 52 details the destruction of Jerusalem and the destruction of the temple. Jehoiachin, who was taken captive by the Babylonians, lives his last days in peace.

Jeremiah's Prophecy

Although Jeremiah's prophecies were about captivity in Babylon, the greater focus of his prophecies is on the promise of God's restoration. Judah was taken into captivity because of its sins, but God in His mercy promises the people's return from captivity. "This whole land shall become a ruin and a waste, and these nations shall serve the king of Babylon seventy years. Then after seventy years are completed, I will punish the king of Babylon and that nation, the land of the

Chaldeans, for their iniquity, declares the Lord, making the land an everlasting waste" (25:11-12). "For thus says the Lord: When seventy years are completed for Babylon, I will visit you, and I will fulfill to you my promise and bring you back to this place" (29:10).

The Fulfillment of Prophecies

The people of Judah were taken into captivity by the Babylonians over three rounds. The first group in 606 B.C., the second in 597 B.C., and the third group in 586 B.C. However, it was when the third group was taken into captivity that the temple and the Kingdom of Judah were destroyed. But just as He promised, God brings them back from exile. The first return (536 B.C.) took place 70 years after the first group was taken into captivity in Babylon. The Zerubbabel Temple was completed in B.C. 516, 70 years after the temple was destroyed. God is faithful to His promises.

The pattern of Jeremiah's prophecies reappears in history in different forms. 1987 is the pivotal moment in world history. Gorbachev, the General Secretary of the then communist state Union of Soviet Socialist Republics (USSR), declared "The Soviet Union is no longer committed to Communism," as he lowered the flag of communism, effectively ending Marxism and Leninism. And just three years later in 1990, the Soviet Union was dissolved. It took 70 years for Communism to collapse after the Communist Bolshevik Revolution began in 1917. 70 years after Russia as a Christian nation was destroyed in 1920, the Soviet Union also collapsed. God is the master of history!

Seeing Jeremiah's prophecy come true in history, I pray and carefully approach the history of our people. After liberation from Japanese occupation in 1945, the two Koreas began a conflict based on ideology and were divided in 1948. The war between the two Koreas broke out on June 25 in 1950, and the ceasefire was signed in 1953. I plead with the Lord that Jeremiah's prophecy also comes true for our nation.

In this context, the two Koreas could resume dialogue in 2015, recognize each other in 2018, end the war in 2020, and establish a unified Korea in 2023. "Lord, have mercy on us and please make this miracle happen!"

Outline

Chapter 1	Jeremiah's calling
Chapters 2-20	Chapters without a specific timeline
Chapters 21-39	Prophecies with a timeline
Chapters 40-44	Prophecies about post-fall Jerusalem
Chapters 45-51	Judgment on Babylon and eight neighboring nations
Chapter 52	The captivity of the people of Judah Summary (appendix)

Voice Outline

JEREMIAH

100-Day Bible Reading Plan

		CHECK
Day 65	Jeremiah 1-13	
Day 66	Jeremiah 14-25	
Day 67	Jeremiah 26-33	
Day 68	Jeremiah 34-45	
Day 69	Jeremiah 46-52, Lamentations 1-5	

LAMENTATIONS OF JEREMIAH

LAMENTATIONS OVER THE DESTRUCTION OF JERUSALEM

The Bible does not tell us who authored the Book of Lamentations. However, the likely theory passed down until the 3rd century B.C. is that Jeremiah was the author. Furthermore, the Septuagint translation has this introductory line before Lamentations 1:1: "And it came to pass, after Israel was taken captive, and Jerusalem made desolate, that Jeremias sat weeping, and lamented with this lamentation over Jerusalem." The Lamentations of Jeremiah are clearly written by a man who witnessed Jerusalem's defeat under Babylon, and Jeremiah seems to best fit the bill.

It is customary to sing the Lamentations of Jeremiah in Israeli funerals. It is about mourning the death of Zion's daughter, the fall of the city of Jerusalem and the temple. Lamentation is a mourning for the suffering Church and at the same time a confession of repentance to God. It is not a complaint about the consequences of sin, but the mourning of sin, repentance, and a call for God's grace. "The steadfast love of the Lord never ceases; his mercies never come to an end; they are new every morning; great is your faithfulness" (3:22-23). "But you, O Lord, reign forever; your throne endures to all generations. Why do you forget us forever, why do you forsake us for so many days? Restore us to yourself, O Lord, that we may be restored! Renew our days as of old" (5:19-21).

In the foreword of the Dutch Bible NBV, it is written as follows: "This little book is so elegant in its literary style and choice of language that it cannot be compared with any other book by the best pagan authors."

An Appendix to Jeremiah

In terms of content, Lamentations of Jeremiah have many similarities with the Book of Jeremiah. So much so that it could even be called the "Appendix to Jeremiah." The Book of Jeremiah foretells the destruction of Judah and Jerusalem and records precisely how this prophecy was fulfilled. The Book of Jeremiah also shows that Jeremiah was honest when he expressed his wishes that the day of calamity would not come, and that every time he thought about that day, his heart anguished in pain.

However, those who heard Jeremiah prophesize that it was better to surrender to Babylon quickly and be taken into exile misunderstood him as a man who was eager for the destruction of Israel. However, in the Lamentations of Jeremiah, it is revealed that he truly loved the nation and people. This book effectively conveys the grief of Judah and Jeremiah when Jerusalem was destroyed.

This book was not written in advance looking at future

events from a distance; it was written while the author witnessed and experienced everything in person. That is why the book is filled with sorrow about Jerusalem's destruction for its sins, the rebellion of God's people, and the prophet's heart which is plagued with sadness. The book also expresses God's sorrow, who has no choice but to judge His people. Seeing the destruction that has overtaken Judah and Jerusalem, Jeremiah wishes his head were waters, and his eyes a fountain of tears (Jer. 9:1). When disaster finally strikes, Jeremiah falls into deep sorrow.

He expresses his mourning in verses 1:1, 2:1, and verse 4:1 by confessing his sadness. He repeatedly expresses his sadness in 1:9, "O Lord, behold my affliction," and in 1:20 and 2:20, "Look, O Lord, and see!" Jeremiah's enemies accused him of turning away and betraying his country, but the Lamentations of Jeremiah shows that he had a deeper love for his people and nation than anyone else.

Structure

The Book of Lamentations is very unique in its structure. It is composed of five chapters and with the exception of Chapter 5, the entire book is poetry. The book is arranged with the 22 letters of the Hebrew alphabet in regular order. The first chapter comprises 22 verses, each verse beginning with a letter of the Hebrew alphabet.

It is structured so that each verse begins with a letter of the Hebrew alphabet, the first verse starting with "Aleph," the second verse with "Bet," and going down the Hebrew alphabet. However, Chapter 3 contains three times as many verses, totaling 66 and it groups three verses into a set, where the first set begins with "Aleph," the second set with "Bet," and so on. Chapter 3 comprises 22 of such sets of three verses, adding to a total of 66 verses for the chapter.

Although Chapter 5 is not arranged in the order of the Hebrew alphabet, it is still composed of 22 verses like Chapters 1, 2, and 4. The first four chapters of the book are in poetry form and the last chapter is in prose. Psalms 119 also has this structure with a total of 22 sets of 8 verses, where the first verse of each set begins with a letter of the Hebrew alphabet in order.

Such an arrangement helped people remember the content of the book as well as memorize the lyrics of the songs of mourning. This type of structure was commonly used to compose poetry at the time.

The Book's Role and Content

Lamentations was a great source of encouragement to godly Jews in their distress. It gave them a spiritual language with which they could express their grief. This book also helped future generations preserve vivid memories of Zion even though they had never once set foot in Jerusalem and were living in captivity in Babylon.

Lamentations also taught them to lament on their sins and turn to God in repentance. Another important aspect of this book is that it empowered them with the hope that God will show His mercy in the future. Lamentations also teaches us to grieve the sufferings of God's Church appropriately.

In Chapter 1, the author mourns over the horrors taking place in Jerusalem with great grief. This grief is deepened by drawing a comparison between the city's current miserable state and its glory days of the past. While the author acknowledges that the suffering of the people as they repent their sins and mourn is God's justice, he pleads to God for mercy. He also asks God to judge the enemy with His justice.

Chapter 2 is an acrostic, just like Chapter 1. The contents are almost the same, and both start with the same tone of sorrow. The cause of all the disasters is God's wrath for their sins. But the author continues to hope that God will listen and show compassion.

Chapter 3 puts verses in groups of three and places them in alphabetical order. Chapter 3 is unique in the sense that its content is more general and may be applied to personal situations. This chapter can be used not only as an intercessory prayer for Israel but also for ourselves when we are praying for our individual concerns.

Chapter 4 is structured just like Chapters 1 and 2 and mourns the destruction of Jerusalem. Although Chapter 5 contains the same numbers of verses as Chapter 1, 2, and 4, it is written in prose form and is not an acrostic. However, its contents are in line with all the previous chapters of the book. The chapter describes disaster while humbly pleading with God to show mercy.

Outline

Chapter 1	The destruction of Jerusalem, sorrow, and mourning
Chapter 2	God's judgment on Zion
Chapter 3	The suffering of the prophet (prayer for mercy)
Chapter 4	A comparison of the former glory and current desolation
Chapter 5	A prayer for restoration and a prayer of repentance

Voice Outline

LAMENTATIONS OF JEREMIAH

100-Day Bible Reading Plan

		CHECK
Day 69	Jeremiah 46-52, Lamentations 1-5	☐

EZEKIEL

HOPE FOR THE TEMPLE

Ezekiel, like Jeremiah, came from a priestly family. He was deported to Babylon along with King Jehoiachin with the second group of exiles. He began his prophetic ministry five years after he was taken captive when he was 30 years old. It was the right age to enter into priesthood. It is written in 29:17, "In the twenty-seventh year, in the first month, on the first day of the month, the word of the Lord came to me," meaning the Lord came in the 27th year of Judah's exile. In other words, it had been 22 years since Ezekiel began his ministry, which also means that Ezekiel was 52 years of age at the time the Book of Ezekiel was recorded.

This book is a message to the children of Judah who were being held captive in Babylon. It also holds spiritual lessons to foreign nations. It reminds the people of the reason they are being held captive in Babylon, God's judgment for all their sins. But it also tells them that if they repent, even now, God can restore them in His mercy and grace. With the exception of Jonah, who was called to go to Nineveh to prophesy, Ezekiel and Daniel were the only Old Testament writers who lived and prophesied in Babylon. Ezekiel prophesied in the early days of captivity and Daniel in the latter days of captivity. Although the Israelites lived in exile in Babylon because of their sins, God remained with them. He gave them vigilance, counsel, comfort, encouragement, and hope.

Judgment on Judah and Jerusalem

The beginning and end of the book of Ezekiel are very mysterious and difficult to understand. The visions recorded in this book are intricately intertwined, but their message is clear as day. It is to show God's people their sins, awaken them, and draw them to repent before the Lord. To have a prophet among them during their desperate time in exile was a great source of comfort to the people.

Chapters 1-24 record the events of before the fall of Jerusalem. The Jews that were taken captive by Babylon before the fall of Jerusalem thought that it was possible for Jerusalem to fall and the temple to be destroyed. However, Ezekiel prophesied that Jerusalem will fall and the temple will be destroyed. The chapter states clear reasons as to why.

Chapters 1-3 present the prophet's vision which serves as the proof of his credentials as a prophet and Chapters 4-24 contain words of rebuke and warning. God makes use of parables and visions to help His people understand His will. In Chapters 25-32, Ezekiel prophesies that God will judge Jerusalem, Judah, as well as the surrounding foreign nations fairly. Jeremiah prophesies the fall of Babylon, and Ezekiel mainly prophesies against the nations of Tyre and Egypt.

Chapters 33-39 prophesy that the Lord will draw them back and restore them. Chapters 40-48 describe the New Jerusalem Temple in all its glory. Ezekiel not only held on to God's promises for the restoration of Israel in its time of exile but also the beauty of the New Testament church and how it would influence the world and reveal the glory of God.

The Book of Ezekiel is written in the first person. In Chapter 1, God calls Ezekiel through the vision of four living creatures, four wings, and four wheels. This image is a vision of the Ark of the Covenant in the temple of God. The Ark of the Covenant is a symbol of God's presence, a place in which to meet with God. The reason God shows Ezekiel a vision of the Ark of the Covenant and meets with him during Babylonian Captivity is to show him that, even though His people may be in exile, God still loves them, has compassion for them, and has a heart for them. God comforts His people and gives them a chance for restoration even if they are in the midst of a tribulation they have brought upon themselves with their sins.

God wanted to show Ezekiel the reasons for Jerusalem's judgment. To do this, he allowed Ezekiel to temporarily move in space. He moved Ezekiel from Babylon to the temple in Jerusalem and showed him how the temple was filled with idols and how the people worshipped those idols. Then God showed Ezekiel how the Spirit of the Lord moved up from the Temple until He finally left the temple (Chapters 8-11). At first, the glory of God filled the temple (10:4). Then, His glory left the temple and stood at the east gate (10:17-19). And later, the glory of the Lord went up from the midst of the city and stood on the mountain to its east (11:22- 23).

Once the glory of God had left the Temple, it was no longer a holy place of worship; instead it was nothing more than a building. But the Israelites, who were not aware of this, believed themselves to be safe because God was in the Jerusalem Temple. He was no longer protecting Jerusalem. Ezekiel receives the bitter news that Jerusalem has been struck down and that the Temple has been destroyed (33:21). And although the glory of God returns and fills the temple, that temple is no longer a building but the New Testament Church built by Christ Jesus (Chapter 43).

God promises that despite being in sin, if the people of Israel turn away from the wickedness in their hearts, throw away their idols, return to Him, He will forgive all their sins and restore them by giving them a new spirit and tender heart. Real change can only come when we turn from our selfish ways and live a God-centered life.

The Prophets

Prophets are watchmen (3:16-21; 33:1-9). A watchman is a person who blows the trumpet of warning after hearing the Word of God. Just like in the Book of Jeremiah, the Book of Ezekiel speaks of false prophets (Chapter 13). False prophets are those who speak the words that people love to hear. They do not rebuke people for their sins but give false hope and fake comfort. Their prophecies are nothing more than fanciful utterings of their own thoughts.

Prophets are intercessors. God does not carry out His work without first showing it to His prophets (Am. 3:7). This is because He wants His prophets to intercede with their prayers. Intercessory prayer is the most important theme in the Book of Ezekiel. God promises His people that even if they are living in serious sin, He will save them for the sake of the people who intercede earnestly with their prayers.

In particular, Ezekiel 22:25-29 speaks of the totality of Israel's crimes. Verse 25 shows the sins of the prophets, Verse 26 the sins of the priests, Verse 27 the sins of the political leaders, and Verse 28 shows the spiritual leaders in collusion with the politicians and their wrongdoings. Verse 29 tells us that while the people were violent, cruel, oppressive toward the needy, and wicked in their ways. Judgment lies before the entire city, just like Nineveh.

However, in Ezekiel 22:30, God says, "And I sought for a man among them who should build up the wall and stand in the breach before me for the land, that I should not destroy it." No matter how serious the sin, God is in search of an intercessor that will not just stand to the side and condemn but instead stand with arms raised to prevent the destruction of the land. God promises that He will restore the land if such a man or woman is to be found.

Chapters 34-37 are filled with God's plan of restoration for Israel. In particular, Chapter 37 tells us that He will restore the Israelites as the dry bones of the valley rise to become a great army. God also speaks of an important principle in

36:37: "Thus says the Lord God: This also I will let the house of Israel ask me to do for them: to increase their people like a flock."

However, God's promise does not mean that things will happen by themselves without us doing our part. God tells us that He will answer when someone comes to Him to repent and prays earnestly for restoration. In such times, He pays attention not to those with many words who are quick to judge but to those who come before the Lord and intercede with their prayers.

Another aspect of the Book of Ezekiel we need to pay attention to is whether the saying, "Break the curse that runs in the family" is correct. In Ezekiel 18:20, it is written: "The soul who sins shall die. The son shall not suffer for the iniquity of the father, nor the father suffer for the iniquity of the son... The wickedness of the wicked shall be upon himself." In other words, each will die as a result of his or her own sins and the sins of a father shall not be passed onto his sons.

Parables

The Book of Ezekiel contains many parables to aid the understanding of its readers.

- **The vine** (Chapter 15). God says to Ezekiel: "How does the wood of the vine surpass any wood, the vine branch that is among the trees of the forest? Is wood taken from it to make anything? Behold, it is given to the fire for fuel." Just like the vine, the people of Jerusalem will be tossed aside for their sins and receive God's judgment. God reveals how their land will become desolate and useless.

- **The adulteress** (Chapter 16). A young child with no one to care for her was taken in, cared for, washed, clothed, fed, and nurtured. She grew up to be a beautiful woman. However, she believed in her own beauty and used her popularity to do detestable and obscene things. She symbolizes Israel who betrayed God's love and care and worshipped idols. God tells us that He will judge such behavior.
- **Two eagles and a vine** (Chapter 17). Chapter 16 speaks of the sins of the people of Judah and Chapter 17 speaks of the sins of the king of Judah. Zedekiah breaks his pact with Babylon and pursues an alliance with Egypt. This resulted in the destruction of Jerusalem by Nebuchadnezzar's army.
- **The furnace** (Chapter 22:17-22). "As silver is melted in a furnace, so you shall be melted in the midst of it, and you shall know that I am the Lord; I have poured out my wrath upon you" (22:22). Israel became as the useless dross left in the furnace due to its sins. However, God will purify Israel with fire and remove (judge) its impurities.
- **Two women** (Chapter 23). A lengthy chapter just like Chapter 16, Chapter 23 uses the metaphor of two women acting like prostitutes to speak about the sins of Israel and Judah who abandoned God and worshipped idols. The chapter tells us that Israel and Judah will eventually be judged and destroyed for their sins.

- **The boiling pot** (Chapter 24:1-14). God speaks to Ezekiel using the same parable of the boiling pot that He used to speak through Jeremiah (1:13). He says that Israel will be surrounded like a boiling pot on top of a fire in due time. Just like meat is taken out of a pot to feast on, the people will either be killed or be taken as captives. The empty pot will be set upon the coals, just like the city will be left to burn in flames.
- **Wicked shepherds** (Chapter 34). The wicked shepherds refer to the evil leaders of Israel. By failing to fulfill their duties, they led Israel into sin and its ultimate destruction. God will remove them from their offices. However, He will send the Messiah to comfort, restore, and enrich them like a good shepherd.

A Vision of Restoration

God spoke to Ezekiel through many visions to deliver His message in a way that can be easily understood. Chapters 8-12 contain visions about Jerusalem's sin and destruction as a consequence of that sin. Here, we will look at two visions about the restoration of Jerusalem. Ezekiel 37 focuses on the restoration of Israel and Chapter 47 focuses on Israel's glory. These visions are prophecies directed at the Church of the New Testament.

- **The dry bones of the valley** (37:1-14). God took Ezekiel to a valley filled with the dry bones of the dead. He blew breath into them and they became alive again. This is a vision of God's promise to restore Israel. The vision helps us envision God's creation of man (Gen. 2:7) and the establishment of the Church with the descent of the Holy Spirit on Pentecost (Act. 2).

- **Water flowing from the Temple** (47:1-12). This scene is a part of the visions that Ezekiel had about the Temple (Chapters 40-47). God shows Ezekiel the Temple, and the water trickling out of the Temple. That water starts at his ankles, then rises up to his knees and waist until it becomes so deep and wide that he has to swim out before it flows into the sea. Wherever this water flows, the water becomes fresh even in the sea. To the left and right of this river, trees and fruits flourish, and healing leaves sprout. This vision was also seen by John the Apostle in the New Testament (Rev. 22:1-2). This vision represents the enrichment of individuals and the Church community and the glory of their blessings through the Spirit of God.

Ezekiel's Symbolic Actions and Signs

The Book of Ezekiel records many symbolic actions taken by Prophet Ezekiel. The actions of a prophet can also be a message God wants to deliver to His people.

- God commanded Ezekiel to surround the map of Jerusalem which he had carved on a brick. This represents the future siege and attack against Jerusalem by the Babylonians (4:1-3).
- After Ezekiel cut off his hair and beard with a sharp sword. He burned one-third of the hair, another third he struck with the sword, and the other third he scattered

into the wind. This represents God's coming judgment on Judah. He showed in advance that they would die by fire, die by the sword, and be scattered in all directions (5:1-4).

- When God ordered Ezekiel to prepare a bag for his exile and leave in secret at night, He foreshadowed how bitter the people's exile to Babylon would be (12:1-6).
- God showed that Jerusalem would be killed by the sword of the adversary when He told Ezekiel to swing his sword in the air and mourn and strike his thighs (21:8-17).
- God told Ezekiel to mark two ways for the sword of Babylon to come and to place a signpost pointing to Jerusalem on one of the ways. This action foretells the attack of the king of Babylon on Jerusalem along the path on which he is being directed (21:18-23).
- After pouring water into the kiln, the placing of a good part of lamb and burning it for a long time showed that God would remove Judah's sin through fierce judgment (24:3-14).
- God tells Ezekiel not to mourn his wife's death. The death of Ezekiel's wife prefigures the utter destruction that is to come (24:15-27).
- When God told Ezekiel to tie the two sticks together, He showed that Israel would be united in the future (37:15-23).

The Lamentations of Ezekiel

The Book of Ezekiel, too, contains lamentations. God tells Ezekiel to take up a lament and recite it.

- **A lament for the princes of Israel** (Chapter 19). This lament foreshadows the destruction of the House of David, Judah's royal family. Josiah's sons and grandchildren (Jehoahaz, Jehoiakim, Jehoiachin, and Zedekiah) are to face disaster and perish. The glorious days of the royal bloodline are over once death finds Zedekiah. Ezekiel's sorrow is expressed through this lament. The lament contains two parables; the first likens the Kingdom of Judah to a brave and regal lion who has now been trapped in a net. The second is that the Kingdom of Judah was like a lush vine that has now dried up, been broken, and burned.

- **A lament for Tyre** (Chapter 27). This is a song to mourn the destruction of the city as a witness to the destruction of the Kingdom of Tyre. Tyre was once famous for its craftsmanship in shipbuilding and was an international trade hub where goods from all around the world were traded. But in an instant, its ships were wrecked and all its glory faded. The greatest cause of its destruction was its arrogance.

Outline

Chapters 1-24	Judgment on Judah and Jerusalem
Chapter 1	The glory of God witnessed by Ezekiel.
Chapters 2-3	Ezekiel's calling
Chapters 4-24	Judgment on Judah The message, signs, visions, parables, and laments about judgment
Chapters 25-32	Judgment on the six neighboring nations
Chapter 25	Judgment on Ammon, Moab, Edom, and Philistine
Chapters 26-28	Judgment on Tyre
Chapters 29-32	Judgment on Egypt
Chapters 33-39	The promise of restoration Israel's return to God
Chapter 34	Shepherds
Chapter 37	The dry bones of the valley
Chapters 40-48	A vision of the Temple The Temple and glory of the New Israel

Voice Outline

EZEKIEL

100-Day Bible Reading Plan

		CHECK
Day 70	Ezekiel 1-11	
Day 71	Ezekiel 12-24	
Day 72	Ezekiel 25-39	
Day 73	Ezekiel 40-48	

DANIEL

GOD'S WISDOM, INSIGHT, AND PROVIDENCE FOR THE NATIONS

The Book of Daniel, along with the Book of Ezekiel, is a great demonstration of how the Israelites being held captive in Babylon maintained their Jewish identity, lived according to the will of God, and how God's will was fulfilled through them. If Ezekiel gave hope to the exiles by preaching the Word and the Lord's promises during the first half of captivity, Daniel inspired hope and courage during the latter half of their time in captivity.

In particular, the question we may ask while looking at the two books is, "Why did God cause Israel's destruction by worldly nations when it was God who made a promise and fulfilled that promise to give them land and children?" Another question that comes up is, "Why did God establish a nation that would ultimately be destroyed?" Though they may have been judged at the hands of foreigners as a result of their sins, God is among them and works through them to do His will and be glorified.

Apocalyptic Literature

The books of Daniel and Ezekiel can be described as "apocalyptic literature" along with the New Testament book of Revelation. It is written in a literary style that encompasses dreams and visions. Revelation refers to the revelation of God's plans for the future. Therefore, these books demonstrate God's sole sovereignty as the master of history, and that all mighty empires will be judged and brought to an end at His appointed time.

These books also show us that the Kingdom of God will ultimately triumph. In particular, the Book of Daniel shows God's everlasting Kingdom and Jesus Christ, the King of kings. As we all know, King Nebuchadnezzar's dream in Daniel Chapter 2 was a preview of a world history that had yet to unfold but that God had shared in advance. The message contained in Daniel Chapter 2 is "King Nebuchadnezzar, you are not the king, but I, Jesus Christ, am King. I gave you this empire but your empire will not last forever. Only my Kingdom will rule over all the earth and be everlasting."

Babylon, Persia, Greece, Rome, all of the great empires of the world, will eventually succumb to King Jesus Christ. Only God is the master of history. History does not revolve around empires but around the Cross on Calvary Hill; the protagonists of history are not emperors or heroes, but only Jesus Christ. The Book of Daniel makes this very clear to Israel, a people in deep despair in exile.

Daniel, a Man of God

Daniel's Hebrew name was 'Daniel' and his Chaldean name was 'Belteshazzar.' He was most likely from the House of Judah, meaning he was royalty. He made a name for himself because of his wisdom and piety. He was a man who revealed the glory of God in a foreign land. He was a legendary figure during his time and many in the heart of Persia, in what is now Iran and Central Asia, still celebrate Daniel.

Ezekiel, a contemporary of Daniel but older in age, surprisingly mentions Daniel and rebukes the prince of Tyre for being arrogant and proudly calling himself wiser than Daniel (Eze. 28:3). He also lists Daniel as one of the three most influential figures, along with Noah and Job (Eze. 14:14,20). Daniel began gaining prominence during Ezekiel's ministry and maintained his good reputation for many years after that. The angel Gabriel calls Daniel a "man greatly loved by God" (10:11).

Daniel lived in the courts of Nebuchadnezzar, one of the greatest kings in history. Daniel had substantial influence over the empire and used that influence for a long time. He was educated on many subjects that were available under the educational system of the time, and was no less learned than a prophet when it came to the Word of God. He was also a politician who served as a servant of a Gentile king; nevertheless, he maintained his intimacy with God, fearing Him and revealing His glory.

If Christians today in similar offices were to justify their lack of commitment to their faith because it is too difficult, Daniel would have no words other than rebuke for them. But for politicians and leaders who fear God, are respected by all, and shine God's glory, Daniel only has words of courage and encouragement. The time for Christian leadership as presidents, ministers, parliamentary members, governors, and mayors like Daniel is now.

God works through prophets like Jeremiah and Ezekiel, and through politicians like Daniel. There are endless different ways and levels to how God works.

Structure

The Book of Daniel can largely be divided into two sections. The first six chapters contain stories from history, making them easy to understand. However, the last chapters mostly comprise prophecies that are a little more difficult to fully understand. Nevertheless, a historical understanding of Israel and its neighboring countries can contribute a great deal to understanding the prophecies. We need to have an understanding of the so-called "inter-testamental period." Babylon, Persia, Greece, the divided nations after Alexander's rule, and the Roman Empire which united a vast area are among the nations of which we need to have an understanding.

The Book of Daniel covers a long span of history from the time of Jerusalem's destruction by Babylon to its destruction by Rome again. Timewise, the book gives us a preview of 600 years of history. With an understanding of the Book of

Daniel, we can not only understand the history of the world during those times but also the sovereignty, providence, wisdom, and insight of God who has been and will be governing all the earth until Jesus' Second Coming.

The Book of Daniel is written in Hebrew from 1:1-2:3, in Aramaic from 2:4-7, and again in Hebrew from Chapter 8-12. Because the Chaldeans accepted Daniel's request in good faith and allowed him to eat vegetables and drink water instead of the king's food and wine, God allowed some parts of His book to be written in the language which the Chaldeans had taught Daniel. This was to make sure that the Chaldeans were rewarded for their help to others. God not only comforted and encouraged His own people in their times of tribulation, but He also comforted and encouraged the people of other nations who respected Him.

Serving Only the Lord

The first half of the book, Chapters 1 through 6, gives us some temporal and spatial background information about our heroes, Daniel and his three friends who lived in Babylon and Persia. When the first round of exiles was taken to Babylon, Babylon selected competent youths from among the Jews and educated them as part of its ambition for world domination. Their plan was to use these educated young men in the management of their empire. So naturally, every young man they selected was one who had been recognized for his excellence. It is said that Daniel and his three friends shone brighter than any others in the group.

Daniel's wisdom shone especially brightly when it came to interpreting King Nebuchadnezzar's dreams (Chapter 2). Nebuchadnezzar had a dream about a huge statue whose head was of fine gold, its chest and arms of silver, its middle and thighs of bronze, its legs of iron, and its feet partly of iron and partly of clay. The dream was a preview of the nations of the world, from Babylon, Medes, Persians, Greece, and all the way to Rome. However, even these mighty empires were broken and reduced to powder with the strike of a single stone. That stone grew larger and larger and became a great mountain that filled the whole earth. This shows how God rules the whole world through His Church. It demonstrates that God alone is the master of history and that only Jesus Christ is the King of kings and Lord of all things.

Though Babylon selected and took young people to fulfill its dream of world domination, God used these young people to reveal His glory in Babylon. Daniel, who interpreted Nebuchadnezzar's dream, and Shadrach, Meshach, and Abednego, who showed God's glory by being tossed in a furnace that was seven times hotter than usual for not bowing in front of the image of Nebuchadnezzar, were not just loyal to God in Babylon but also glorified His name (Chapter 3).

Nebuchadnezzar's second dream was also interpreted by Daniel (Chapter 4). The author of Chapter 4 is the king himself. Because he in person wrote down his own experiences, the words are exactly as they were published. God has Daniel record this as well.

Nebuchadnezzar talked honestly about his arrogance.

He experienced firsthand that only God is ruler over all the earth. So he, in a decree, informed the people and the nations that he knows that the Most High rules the kingdom of men and gives it to whom he wills (4:32). He ends his words like this:

"Now I, Nebuchadnezzar, praise and extol and honor the King of heaven, for all his works are right and his ways are just; and those who walk in pride he is able to humble" (4:37).

On the night that Daniel interpreted the writings on the wall at King Belshazzar's grand feast, Babylon was captured by King Darius of the Medes, and Babylon's dream of world domination was shattered (Chapter 5). A new empire, Persia, emerged. Babylon's destruction had long been and often foretold, a very long time ago by Isaiah, and more recently by Jeremiah and Ezekiel. On the night that Belshazzar became aware of the mystical writings, he was killed. The Babylonian Empire fell, immediately fulfilling the interpretation of the writing (5:30-31).

Daniel maintained a position of influence in the Persian Empire as he had in the Babylonian Empire. God shut the mouths of lions in the lions' den dug out by Daniel's enemies. Daniel revealed God's glory even more by serving only Him in all situations (Chapter 6).

The Messianic Prophecies

The second half of the Book of Daniel, Chapters 7-11, differs greatly in both content and form from the first half of the book. The timeline of Daniel's vision in Chapter 7 actually comes before Chapter 6. Chapter 6 covers events from King Darius' reign during the time of Persia and Medes after the fall of Babylon. Chapter 7 takes place in the first year of Belshazzar, the last king of Babylon, just before the time of King Darius. Daniel's vision of the four beasts foretells the swift transitions that will take place from Babylon, Medes and Persia, to Greece, and the great Roman Empire, as well as future events.

The vision of the ram and the goat in Chapter 8 refers to events that will soon occur in the Persian and Greek Empires. Beginning in Chapter 8, the book continues again in Hebrew. The prophecies in Chapter 8 are fulfilled with the death of Alexander and the division of the Greek Empire into four.

Chapter 9 comprises Daniel's intercessory prayer. Daniel searches Jeremiah's prophecy in the Book of Jeremiah and finds the passage in which God promises to return them to Jerusalem after 70 years in Babylonian Exile. All that he can do is to ask God for the prophecy to be fulfilled. Intercessors are those who put the Lord in remembrance and give Him no rest until He fulfills His promises (Isa. 62:6,7). Intercessors have the privilege of moving God's throne. God promises to answer Daniel's prayer. However, His promises go beyond the simple return from exile in Babylon and clearly point to the coming of the Messiah. Chapter 9 contains the clearest and most explicit Messianic prophecy in the Old Testament.

Young Heroes

Chapters 10-12 are the conclusion of the Book of Daniel.

Unlike previously seen in Chapters 7 and 8, the visions and prophecies in these three chapters are given to Daniel through explicit words, not signs or symbols. Chapter 10 contains introductory content related to prophecies, Chapter 11 has detailed information on the prophecies, and Chapter 12 provides the conclusion of the prophecies.

These prophecies will be fulfilled some 300 years after Daniel's time when Alexander has died and the empire is divided into four and is warring against each other with Palestine at the center of that conflict. In particular, they are about the wicked deeds of Antiochus IV Epiphanes, against Israel and his demise. However, the prophecies foretell events that will take place a little further down the road. To be exact, the prophecies also point to the coming of Jesus Christ and His Church.

It is written in Daniel 11:32. The people who know their God shall stand firm and take action." It tells us that no matter how hard the wicked try to overpower and swallow the people of God, His people will not just have the mighty power to resist and not be swayed, but they will display valor that reflects the glory of God. These words are manifested in the actual historical time and space between Chapters 1-6, during which Daniel and his three friends lived.

In the last days, it is necessary to reveal God's glory in such a world that is like the Babylon Empire where God and His Word are ignored. If God showed His glory through young heroes like Daniel and his three friends in Babylon, we must pray for young heroes who fear only God and rely only on the Holy Spirit to emerge. We must pray earnestly that young men and women who devote and begin preparing themselves in their teens and begin shining God's glory from their 20s to past their 80s are found.

These heroes are characterized as the "people who know their God." There is nothing more important than knowledge of God. We must pray to know God through the revival of the Word.

Outline

Chapters 1-6	A historical night
Chapter 1	Daniel and his three friends - the heroes emerge
Chapters 2-4	Nebuchadnezzar's dreams - God's glory
Chapter 5	Belshazaar's vision - the big change
Chapter 6	Darius' decree - the great reversal
Chapters 7-12	A prophetic light
Chapter 7	The vision of the four beasts
Chapter 8	The vision of the ram and the goat
Chapter 9	Prayers and visions - the seventy weeks
Chapters 10-12	A vision on the future of Israel

Voice Outline

DANIEL

100-Day Bible Reading Plan

Day 74	Daniel 1-12	CHECK

The Minor Prophets

The 12 books from Hosea to Malachi are called the "Minor Prophets," not because they are inferior in authority, content, or importance compared to the Major Prophets, but because they are smaller in terms of their size. The Minor Prophets record the ministries of outstanding prophets that were no less robust than those of the Major Prophets.

The same is true today. It should not be easily concluded that ministers who are famous for the size of their congregation or organization, lectures, or writings are better or more successful than those who are not. There are many hidden heroes among the lesser-known ministers who glow brightly in the work they do.

These 12 prophets who make up the Minor Prophets are such people. Among them, Hosea, Joel, Amos, Obadiah, Jonah, Micah, Nahum, Habakkuk, and Zephaniah were active before the Babylonian Exile; Haggai, Zechariah, and Malachi were active after the return from Exile. None of the Minor Prophets was recorded during the Babylonian Captivity. The only two prophets that ministered during this period are Ezekiel and Daniel who are classified as Major Prophets.

HOSEA

GOD'S LOVE

The author of this book is Hosea. Hosea and Joshua are originally the same name, meaning "salvation." The prophet Hosea is the quintessential figure of someone who embraced the world with God's love. He was a contemporary of Amos, was older than Micah, and similar to Isaiah in age. During the service of his long ministry, he foretold the destruction of the Northern Kingdom of Israel. Hosea wept over the destruction of the Northern Kingdom. The destruction of the Northern Kingdom is used as a warning for the Southern Kingdom of Judah.

The purpose of the Book of Hosea is to tell those who have abandoned God in order to worship idols to now return to the Lord and in doing so, know that they will be restored through God's blessings. What is interesting about this book is that God demonstrates His message through the example of Hosea's family.

Hosea's Love for Gomer

Chapters 1 to 3 tell the story of how Hosea got married and

had three children by God's command. Gomer, Hosea's wife, was an unclean woman. God makes Hosea provide his three children with names whose meanings reflect the situation at the time of their birth.

The name of Hosea's first child, "Jezreel," means, "God scatters and sows." We see that God does, in fact, judge Israel for its idolatry: Israel is destroyed by the Assyrians and its people are taken and scattered throughout the Assyrian Empire. The name of his second child, "Lo-Ruhamah" means "no mercy." The name of his third child, "Lo-Ammi" means "not my people." All three names show how Israel left God in pursuit of idol worship.

In Hebrew, "Lo-" means "No." But God is a God of compassion and love. He says that He will love even those the Israelites and forgive and restore them. So God tells Hosea to change the names of his three children: his first, from Jezreel to Israel; his second, "Lo-Ruhamah" to "Ruhamah," to show His mercy for those who did not have His mercy; and his third from "Lo-Ammi" to "Ammi," to show that those who were not His people are now His people.

Hosea's Wife, Gomer

Chapter 2 explains the process by which God restores His people. In Hosea 2:6, God says, "I will hedge up her way with thorns, and I will build a wall against her, so that she cannot find her paths." When people leave God and live according to their desires, He blocks their path with thorns so that they may return to Him. This shows God's desire to have people return to Him even if it is to rid themselves of their suffering. Here, God is telling us that He will build a wall until we have nowhere else to go and finally seek His grace in our despair.

In Verses 14 and 15, God says that He will take the people into the wilderness, comfort them with His Word, and, at last, return His vineyard to them and make the Valley of Achor a gate of hope. The wilderness is a land that leaves people with no choice but to wander in hardship, fear, and anxiety. It is a place in which stability is nowhere to be found. But God tells them He will provide them comfort in those lands. The Valley of Achor means the "valley of tribulation." God tells us that though we may leave Him and wander off to live as we please only to end up in despair, He will have mercy on us and turn our despair into a gateway to hope.

Furthermore, God tells His people that He will betroth them. He says this not once but three times, showing His determination that stems from love, grace, and compassion. "And I will betroth you to me forever. I will betroth you to me in righteousness and in justice, in steadfast love and in mercy. I will betroth you to me in faithfulness. And you shall know the Lord"(2:19-20).

God embraces us with His love and wants to restore us. As He rebukes Israel and Judah for going against Him and seeking help from their neighbors, He likens them to a wife who has abandoned and left her husband. That is the reason why He tells His message to the people of Israel through Hosea's marriage: "And I will sow her for myself in the land. And I will have mercy on No Mercy, and I will say to Not

My People, 'You are my people'; and he shall say, 'You are my God'" (2:23).

In Chapter 3, Hosea pays to bring back his unclean wife who had left him for fifteen shekels of silver, a homer and a lethech of barley. Israel and Judah trusted their allies for political protection. The prophet criticizes their actions and tells them that their trust must only lie in God. Nevertheless, Israel and Judah bypassed God and formed alliances with their foreign neighbors. Their actions were no different to selling their integrity as God's holy people and prostituting themselves.

God wished for Israel to come to terms with their actions through the example of Hosea's marriage. Later, God plucks Israel from its very roots and scatters them across the foreign lands of Assyria. Indeed, the Northern Kingdom of Israel is conquered by the Assyrians in the year 722 B.C. and its people are exiled. But God will bring them back from captivity and restore them.

God's Love toward Israel

In Chapters 4-14, we observe three aspects of God. Chapters 4-7 reveal a God who is holy. In these chapters, God points out all the sins of Israel and urges them to live holy lives before Him who is holy. Israel's greatest sin is its "failure to know God." Through these chapters, God tells the Israelites that He wishes for them to turn back from their ways that do not recognize Him and to once again know Him.

For it is written in Hosea 6:3, "Let us know; let us press on to know the Lord," in 6:6, "For I desire steadfast love and not sacrifice, the knowledge of God rather than burnt offerings," and in 4:6, "My people are destroyed for lack of knowledge."

Chapter 7 illustrates the sinfulness of the Israelites through four metaphors.

First, they are likened to a "heated oven" (7:4). The metaphor speaks of their state as being full of evil thoughts.

Second, they are likened to a "cake not turned" (7:8). A cake that is baked only on one side will be raw on the other side and cannot be eaten. God tells us that Israel is in such a state.

Third, they are likened to a "dove, silly and without sense" (7:11). Doves find their homes well, but foolish doves go elsewhere. This metaphor accurately illustrates how the Israelites should have gone to the Lord for help but instead went to foreign nations.

Fourth, they are likened to a "treacherous bow" (7:16). At first, it is aimed at the target, but in the end, it shoots in the wrong direction. It illustrates how the Israelites directed themselves to the Gentiles instead of turning to God. Nevertheless, God is holy and calls for them to repent of all their sins and return to Him.

Chapters 8-10 reveal a God who is just. In these chapters, God shows the people just how painful are the consequences of sin. Hosea 8:7 tells us, "For they sow the wind, and they shall reap the whirlwind." What they sowed in vain came back to them as a life of even greater vanity. People who reject God's Word will become "wanderers among the nations," and their royal bloodline will be cut off. God desperately wants them to return to Him. He wants them to have a single heart and not one that is divided in two.

Chapters 11-13 reveal a God who is love. Despite the Israelites living a life away from Him, God treats them with the same unchanging love. He says, "I led them with the bands of love" (11:4). He shows them the love of a loving father who teaches his children to walk and heals in his arms when they fall. God expresses His love with the words, "My heart recoils within me; my compassion grows warm and tender" (11:8). He is a father who does not anger but whose heart aches and wants to take care of us when we sin.

In Chapters 12-13, God points to Ephraim's sin. Indulging in abundance, they do not regard sin as such and become arrogant with the wealth and power it has accumulated, forgetting God. God tells us to take care of the poor, the orphans, widows, and strangers with our wealth.

A Promise of Abundance for Those Who Repent

The tone of Chapter 14 is quite different from the chapters that come before it. If previous chapters were about reproof, wrath, and warning against sin, this chapter consists of the counsel of repentance and promises of restoration through God's mercy. We could consider this chapter a guidebook for those who repent. This chapter speaks of the promise of the forgiveness of sins. When we proceed to confess all our sins with our lips, God will heal and restore us.

First John 1:9 says, "If we confess our sins, he is faithful and just to forgive us our sins and to cleanse us from all unrighteousness."

Hosea 14:5-8 lists the ways in which God will restore us. As we plunge deeper into sin and further into ruin, God continues to tell us to repent, to turn around, and come back to the Lord. He promises to restore us with great blessings, abundant fruits, and a powerful and beautiful life.

In the Book of Hosea, we can see the heart that God has for people who have sinned against Him unilaterally. He continues to give them opportunities, forgive them, restore them, and ultimately lead them to great blessings.

Outline

Chapters 1-3	Hosea's love for Gomer The antitype of God's love, Hosea's marriage
Chapter 1	Hosea's children, two sons and one daughter
Chapter 2	Hosea's wife, Gomer
Chapter 3	Buying his wife back with fifteen shekels of silver, a homer and a lethech of barley
Chapters 4-14	God's love for Israel
Chapters 4-7	Israel's sin (God is holy)
Chapters 8-10	Judgment on Israel (God is just)
Chapters 11-13	Israel's restoration (God is love)
Chapter 14	A promise of abundance for those who repent

Voice Outline

HOSEA

100-Day Bible Reading Plan

		CHECK
Day 75	Hosea 1-14	

JOEL

THE DAY OF THE LORD

The Bible does not tell us who the Prophet Joel is or when he ministered as a prophet. Other than Acts 2:16, which tells us that Joel's prophecy was fulfilled by the amazing work of the Holy Spirit who filled Peter and the people after the Pentecost, the Bible does not provide any other details.

In general, the Prophet Joel is thought to have been a contemporary of Amos. The reason is that Joel also prophesied about locust swarms, famine, and judgments of fire, just as Amos did (Am. 4:7-11; 7:1-6). Amos served as a prophet in the Northern Kingdom of Israel and Joel in the Southern Kingdom of Judah. It is assumed that Joel ministered with Hosea and Obadiah around the same period.

The Day of the Lord

The Book of Joel mentions the "day of the Lord" a total of five times (1:15; 2:1,11,31; 3:14). It tells us that the day of the Lord is very near. The book tells us that the day of the Lord is a sad day, a day of destruction, and a terrifying day for the inhabitants of the land. It is expressed as a fearful day of darkness and gloom, a day of clouds and thick darkness. The day of the Lord may be what is right now, or it may be just a prelude to a greater day of judgment. But one thing the book tells us is that we must always be awake and cry out to the Lord.

Joel 1:1-2:11 contains prophecies about the days of disaster. The content is tremendous with no other verses coming close to it. God tells us to pass on the content of the book from generation to generation. In other words, God is telling us that what the book contains is more than just an interesting story. He commands us to "teach" it to future generations. He wishes for us to use the book as a lesson and learn how to fear God and hate sin.

In particular, the book speaks of the devastation of nature caused by the swarms of locusts. The cutting locusts, the swarming locusts, the hopping locusts, and the destroying locusts leave nothing behind, destroying everything (1:4). The calamities caused by natural disasters provide an opportunity for all the people to repent, and show them that it is time to go before God and seek His face. In Joel 1:14, God says to His people, "Consecrate a fast; call a solemn assembly. Gather the elders and all the inhabitants of the land to the house of the Lord your God, and cry out to the Lord."

Return to the Lord

In Joel 2:12-14, the prophet says: "'Yet even now,' declares the Lord, 'return to me with all your heart, with fasting, with weeping, and with mourning; and rend your hearts and not your garments.' Return to the Lord your God, for he is gracious and merciful, slow to anger, and abounding in steadfast love; and he relents over disaster. Who knows whether he will not turn and relent, and leave a blessing behind him, a grain offering and a drink offering for the Lord your God?"

These words explain God from five different perspectives. First, He is gracious; second, He is merciful; third, He is slow to anger; fourth, He is abounding in steadfast love and therefore relents over disaster; and fifth, He is One to go beyond all these and bless us. In general, we have to change, cancel, or postpone plans when they become unworkable or when we do not have the ability to make them happen. However, when it is God who turns back from His plan; it is entirely out of the compassion in His heart. If we rely on God's character and repent, earnestly seek His grace, even if He has made plans to judge us, God tells us that He will change His plans and refrain from judging us.

The Book of Joel explains that even in the midst of our sins and iniquities, if we return to the Lord, earnestly cry out to Him, and trust in His character, He will not only spare us from disaster out of the compassion in His heart, but that He will go further to bless us. When we come to God to repent, our hearts should be centered not around our own actions, but be founded in prayer and on the trust that we have in God's compassionate character.

Restoration to a Bountiful Life

In Joel 2:18-32, God promises to show mercy should the

people repent despite all their sins. In particular, Verses 18-27 explain the five different ways in which God will do this.

First, He promises to give His people food so that they can live a bountiful life. Second, He tells them that He will never let them be put to shame by foreign nations again. Third, He says that He will drive out the armies that tormented Israel into dry and desolate lands so that they may never do so again. Fourth, He says that He will give them the early rain and the latter rain to the Israelites who repent and return. And fifth, He promises to restore to them the years that the swarming locust, the hopper, the destroyer, and the cutter.

The greatest surprise of all is that God says that He will pour out the Holy Spirit in Verses 28-32. In the Book of Acts, this is clearly stated as being "in the last days." It is written in Acts 2:17, "And in the last days it shall be, God declares, that I will pour out my Spirit." Here, the "last days" refers to the period from when Jesus came to this earth until when He comes again. Through the Prophet Joel, God promises a life rich in spirituality with the pouring out of the Holy Spirit on all flesh in the last days.

The Valley of Jehoshaphat

In Chapter 3, the Lord says that when the time comes, the Lord will punish the enemies of His people, vindicate them, and restore Jerusalem to glorious prosperity and give it eternal life. The Valley of Jehoshaphat is the court in which God will enter into judgment with the nations on behalf of His people (3:2).

The crimes of the nations are as follows: First, they scattered the Israelites among the nations and divided up their land; second, they sold young Jewish men and women to traffickers; third, they stole the Lord's silver and gold and took God's treasures to their temples.

For their crimes, the nations were sentenced as such: First, the return of God's people by the hand of God; second, suffering just as God's people had to suffer; third, God's direct judgment. For His people, however, God will be a refuge and a fortress,

The aftermath of the nations' judgment is to be as follows: Egypt will suffer desolation and Edom will become a desolate wilderness. But Judah will remain forever and Jerusalem will be passed onto generations. Though these promises were partially fulfilled through the Israelites, they will come to complete fruition with the Church of the New Testament.

The Book of Joel underlines God's sovereignty in the making of history. The wicked who rebel against God will be destroyed, but He promises to be merciful to those who trust in His character, repent and earnestly seek His face despite all their sins.

Outline

Chapters 1-2:11	Prophecies about the day of the Lord and the day of disaster
Chapter 2:12-17	Call to repentance
Chapter 2:18-32	God who does amazing works
Chapter 3	The Valley of Jehoshaphat, God who vindicates

Voice Outline

JOEL

100-Day Bible Reading Plan

		CHECK
Day 76	Joel, Amos, Obadiah, Jonah	

AMOS

GOD'S RIGHTEOUSNESS

This book was written by the Prophet Amos. When God called him, Amos was a shepherd. His town, Tekoa, is a small town about 10 kilometers southeast of Bethlehem. God called on him to deliver a message to the Northern Kingdom of Israel.

Amos served the Lord during the same period as Hosea, Joel, and Jonah, and a little before the time of Isaiah. This is explained to us in Amos 1:1, "The words of Amos in the days of Uzziah king of Judah and in the days of Jeroboam the son of Joash, king of Israel, two years before the earthquake." Unlike the Prophet Isaiah who lived in the royal courts as a member of the royalty, Amos lived and worked as a farmer in the countryside.

Word of Warning

The name Amos has the meaning of "heavy load" or "carrying a burden." His message, as his name suggests, carries with it a warning of significant weight. Amos is a simpler and less polished prophet compared to the other prophets. He was a Judean who prophesied mainly at Bethel to Israel (7:10-15).

Though Amos faced opposition from Amaziah the priest of Bethel during his ministry, he did not back down. He rebuked sin and boldly proclaimed God's judgment while encouraging people to repent. He did the task with which the Lord had entrusted him; he was bold, faithful, and unshaken.

Though the books of Amos and Hosea carry the same message directed to the same people, the angle they take with which to deliver this message is the exact opposite. The Book of Hosea conveys God's amazing and unconditional love and the Book of Amos conveys God's justice.

Additionally, the Prophet Amos and Prophet Joel were contemporaries; thus, their books also resemble each other in content and form. They first show the people their faults and reveal their wounds; they then present the cure promised through God's grace. This period was during the reigns of Uzziah in the Southern Kingdom of Judah and Jeroboam in the Northern Kingdom of Israel when both prospered.

A Solemn Warning

This book was written as a solemn warning against the sins of the Northern Kingdom of Israel. Their sins can be divided into five major categories.

The first was idolatry. The second was the oppression of the poor. The growing gap between the rich and poor was a real problem at the time. The third was the unfair trials held by its leaders (5:10-13). Undue coercion and persecution of the people were rampant at the time. The fourth was their extremely extravagant lifestyles (6:4-6). The rich and powerful used their wealth to splurge in extravagance and debauchery. The fifth was dishonest transactions (8:4-6). Exchanging bribes and dishonest transactions ran rampant throughout the nation.

God warned the people against these five sins through the Prophet Amos. But in the second half of the book, God surprises us by having mercy on the people following His harsh judgment.

Declaration of Judgment on Eight Nations

Chapters 1-2 contain warnings for eight nations. They warn the two Kingdoms of Judah and Israel as well as six other nations surrounding them about God's impending judgment. Initially, these judgments include judgments on Gaza, Tire, Edom, Ammon, and Moab from the Damascus and Philistine regions.

There are four recurring statements that appear in the prosecution of the sins of these eight nations. The first is "Thus says the Lord." Regardless of whether the people choose to believe in God or not, God is not only the God of Israel but the God of all nations (Psalm 117:1). The Book of Malachi refers to the "Lord of armies" 20 times, also showing that God is the God of the nations.

The second is "for three transgressions… and for four." We could consider this to mean "three or four sins" or "third and fourth sins," as in "a lot of sin." While one or two is used to represent a small number, three or four is used to represent a large number. Another meaning could also be that there are many sins, but the fourth sin is especially grievous. God specifically addresses this fourth sin separately. The common characteristic of all the fourth sins is that they have to do with "persecution," because persecution is the most serious of sins.

The third recurring statement is, "I will not revoke the punishment." This statement shows that God has given the people plenty of opportunities to turn back by delaying the execution of judgment but that he cannot wait any longer and has no choice but to deliver justice. God issues a very stern statement.

The fourth reoccurring statement is "I will send a fire." God here is telling the people that he will turn houses and cities into piles of ash with fire.

The Proclamation of Judgment against Eight Nations

Damascus' sin was cruelty (1:3-5). Located in the southernmost part of the Philistine region, Gaza's sin was selling Israelites to Edom as slaves (1:6-8). Tyre served as an agent in the slave trade (1:9-10). Edom's sin was hatred and an unforgiving heart; they persistently chased God's people and treated them without mercy (1:11-12). Ammon brutally slaughtered its neighboring countries and waged war (1:13-15). Moab's sin was to burn the dead again (2:1-3). Judah rebelled and disobeyed God's Word (2:4-5).

The book covers the sins of other nations in two or three verses but the sins of the Northern Kingdom of Israel are detailed over 11 verses. Israel committed five sins: bribery, persecution of the poor and needy, unholiness, idolatry, and the refusal to heed the Word of God (2:6-16).

Three Sermons on Judgment

In Chapters 3-6, Amos deals in particular with the sins of the Kingdom of Israel. He starts each of these sermons with "Hear this word that the Lord has spoken against you, O people of Israel" (3:1; 4:1; 5:1). They are referred to by name because unlike the other nations, they knew God's name and were a chosen people who were called by His name. However, they continuously refused to listen to His Word. And now they are being prosecuted and told to "listen" to God's closing statement.

The first sermon addresses Israel's privileges and responsibilities (Chapter 3).

"Though the grace of the Lord has been with you until now, do not expect it to remain with you before you first reconcile with God. Know that your evil deeds are the cause of your judgment. All tribulations that you face are by God so that you may be brought back to repentance. You have been warned previously through the prophets that I had sent for you." God then tells His prophet to notify Israel's neighboring nations of Israel's impending judgment. This is a warning for them too.

The second sermon addresses Israel's failure to heed God's warnings (Chapter 4). God tells them that oppressors will be humbled and the idolaters become more stubborn. God laments that the people have no intention to turn from their ways despite the many opportunities He provided for them to repent through their tribulations. Still, God wishes to give them another chance to change.

The third sermon is a lament for Israel (Chapters 5-6). God wants Israel to seek Him and stop their worship of idols. He also gently explains to them why they must prepare to meet Him. He is explaining to them that there is no other way for salvation other than to repent and return to Him. Continuing to disregard God's warnings and opportunities to turn back will only lead to judgment in the end. And with judgment, will come thorough devastation.

Five Visions

In Amos 7:1-9:10, God gives us five visions of judgment. Again, there is a common thread among these visions. The visions each start with "This is what the Lord God showed me." The Lord shows Amos the present, the future, and what He will do in that future, for God always shows His servants what He will do in advance (3:7).

In addition to delivering God's messages of warning to the people, the prophet's role is to intercede. It is not only to deliver this message, but to come before God with intercessory prayer. If a prophet does not warn the people and only slanders, judges, gossips, and observes from behind the scenes, he is no longer of use to God as a messenger. God hears Amos' intercession and decides to overturn His judgment.

The first vision is of judgment by locusts (7:1-3). However, through Amos' earnest intercession, God decides against this judgment.

The second vision is of judgment by fire on all earth. But again, God relents and overturns this judgment with Amos' earnest intercession (7:4-6).

The third is of judgment by a plumb line (7:7-9). God shows Amos a plumb line set to determine whether the wall has been built correctly. The plumb line represents the Word of God. God weighs the lives of His people against His Word and tells Amos that He will destroy what needs to be destroyed without hesitation.

The fourth vision is of a basket of summer fruits (Chapter 8). God shows that just as ripe summer fruits might be good now, they will soon begin to rot. And so too will Israel be deserving of judgment with its rottenness.

With the fifth vision of the destruction of the altar, God warns them ahead of time that Israel too will be destroyed by its sins (9:1-10).

The Restoration of Israel

In Amos 9:11-15, God finally gives Israel the promise of the blessings of restoration following its judgment. He makes five promises of restoration. The first is that the Kingdom of David will be restored through the Messiah (9:11); the second is that the Kingdom of David will expand into vast territories with the joining of people from all nations (9:12); the third is that everything will become bountiful (9:13); the fourth is that the captives will return and rebuild (9:14); the fifth is that they will be deeply planted in the ground and never be plucked out again (9:15).

Through the Book of Amos, God tells us to do what is just and fair, and to take care of the poor and afflicted.

Outline

Chapters 1-2	The proclamation of judgment against eight nations
Chapters 3-6	Three sermons The sinful past of Israel and the judgment on its present and future
Chapters 7-9:10	Five visions The description of Israel's judgment
Chapters 9:11-15	Five promises The restoration of Israel

Voice Outline

AMOS

100-Day Bible Reading Plan

		CHECK
Day 76	Joel, Amos, Obadiah, Jonah	

OBADIAH

THE DESTRUCTION OF EDOM

The Book of Obadiah is the shortest book in the Old Testament with only one chapter and 21 verses. It records the very significant event of Edom's destruction. Edom, who were descendants of Esau, always hated Judah. When Nebuchadnezzar's army invaded Judah to destroy Jerusalem, Edom stood on the side of Babylon and aided the destruction of Judah. In its days of despair, Judah looked for help from his brother Edom, but Edom stood and watched, rejoicing in the destruction of Jerusalem. The Book of Obadiah proclaims the judgment against Edom for these actions.

As Verse 1 suggests, the title of this book is "Obadiah's revelation." The Bible does not tell us about the Prophet Obadiah. A revelation does not include the prophet's thoughts or opinions but simply states what has been shown by the Lord. This is the most important principle for the deliverer of any message. Obadiah only speaks of the sins of Edom.

Reasons for Judgment against Edom

This book is a declaration of war against Edom. God sent his messengers to the nations to report, "Rise up! Let us rise against her for battle!" (1:1). Edom ultimately loses this war and becomes small among the nations (1:2).

The first reason for judgment against Edom was its pride (1:3). They were proud, relying on the following five things.

1. Edom was located at high altitude. It was situated on an impregnable natural fortress. They believed it was impossible for anyone to tear them down. But God brings them down (1: 4). When we fall prey to our pride, we exalt ourselves and fall into a false sense of comfort.
2. They trusted their wealth and riches. But even those were not able to protect them (1:6).
3. They trusted their alliances with their neighboring nations. But their neighbors did not keep their word of Edom's day of trouble (1:7).
4. They trusted the tactics of their wise men (1:8). But their tactics were foolish and bound to fail.
5. They trusted their warriors (1:9). But even the mightiest of warriors will lose morale and lose the battle. Ultimately, Edom will be destroyed and annihilated.

Edom's second serious sin was that it just watched, rejoiced, and ridiculed its brother in distress. It went so far as to aid Babylon when it partook in the invasion of Jerusalem.

Verses 11-14 describe Edom's sin in detail.

"On the day that you stood aloof, on the day that strangers carried off his wealth and foreigners entered his gates and cast lots for Jerusalem, you were like one of them" (1:11). Then, God lists eight actions that Edom must not take.

1. Do not gloat over the day of your brother in the day of his misfortune.
2. Do not rejoice over the people of Judah in the day of their ruin.
3. Do not enlarge your mouth (boast) in the day of distress.
4. Do not enter the gate of my people in the day of their calamity.
5. Do not gloat over his disaster in the day of his calamity.
6. Do not loot his wealth in the day of his calamity.
7. Do not stand at the crossroads to cut off his fugitives.
8. Do not hand over his survivors in the day of distress.

But in reality, Edom violated all of these things and not only turned a blind eye to its brother, the Kingdom of Judah, in his day of calamity but also cooperated with the enemy to destroy and loot its brother.

In Verse 15, God says, "As you have done, it shall be done to you" Then, in Verses 17-21, He promises to restore His people. God says He will destroy Edom, who had helped Babylon destroy the Kingdom of Judah, in the same way and promises to restore the people of Israel and bring them back to the land.

The Promise of Restoration

These words are reminiscent of Genesis Chapter 14. Upon hearing the news that his nephew Lot had been taken captive during the wars in the Near East at the time, Abraham immediately gathered everyone in his household to rescue Lot.

Perhaps, his neighbors tried to stop him and said: "Be thankful that you are safe amid this war. How do you think that a civilian like yourself can head up against the joint forces and save your nephew?" Or they may have said, "Don't even think about going there to help." Or Abraham could have judged Lot for his misery and thought, "What did I say from the very beginning? Did not I tell him that those lands were not suitable for the righteous? Of course, he is facing hardship for going against God's will." He could easily have just sat there thinking of all the ways Lot brought his hardship upon himself.

But Abraham did not react in this way. He neither questioned the cause behind Lot's misery nor listened to his neighbors' dissuasions. He went with his heart and took all the men of his household simply to save his nephew in trouble. He did not sit on the sidelines and judge his brother's misfortune and did not question its cause. He neither slandered nor mocked his nephew.

Abraham risked his life to help his brother in tribulation. God valued his actions and gave him victory. When we see a brother in suffering, it is God's will that we lay down our lives to help the brother in need. God is not pleased with bystanders who judge, assign blame, slander, or mock. He is pleased with those who sacrifice everything they can to help a brother during hardship. True beauty lies in helping those in need with all our strength without any calculations of our own ability.

In a self-centric age such as today where no one cares about the difficulties of one's neighbors and brothers, Obadiah delivers a stunning message.

"A new commandment I give to you, that you love one another: just as I have loved you, you also are to love one another. By this all people will know that you are my disciples, if you have love for one another" (John 13:34-35).

"By this we know love, that he laid down his life for us, and we ought to lay down our lives for the brothers. But if anyone has the world's goods and sees his brother in need, yet closes his heart against him, how does God's love abide in him? Little children, let us not love in word or talk but in deed and in truth" (1 John 3:16-18).

Outline

Chapter 1:1-16	Judgment on Edom
Verses 1-2	Proclamation of judgment
Verses 3-14	The two reasons for judgment
Verses 15-16	The results of the judgment
Chapter 1:17-21	The restoration of Israel

Voice Outline

OBADIAH

100-Day Bible Reading Plan

		CHECK
Day 76	Joel, Amos, Obadiah, Jonah	☐

JONAH

GOD'S COMPASSION

Although the Book of Jonah is categorized as a Prophetic Book, it is closer to a story than a prophecy. It does, of course, contain a single prophecy. Other than this one line, "Yet forty days, and Nineveh shall be overthrown!" (3:4), the book contains stories about events that take place before and after the prophecy. Jonah, along with Moses and a few other authors of the books of the Bible, records his own mistakes. However, this is not to stress his shortcomings but rather to reveal the glory of God by showing God's forgiveness and compassion despite himself.

According to 2 Kings 14:25-27, Jonah was from Gath-Hepher in the region of Galilee, a city belonging to the tribe of Zebulun of Israel. He delivered a message of God's mercy toward Israel in the days of Jeroboam II.

The Book of Jonah was written to serve multiple purposes. The first was to explain that God loves not only Israel but all the nations. The second was to show that to obey and rely on God is a joyful and blessed way to be in Jesus. God's love and mercy are for all the nations. God wishes for His people to know this.

Through this book, God tells us that He forgives all sins and provides salvation if we repent and return, regardless of the seriousness of our sins. For example, when Ahab, said to be the evilest king of all the kings of Israel, heard the message of God's judgment and fasted, repented, and earnestly sought God's grace, God delayed Ahab's judgment to his son's generation. Had Ahab's son repented before God as his father had, God would have delayed judgment on him as well and completely erased the sin. This is because no matter how great a sin, God does not allow its consequences to continue for more than three or four generations.

A Missionary without God's Heart

Another important topic addressed in the Book of Jonah is missionaries who have been commissioned to preach the Gospel. The most difficult element of missions is not the obstinacy of the people in the mission field. It is not the physical conditions, such as harsh climates or poor food. It is not the lack of strategy or knowledge, nor is it the lack of finances. It is the missionary himself who does not have the heart of God. Jonah was such a missionary.

He approached the people with God's righteousness and not His love. He considered Nineveh to be deserving of judgment and destruction due to its sins. Moreover, Nineveh was a nation that had harassed Jonah's home of Israel from time to time. Within, he may even have rejoiced at the news of Nineveh's coming destruction. But Jonah knew how God is pleased with those who forgive. So Jonah left Nineveh, disobeying God's orders because he knew that God would surely forgive the people of Nineveh once they heard the message of judgment and turned back from their sins to repent.

Jonah was a dedicated missionary equipped with a passion for God, but he lacked God's love. He is a good representation of a missionary who lacks God's fiery heart of love and only cries out righteousness.

The God Who Prepares

God is He who prepares. In Jonah 1:4, God prepared a "great wind" to hurl up upon the sea when Jonah disobeyed him and ran away. When Jonah went to the Port of Joppa and found a ship going to Tarshish, the opposite direction to Nineveh, he must have felt good and thought to himself, "The heavens are on my side."

However, God prepared a great storm and shook the ship on which Jonah was sailing. Jonah turns to the crowd on the ship, "Pick me up and hurl me into the sea; then the sea will quiet down for you, for I know it is because of me that this great tempest has come upon you" (1:12). On the surface, it appears as though Jonah displayed an amazing act of selflessness by being willing to sacrifice himself on the ship. But in fact, he had an ulterior motive. He was willing to give up his body to ensure the destruction of his enemy, Nineveh.

But when Jonah fell into the sea, God prepared a "great fish" to swallow him. In Chapter 4, God prepares a plant to put a shade over Jonah's head. Jonah was glad because of the plant. But the next day, God prepares a worm to eat the leaves of the plant and they are eaten away in an instant. God also prepares a scorching east wind. This confuses Jonah and he becomes exceedingly angry.

God is one to prepare in ways like this. When He makes a plan, He sufficiently prepares and equips those who obey His will to handle His work. If we obey the Word and do our best, He prepares us so that we may not be lacking in any aspect, be it in terms of the environment, people, finances, or ability to work.

In the Book of Acts, we can see God making preparations in many places. When Cornelius prays before the Lord, God tells him to invite Peter. Given the culture of the times, Cornelius thought that Peter would not answer an invitation from him, a Gentile. Regardless, he trusted and obeyed the Word of God. And God responded by moving Peter's heart to accept Cornelius' invitation before the messenger arrived. We must have faith that God will prepare and take care of the rest when we do our utmost.

A Chance

God is one who gives chances. The Kingdom of God shows just how there is always another opportunity. In Jonah 3:1, it is written, "Then the word of the Lord came to Jonah the second time." We need to think about why it is specified as "the second time." Jonah disobeyed God and went in the opposite direction the first time, but God gave him a second time after Jonah repented in the great fish. The second time here means a second chance, meaning the third and fourth times all count as a second chance.

These verses tell us that our lives do not come to an end with a single mistake or sin, but that we will always be given another opportunity to serve God's Kingdom when we repent and return. God planned to judge Nineveh but did not do so and gave them another chance when they turned and repented. The God of wisdom softened Jonah the stubborn missionary's heart and gave him another chance.

The Unparalleled Repentance Movement

Another peculiarity to note is that this repentance movement which took place in Nineveh is unparalleled in history. When the king of Nineveh repented, he not only repented himself but ordered all his subjects and servants, including children and beasts, to fast and repent.

"The word reached the king of Nineveh, and he arose from his throne, removed his robe, covered himself with sackcloth, and sat in ashes. And he issued a proclamation and published through Nineveh, "By the decree of the king and his nobles: Let neither man nor beast, herd nor flock, taste anything. Let them not feed or drink water, but let man and beast be covered with sackcloth... Who knows? God may turn and relent and turn from his fierce anger, so that we may not perish" (3:7-9).

There has never been a time in history when an entire nation has joined in repentance. What we find here is that if we go before the Lord wholeheartedly and repent, He will forgive all our sins no matter what circumstances we may be in. Even if we are in judgment, He will reverse His decision and bring us back to salvation.

In the kingdom of God, there is no despair; there is only hope. God is a God who never fails to give us hope when we repent and earnestly seek the grace of the Lord. We always have a chance in the Kingdom of God. No matter how big the mistake or how grave the sin is, if we repent and turn around, He gives all of us another chance.

- Name: Jonah
- Address: Gath-Hepher in the region of Galilee, a city belonging to the tribe of Zebulun of Israel
- Occupation: Missionary
- Strengths: Passionate; active worshipper. Strong sense of patriotism for Israel
- Weaknesses: Hot-tempered and stubborn. Has an obstinate heart and often says he wishes to die. Doesn't have the heart of God (the greatest flaw)
- Overall evaluation: questionable character as a missionary. In need of further internal healing and training. Not yet prepared.
- God's remarks: I will use him regardless. I will give him a chance now.

Outline

Chapters 1-2	God calls Jonah the first time
Chapter 1:1-3	Jonah's disobedience
Chapter 1:4-17	The great wind, the tempest, and the great fish
Chapter 2:1-9	Jonah's prayer of repentance
Chapter 2:10	Jonah is saved
Chapters 3-4	God calls Jonah a second time
Chapter 3:1-4	Jonah's obedience
Chapter 3:5-10	The great city, the great repentance, and the great pardoning
Chapter 4:1-3	Jonah's prayer of protest
Chapter 4:4-11	Jonah is rebuked

Voice Outline

JONAH

100-Day Bible Reading Plan

		CHECK
Day 76	Joel, Amos, Obadiah, Jonah	

MICAH

JUDGMENT AND RESTORATION

The author of this book is the Prophet Micah. He is introduced as a person of Moresheth-Gath, a region about 30 kilometers southwest of Jerusalem. As stated in 1:1, he ministered during the same period as the Prophet Isaiah (Isa. 1:1), and his prophecy is similar to that of Isaiah as well. For example, Isaiah 2:2-3 and Micah 4:1-2 use almost the same words.

Isaiah speaks of "Judah and Jerusalem," and Micah speaks of "Samaria and Jerusalem." Samaria is the center of the Northern Kingdom of Israel, and Jerusalem is the center of the Southern Kingdom of Judah. Although the Book of Micah speaks of the reigns of the kings of Judah, its words are targeted at both the Southern Kingdom of Judah and the Northern Kingdom of Israel.

Micah was the last prophet to minister during the time of the Northern Kingdom's destruction. Micah ministered primarily to the people and Isaiah primarily to the royal court.

The purpose of the Book of Micah is to enlighten Israel of

its sins by listing them on paper and to prophesy about the consequences of those sins. But the book also encourages the people with God's promise of restoration by His grace. Micah prophesies two big events: one the destruction of Jerusalem (3:9-12), and the other the birth of the Messiah (5:2).

In summary, the Book of Micah prophesies that the Northern Kingdom of Israel will be destroyed by Assyria with the vision of Assyria conquering its cities and bringing the nation to ruin. At the same time, it criticizes the greed of the rich in the city, the economic troubles of the nation, and the hardship of the poor in a society that had lost its sense of equity. In particular, Micah woefully grieves over the greed of the priests.

The Declaration of Judgment

The seven chapters that comprise the book can be divided into three sections.

Chapters 1-3 lay out the sins of Jerusalem and Samaria, and the judgment to soon come upon them. Samaria and Jerusalem were not centers of godly worship, but rather centers for idol worship. These idols will be broken, burned, and shattered.

Micah exposes all the people's sins one by one (2:1-11). They plan evil from where they sleep. Their entire mind is devoted to doing evil. They use their wealth, power, and influence to swiftly execute their evil schemes, sparing no means. They also reject the prophets and oppress the poor.

Through the Book of Micah, God specifically warns

leaders of the judgment and justice that await them for their corruption and instills hope in the people that God will bring salvation. People instinctively try to use their power for evil. Those with power covet others' wealth and property and try to seize them illegally. Micah sends a serious message of warning against such actions.

God wants those with power to help those who are weak, poor, and in trouble. He wants them to rule the country with justice and fairness, and to support the powerless. The wealthy are rich because He gave them wealth so that they may help those who are poor and in need to uplift them. Because the leaders of Micah's time did not use their power nor the rich use their wealth in the way that was intended, God tells them that judgment is imminent.

The Northern Kingdom of Israel will be destroyed by the king of Assyria and the Southern Kingdom of Judah will be as a candle in the wind. The Prophet Micah sings his lament amid great sorrow as the chief mourner (1:8-16).

Three Promises

Chapters 4-5 reveal the promises of God's grace that will soon descend and the restoration that will take place in the days to come.

Micah 4:1 sets a contrast with the last verse of Chapter 3 by starting with the verse with the word "but" (the word "but" is not included in the English translation of the Bible). Chapters 4-5 lay out four events that will take place in the future.

1. The nations will come to Jerusalem to hear the Word, and there will be true peace on all the earth. "They shall beat their swords into plowshares, and their spears into pruning hooks" (4:3), means that the war will come to an end, and "they shall sit every man under his vine and under his fig tree" (4:4) means that fear shall dissipate and peace shall take its place.
2. The captives will return and ultimately Jerusalem will reign victorious.
3. The Messiah will come out of Bethlehem to restore the people (5:2).
4. Those who keep their faith through all tribulations will be used by God for His holy purpose. They shall not wait for man or rely on him but they will be like dew and showers that only wait for and rely on God's grace (5:7). They will receive God's blessing and bless the nations with it. They will be like a lion (5:8). They shall be lifted up over their adversaries with God's strength and trample over their enemies (5:9).

Call for Repentance

That is why Micah urges us to repent our current ways of living in Chapters 6-7. Just as Micah 1:2 started with the words, "Hear, you peoples, all of you," Micah 6:1 begins with, "Hear what the Lord says." If Chapter 1 urges the people to hear God's judgment for their sins, Chapter 6 lists their sins to urge them to repent. Micah urges the people to listen to the Word of God.

Micah 6:3-5 contains a very moving message from God.

"O my people, what have I done to you? How have I wearied you? Remember all that I have done for you! For I brought you up from the land of Egypt and guided you through the wilderness. O my people, remember what happened from Shittim to Gilgal. What else do you have to know other than to be moved by the salvation, love, and grace that I have given you?"

What does God want from us? We need to look no further than the amazing essence of Christianity (6:6-8). He does not wish for us to live a religious life. He is not concerned with the religious rites or the offering of our wealth, treasures, or bodies which are generally associated with being religious. That is not the kind of piety that God wants from us.

God wishes for us to be just, love the Son of Man, and to walk humbly with Him. What God wants from us is summed up in the Ten Commandments: to love God and love our neighbors!

God wants his people to live holy lives. A holy life does not mean conspicuous worship but a life that is pure, humble, and obedient. He wants us to be just and not oppress the poor in unjust ways. What God desires from us is to exercise the right kind of leadership.

The end of Chapter 6 also tells of the actions and consequences of being a worldly rich person who lives in the ways of this world.

God strictly criticizes those who accumulate wealth through unjust means and use that wealth only to benefit themselves. Wealth must be accumulated in the right way and must mainly be used to help the poor and those in need while spending minimally for oneself. God tells us that this is the way for a holy rich person to live.

In Micah 7:1-6, we hear Micah's lament, "Woe is me!"

"The godly has perished from the earth, and there is no one upright among mankind. Many seek to harm and do evil unto others. Leaders and judges ask for bribes and those with power collude with them to do evil. There is no one left to trust. Children treat their parents with contempt and rise up against them. There is only fighting in households."

Micah 7:7-13, brings greater pain to our souls when we look only to the evil around us. In such times, we must look to God. This will bring us hope. Micah's confession during such times is, "I will look to the Lord; I will wait for the God of my salvation; my God will hear me!" We must trust in God and look to His salvation. God will surely answer our prayers.

Micah concludes the book with a beautiful confession (7:18-19).

> Who is a God like you?
> Pardoning iniquity and passing over transgression
> For the remnant of his inheritance?
> He does not retain his anger forever,
> Because he delights in steadfast love.
> He will again have compassion on us;
> He will tread our iniquities underfoot.

You will cast all our sins
Into the depths of the sea.

After reading Micah's confession, we can imagine a sign on the beach that reads:
"No fishing - Owner of the property"

As such, God cast all our sins into the depths of the sea. The deepest water is in the Mariana Trench in the Pacific Ocean. At its deepest the trench goes down 11,000 meters, with an average depth of 7,000-8,000 meters. It is deeper than the height of the Himalayas. Like this, God casts our sins so they may never resurface again.

Outline

Chapters 1-3	The declaration of judgment
Chapters 1-2	Judgment on the sins of the people
Chapter 3	Judgment on the sins of leaders
Chapters 4-5	The promise of restoration (three promises)
Chapter 4:1-5	The promise of the Kingdom soon to come
Chapters 4:6-5:1	The promise of Israel's return from captivity
Chapter 5:2-15	The promise of the Coming King
Chapters 6-7	Call for repentance
Chapter 6:1-9	God's first call to repentance
Chapters 6:10-7:6	God's second call to repentance
Chapter 7:7-20	Promise of salvation

Voice Outline

MICAH

100-Day Bible Reading Plan

Day 77	Micah, Nahum, Habakkuk, Zephaniah	CHECK ☐

NAHUM

NINEVEH'S IMMINENT JUDGMENT

The Book of Nahum is full of prophecies of Nineveh's judgment. Nineveh was a central city in the Assyrian Empire and dominated the world at that time. It was also the place of Jonah's surprising repentance not long before that. The people of Nineveh experienced firsthand how their repentance could change the entire course of the nation. However, they forgot God's compassion and mercy that came with their repentance and sinned again. They could not abandon their imperialist ambitions and continued in their evil ways.

The Prophet Nahum proclaims the destruction of Nineveh about 150 years after the Prophet Jonah delivered the same message. And 18 years after Nahum's proclamation of the destruction of Nineveh, Nineveh and Assyria were destroyed just as Nahum had prophesied.

The Cause of Destruction

The Book of Nahum has three chapters. Chapter 1 proclaims Nineveh's destruction and tells readers about God's judgment. Chapter 2 describes Nineveh's destruction and how its judgment will take place. Chapter 3 explains why Nineveh is bound for destruction.

Nahum 1:2 tells us that the cause of Nineveh's destruction was that it had made God its adversary and enemy. In Verse 14, Nahum tells us that Nineveh made idols and did evil. To serve an idol is to set God as an adversary and enemy. The Lord is a jealous and avenging God. He is fiercely angry and determined to judge those who do evil.

Moreover, in Nahum 3:1, God calls Nineveh "the bloody city" after the city commits barbaric murders and sheds the blood of innocents. The city is filled with blood, lies, and violence, the stench of which it is impossible to rid. Furthermore, the city was rampant with idolatry, which is spiritual perversion, and the practice of magic. Though it enticed many nations with such, these things ultimately paved the way for its destruction.

God also discloses the way in which Nineveh's destruction will come through the Book of Nahum. It is written in 1:8, "With an overflowing flood he will make a complete end of the adversaries, and will pursue his enemies into darkness," in 1:9, "He will make a complete end," in 1:12, "Though they are at full strength and many, they will be cut down and pass away," and in 1:14, "No more shall your name be perpetuated."

Furthermore, Nahum prophesies that "The river gates will be opened; the palace will be melt away" (2:6), "Nineveh, rich in silver and gold and precious things will become desolate and ruined" (2:9-10), "the Lord of hosts will be against Assyria and burn Nineveh to the ground" (2:13).

War and Water

A keyword to describe Nineveh's destruction is "war." Nineveh falls by the hand of Babylon. Nahum paints the picture of a fearsome army (2:3-5). Its lavish cities are hollowed (2:7-10), and surrounding nations formerly oppressed by Assyria rejoice (2:11-12). The death toll of Nineveh's destruction will be so great that they will stumble over heaps of corpses (3:3).

Another keyword is "water." The river gates will be opened and its palace will be flooded and destroyed (2:6). God will make a complete end of them with an overflowing flood (1:8). Historical evidence backs the destruction of the Assyrian Empire, a vast empire that lasted for 520 years. In the year 609 B.C. the empire was brought to ruin by Babylon and was wiped out without a trace. Sometime between the years 612 and 609 B.C., the Assyrian Empire lowered its flag and disappeared into history. For many years, many thought that the Assyrian Empire was nothing but a myth.

It was not until the mid-19th century when British archaeologist Austin Henry Layard began excavating Nineveh that the existence of the historical Assyrian Empire was proven. Through his excavations of the ruins, Layard discovered that the walls surrounding the city of Nineveh were 13 kilometers in length and 60 meters in height, wide enough for two chariots to run side by side. He also found temples that would have shone in gold and silver and reached over 30-stories high. But the magnificent city was completely swallowed by water, just as the Lord had prophesied.

The overflowing flood and mud that followed completely buried the 60-meter wall and left the vast city under 6 meters of earth. The flood and mud reaching 66 meters in height completely wiped the enormous city of Nineveh from history without a trace. The existence of Assyria and Nineveh lay buried and hidden deep underground for 2,455 years from 609 B.C. until its excavation in 1836 A.D.

A Fair Trial

The Book of Nahum tells us that no matter how strong Nineveh may be, it will fall because it has made God its adversary. Nahum explains this with an example from history (3:8-10). The city called "No-amon (Thebes)" was a city gifted with a fortress from the heavens. It lay between rivers next to the sea. The sea was its fortress and defensive wall. It had mercenaries from Cush, and Egypt was its strength. But No-amon fell helplessly. The city, once considered the strongest and safest of cities, fell and its residents were taken as captives. Although the city is not recorded in history, it is clear that No-amon was a famous city in Nahum's time.

The prophet asks, "Even such a great city as No-amon could not escape God's judgment; are you better, Nineveh?" Even Nineveh's trusted warriors will not be able to display valor on the day of despair. The strong walls and garrisons they so greatly relied on will be rendered useless as though they were built of sheets of paper. No matter how much food they store in preparation for the day of war, their efforts will be in vain.

We are told that the rich fled the uncertainty of war, taking every last bit of their wealth with them (3:16). Neither the king nor the leaders they relied on were able to shield them from the war. God says, "Your princes are like grasshoppers, your scribes like clouds of locusts" (3:17).

The Book of Nahum concludes with the following sad news (3:18-19).

> Your shepherds are asleep, O king of Assyria;
> your nobles slumber.
> Your people are scattered on the mountains
> with none to gather them.
> There is no easing your hurt; your wound is grievous.
> All who hear the news about you clap their hands over you.
> For upon whom has not come your unceasing evil?

As prophesied in the Book of Nahum, just as the Lord said, even the greatest of cities that once dominated the world will be completely destroyed if they engage in unjust and illegal actions and their name will not be perpetuated. What we find again through the book of Nahum is that God is the master of all history and that He is a fair judge.

Outline

Chapter 1	Declaration of Nineveh's fall
Chapter 2	How Nineveh failed
Chapter 3	Why Nineveh failed

Voice Outline

NAHUM

100-Day Bible Reading Plan

		CHECK
Day 77	Micah, Nahum, Habakkuk, Zephaniah	☐

HABAKKUK

THE RIGHTEOUS SHALL LIVE BY FAITH

The Prophet Habakkuk is the author of this book. However, the Bible does not provide any information about the prophet. This prophetic book was not addressed to any particular individual or group, but to Judah as a whole before it was conquered by Babylon. Seeing no mention of the destruction of the Northern Kingdom of Israel by Assyria, but instead descriptions of the imminence of the Babylonian threat, scholars assume that the book was written after King Hezekiah and before Jerusalem fell to the hands of Babylon.

The Book of Habakkuk consists of three chapters. Chapters 1 and 2 are in the form of the Prophet Habakkuk's questions to God and God's answer to those questions. Chapter 3 contains Habakkuk's prayers and praise to the Lord.

The First Question and Answer

Habakkuk agonizes over the reality that the good and holy suffer while the wicked prosper; the same profession of concern that is expressed in Psalm 37. Thus the prophet questions the Lord. In Habakkuk 1:2, Habakkuk cries out, "O

Lord, how long shall I cry for help, and you will not hear? Or cry to you 'Violence!'" He continues to ask similar questions in Verse 3, "why?" or "how long?" and continues to repeat his questions of "why?" in Verse 13, questioning God about the iniquities he has to witness.

In Habakkuk 1:3-4, the prophet asks, "Why do you make me see iniquity, and why do you idly look at wrong? Destruction and violence are before me; strife and contention arise. So the law is paralyzed, and justice never goes forth. For the wicked surround the righteous; so justice goes forth perverted."

Habakkuk cried with those suffering injustice, with the distressed and oppressed. His heart broke watching good people suffer. The wicked were strong and parading the streets. The Law was not enforced and justice was lost. Habakkuk was heartbroken to see all this happening out in the open.

God answers Habakkuk's questions in Verses 5-11. He tells Habakkuk that He used Babylon as a tool to judge the evil deeds of His people. He tells him, "You and your people, look at the nations. Watch them. You will be amazed to see my wonders among you. I will have the Babylonians, infamous for their cruelty, judge the wicked. They will come and judge those who do evil and take them captive."

God says that He will use Babylon as the "executor of His righteousness" against an evil Israel. The Babylonians are fierce and impatient, fearsome and terrifying. Their warhorses are faster than leopards and fiercer than the ferocious wolves of the night after a long day of hunger. They are like eagles that come down like lighting to snatch their prey. They are terrifying executors that will exile the captives into the land of Babylon.

The Second Question and Answer

Hearing God's answer, Habakkuk became more confused and asks God another question (1:12-17). "But why would the Lord, of all the tools He could use, use Babylon to judge the sins of the people of Judah? If anything, Babylon is more wicked than the people, but why use it?" In essence, he was asking God, "Should not the people You use as a tool to judge the wicked be good? How is it that You are using people considered even more wicked?"

In particular, Habakkuk asks, "You who are of purer eyes than to see evil and cannot look at wrong, why do you idly look at traitors and remain silent when the wicked swallows up the man more righteous than he?" (1:13).

Habakkuk knew exactly who God is. He was asking, "God, you are pure and righteous. Why are you judging wicked with the even more wicked?" The prophet's heart was filled with discontent and lament. "Are you using a people who do not know the slightest bit about You to judge Your people? How am I supposed to give meaning to this?"

The prophet's heart is broken seeing all the evil and falls into greater confusion seeing an even greater evil take place. He says, "I will look out to see what He will answer concerning my complaint" (2:1).

God responds, "Write the vision; make it plain on tablets, so he may run who reads it. For still the vision awaits its appointed time; it hastens to the end—it will not lie. If it seems slow, wait for it; it will surely come; it will not delay... The righteous shall live by his faith" (2:2-4).

We will live in strength and peace by the faith we have in what God has promised. Faith is not to respond to the things that our eyes see but rather to respond in accordance with God's word and promises.

God uses Babylon to test the faith and patience of His people. And He says that Babylon, who was used to judge His people, will in time be judged for their pride. God says that He will lower the Babylonian Empire and destroy it. He tells us that it will eventually perish due to its endless greed for world domination and insatiable ambition.

He also tells us that it is not only Babylon that will be judged, but that all the nations around Judah which act similarly will be judged in the same way (2:5-8).

Habakkuk 2:9-11 describes the common trait of these nations as their coveting of the wealth of others and desire for unfair gains. Verses 12-14 describe their people as those who harm others and oppress them, and those who collect wealth through injustice and looting. Also, in 2:15-17, we are told that they are those who make their neighbors drink to shame them. God will in time judge these people and nations for their actions. As it is written in Verse 14, "For the earth will be filled with the knowledge of the glory of the Lord as the waters cover the sea," the entire world will acknowledge

God's righteousness and glory.

Habakkuk's Prayer and Praise

Habakkuk finally and fully understands God's holiness, righteousness, and power through the answers he receives from God to his questions in Chapters 1-2.

In Chapter 3, Habakkuk goes before the Lord to raise his prayers and praises to God after hearing the answers to his questions. He professes God's glory, power, and governance. He stands before the Lord deeply moved, full of joy and gratitude.

In particular, Habakkuk prays that God will once more show the power that He demonstrated at the time of the Exodus and that He will reignite a revival. In 3:2, Habakkuk prays earnestly for God to allow a revival in His compassion by professing, "O Lord, in the midst of the years revive it; in the midst of the years make it known; in wrath remember mercy."

Habakkuk did not dwell in the gloomy and discouraging circumstances of the present day. He believed in God's mercy and power. He believed that it was the time for revival and truly believed that a revival would surely come. Like Habakkuk, now is the time for us to pray for a revival. Instead of speaking negatively or being disheartened by our perceived depressing circumstances, we must cry out, "Lord, give us a revival! Give us a revival in the coming years! Even in Your wrath, do not forget mercy!"

Habakkuk further processes his faith by proclaiming that

he will continue to rejoice in the Lord even if everything is to disappear. "Though the fig tree should not blossom, nor fruit be on the vines, the produce of the olive fail and the fields yield no food, the flock be cut off from the fold and there be no herd in the stalls, yet I will rejoice in the Lord; I will take joy in the God of my salvation" (3:17-18).

We must profess that all of our satisfaction and joy lies with God, even if materially and environmentally we may not be fully satisfied. Habakkuk makes the decision not to be depressed and disheartened by looking only at his present condition. Rather, he chooses to rejoice. His joy lies only in God. It is just like what the Apostle Paul wrote from inside his cell to his brothers in Philippi: "Rejoice in the Lord always; again I will say, rejoice."

In 3:19, the prophet says, "God, the Lord, is my strength; he makes my feet like the deer's; he makes me tread on my high places." Deer have shorter front legs and longer hind legs, optimized for climbing to high places. The Lord tells us that He will make our feet like those of the deer so that we also may walk on high places. He tells us that He will give us a life full of joy and satisfaction that goes beyond our present circumstances. That is the message of gratitude and victory with which the Prophet Habakkuk concludes his book.

Outline

Chapters 1-2	Questions and answers What God wants
Chapter 1:1-4	Habakkuk's first question
Chapter 1:5-11	God's first answer
Chapters 1:12-2:1	Habakkuk's second question
Chapter 2:2-20	God's second answer
Chapter 3	Prayer and Praise Who is God?
Chapter 3:1-15	Reveal Your glory and might once again
Chapter 3:16-19	I will rejoice only in the Lord

Voice Outline

HABAKKUK

100-Day Bible Reading Plan

		CHECK
Day 77	Micah, Nahum, Habakkuk, Zephaniah	

ZEPHANIAH

THE REMNANT IN ZION ARE SAVED

The Book of Zephaniah takes place at the end of all the other Minor Prophets because, chronologically speaking, he was the last prophet to minister among those who were active before the period of exile. His ministry took place during the reign of King Josiah when the Prophet Jeremiah's ministry was just beginning. The book carries with it a very stern tone. Hence, it is believed that Zephaniah ministered before the twelfth year of King Josiah when the king started a national revival movement at the age of twenty because syncretic idol worship and corruption and injustice were rampant in the Kingdom of Judah before the revival. We can assume that the Book of Zephaniah had a positive impact on Josiah's revival efforts.

Zephaniah, like the Prophet Isaiah, was of royal birth. He introduces himself as the son of Hezekiah in Zephaniah 1:1. The godly and God-fearing King Hezekiah was Zephaniah's great-grandfather. God used two different prophets and worked with them through Josiah's revival movement. He called Zephaniah immediately before the revival movement and Jeremiah at the beginning of the movement. The young King Josiah, the Prophet Zephaniah from the royal family, and Jeremiah the young prophet from a priestly family were at the center of a remarkable revival in the final chapter of the Kingdom of Judah.

Zephaniah's Message

Through Zephaniah, God speaks about the last standing Kingdom of Judah after the Northern Kingdom of Israel was destroyed by Assyria and its people were taken captive. The prophet prophesies that Judah and Jerusalem will be destroyed by the Chaldeans. He cries out to the people to repent, enumerating the sins that have brought God's wrath upon them and caused the destruction of the kingdom.

It also warns Judah's neighboring nations that they, like Judah, will be destroyed. And it prophesies that in time the people of Judah will return from captivity. It comforts those who want to stay loyal and live faithfully before the Lord amid all the sin around them.

The Book of Zephaniah mentions the phrase "the day of the Lord" a total of twenty times, the word "desolation" seven times, and the word "remnant" four times.

Judgment on the Day of the Lord

The Book of Zephaniah is composed of three chapters. Chapter 1 talks about God's judgment that will come upon Judah, Chapter 2 about God's wrath on the nations, and Chapter 3 about the restoration of Judah post-judgment.

We can summarize each chapter as follows: Chapter 1, "look inside"; Chapter 2, "look around"; and Chapter 3, "look beyond."

Chapter 1 describes why and how God will judge Judah. Zephaniah begins his prophecies without an introduction. "I will utterly sweep away everything from the face of the earth, declares the Lord" (1:2). How stern His words are! They remind us of His words before Noah's Flood: "I will blot out man whom I have created from the face of the land, man and animals and creeping things and birds of the heavens, for I am sorry that I have made them" (Gen. 6:7).

Verses 3-6 list everything that will be eradicated: man, beasts, birds of the air, fish of the sea, the rubble, the wicked, idols and idolaters, criminals, traitors and those who have turned back from the Lord, and those who neither search for nor seek the Lord.

Verses 7-13 are God's warning of the day of judgment. He states those who are to be judged and what their crimes are. The royalty is guilty of being concerned with fashion, and their preoccupation with glamour and extravagance (1:8). The nobility and their servants are guilty of abusing their power and amassing wealth through unjust means (1:9). God declares that both merchants and the rich will go bankrupt (1:11). The Mortar mentioned in Verse 11 is the place where the goldsmiths and merchants lived (Ne. 3:32).

God also explains that those who are spiritually lukewarm, the prodigal and extravagant, and atheists (1:12) are also subject to judgment. These are people whose hearts sunk like dead weight due to a lack of anticipation and faith in God. Like this, God judges those who are spiritually weary and fatigued as a result of their unbelief in God.

Verses 14-18 contain God's words of warning about "the day of the Lord."

- **"The great day of the Lord is near."** It is not the event of a distant future. It is imminent.
- **"A day of wrath is that day."** Mighty men will cry aloud on that day. It is a day of tribulation and suffering.
- **"A day of ruin and devastation is that day."** Fortified cities will come crashing down and countless men will be slain.
- **"No one shall be able to escape that day."** No riches will be able to deliver them on that day.

Judgment on Judah's Neighbors

In Chapter 2, God promises to save the humble and those who earnestly seek the Lord, even in such a day of wrath. The warning of God's fearsome judgment in Chapter 1 is not to drive the people into despair, but to make them repent and seek the face of the Lord.

As written in 2 Corinthians 7:10, "For godly grief produces a repentance that leads to salvation without regret, whereas worldly grief produces death," God does not wish to drive His people into despair but to give them hope. "For he says, 'In a favorable time I listened to you, and in a day of salvation I have helped you'" (2 Cor. 6:2).

Zephaniah urges the people to put all else aside and do the following: "Seek the Lord, seek righteousness; seek humility;

seek His mercy; seek His grace" (2:3).

Verses 4-15 tell us that God will judge the nations surrounding Judah in the same way that He did Judah. He judges the cities of Gaza, Ashkelon, Ashdod, and Ekron (2:4-7). Another Philistine city, Gad, is not included here because it already was a part of Judah. Verses 8-11 list the judgments against Moab and Ammon. Their sin was mocking and criticizing the people of God, as well as their pride. Verses 12-15 contain judgments against Cush, Assyria, and Nineveh, cities central to the Assyrian Empire. The Cushites were an Arabian people. Nineveh, a particularly prosperous city, was to soon become desolate.

Judgment on Jerusalem

Chapter 3 brings us back to Jerusalem from the surrounding nations. Verses 1-7 contain reproof and warnings against Jerusalem. The chapter describes the entire city as very evil. Its inhabitants do not heed God's commands, do not follow instruction, do not trust in God, and do not bring themselves close to the Lord. It also explains in detail the wickedness of the leaders of Jerusalem (3:3-4). Its princes are like roaring lions, abusing their power, and its judges are like wolves of the night, cruel and greedy. Its prophets are frivolous and cunning; its priests defile the temple, violate the Law, and even abandon their duties as priests.

Jerusalem enjoyed greater privileges and advantages than any other nation. God was among them and spoke to them. He also showed Israel firsthand that He is the ruler of nations.

As such, they were in a position to better worship and serve God than any other nation. Nevertheless, they got up each dawn, eager to make all their deeds corrupt (3:5-7).

In Verses 8-13, we see a God waiting for Israel's return to Him even though they have turned their backs to His goodwill. He will also kindly judge the nations oppressing His people and correct what is wrong.

Verses 14-20 contain the promise of restoration that will come after judgment. He promises to restore those who have decided to seek God, set the Word of God as the standard of their lives, placed their hope in God, abandoned pride, and committed to living in humility and holiness even after judgment. He promises them, "I will erase the judgments against you. I will drive out your enemies. I will be with you and you shall never again fear evil." He tells them, "Sing joyfully. Rejoice with all your heart and do not be afraid. Do not let your hands grow weak."

God's Touching Confession to Us

God comforts those who have remorse and sorrow for their sins. He brings the captives back. He honors His people so that His name will be known and praised among all the people.

"The Lord your God is in your midst, a mighty one who will save; he will rejoice over you with gladness; he will quiet you by his love; he will exult over you with loud singing" (3:17).

Outline

Chapters 1-3:8	The judgment on the day of the Lord
Chapter 1:1-3	Judgment of nations
Chapters 1:4-2:3	Judgment of Judah
Chapter 2:4-15	Judgment of Judah's surrounding nations
Chapter 3:1-7	Judgment of Jerusalem
Chapter 3:8	Judgment of nations
Chapter 3:9-3:20	Salvation on the day of the Lord
Chapter 3:9-13	Promise of change
Chapter 3:14-20	Promise of restoration

Voice Outline

ZEPHANIAH

100-Day Bible Reading Plan

		CHECK
Day 77	Micah, Nahum, Habakkuk, Zephaniah	

HAGGAI

CONSTRUCTION OF THE SECOND TEMPLE

The Prophet Haggai was a Levite who returned to Jerusalem with Zerubbabel, part of the first group of exiles to return from Babylon. The Book of Haggai is addressed not only to Zerubbabel the governor and Joshua the high priest, but to all the people of Judah who returned from captivity. The primary purpose of the Book of Haggai is to encourage the returning Jews to rebuild the temple after its construction had been halted due to various complications.

Structure

The Book of Haggai consists of two chapters. The book comprises four sermons, and the exact dates on which these sermons were delivered are recorded.

- First message (1:1-15) June 1, 520 B.C. - Rise and build the temple
- Second message (2:1-9) July 21, 520 B.C. - I will be with you
- Third message (2:10-19) September 24, 520 B.C. - I will bless you starting today

- Fourth message (2:20-23) September 24, 520 B.C. - I choose you as a signet (A promise to Zerubbabel)

The Book of Haggai explains the things that need to take priority in our lives. The Israelites returned from captivity and tried to rebuild the temple, but had to stop due to a number of hindrances and the opposition they faced. But even in the midst of this, they found time to build their own houses in which to live. God severely rebuked their actions through the Prophet Haggai.

In the end, they obeyed God's Word and resumed the construction of the temple.

The First Message

There is an important meaning behind the words of Haggai 1:1: "The word of the Lord came by the hand of Haggai the prophet to Zerubbabel the son of Shealtiel, governor of Judah, and to Joshua the son of Jehozadak, the high priest." It was in the first year of Cyrus (536 B.C.) that the Israelites returned from exile in Babylon. After their return, God did not speak to them for some time until He spoke through the Prophet Haggai on June 1, 520 B.C when He broke His silence after 16 years.

This reminds us of the days of young Samuel, "And the word of the Lord was rare in those days; there was no frequent vision" (1 Sam. 3:1), and when God only spoke to Abraham after he turned 99 years-old after speaking to him at age 86 (Gen. 16:16; 17:1).

It is truly sad to be without the Word of God because

"His word is a lamp to our feet and a light to our path" (Psa. 119:105). Without the Word, we live not according to God's will either in terms of the purpose and direction or the specifics of our lives, but rather simply live it as we please. That can only result in a life that lacks purpose, direction, conviction, and stability. We must hear the Word of the Lord, because it is the only way to ensure that we are headed in the right direction and that we are doing what is right.

Thankfully, the Lord begins speaking to the Israelites who have returned from captivity. His voice helps them to assess their lives. Though they tried to rebuild the temple after returning from captivity, they halt due to external difficulties. And even though they felt a need to rebuild the temple, they assumed that it was not yet time and went about their daily lives.

It is easy for anyone to fall into this trap. Even though we are fully aware of what tasks should take precedence over other tasks, we habitually live with our priorities all out of order.

Priorities are extremely important. At times they may not appear so pressing, especially if the situation or conditions are not yet ready. Tasks that are of lower priority, though unimportant, may require immediate attention. By nature, we have a tendency to prioritize what is urgent. Unfortunately, such a life is an ineffective life.

That is when we need the Word of God. We can place checks to reflect on our lives and see patterns of our behavior as they are, using the Word. Grace comes from going and staying before the Lord on a consistent basis. However, if we habitually go to church and make time for sermons and prayers only as sequences in a religious ritual, we do not have access to the Word of God. We do not have discerning eyes to look back on our lives. When we stop performing religious acts out of habit and stand in the presence of the Lord who is a person, we begin to hear His voice.

When we are told that the Word of the Lord was rare, it is not because the Lord is not there or because He does not speak. God is with us everywhere and always. His words are rare because we become so wrapped up in everyday trifles that we do not have time to hear His Word. God is silent because He knows that the people do not have room in their hearts to listen to His voice.

In Chapter 1 Verses 2-11, Zerubbabel the Governor, Joshua the High Priest, and the remaining people listen to the Word of God. God repeats twice, "Consider your ways" (1:5,7). He tells them to take a look at what they are experiencing. They are living in dire poverty. God tells them that it is because they have mixed up their priorities in life (1:4,9). Thus he gives them the solution. He says, "Go up to the hills and bring wood and build the house" (1:8). He is telling His people to set their priorities straight.

We see the people fearing God in Verses 12-15. They heed God's Word and resume the construction of the temple that had been halted for some time. After hearing God, they swiftly take action and resume building just 24 days later. God encourages the people who listen to him with the words,

"I am with you" (1:13; 2:4) twice. He tells them, "I will be with you to strengthen your hands and make your work prosper. I will protect you from your enemies and help you."

Although the temple is referred to as a physical building in the Book of Haggai, the message God sends us within these verses refers to a God-centric life rather than an actual temple or church building.

To be temple-centered means to be God-centered. To live a God-centered life means to live a life of the Word and prayer, a life seeking the power of the Holy Spirit, and a life that first seeks God's will. If we reorganize our priorities and begin living a God-centered life, God blesses us and helps us to live an abundant life.

God tells us in Matthew 6:33, "But seek first the kingdom of God and his righteousness, and all these things will be added to you."

Second Message: Six Rounds of Encouragement

One month after the construction of the temple began, God spoke again. The first message contained words of rebuke, but this second message contained words of encouragement. These are the words Israelites hear as they are building the temple. The returnees from Babylon included some that were older. The temple built by Solomon was destroyed in 586 B.C., and the temple was being rebuilt 66 years later in 520 B.C. Those who were just boys and girls at the time of the construction of Solomon's temple would have been 80 to 90 years old when the temple was being rebuilt. The Bible tells us that the elders wept and mourned rather than act thrilled that the temple was being rebuilt. It was because the new temple was so starkly undistinguished in comparison to Solomon's (2:3; Ezra 3:12).

Zerubbabel and Joshua had heard of Solomon's temple, but never seen it. The second generation captives were filled with delight, rejoiced, and praised God as they saw the temple go back up (Ezra 3:10-12). Ezra 3:13 describes the scene as follows: "The people could not distinguish the sound of the joyful shout from the sound of the people's weeping, for the people shouted with a great shout, and the sound was heard far away."

However, they became depressed, disheartened, and lost joy upon hearing the deep sighs of the elders. They gradually lost their motivation. Elders should not speak of the former glories of days past and compare them with the present. It cannot be considered wisdom if it brings the young generation down rather than encourages and supports them. For it is written in Ecclesiastes 7:10, "Say not, 'Why were the former days better than these?' For it is not from wisdom that you ask this."

It is also important not to fall into the trap of comparison by comparing those who are not able to do much work on the temple with others who are doing a much better job than they are. Such comparisons stem from the pride in our hearts. God is pleased with us as long as we serve Him faithfully with all our strength. God tells Zerubbabel and Joshua, "I will rejoice and be glorified by the temple that you build with all your strength" (1:8).

It was in such a time that God encouraged the workers responsible for the construction of the temple to press on and rebuild the temple through the Prophet Haggai.

First Encouragement

"Who is left among you who saw this house in its former glory? How do you see it now? Is it not as nothing in your eyes? Yet now be strong, O Zerubbabel, declares the Lord. Be strong, O Joshua, son of Jehozadak, the high priest. Be strong, all you people of the land, declares the Lord" (2:3-4). He goes on to encourage them further. "I am with you just as I was with you when you came out of Egypt by my power. The Holy Spirit will remain among you to give you wisdom and strength. Therefore, I say, do not be afraid" (2:5).

Second Encouragement

"Yet once more, in a little while, I will shake the heavens and the earth and the sea and the dry land. And I will shake all nations" (2:6-7). God will use all nations to accomplish His work. At those times, there will be a holy uprising. Jerusalem was in uproar with the news of Jesus' coming (Matt. 2:3) as well as with the descent of the Holy Spirit on the day of Pentecost (Acts 2:6).

In every city Paul and his team set foot on, there was an uproar. About Paul, people said, "For we have found this man a plague, one who stirs up riots among all the Jews throughout the world and is a ringleader of the sect of the

Nazarenes" (Acts 24:5) and referred to Paul's team as "men who have turned the world upside down" (Acts 17:6).

I like to call these uprisings "holy revolutions." True revolution moves us from darkness to light, from death to life, from curse to blessing, from bondage to freedom, from injustice to justice, from lies to truth, from hate to love, from sadness to joy, and from sickness to health.

God has said, "I will shake the heavens and the earth and the sea and the dry land and all nations." And this shaking will occur on the level of the individual, family or the church community, city, region, and nation.

Third Encouragement

"In a little while, the treasures (the love) of all nations shall come in" (2:7). This verse tells us that the Messiah for whom all nations have longed for and loved is to come.

Fourth Encouragement

"I will fill this house with glory" (2:7). God's glory filled the premises both after Moses completed the Tabernacle on Mount Sinai and after Solomon completed the temple. The Temple of Zerubbabel was also to be filled with the glory of God. Generally, we refer to the Temple of Solomon as the "First Temple," and the Temple of Zerubbabel as the "Second Temple."

Fifth Encouragement

"The latter glory of this house shall be greater than the

former" (2:9). The glory of God's temple is not measured by its gold or silver or jewel ornaments, or by the size of its structure. All those things belong to God. What is important is its use. A temple must act on the will of God and reveal His glory. Though the Temple of Zerubbabel may lack the outward magnificence of the Temple of Solomon, it will be used to bring glory to God.

Sixth Encouragement

"In this place I will give peace" (2:9). Jesus said, "Peace I leave with you; My peace I give to you. Not as the world gives do I give to you" (John 14:27). The peace of the Lord is the power to maintain an inner quiet that transcends any given situation. A beautiful life is one in which you can maintain your inner quiet regardless of the circumstances. This is a gift that we all truly need.

Third Message

Haggai 2:10-19 explains that God wants us to do the right thing in the right way. Rebuilding God's temple is the right thing to do, but if one works from unclean hands the Lord will not accept it. When our lives are holy, our offerings are also holy and God will accept them.

But if our lives are not holy, our offerings are not holy and God will not accept them. This means that we must make sure not only to keep ourselves pure on the outside, but also that we must maintain purity on the inside. God accepts holy gifts offered through holy lives.

He tells us to keep our lives pure and to build the temple. "So if you are offering your gift at the altar and there remember that your brother has something against you, leave your gift there before the altar and go. First be reconciled to your brother, and then come and offer your gift." (Matt. 5:23-24).

Actions are important, but one's heart and attitude are also just as important.

Fourth Message

In Haggai 2:20-23, God promises Zerubbabel a blessing for the future. In the future, God will shake nations. He will overthrow the thrones of many kingdoms and render them powerless.

But He will protect and sustain His servants who depend on Him. Although many will fear, be shaken, and fall to natural disasters, financial troubles, and diseases, God's people who rely on Him will be safe under His protection.

Outline

Chapter 1	The first message (rebuke) Construction of the second temple begins
Chapter 2:1-9	The second message (encouragement) The glory of the second temple
Chapter 2:10-19	The third message (rebuke) The blessings of now for obedience
Chapter 2:20-23	The fourth message (encouragement) The blessings of future for obedience

Voice Outline

HAGGAI

100-Day Bible Reading Plan

		CHECK
Day 78	Haggai, Zechariah, Malachi	

ZECHARIAH

THE MESSIAH, ISRAEL'S SAVIOR

The Book of Zechariah, along with the Book of Haggai, contains the message of two prophets delivering the same message to the Israelites who returned from exile in Babylon at the same time. These two books are a source of encouragement to the Israelites who returned from Babylon, began the reconstruction of the temple, stopped work due to obstacles, and as a result are discouraged, disheartened, and fatigued.

The pre-captivity prophets used the dates of the kings of Israel and Judah, but these two books use the dates of the kings of the Persian Empire since they were under the control of the Persian Empire at the time of the books' writing.

Zechariah 1:1 introduces the prophet as "Zechariah, the son of Berechiah." The Prophet Zechariah appears in Jesus' words in Matthew 23:35, "So that on you may come all the righteous blood shed on earth, from the blood of righteous Abel to the blood of Zechariah the son of Berechiah, whom you murdered between the sanctuary and the altar." There is no historical record mentioning Prophet Zechariah being killed by the Jews. However, the Jewish historian Flavius Josephus writes that the Jews may have concealed the killing to try to hide an incident that was a national disgrace.

Zechariah's prophecy that Christ would be sold and wounded and killed in the house of his friends was fulfilled through his own life as well. He was likely killed between the temple and the altar while fleeing to the court of the priest to escape from those persecuting him.

Eight Visions, Four Messages, and Two Warnings

The Book of Zechariah consists of visions, messages, and warnings. Chapters 1-6 contain eight dreams, Chapters 7-8 four messages, and Chapters 9-14 two prophetic warnings.

It was the eighth month of the second year of King Darius when the Word of God was first given to Zechariah. In the sixth month of that year, Haggai delivered his first sermon. Two months after the Israelites began to obey the Word given through Haggai, God also spoke through Zechariah. When we obey the Word of God, we are able to hear His voice more abundantly. God's grace is added to those who hunger for Him. It is written in Luke 1:53, "He has filled the hungry with good things, and the rich he has sent away empty."

His first sermon was titled "Do not take after your ancestors" (1:3-6). It is not easy preaching a sermon with that title. It would have been much easier to preach a sermon titled "Take after your ancestors." Nevertheless, Zachariah obeyed. It is not the preacher's job to speak as he wants. As it is written, "The Word of the Lord came to the prophet," and thus it is the preacher's duty to deliver the Word of God.

He tells the people not to imitate their ancestors who brought suffering upon themselves by refusing to heed and listen to the Word of God. If the Word was the standard at that time, it still remains the standard today. God's Word is unchanging. That is why God tells them not to follow in the footsteps of their ancestors. He promises, "Return to me… and I will return to you" (1:3).

His second sermon carries a completely different tone from the first sermon (1:7 - Chapter 6). This time, the Lord's Word came to Zechariah on the 24th day in the eleventh month of the second year of Darius, three months after he gave his first sermon. Although the first sermon was short, his second sermon was long. God spoke to him through eight different visions. God uses visions to awaken His audience and make sure that His will is deeply engrained in their hearts. With the second sermon, God consoles the returnees from exile and encourages them to resume the construction of the temple. This sermon is a message of hope from God to remind the people that they have not been abandoned and that God is always with them and taking care of them.

The second sermon also gives us a glimpse of the future King who will establish an everlasting kingdom. When the visions become too difficult to understand, Zechariah asks God five times, "What are these, my lord?" (1:9, 19; 4:4; 5:6; 6:4). These are the same questions that Ezekiel and Daniel asked. If we wish to know the secrets of God's Kingdom, we should not ask the angels but instead ask our questions for Jesus, for

He is the only One who is worthy to take the scrolls and open its seals (Rev. 5:9).

The Eight Visions

1. **A vision of four horsemen** (1:7-17). The vision depicts Christ riding on a red horse, and three angels of the Lord riding on red, sorrel, and white horses. This vision tells us that after God brings His people back from captivity, He will rebuild a prosperous Jerusalem. In time, Christ will come to judge the nations and restore Israel.
2. **A vision of four horns and four craftsmen** (1:18-21). The four horns represent the forces and the four nations interfering with the rebuilding of the temple. The four craftsmen represent the angels of the Lord who will judge the horns, the forces and nations interfering with the construction of the temple.
3. **Measuring line** (Chapter 2). God will rebuild Jerusalem and restore its former glory. As the number of its inhabitants increases once again, Jerusalem will become a vast city without walls. God will safeguard it by Himself becoming a wall of fire surrounding the city (2:4,5). He will be the city's glory. Twice, He says, "I will dwell in your midst" (2:10-11). God will look after His people. "He who touches you touches the apple of his eye" (2:8). This vision was a great source of comfort for the people as it was for the Church of the New Testament.
4. **The clothing of Joshua with new vestments** (Chapter 3). God promises that His people will be made holy in

garments He considers pure. There is also a promise for those who faithfully carry out the responsibilities of the office the Lord has entrusted to them (3:7). His people will rule the House of God, protect His courts, and interact with His angels. In other words, God will build a strong Church, restore worship, and be honored. In the vision, Joshua the high priest not only represents all ministers, intercessors, and people of God, but also our Lord Jesus Christ. The Lord says, "They are men who are a sign: behold, I will bring my servant the Branch" (3:8). The Lord will come and settle all sins with the cross, and we will be reconciled to God and with our brothers (3:9-10).

5. **The lampstand and olive tree** (Chapter 4). This vision shows that the Holy Spirit will descend upon Zerubbabel and Joshua in power and that they will finish the work entrusted to them. The vision also shows how the Church will burn bright through the anointing of the Holy Spirit that comes from Jesus, the olive tree to shine Christ's glory on the entire world.
6. **The flying scroll** (5:1-4). The scroll is nine meters in length and four and a half meters in width. In it, the scroll contains words of warning that God will definitely judge the sins of each and every individual.
7. **The woman in a basket and the transport of the basket** (5:5-11). The basket here is a basket used to weigh grain. The woman here represents the sin and wickedness of the people of Israel. The woman sitting inside the basket

symbolizes how the sins of Israel fill the basket as though it was being filled with grain. The leaden weight on its opening represents the people of Israel who refuse to repent. The basket is moved to show that the people of Israel will be transported to Babylon as a result of their sins.

8. **The four chariots** (6:1-8). Though the four chariots represent the four great empires of the time, they also represent God's providence, wisdom, and insight over all the earth. This vision tells us of God's judgment that will be cast upon the nations and proclaims God's sovereignty over all the earth.

Up until this point, God uses visions to disclose His will. However, in 6:9-15 God speaks through a model. Joshua is used to represent the image of Jesus Christ. Furthermore, the Branch in 6:12, "Behold, the man whose name is the Branch" also refers to Jesus Christ. If Joshua was the one to rebuild the temple, Jesus is the One who will establish the Church and proclaim peace. This peace is peace with God, peace among Christians, and peace in the world.

Four Messages

Chapter 7 to Chapter 8 is completely different from the previous section of the book. Three months after the first sermon, God speaks through visions. Two years after that, God speaks through messages. These messages are presented in the form of questions and answers.

The returnees from captivity send Sharezer and Regemmelech to the priests to ask questions about prayer and fasting: "Should I weep and abstain in the fifth month, as I have done for so many years?" (7:3). But God only wanted the Israelites to come and worship before Him once a year on the Day of Atonement.

However, the Israelites wanted another day to remember the destruction of Jerusalem and the temple in Jerusalem, and had been holding a feast in commemoration. What they wanted to know was whether they had to continue observing those days. The question is answered in four parts and each of the answers begins with, "Then the word of the Lord of hosts came to me."

- First message (7:4-7) - The Israelites did not fast as intended. They focused on its form and rituals rather than the essence of fasting. God criticizes them and tells them they fast not for Him, but for themselves. The purpose of fasting is to repent of our sins and to put our lives back on the right track.
- Second message (7:8-14) - Proper fasting means listening to God's Word, obeying it, and loving our neighbors. What God wants from us is to do justice, to love the Son of Man, and to walk humbly with God (Micah 6:8).
- Third message (8:1-17) - God tells the people that if they fast correctly, He will be with them, protect them, restore Jerusalem, reform their lives, make them wealthy and prosperous again, restore their reputation, and smooth their paths. God encourages them with the words, "Let

your hands be strong and fear not" (8:9,13,15). He tells them they will have plenty to eat unlike before. He also tells them not to do what He hates.

- Fourth message (8:18-23) - Here, God speaks to those building the temple. He answers questions about days of fasting. He tells them that the past days of fasting will turn into days of joy and happiness. The nations will come to Jerusalem in search of God's grace. Those who wish to know the Lord more earnestly will live in communion with the Lord.

Two Warnings

In Chapters 9-14, God provides two warnings. The first is a severe warning against Jews who reject the Messiah; the second is a blessing for His people who welcome and serve the Messiah.

The First Warning (Chapters 9-11)

Zechariah's sermon in these chapters is titled "The Strict Words of the Lord." It starts with words of judgment against Israel's neighboring nations. This is so that He may surround, protect, and have mercy on Israel, just as in His words in Zechariah 9:8: "Then I will encamp at my house as a guard, so that none shall march to and fro." The Lord judges Israel's evil neighbors: Damascus, the capital of Aram, Tyre and Sidon, and the four city-states of Philistia (Ashkelon, Gaza, Ekron, and Ashdod).

The salvation granted to the returnees was only made

possible through the blood of the covenant and the promise of the Messiah. They will be blessed in the land (9:9-17) through God's mercy and grace. Although they are surrounded by enemies and dangers, God will bless them and they will be triumphant externally and prosperous internally (Chapter 10). And they will receive their most amazing blessing through the coming of the long-awaited Messiah. However, God will thoroughly discard those Jews who reject the Messiah who will come as the true shepherd of this world and hand them to destruction (Chapter 11).

Second Warning (Chapters 12-14)

The second warning begins with "The oracle of the word of the Lord concerning Israel" (12:1). Like the first, it is a rather strict statement. In particular, the sermon explains various things that will happen "on that day" as well as the judgment that will take place "on the Day of the Lord." Chapters 12-13 mention "that day" ten times, and in Chapter 14, "that day," used to refer to the "Day of the Lord," is repeated seven times. The words should weigh heavy on the hearts of the enemies of Israel; however, to Israel, they are a source of comfort that were written to benefit them.

The friends of Israel will succeed, but its enemies who wish harm will be put to danger and eventually face destruction. God will protect, strengthen, and bring salvation to His people (Chapter 12).

When the Messiah comes, He will first forgive the sins of His people and correct their behavior. When He faces suffering, His disciples will scatter. Unbelieving Jews will be rejected, but believers will be tried and preserved (Chapter 13). "The Day of the Lord" is a day of judgment and mercy. There will be mercy for His people and judgment for His enemies. A great crowd will come before the Lord and He will purify them and make them a godly people (Chapter 14).

The words of 14:20-21 speak of an amazing thing that will happen in the last days. Previously, holy objects were limited to those in the temple. However, when the time comes, vessels in the temple and the vessels in the homes of people will be equally holy. If we give all we have to God, we will live in holiness. God tells us that it is not a certain occupation itself that is holy but that anyone who worships Him does holy work regardless of his or her occupation.

Abraham Kuyper, the Dutch theologian and prime minister, said:

"Whatever man may stand, whatever he may do, to whatever he may apply his hand - in agriculture, in commerce, and in industry, or his mind, in the world of art, and science - he is, in whatsoever it may be, constantly standing before the face of God. He is employed in the service of his God. He has strictly to obey his God. And above all, he has to aim at the glory of his God."

Outline

Chapters 1-6	Eight visions
Chapters 7-8	Four messages
Chapters 9-14	Two prophetic warnings

Voice Outline

ZECHARIAH

100-Day Bible Reading Plan

		CHECK
Day 78	Haggai, Zechariah, Malachi	

MALACHI

THE MESSIAH'S ANGEL

Malachi is the last book in the Old Testament. It is the last book not only in terms of the order, but also in terms of chronology. At each step of the way, God sent His prophets to witness for Him and His Kingdom as well as to reveal His power and glory. All these prophets unanimously testified for the Messiah to His people.

As we read this book, we hear the testimony of the last witness of the Old Testament. The Book of Malachi is referred to as the "Seal of the Prophets" because the era of the prophets goes into a long hiatus with the era of the second temple that followed the age of Solomon's Temple. However, the book introduces Elijah who is preparing for the coming of the Messiah of the New Testament and leaves us with great hope and anticipation.

God's Love

The Book of Malachi is titled "The oracle of the warning of the Lord to Israel by Malachi" (1:1). This book is a message of warning from God.

As the Israelites returned from captivity, the thrill of grace for God's great love grew dull, and their faith became a formality. Although the temple was completed through Haggai and Zechariah, their lives became legalistic and religious, and they fell into a pattern of religious mannerism. The Book of Malachi reproves the spiritual conditions of such people, awakens them, and calls upon them to restore their faith.

What caused the hearts of the people to grow bitter, hard, and cold? The Book of Malachi tells us that it is because of sin. Sin makes us unable to see ourselves as we are. The Book of Malachi also contains words of harsh criticism for the temple for its neglect and performing worship as a mere formality. God criticizes the lies and unfair dealings tied to material things and rebukes the people harshly about tithing.

However, He does so as though God Himself were sitting next to us and talking to us kindly to convince us face to face. He tells us that the worship He desires is neither the formality of worship nor our offerings. He desires us to worship Him with our hearts full of love.

There are two main evils mentioned in Malachi. One is "formalism" and the other is "skepticism." These evils were passed on to the New Testament, with the Pharisees continuing the evil of formalism and the Sadducees of skepticism.

Passing the Baton between the Old and New Testaments

The book of Malachi serves as a baton between the New and Old Testaments that begins with the coming of Jesus. Indeed, Chapters 3 and 4 foretell the Lord's coming. The Messiah will come to cleanse and heal the people. God also tells us that His servant will pave the path for the Messiah's coming.

Malachi 4:5-6 and Luke 1:17 are connected to each other. "Behold, I will send you Elijah the prophet before the great and awesome day of the Lord comes. And he will turn the hearts of fathers to their children and the hearts of children to their fathers, lest I come and strike the land with a decree of utter destruction" (Mal. 4:5-6). "And he will go before him in the spirit and power of Elijah, to turn the hearts of the fathers to the children, and the disobedient to the wisdom of the just, to make ready for the Lord a people prepared" (Luke 1:17).

The Book of Malachi prophesies the coming Messiah and serves as a bridge between the New Testament age and the Old Testament age.

The First Dialogue (1:2-5)

Like the Book of Habakkuk, the Book of Malachi is structured as a dialogue between God and the Israelites. God says, "I have loved you" (1:2). The motive behind all of God's actions is love.

But rather than think about how to repay that love, the people question Him instead, "How have you loved us?"

(1:2). In other words, they are saying, "Yes, we are back from captivity but we are still living in poverty and our lands have been devasted. I look around everywhere and I still cannot see your love."

In response, God presents concrete evidence from their own history. "I have loved Jacob but Esau I have hated." Esau may have done something deserving of the Lord's hate but it does not mean that Jacob did something deserving of God's love. God's love is only the result of His one-sided and unconditional love as well as His absolute sovereignty.

The Second Dialogue (1:6-14)

God said, "I am the Father, but where is your respect for me? I am the owner, but where is your fear of me?" God is our Father and Lord, and we are His children and servants. Therefore by nature, we must honor and fear God. But the people who fail to do these most basic things turn around and question God, "How have we despised your name and defiled you?"

They do not take time to self-reflect and therefore are not aware of the true gravity of their actions. They have ignored God's Word and therefore do not realize the problem within their actions. When we do not have intimacy with God and neglect the Word, our spirit becomes desensitized and we lose our ability to discern and judge.

So, when they gave their offerings to God, they offered animals that were flawed and blind. Their spiritual senses had become dull, so they could not experience the living God and instead just engaged in the tradition and formality of worship. They did not have the fear of God in their hearts. Nevertheless, they asked for God's grace. So God tells them, "Why would I receive the offering of your hands?" He does not answer their prayers nor accept their worship.

A Priest's Duty (1:6; 2:1)

A priest's greatest duty is to serve God. But the priests of the day neither honored nor feared God, let alone serve Him (1:6-14).

A priest's second duty is to instruct the people through the Word so that they may serve God and live in holiness. However, the priests of the time were not faithful to their duties, and they broke Levi's covenant. They ignored and neglected the Word of God. As a result, their blessings became a curse (2:2). They were to be ignored and despised by the people (2:9). God was not to accept their service (2:3). They lost their privilege to serve God.

The sins of the priests ultimately caused the people to live in sin (2:10-16). God tells them, "Guard yourselves in your spirit, and do not be faithless" (2:16). The message here is the same as that of Proverbs 4:23, "Keep your heart with all vigilance, for from it flow the springs of life." Sin starts in our hearts. Therefore, we must guard our hearts more so than anything else. The best way to do this is to heed the Word of God (Prov. 4:20-21).

The Third Dialogue (2:17-3:6)

God says, "You have afflicted God with your words." Without the Word of God in their lives, they cannot guard their hearts. As a result, their words and actions lead them into sin. The words of their mouths are negative, resentful, thankless, and slanderous.

They see the wicked prosper and believe that God will be generous even if they do evil. They deny the justice and fairness of God and then turn around and ask, "Where is the God of justice?" What they are actually saying is, "There is no God of justice." Their words torment God. Still, they ask, "How have we wearied him?" (2:17).

God responds directly to those with such arrogant and atheistic minds. "Here is the God of justice. I will soon emerge. I will judge those who spew words without thought" (3:1-6).

The Fourth Dialogue (3:7-12)

When God says to the people, "You are robbing me," they ask, "How have we robbed you?" God tells them, "You have robbed me in your tithes and contribution that was meant to be returned to me." They did not fully understand tithing. They thought they were taking a part of "what is mine" and giving it to God. But tithes are God's from the beginning. Deuteronomy 26:12-15 refers to tithes as "sacred." Tithes are set apart from the beginning as God's and do not belong to us. We are not giving back a tenth of what is ours; they are God's from the beginning.

God tells us that we should not think of tithing as giving "what is ours." He says, "You have robbed me." Not paying tithes properly is not a matter of "I have not been practicing my faith properly" or "I did not give to God what is mine." It is a matter of "I have robbed God of what is His."

We must think about why it is that God places such importance on tithing. It is not because He is short on money or that He cannot do His work without our tithes. The Bible tells us the "whole world belongs to Him." He tells us, "The silver is mine, and the gold is mine" (Hag. 2:8).

It is entirely due to God's love for us. He tells us to tithe through His grace because He wants to bless us. "Bring the full tithe into the storehouse, that there may be food in my house. And thereby put me to the test, says the Lord of hosts, if I will not open the windows of heaven for you and pour down for you a blessing until there is no more need" (3:10).

Tithes are the "key to the doors of the heavenly warehouse," and they are our "guarantee for the blessings of God" that is poured so abundantly into our lives that we do not have place to store it all.

Furthermore, God says in Malachi 3:11-12, "I will rebuke the devourer for you, so that it will not destroy the fruits of your soil, and your vine in the field shall not fail to bear, says the Lord of hosts. Then all nations will call you blessed."

God tells us that he will stop the devourer if we tithe. At times, we have unexpected expenses or suffer an injury or disease without notice. God protects us from such ills and protects us from theft. God makes sure that our fruits do not fall before the time for their harvest has come. He blesses our lands and He says that if we pay our tithes, He will ban grasshoppers. He blesses our land and blesses our environment so that we may live an abundant life. Tithes are like the water used to prime the fountain of blessing that God made to bless us.

The Fifth Dialogue (3:13-4:3)

The Lord says to the people, "Your words have been hard against me," and the people ask, "How have we spoken against you?"

The following are their hard words spoken against God (3:13-15).

- "It is vain to serve God." There is no use in going through the trouble of serving God; all we get in return is greater trouble.
- "What is the profit of our keeping his charge?" What have we gained by heeding His Word? He said that we would prosper by tithing but it has only returned to us as a loss.
- "We call the arrogant blessed. Evildoers not only prosper but they put God to the test and they escape."

God answers them (3:16-4:3). God will come to judge them. He will separate the good from the bad, those who serve Him from those who do not, and judge accordingly.

The Prophet Elijah to Come (4:4-6)

Malachi 4:1-3 speaks of the coming Messiah. Verses 4-6 speak of Elijah, who comes to prepare the way for the

Messiah.

When the Messiah comes, He will judge good and evil. Therefore, we must prepare for His coming and reflect upon our lives. Just as John the Baptist prepares the way for the Lord to come, we must make preparations in our own lives for when we meet the Messiah. We must always remember the Word of God. We heed and obey the Word. We must be diligent in how we respond to the Word.

Outline

Chapter 1:1-5	God's love
Chapters 1:6-2:9	The sins of the priests
Chapters 2:10-3:15	The sins of the people
Chapter 3:16-18	The book of remembrance
Chapter 4:1-3	The Messiah to come
Chapter 4:4-6	The Prophet Elijah to come

Voice Outline

MALACHI

100-Day Bible Reading Plan

		CHECK
Day 78	Haggai, Zechariah, Malachi	

ΚΑΤΑ ΜΑΘΘΑΙΟΝ

The Genealogy of Jesus Christ

(Lk 3.23–38)

νενέσεως Ἰησοῦ Χριστοῦ υἱο

ι ἐγέννησεν τὸν Ἰσαάκ, Ἰσαὰ
Ἰακὼβ δὲ ἐγέννησεν τὸν Ἰο
τοῦ, 3 Ἰούδας δὲ ἐγέννησεν
τῆς Θαμάρ, Φάρες δὲ ἐγέννησε
γέννησεν τὸν Ἀράμ, 4 Ἀρὰ
άβ, Ἀμιναδὰβ δὲ ἐγέννησεν
ἐγέννησεν τὸν Σαλμών, 5 Σα
όες ἐκ τῆς Ῥαχάβ, Βόες δὲ
ῆς Ῥούθ, Ἰωβὴδ δὲ ἐγέννησε
ἐγέννησεν τὸν Δαυὶδ τὸν βασιλ
ἐγέννησεν τὸν Σολομῶνα ἐκ τῆ
ὲ ἐγέννησεν τὸν Ῥοβοάμ, Ῥο
βιά, Ἀβιὰ δὲ ἐγέννησεν τὸν Ἀσ

THE NEW TESTAMENT

The Four Gospels

The Books of Matthew, Mark, Luke, and John are referred to as "the Gospels." Gospel means "blessed news, good news." These four books are called the Gospels because they deliver such news.

The most stunning news of them all is "Jesus Christ." These books have Jesus Christ as their focal point. They record the life, words, and ministry of Jesus, who came to earth, did miracles, taught the Word, suffered in our place, died on the cross, rose from the dead in three days, and ascended to heaven.

In particular, the three books of Matthew, Mark, and Luke take a significantly similar approach in records and are, therefore, called the "Synoptic Gospels." Forty-five percent of the Gospel of Matthew, seventy-six percent of the Gospel of Mark, and forty-one percent of the Gospel of Luke overlap with each other. In particular, ninety-four percent of the Gospel of Mark is contained in Matthew's Gospel. Content that is only recorded in the Gospel of Matthew makes up twenty percent of the book, three percent of the Gospel of Mark, and thirty-five percent of the Gospel of Luke. If the Synoptic Gospels are interdependent, we can consider the Gospel of John to have been written independently. Ninety percent of John's Gospel is not in the other three Gospels.

Understanding the Gospels 1 - A Vertical and Horizontal Understanding

It is important to have a horizontal view of the Gospels to gain a better understanding of them. That is, one must look closely at the context of the text and consider the same event or message alongside the other Gospels. This is because the message emphasized in each book may be different, even regarding the same event. Each book has its own character through which the Holy Spirit speaks.

Yet, we also have to take a vertical view of the Gospels and consider them from a historical perspective. That is, we have to understand the historical realities Jesus had to face as well as the times during which the Gospels were written. We have to understand that the authors not only considered the life of Jesus on a linear, historical axis when they recorded the Gospels; we also need to look at the before and after of the context as well as the event and message. Though the Gospels are a record of past events, they are surprisingly written in the present tense. This emphasizes that they are a message that God is giving to us in this very moment.

Understanding the Gospels 2 - A Temporal and Spatial Understanding

Because the Gospels are neither a biography nor a history book, they are not recorded in chronological order. Although the Gospel of Luke is organized by chronology relative to the others, the Gospels of Matthew, Mark, and John are generally organized by theme. Therefore, trying to understand each chapter in temporal order will interfere with an accurate understanding of the message as a whole.

Rather, it is beneficial to consider the Gospel using the elements of time and space. They are interwoven in the Gospels. Taking a temporal view of the Gospels, we can see that the record of Jesus' 30 years as a private person is brief whereas the records of His ministry (public life) during three and a half years make up a majority of the content of the Gospels. A significant portion of Jesus' ministry is centered around the Passover. Jesus' public ministry took place over four Passovers, and it is useful to use each of these Passovers as a baseline when considering His ministry. At each Passover, Jesus heads to Jerusalem and then goes north side to do His ministry there. It is recorded across the Gospels.

We also need to have a spatial view of the Gospels in order to understand them. That is, we need to consider the place of His ministry, the stage on which His ministry took place. Of course, Jerusalem is at the core of His ministry, but He also often ministered in the northern region of Galilee as well as the central region of Samaria from time to time. He also ministered in Perea to the east as well as the foreign regions of Tyre and Sidon to the north. It is important to look at His ministry in these regions.

Jerusalem is a place of great importance in Jesus' ministry. It was the city at the center of Judah and was also home to the Temple. It was the center of politics, economy, education, and religion, as well as the home to Roman politicians, and a point of contact for Roman culture. It was also the main stage for the Pharisees, Sadducees, scribes, and groups of priests.

In the course of His public life, Jesus always visited the temple in Jerusalem during the Passover, a holiday observed once a year. Discipleship training was always at the center of all such journeys, His words, and ministry. Jesus focused more on discipleship training than on ministering to the public. He did not have set subjects; instead, His classes were "dynamic," teaching through the events that took place in each situation. His teaching method of speaking through the events of everyday life offered a very effective education that enabled people to directly apply His teachings in their individual lives.

Jesus, the Lion, the Servant, the Man, and God

The four Gospels show and emphasize different aspects

of Jesus. The Gospel of Matthew highlights the image of Jesus as king. In particular, it places emphasis on the image of Jesus as the "lion" of the tribe of Judah. The Gospel of Mark emphasizes Jesus as a "servant" who came not to be served but rather to serve. The Gospel of Luke emphasizes His image as a "man" who offered himself as a sacrifice for the redemption of the entire world. The Gospel of John emphasizes Jesus as God who came to reveal that God is His Father.

Ezekiel 1:10 describes Jesus as follows: "As for the likeness of their faces, each had a human face. The four had the face of a lion on the right side, the four had the face of an ox on the left side, and the four had the face of an eagle." As such, each of the Gospel books introduces an image of God. The Gospel of Matthew introduces Him as the Lion who is king, the Gospel of Mark as an ox that is a servant who comes to serve, the Gospel of Luke as a sacrifice who comes to redeem man and the whole world, and the Gospel of John as an eagle that rises high and looks straight into the sun. The Gospels of Matthew and Mark set a contrast between Jesus as the reigning king and the servant who serves; the Gospels of Luke and John contrast Jesus' human nature as man against His divine nature as God.

Furthermore, the four Gospels, although written for all people from all generations, introduce Jesus to a specific group each in its unique way. The Gospel of Matthew introduces Jesus to the Jews, the Gospel of Mark to the Romans, the Gospel of Luke to the Gentiles, and the Gospel of John to all nations.

The Gospels of Matthew and Luke begin with the birth of Jesus. The Gospel of Mark begins with Jesus' baptism, and the Gospel of John begins with the Word in the beginning.

Matthew and John are disciples of Jesus; Mark and Luke are disciples of the disciples of Jesus. That is, Matthew and John share stories of the Jesus they experienced firsthand while Mark and Luke share the Jesus they heard of from the apostles. However, what is clear is that the author of all four of the Gospels is God the Holy Spirit. While the circumstances and experiences of each of the authors are woven into their respective texts, they all fundamentally share the same message from God.

MATTHEW

JESUS CHRIST WHO CAME AS THE KING OF THE KINGDOM OF GOD

The Gospel of Matthew focuses on introducing Jesus as the One who came as King against the backdrop of the coming of the Kingdom of God. In this sense, the Gospel of Matthew can be divided into five sections. Each of these sections is separated by the words "Jesus finished these sayings" that appear in Matthew 7:28; 11:1; 13:53; and 19:1. Using these verses as separators, we can summarize the content of each section as follows:

- What the life is as a citizen of the Kingdom of God (1:1-7:29).
- How the ministers of the Kingdom of God should live (8:1-11:1).
- What kind of kingdom the Kingdom of God is (11:2-13:53).
- What relationships and discipleship mean in the Kingdom of God (13:54-19:1a).
- How the Kingdom of God reaches completion (19:1b-28:20).

The book talks about Jesus Christ, His Kingdom, His citizens, and His Great Commission under the greater theme of the Kingdom of God.

The Kingdom of God

Chapter 1 first lists Jesus' genealogy. It tells us that Jesus Christ came to earth as the legitimate King of the Jews and all mankind through the line of David. This book contains the phrase, "the son of David" more than any other one of the Gospels (1:1; 15:22; 21:9; 21:15).

Chapter 2 talks about who the King is. When the wise men said that they came to worship him who came as the king of the Jews, a commotion arose in all of Jerusalem. This made Herod very afraid. To counter this threat, Herod ordered the killing of all boys under the age of two.

Chapter 3 explains Jesus' coming as King and prepares us to receive Him. John the Baptist's primary ministry was to preach the coming of the King Jesus Christ and prepare people to meet this King. His message, "Repent, for the kingdom of heaven is at hand" tells us how we should serve the King our Lord.

Chapter 4 marks the beginning of Jesus' ministry. The three core components of His ministry are, "teaching, preaching, and healing."

Chapters 5-7 are called the 'The Sermon on the Mount,' and they explain how the citizens of God's Kingdom should live on this earth.

Chapter 10 sets the principles by which the ministers of the Kingdom of God must abide.

Chapter 13 is the "parable chapter." It explains the Kingdom of God through parables. Jesus describes the secrets of the kingdom of heaven with seven parables: the parable of the sower, the parable of the mustard seed, the parable of the leaven, the parable of the tares, the parable of the hidden treasure, the parable of the pearl, and the parable of drawing in the net.

Chapter 17 describes the event that took place on the Mount of Transfiguration. It describes the transformation of His appearance: how his face shone like the sun and his clothes became as white as light. Jesus also speaks with Moses and Elijah on the mountain. Moses and Elijah are representative figures of the Old Testament, or of "the Law and the Prophets." All the books of the Old Testament are centered on Christ Jesus.

Chapter 18 explains the principle of discipleship: a life of service, restoration, and forgiveness.

Chapter 21 describes Jesus' entry into Jerusalem as King at last.

Chapter 24 is called "the end of the age chapter" and talks about when and how the Kingdom of God will arrive.

Chapter 25 describes another aspect of the Kingdom of God through parables. The three parables presented to explain Heaven are the parable of the ten virgins, the parable of the talents or minas, and the sheep and the goats.

In Chapter 27, Jesus refers to Himself as King before Pontius Pilate. He shows that He is King over the cross and over Pilate.

And the final chapter, Chapter 28, concludes with the Great Commission. The resurrected Jesus, who is the Church, with all power that has been given to Him in Heaven and on earth, commands His people. Because Jesus Christ is not just the King of the Jews, but the King of all nations, He commands us to "go and make disciples of all nations." Jesus in the Gospel of Matthew appears as the King, dressed in purple and wearing a crown of gold.

The Church: Partners of Jesus Christ

The Gospel of Matthew shows a particular interest in the Church. This is why the Gospel of Matthew is the only one of the Synoptic Gospels to use the word "church." After Peter's profession of faith at Caesarea Philippi, Jesus speaks His most important words about the church (16:13-19). The church is not a building. Its identity lies in the fellowship of believers; furthermore, it is the Church's mission to influence the world to establish the Kingdom of God.

The Church is where two or three are gathered in the name of the Lord. The Church's mission is to make disciples in each nation: to make disciples in every nation and in every area of society of every race by the Lord's authority (28:18-20). It is also the Gospel of Matthew that uniquely states it is the Church's duty to reconcile Christians with each other (18:17). Christ the King called upon the Church as His partner in establishing the Kingdom of God.

The Jews: Matthew's Target Audience

Matthew wished for the Jews to be the first ones to believe in the Lord and come before Him. When a Canaanite woman asked Jesus for help, Jesus answered, "I was sent only to the lost sheep of the house of Israel" (15:24). As Jesus sent out His twelve disciples, He also instructed them: "Go nowhere among the Gentiles and enter no town of the Samaritans, but go rather to the lost sheep of the house of Israel" (10:5-6).

Jesus, of course, is not saying that it is only the Jews who need the Gospel. Just as Jesus said, "Go and make disciples of all nations," Jesus came to save the entire world (28:19). What the Gospel of Matthew does emphasize is God's heart toward the Jews and it doesn't alienate the Gentiles.

On the other hand, the Gospel of Matthew has harsh words of rebuke for the scribes and Pharisees. Jesus warns us to be careful in regard to their instructions (16:12). There is no other place in the Bible that the scribes and Pharisees are criticized as severely as they are in Matthew 23.

To Fulfill What the Lord Had Spoken by the Prophet

What is worth noting in the Gospel of Matthew is that, by quoting the Old Testament saying, "All this took place to fulfill what the Lord had spoken by the prophet," the Gospel, Jesus' work, was foretold through prophets long ago.

Jesus' coming to this earth by virgin birth (1:22-23), being born in Bethlehem (2:5-6), fleeing to Egypt (2:14-15), the killings of countless boys by Herod (2:16-18), and returning from Egypt to live in Nazareth as prophesied in the Old Testament were all to fulfill what the Lord had spoken (2:23). As was John the Baptist's ministry was prophesied in the Old Testament (3:3).

These verses show us that the coming of Jesus was planned

by God even before creation, and that all took place in His providence. "He was foreknown before the foundation of the world but was made manifest in the last times for the sake of you" (1 Pet. 1:20). "But when the fullness of time had come, God sent forth his Son, born of woman" (Gal. 4:4). Furthermore, He planned for our salvation through Christ Jesus. "He lavished upon us in all wisdom and insight" (Eph. 1:9).

In particular, all decisions made during Jesus' life and ministry are entirely to obey God's Word spoken through the Old Testament prophets. Even when the Lord moves his residence in Chapter 4, He does so in obedience to the Word (4:12-16). When deciding where to live, he did not decide based on the criteria of this world; he did so according to God's criteria. Here, Jesus reveals the standards by which the citizens of the Kingdom of God must live. We must not make decisions on where to live based on human thought and criteria as Lot did. Instead, like Abraham, we must base our decisions on God's perspective and criteria (Gen. 13).

Chapter 8 records Jesus' healing ministry (8:16-17). He healed the wounds of people and through His acts of healing and obeyed the words of the Old Testament. When selecting a ministry, it is important that we choose the one that God has intended for us. Our ministry must be dictated by the Word of God and not by the popularity of the work or our own wishes.

In Chapter 13 as well, Jesus mainly speaks in parables in order to obey God's words in the Old Testament (13:34-

35). Even when we are preaching the Word of God, we must convey the message God wants and not the message we choose. Our focus should be conveying God's will, not how much popularity we will gain from speaking a certain message.

In Chapter 21, Jesus rides in on a donkey when he enters Jerusalem as King on Palm Sunday. The chapter introduces Jesus riding humbly on a lowly donkey rather than a horse or carriage (21:1-5). The reason that Jesus entered Jerusalem in this manner was also to obey the words of the Old Testament.

Finally, in Chapter 26, when people armed with clubs and swords under Judas Iscariot's plot to turn over Jesus, Peter pulls out his sword and cuts of Malchus' ear. Jesus says to him, "I have not been captured due to a lack of strength. Do you think that I cannot appeal to my Father, and he will at once send me more than twelve legions of angels? But how then should the Scriptures be fulfilled, that it must be so" (26:51-54). Jesus tells Peter that the reason He did not use His power and authority and allowed them to arrest Him without any resistance is so that He may fulfill the prophecies of the prophets.

Thus the Gospel of Matthew focuses on how Jesus fulfilled the will of God by obeying His will. Also, it describes the Jesus who came as King, quoting the Old Testament more than 130 times to do this. Only the Gospel of Matthew talks about the wise men, Jesus' flight to Egypt, and the Sermon on the Mount, all so as to explain that Jesus is King and to describe the Kingdom over which He is King. The Gospel of Matthew was recorded to specifically emphasize the relationship between Jesus Christ and the Old Testament more than any other Gospel.

Ten Teachings of the Sermon on the Mount

1. Beatitudes given to the citizens of the Kingdom of God (5:3-12)
2. Christian life that impacts the world (5:13-16)
3. The true meaning of God's Law (5:17-48)
4. The correct motive for relief, prayer, and fasting (6:1-18)
5. The correct purpose for serving God (6:19-34)
6. Warning against judgment; do not judge your neighbors (7:1-6)
7. Invitation to a life of prayer; the privilege and blessing of prayer (7:7-12)
8. Two roads: the wide road and the narrow road (7:13-14)
9. The importance of fruit; tell a tree by its fruit (7:15-20)
10. The importance of action; obedience to God (7:21-29)

Another Structure

The Gospel of Matthew can be divided into three parts using the phrase "From that time Jesus began." This appears in 4:17 and 16:21.

"From that time Jesus began to preach, saying, 'Repent, for the kingdom of heaven is at hand'" (4:17). "From that time Jesus began to show his disciples that he must go to Jerusalem and suffer many things from the elders and chief priests and scribes, and be killed, and on the third day be raised" (16:21).

Using these two verses, we can organize the Gospel of Matthew as follows:

- The King and His Kingdom are prepared (1:1-4:16)
- Principles of the King's Kingdom (4:17-16:20)
- The emergence of the King - The Kingdom is not built on political power but on suffering, death on the cross, and the resurrection (16:21-28:20).

Outline

Chapters 1-7	The beginning of the Kingdom of God
Chapters 8-11:1	Ministers of the Kingdom of God
Chapters 11:2-13:53	Parables about the Kingdom of God
Chapters 13:54-19:1a	Discipleship in the Kingdom of God
Chapters 19:1b-28	The completion of the Kingdom of God

Voice Outline

MATTHEW

100-Day Bible Reading Plan

		CHECK
Day 79	Matthew 1-10	
Day 80	Matthew 11-18	
Day 81	Matthew 19-28	

MARK

THE AMAZING JESUS

The Gospel of Mark focuses on "the Jesus Christ who came as a servant to serve on this earth." This Gospel contains the most realistic record of Jesus, so much so that we could consider it to be a documentary on Jesus. This is because Mark was the interpreter and spiritual son of Peter, Jesus' closest disciple. More than any other, Mark was deeply moved by the Lord Jesus with every sermon he interpreted for Peter about the life, teachings, and ministry of Jesus.

The Gospel of Mark is composed of 16 chapters, 109 sections, and 678 verses. Among them, 93 sections and 606 verses are the same as those of the Gospel of Matthew. Only four sections and 24 verses in the Gospel of Mark are not found in the Gospel of Matthew and Luke. It is generally agreed that the Gospel of Mark was already in existence at the time of the Gospels of Matthew and Luke's writing. Therefore, it can be seen that these Gospels were written based on the Gospel of Mark. These Gospels cover the same topics yet approach them from different angles.

It is worth noting that the Gospel of Mark is based on

Peter's sermons. Therefore, reading the book through the eyes of Peter will enable us to be more deeply moved by its words.

Dramatic Portrayal

The Gospel of Mark describes the life of Jesus in a most vivid, concise, and dramatic way. It is based on facts. The book starts by emphasizing that Jesus is the Son of God from the very beginning. Mark 1:1 starts with the words, "The beginning of the gospel of Jesus Christ, the Son of God," to introduce the great wonder of the Lord Jesus Christ. The book uses the word "amazing" 19 times to describe Jesus, reflecting just how amazed Jesus' disciples were with Him. The book vividly expresses how amazed, touched, and moved Jesus' close disciples were with His work, words, and character.

At the same time, the Gospel of Mark records the humanity of Jesus. Mark 6:3 introduces Jesus' occupation as the son of a carpenter; Verse 31 tells us that Jesus grew tired and rested; in Verse 34, Jesus shows compassion for the people; In Chapter 7 and 8, Jesus sighs in deep grief; Chapter 10 records His love for the rich young man; Chapter 11 expresses Jesus' hunger, recording His feeling of hunger. All these indicate that Jesus came to this earth as man.

A Vivid Record

Overall, the book is based on realism, using simple sentences to record events. The sentences are raw and unrefined. The word "and" is used quite often, like in children's speech. This word appears 34 times and the word, "immediately" appears 41 times, indicating the quick progression of events in the book.

Furthermore, Mark describes the events as though he was live broadcasting just as the events were taking place before his eyes. For example, in Chapter 1, Mark records that Jesus went to the synagogue in Capernaum in the morning to preach the Word, and at lunch, He ate at Peter's house (Peter's house was opposite the synagogue in Capernaum). He further records that Jesus healed many sick people who flocked in front of the house in the late afternoon. The next day, He woke up early in the morning to go to a quiet place to pray, and then stepped out to evangelize and heal the sick again.

In Mark 1:35 it is written, "And rising very early in the morning, while it was still dark, he (Jesus) departed and went out to a desolate place, and there he prayed." The verse describes Jesus' actions as if we were a direct witness to them. It is as though these verses record Jesus' daily schedule.

In addition, the book contains several places where words spoken by Jesus were recorded in the original Aramaic even though the book itself is written in Greek. These include "Talitha cumi" in 5:41, "Corban" in 7:11, "Ephphatha" in 7:34, "Abba" in 14:36, and "Eloi, Eloi, lema sabachthani?" in 15:34.

Structure

- **Jesus as a servant** - four identities (1:1-13)

  The Son of God (1:1), Lord (1:3), The Mighty One (1:7), My

Son (1:11)

- **The servant's ministry** - a ministry with authority (1:14-8:26)
  First message (1:14-15), first ministry with authority (1:21-2:12), Jesus calls four men to be His disciples (1:16-20), Jesus selects twelve disciples (3:7-19), Jesus sends them out (6:7-13)
- **The servant's suffering** (8:27-15:47) - Jesus foretells the cross three times (8:31-9:1; 9:2-13; 9:30-32).
  Passion Week (Chapter 11 - Chapter 15)
  - Day 1: Triumphal entry (11:1-11)
  - Day 2: Cleansing of the temple and cursing of the fig tree (11:12-19)
  - Day 3: The Mount of Olives sermon (11:20-13:37)
  - Day 4: Visit to Bethany, the betrayal of Jesus (14:1-11)
  - Day 5: The Passover feast, prayer at the Gethsemane, the arrest of Jesus, Peter's denial (14:12-72)
  - Day 6: Jesus' trial before Pilate, the Crucifixion, the burial (Chapter 15)
- **The servant's victory** - Four victories (16:1-20)
  - The resurrection (Verses 1-8): the empty tomb
  - The appearance (Verses 9-18): Jesus appears to Mary Magdalene, two disciples walking into the country, and the eleven disciples; the Great Commission
  - Ascension (Verse 19): Jesus is taken up into heaven and seated at the right hand of God
  - The Lord's work (Verse 20): The disciples go out to spread the Gospel while the Lord works with them

Suffering, Death, and Resurrection

The Synoptic Gospels place Jesus' suffering at the center of the Gospel. The work and words of Jesus during the Passion Week as well as his arrest, suffering, crucifixion, and resurrection cover over one-third of the books. Based on this background, the Gospel of Mark focuses on Jesus' being the Son of God as well as His being a servant. In this book, we see the servant Jesus through the suffering He endures.

Jesus hides the fact that He is the Messiah on several occasions. This is so that He can first show to the people that He is the suffering servant who accomplishes God's purpose through His death. However, His disciples do not realize that Jesus is suffering. This is because the disciples did not have an understanding of the "suffering servant who serves." The Gospel of Mark records Jesus' image of the suffering servant countless times to show us how the Lord served us through His suffering.

There are times when the Lord ordains the blind once to heal them, but there are other times when He ordains them twice. Jesus lays his hand on the blind man and asks, "What do you see?" The blind man answers, "I see something that looks like a tree walking." Then the Lord lays his hands on the blind man again and he is able to see clearly. This goes for when we pray. We also need to try again and not give up just because our prayers were not answered the first time. When praying for the sick or ministering for the Kingdom of God, we should not be afraid of trying many times over.

The Gospel of Mark explains the work of Jesus by

segmenting His ministry by region. His ministry in the region of Galilee (1:1-6:13), His ministry in the region north of Galilee (6:14-8:30), His ministry as He heads to Jerusalem (8:31-10:52), and the Passion week in Jerusalem (11:1-16:8) are examples of this kind of segmentation.

He Works for Us

Mark 1:1 is what sets the Gospel of Mark apart from the rest. It is written, "The beginning of the gospel of Jesus Christ, the Son of God." This verse is in contrast with the words of Genesis 1:1 that say, "In the beginning, God created the heavens and the earth." These verses tell us that God who created the heavens and the earth is among us and works for us.

Other verses that set a good contrast to Mark 1:1 are John 1:1 "In the beginning was the Word" and 1 John 1:1 "That which was from the beginning… concerning the word of life."

John 1:1 tells us that the Word, who was from the beginning and who is God, came as man. 1 John 1:1 tells us that God who became man relates to man. This extends beyond the relationship between God and man and tells us that we are all in relationship with each other through the Word.

The Gospel of John teaches us, "for God so loved the world," and the Book of 1 John teaches us "to love one another." It is telling us that because we have received the amazing love of God, we must be in relationship with one another. John speaks of God's vertical love whereas 1 John explains God's horizontal love.

The Gospel of Mark is unique in that it begins with the Gospel and ends with the Gospel (16:19-20). Mark begins by describing John the Baptist preaching the Gospel of Jesus Christ who came to this earth in 1:1, and concludes with disciples' preaching of the Gospel of Jesus Christ who is to come again.

Outline

Chapter 1:1-13	Jesus as servant Jesus described through four identities
Chapters 1:14-8:26	The ministry of the servant Four ministries with authority
Chapters 8:27-15:47	The suffering servant Suffering and the cross
Chapter 16:1-20	The triumph of the servant Four victories

Voice Outline

MARK

100-Day Bible Reading Plan

		CHECK
Day 82	Mark 1-9	☐
Day 83	Mark 10-16	☐

LUKE

THE MESSIAH WHO CAME AS THE SON OF MAN

The Gospel of Luke places particular emphasis on the humanity of Jesus, the Son of Man. This book is often referred to as the "most beautiful book ever written" because of the beauty of both its content and its prose.

The author of this book, Luke, was a physician. We know this through the words of Colossians 4:14, "Luke the beloved physician greets you." Luke is uniquely the only Gentile: the only non-Jew author among the authors of the Gospels.

A Detailed Record

If a pastor sees the best in man, and a judge sees the worst in man, a physician sees man for what he is. In that sense, it is evident that God used Luke to record His Gospel so that he may do so with great attention to detail and sensitivity for accuracy. For example, Luke 3:1-2 shows just how much attention Luke paid to record the ministry of John the Baptist accurately. Luke describes the period in which John the Baptist ministered by presenting as many as six historical contexts.

The first is that John the Baptist's ministry took place on the fifteenth year after Tiberius became the emperor of Rome. Second, it was when Pontius Pilate was governor of Judea; third, Herod was the Tetrarch of Galilee; fourth, Herod's brother Philip was the Tetrarch of Iturea and Trachonitis; and fifth, Lusania was Tetrarch of Abilina. The final historical context given is that Annas and Caiaphas were the high priests of the time when the Word of God came to John, proving that the Gospel was accurately recorded based on historical facts.

Luke's detailed account does a good job of revealing God's heart. God works in the specifics of historical context and shows great interest in our daily lives. God calls John the Baptist into a specific historical situation and entrusts His work to him. John the Baptist's primary ministry was to prepare the way for the coming Messiah, and the historical context in which his ministry took place was by no means accommodative.

Nothing seemed to be ready for John the Baptist to do his job. He was in a world where the emperor sitting on the throne claimed he was a man of divine powers, and incompetent and immoral politicians ran rampant. Even spiritual leaders, just like the politicians, only tried to maintain their position and power, showing no interest in the spiritual condition of the people of God. Given the environment in which he had to work, John the Baptist could easily have said, "It is too difficult to minister," "The hearts of the people are hardened and they are uninterested in the

Gospel," or "This is too challenging." It was into this specific historical context that God sent John the Baptist.

Neither the context nor God's calling has changed; it remains the same today. We have been given the work of preparing the way for Jesus Christ who is to come again. God challenges and encourages us through the Gospel of Luke. God, who worked through John the Baptist, still works through us now. What we need is faith and obedience like that of John the Baptist.

We must pray for the Lord to open our eyes so that we can see history and the current world clearly. We must also pray that we may be able to see God in action in times like today. Above all else, we must seek to have the faith that John the Baptist had.

A Gospel Written for the Gentiles

The Gospel of Luke specifically mentions the ministry of seventy people. Chapter 10 describes a scene in which the Lord sends 70 disciples, a truly unique occurrence. This scene is reminiscent of the seventy races in Genesis 10. The Gospel of Luke accurately depicts God's heart and His wish for the salvation of even the Gentiles. The most amazing characteristic of Luke's Gospel is that it is a "Gospel written for the Gentiles."

The Gospel of Luke records the date according to the regnal years of Roman emperors. Unlike the Gospel of Matthew, Luke's Gospel avoids quoting the Old Testament to explain Jesus as the fulfillment of Old Testament prophecies as much as possible. Also, Hebrew names mentioned in the book were always written using their Greek names to allow Greek readers to understand them. For example, "Simon the Canaanite" was recorded as "Simon the Zealot" and Calvary was recorded by its Greek name "Kranion" rather than its Hebrew name of "Golgotha." The book also explains that the name carries the meaning of "a place of skull."

Even for Jesus, the book does not use the word "Rabbi." Instead, it consistently uses the Greek word meaning "teacher." It does not start the genealogy of Jesus with Abraham, the ancestor of the Jews, but begins with Adam, the ancestor of mankind, and explains that Jesus is the Savior of all the earth.

A Jesus Who Prays

Another characteristic of Luke's Gospel is that it is the book that most often describes Jesus when He is praying. When Jesus had been baptized by John and was praying, the heavens opened, the Holy Spirit descended, and the voice of God rang out (3:21-22). The busier He was with His ministries, the more He prayed (5:15-16). He prayed all night on the mountain before He made an important decision to select His twelve apostles (6:12-13).

It was when Jesus was praying alone that He first told his disciples about who the Lord is as well as His death and resurrection (9:18-27). When Jesus took Peter, James, and John to the mountain and prayed together, the appearance of His face was altered, and His clothing became dazzling white.

(9:28-36). After watching Jesus finish praying in one place, the disciples also wanted to learn to pray as He did. He taught them the way to pray; that prayer is the "Lord's Prayer (11:1-4)."

Also, before He bore the cross, Jesus knelt in front of His Father on the Mount of Olives and prayed earnestly. "And being in agony he prayed more earnestly; and his sweat became like great drops of blood falling down to the ground" (22:44).

We also know that Jesus prayed for Peter and His disciples, as it is written in 22:31-32, "Simon, Simon, behold, Satan demanded to have you, that he might sift you like wheat, but I have prayed for you that your faith may not fail. And when you have turned again, strengthen your brothers."

In particular, 5:15-16 describes the life of prayer that Jesus led. It is written, "But now even more the report about him went abroad, and great crowds gathered to hear him and to be healed of their infirmities. But he would withdraw to desolate places and pray." Luke emphasizes that Jesus always took the time to pray even as He gained fame and His ministry grew.

Prayer was Jesus' lifestyle. Jesus sets the example for how to lead a life of prayer. Through the parable of the friend who comes at night asking for help (Chapter 11) and the parable of the unrighteous judge (Chapter 18), Jesus shows us just how important it is to pray. Jesus says to His disciples, "Rise and pray that you may not enter into temptation (22:46)." He tells us that the Holy Spirit will be given to those who ask, and emphasizes the importance of asking through prayer (11:13).

The Universal Gospel

Luke's Gospel is also referred to as the "women's Gospel" because it gives the special status to women. Luke's Gospel does more to describe the service of women to the Lord than any of the other Gospels and gives authority to the ministries of women: Mary, Elizabeth, Anna, the leprous widow, the woman who anointed and wiped Jesus' feet at the house of Simon, Mary and Martha, and Mary Magdalene. Luke's Gospel set the standard for value given to women in the Kingdom of God and for the Gentiles of the time who belittled women.

This Gospel can also be called the "Gospel of praise." It contains far more verses of praise than do all the other Gospels combined. These include Mary's song of praise (1:46-55), the praise of Priest Zechariah, the father of John the Baptist (1:68-79), the praise of angels (2:14), Simeon's song of praise (2:29-32), and the praise of the crowds as Jesus entered Jerusalem (19:38).

The Gospel according to Luke is also referred to as the "universal Gospel." This book emphasizes that it is not certain groups that need care, but that it is everyone who is in need of God's love. The book repeatedly tells its readers that Jesus Christ removed barriers and discrimination and is there for all of humanity.

Jesus explains the universality of the Gospel by teaching that the Kingdom of God is also open to the Samaritans (9:51-56); He tells the parable of the good Samaritan (10:25-37); He tells the story of the foreigner who expressed gratitude among the lepers who were healed (17:11-19); He refers to the widow of Zarephath and Naaman as exemplary figures (4:25-27); He praises the faith of the centurion who is a foreigner (7:2-10); He explains that people will come from east and west, and from north and south, and attend the feast at the Kingdom of God (13:29).

Jesus also expresses a special concern for the poor. This is expressed in His words about gifts from the poor (2:24), in His preaching the Gospel to the poor (7:22), in His parable about the rich man and the poor man (16:19-31), and in His words saying, "Blessed are you who are poor" (6:20). In this way, the Gospel of Luke explains that the Gospel is for all people: the poor, the marginalized and weak, the women, and the foreigners. In particular, the book often describes Jesus as a friend of tax collectors and sinners. Examples include the account of the woman who wipes Jesus' feet with her tears (7:36-50) and Jesus passing through Samaria on His way to Jerusalem (9:51-56).

At the time, when a Jew was going from Galilee in the north to Judea in the south, he would not pass through the shortest route which was through Samaria, but instead take the longer path. Likewise, when people from the south would go up north, they would not go through Samaria and instead go around it. This was because the Samaritans were a people who had historically been in contact with the Gentiles and were therefore treated as a foreign people and not as purebred Jews. But Jesus made sure to pass through Samaria; He never alienated them.

In the parable of the prodigal son in Chapter 15, the second son, who is the prodigal son, is accepted and restored through love. Jesus describes the extent of His love with his words about lepers in Chapter 17, the prayers of Pharisees and tax collectors in Chapter 18, Zacchaeus the tax collector in Chapter 19, and the repentant criminal in Chapter 23. He also tells us that they also will be among the saved in the Kingdom of God.

In this respect, the Gospel according to Luke is the best expression of the Gospel in the broad sense that transcends race, class, and gender, and brings together both the rich and the poor as the people of the Kingdom of God.

Outline

Chapters 1-4:13	The Messiah who came as the Son of Man: His preparation
Chapters 4:14-19:27	The message and ministry of the Son of Man His message (The Kingdom of God) His ministry (Not for the righteous but for the sinner; not for the well but the sick)
Chapters 19:28-23	The suffering and death of the Son of Man: His obedience
Chapter 24	The resurrection and ascension of the Son of Man: His commission

Voice Outline

LUKE

100-Day Bible Reading Plan

		CHECK
Day 84	Luke 1-9	
Day 85	Luke 10-19	
Day 86	Luke 20-24	

JOHN

MESSIAH WHO CAME AS THE SON OF GOD

The Gospel of John offers food for the spirit, nourishment for the heart, and rest for the soul. The Gospel of John is at times likened to an eagle because just like the eagle looks straight into the sun more than any other creature, this book directs us to look to God and Jesus. Furthermore, just as the eagle looks down with its sharp eyes from a high place, this book allows us to have keen insight into the world with the eyes of God's heart.

Characteristics of John's Gospel

The Gospel of John differs from the other Synoptic Gospels in many ways. It skips much of the content that is covered in the other Gospels. Although it would seem that John's Gospel would contain more details about events such as Jesus' birth, baptism, temptation, the Last Supper, prayer in Gethsemane, and ascension than any other book, it contains no record of them. What is most surprising is that it records none of Jesus' parables.

In other Gospels, the center of Jesus' ministry lies in

Galilee and His ministry in Jerusalem took place when He went up there occasionally. In the Gospel of John, however, Jesus' ministry is recorded as having taken place mainly in Jerusalem and Judea, with infrequent trips to Galilee. The Lord was in Jerusalem every year during the Passover. That is why the Passover is mentioned three times in the Gospel of John. He cleanses the temple (2:13), feeds five thousand with five loaves and two fish (6:4), and then goes again to bear the cross. He is also recorded as having been in Jerusalem for a feast of the Jews (5:1), the Feast of Booths (7:2,10), and for the Feast of Dedication during the winter season (10:22).

There are several passages that are only written in the Gospel of John. Turning water into wine at a wedding in Cana in Galilee (2:1-11), Nicodemus' visit to Jesus (3:1-15), His interaction with a woman at a well in Samaria (4:7-42), the resurrection of the dead Lazarus (Chapter 11), Jesus' washing of His disciples' feet (Chapter 13), and above all, the mention of the Holy Spirit as the Comforter in several places (Chapters 14-17) are among those unique passages. All these events make up a very important part of the Christian faith.

John's Gospel also contains very vivid descriptions of some of Jesus' disciples. The book describes Thomas' words about the risen Jesus (11:16; 14:5; 20:24-29), the purity and passion of Andrew the Evangelist (1:40-41; 6:8-9; 12:22), Philip's clever personality (6:5-7; 14:8-9), and Judas criticizing a woman for pouring expensive oil on Jesus' feet (12:4-6).

It is clear that the person who wrote the Gospel of John knew the streets of Jerusalem like the back of his hand. He makes references to the Sheep Gate and the Pool of Bethesda right next to it (5:2), the Pool of Siloam (9:7), the colonnade of Solomon (10:23), the brook Kidron (18:1), a stone pavement called Gabbatha (19:13), and the place of a Skull, which in Aramaic is called Golgotha (19:17). Jerusalem was destroyed in A.D. 70, and the Gospel of John was written about 30 years after that; however, it remembers and records everything with great accuracy.

Authored by John

John, who authored the Gospel of John, is the son of Zebedee and the brother of James. He grew up in a relatively wealthy home; His mother Salome could be considered the originator of what we call a "helicopter mom" today. But Jesus is not swayed by John's upbringing and handles it with wisdom. John and James, along with their other partners, Peter and Andrew, are the first to be called disciples. These brothers were so extreme, closed off, and intolerant that they were given the name "Boanerges," which means "Sons of Thunder" (Mark 3:17).

Jesus was closest to these three men: Peter, James, and John. Whenever there was an important matter, He took them with Him (Mark 5:37; 9:2; 14:33). John had the privilege of being closer to Jesus than anyone else. Even at the Last Supper, he leaned back against the arms of Jesus (13:23-25). He was a witness who saw and heard Jesus' actions, words, as well as His last hours (19:35). That is why he writes, "This is the disciple who is bearing witness about these things, and who has written these things, and we know that his testimony is true" (21:24). John was a member of the leadership team among the twelve apostles. It was the same at the Early Church. Peter, James, and John were called "the pillars of the Church" (Gal. 2:9).

Abba Father

The Gospel of John focuses on the divinity of Jesus as the Son of God. By introducing God as the Father more than 130 times, John shows us that Jesus is the Son of God.

In 1:18, the Gospel of John introduces Jesus as the only begotten Son in the arms of the Father. On several occasions, Jesus calls God "Abba Father," an Aramaic word meaning "Dad." At the same time, Jesus explains to us that God is also our Father. When Jesus says in 14:6, "I am the way, and the truth, and the life. No one comes to the Father except through me," He emphasizes God as the Father rather than Himself as the way, truth, and the life. We can expand Jesus' statement as follows: "God is My Father, but at the same time, He is your Father. I want all of you to have a deep encounter with Him who is both My Father and your Father. And the way to meet our Father is through Me."

Rather than introducing God as a terrifying judge or king, the Gospel of John introduces Him to us as the Father who understands us best, cares for all our needs, cares for us as individuals, helps us, loves us, and sustains us.

Seven Signs

The Gospel according to John does not describe the acts of Jesus as miracles, but as "signs." He uses this word to show that Jesus' ministry is a sign and proof that Jesus is the Son of God. We will take a look at the seven main signs of Jesus' ministry.

1. Turning water into wine (2:1-11)
2. Healing an official's son (4:46-54)
3. Healing a man who was crippled for 38 years (5:1-18)
4. Five loaves and two fish (6:1-15)
5. Walking on water (6:16-21)
6. Healing a man who was blind from birth (9:1-41)
7. Raising Lazarus (11:1-57)

All of these amazing acts prove that Jesus is the Son of God and that the One who sent Him is God. After doing each of these signs, Jesus gives a long sermon. After the sign of the five loaves and two fish, Jesus preaches that He is the "bread of life" (Chapter 6). After healing the blind man, He tells us that He is the "light of the world" (Chapter 9). And by raising Lazarus from the dead, Jesus shows that He is "the resurrection and the life" (Chapter 11).

The miraculous signs in the Gospel of John are more than just extraordinary events. Just as Hebrews 13:8 tells us, "Jesus Christ is the same yesterday and today and forever," Jesus is with us always, transcending time and space.

The Gospel of John was recorded so that we may believe that Jesus is the Son of God. "Now Jesus did many other signs in the presence of the disciples, which are not written in this book; but these are written so that you may believe that Jesus is the Christ, the Son of God, and that by believing you may have life in his name"(20:30-31).

Sent from God

The phrase "sent from God" appears over 40 times in the Gospel of John. In 1:6, John the Baptist is introduced as "a man sent from God." This goes not only for John the Baptist but for all of us: we each are here because we have been sent from God. Not one among us is here on his or her own accord or by chance. None of us were born a mistake, and our existence is not the result of random evolution. We are in this world because we have been sent from God. Having been sent from God means that we all have been "sent with a calling." That is how special each one of us is!

Jesus tells us, "I can do nothing on my own. As I hear, I judge, and my judgment is just, because I seek not my own will but the will of him who sent me" (5:30). The trait that those who have been sent must possess is "obedience." Jesus set us a very good example of what obedience is.

Jesus came to earth because God sent Him and while here, He only did the work that God sent Him to do. None of his actions or words was decided on His own; He first sought the will of God and obeyed accordingly. This is because God sent Jesus to this earth and He gave Jesus a calling. In 8:28-29, Jesus says, "I do nothing on my own authority, but speak just as the Father taught me. And he who sent me is with me. He has not left me alone, for I always do the things that are pleasing to him."

Jesus' words in John 17:4 bring a conclusion to the entire discussion: "I glorified you on earth, having accomplished the work that you gave me to do." Jesus' life's purpose is to glorify God on earth. And the focal point of all ministries should be "to do the will of God who sent us to this earth."

It is my hope that we can confess as Jesus did when we go to meet our Father on the last day. We must make it our life's purpose to not live according to our own will and heart's desires but to live only by the will of God who sent each one of us to this world.

Seven Witnesses for Jesus

Who will witness that Jesus is the Son of God and that He has been sent for the salvation of the entire world? The Gospel of John presents seven witnesses.

1. The testimony of John the Baptist (1:7,8,15,29-34; 5:33).
2. The testimony of Moses (5:46).
3. The testimonies of the twelve disciples (15:27).
4. The testimony of God the Father (5:37; 8:18).
5. The Holy Spirit's greatest work on this earth is to testify for Jesus (15:26).
6. The testimony of the Bible (5:39).

   The Bible is a witness both to the Jesus who came to earth and to the Jesus who is to come. Each verse of the Bible is a revelation of Jesus Christ. For example, we find Jesus who is the Light in the words of Genesis 1:1 that say, "Let there be light." We see Jesus the Son who died on the cross as Isaac is being sacrificed in Genesis 22, and in Genesis 24, we see Jesus the bridegroom as we read of Isaac taking Rebekah to be his wife. The manna of the wilderness shows us Jesus who is the bread of life; the water flowing out of the rock in the desert shows us Jesus who is the living water. As such, the entire Bible serves as a testimony for Jesus.

7. Jesus' work itself is a testimony (5:36).

Jesus said, "Not that the testimony that I receive is from man" (5:34). He never tried to gain recognition from man; He was already made content through God the Father. He did not try to please man but only pleased God the Father (2:23-25). The Apostle Paul said, "For am I now seeking the approval of man, or of God? Or am I trying to please man? If I were still trying to please man, I would not be a servant of Christ" (Gal. 1:10). We must also work not to please man but only to do what is pleasing to our God.

The Seven "I Am" Statements

The Gospel of John contains seven "I am" statements. The following are seven answers to the question, "Who are you, Jesus?"

1. I am the bread of life (6:35,41,48,51).
2. I am the light of the world (8:12; 9:5).
3. I am the door of the sheep (10:7,9).
4. I am the good shepherd (10:11,14).
5. I am the resurrection and the life (11:25).
6. I am the truth, the way, and the life (14:6).

7. I am the grapevine (15:1,5).

As seen above, Jesus knew exactly who He was and what His calling was. His words help a great deal to understand ourselves and what our calling is. The Gospel according to John is an amazing book that enables us to find what we will live for and how we will live on this earth.

Summary of Content

- Chapter 1: Introduction - seven aspects of Jesus
  - God who was from the beginning
  - God who is the Word
  - God who is the light of the world
  - The Word became flesh
  - God who is full of grace and truth
  - God who is the only God
  - The Lamb of God
- Chapters 2-12: Jesus' public ministry, seven signs
  - Turning water into wine
  - Healing an official's son
  - Healing a man who was crippled for 38 years
  - Feeding 5000 people with five loaves and two fish
  - Walking on water
  - Healing a man who was blind from birth
  - Raising Lazarus
- Chapters 13-17: Jesus' personal ministry, seven ministries
  - Loving His disciples in the world until the end
  - Washing His disciples' feet
  - Foretelling Judas Iscariot's betrayal

- The new commandment - Love one another
- Foretelling of Peter's denial
- Promising to send the Holy Spirit the Helper
- Engaging in intercessory prayer for His disciples

• Chapters 18-20: The completion of Jesus' ministry, seven incidents
  - Jesus' arrest and Passion
  - Standing before Pilate
  - Bearing the cross
  - Crucifixion
  - Burial in Joseph of Arimathea's tomb
  - Rising from the dead in three days
  - Appearing to His disciples

• Chapter 21: Conclusion - Seven words spoken in relation to Peter
  - Children, do you have any fish?
  - Cast the net on the right side of the boat!
  - Bring some of the fish that you have just caught!
  - Come and have breakfast!
  - Simon, son of John, do you love me?
  - Feed my lambs!
  - Follow me!

Outline

Chapter 1	Introduction (seven aspects of Jesus)
Chapters 2-12	Jesus' public ministry (seven signs)
Chapters 13-17	Jesus' private ministry (seven ministries)
Chapters 18-20	The completion of Jesus' ministry (seven incidents)
Chapter 21	Conclusion (seven words spoken in relation to Peter)

Voice Outline

JOHN

100-Day Bible Reading Plan

		CHECK
Day 87	John 1-11	
Day 88	John 12-21	

ACTS

GOD'S MASTERPLAN FOR THE WORLD

There are two main ways of recording history. One of them is to record events in chronological order, using sequential time (Chronos); the other is to record events by a qualitative character of time, to the special position an event has in a given period in detail (Kairos). The latter opens a few important windows into history to reveal a story. In this manner, the Book of Acts was recorded.

The book does not record the actions of all the apostles, only those of three. And even among the three, the greater focus is on Peter. The remainder of the book is focused on Paul. Acts 12:2 briefly mentions that James the brother of John was killed by Herod, becoming the first martyr. It also mentions John several other times. However, the book does not record any direct words from John.

In this way, the Book of Acts focuses on Peter in the first half and Paul in the second half. However, the book is not an introduction to the entire lives of Peter and Paul, but the focus is on how the Gospel of our Lord was spread by those who obey Him.

There is no mention in the book as to who the author of the book of Acts is. However, it has been widely accepted since the early days of the Church that Luke, the physician, is the author. In particular, "the first book" mentioned in Acts 1:1 refers to the Gospel of Luke. Luke uses his keen insight as a physician to record the works of Jesus in Luke and the ministries of Peter and Paul in the Book of Acts.

The book of Acts occupies a very important place in the New Testament because it is through this book that we understand the structure of the Early Christian Church. It shows us the process of the Early Church's formation, how the Gospel spread, and how the Church established itself. The Book of Acts explains to us that the Christian faith is not mere theory or religious belief; rather it is a spiritual and real existence that manifests in our lives in concrete terms. That is why many churches today find their role model in this book. God gifted us the Book of Acts so that we may maintain the Church in its original essence, unchanged and unaltered.

Structure

The entire book is structured to reflect Acts 1:8, "But you will receive power when the Holy Spirit has come upon you, and you will be my witnesses in Jerusalem and in all Judea and Samaria, and to the end of the earth." This verse explains how the Kingdom of God is formed, expanded, and how the Church is built to stand firm as those who have been gifted with the Holy Spirit continued to preach the Gospel.

Acts 1:1-6:7 describes the events that took place as the

Gospel was preached in Jerusalem. Chapter 6 Verse 7 concludes with, "And the word of God continued to increase, and the number of the disciples multiplied greatly in Jerusalem, and a great many of the priests became obedient to the faith."

Acts 6:8-9:31 explains how the Gospel spread to all of Judea and Samaria, and records Stephen's martyrdom as well as how the Gospel was preached in Samaria. The section concludes in Chapter 9 Verse 31 with, "So the church throughout all Judea and Galilee and Samaria had peace and was being built up. And walking in the fear of the Lord and in the comfort of the Holy Spirit, it multiplied."

Acts 9:32-12:24 covers Paul's conversion on the road to Damascus, his ministry of preaching the Gospel in Antioch, and Peter's preaching the Gospel to Cornelius, the first Gentile Christian. This section concludes with the words, "But the word of God increased and multiplied."

Acts 12:25-16:5 describes the spread of the Gospel to Asia Minor and Galatians by Paul and Barnabas. It ends with, "So the churches were strengthened in the faith, and they increased in numbers daily."

Acts 16:6-19:20 records the journey of the Gospel from Asia to Europe, Macedonia and Achaia, and all the way to today's Greece through a missionary team led by Paul. This section ends with the words, "So the word of the Lord continued to increase and prevail mightily."

Acts 19:21-28:31 describes the course of Paul's journey to Rome, the center of the world at that time. The section concludes by stating that Paul lived there, "Proclaiming the kingdom of God and teaching about the Lord Jesus Christ with all boldness and without hindrance."

The Men and Women of Acts 29

The Book of Acts concludes with the Apostle Paul's final arrival in Rome after a long journey of tremendous adversity. The book ends as though to foreshadow a part two of the book, leaving us with many lingering questions.

We find ourselves asking questions such as: "What ended up happening to the Apostle Paul? What happened to the metropolis of Rome? Was his journey to Rome able to reveal the power of the Holy Spirit as his first, second, and third missionary journeys had? Did the Romans ever hear the Gospel? What was the outcome of Paul's trial?"

Moreover, after Chapter 12 there is no mention of Peter who had the spotlight starting in Chapter 1. The book does not mention him any further other than to say that Peter was at an important meeting in Jerusalem in Chapter 15. So, we find ourselves asking, "How did Peter continue his ministry? Where might have his last place of ministry been?"

However, the Holy Spirit wants us to focus on how God's Gospel was spread in the Book of Acts, not to dwell on either Peter or Paul. He wishes for us to pay attention to how the Gospel was preached with the power of the Holy Spirit through those who were obedient to Jesus Christ. He wants us to keep our eyes on who will follow in the footsteps of Peter and Paul to spread the Gospel. That is the reason why the Book of Acts concludes as though it is part 1 of a two-part series.

God is looking for someone to spread the Gospel after Peter and Paul. The Holy Spirit wants to write Acts 29 with the acts of such people. These people are called the "men and women of Acts 29."

Growth

Reading through the Book of Acts, the word, "growth" appears many times. The book describes the process by which God's Church grows and expands. In the Synoptic Gospels, Jesus describes the Kingdom of God with the parables of the mustard seed and leaven. They tell us that the Kingdom of God is like a small mustard seed that grows into a large tree. They tell us that the Kingdom of God expands just as leaven spreads through the dough. As such, the Book of Acts describes the expansion and growth of the Kingdom of God in great detail.

It is written in 2:47 that the number of believers increased day by day. In 5:14, it is written that "more than ever believers were added to the Lord, multitudes of both men and women." In 6:7 we are told that wherever the word of God continued to increase, the number of the disciples multiplied greatly. In 9:31, it is recorded that the church throughout all Judea and Galilee and Samaria was being built up, and it multiplied walking in the comfort of the Holy Spirit. In 16:5, it is written that the churches were strengthened in faith, and they increased in numbers daily. In this way, the Acts of the

Apostles tells us that it is by principle that churches expand their reach wherever the Gospel is preached.

The Book of Acts also places a high degree of significance on numbers. In Chapter 2, we are told that Peter's sermon increased the number of believers by three thousand, and in 4:4, five thousand men came to believe in the Lord after witnessing the lame man at the temple be healed in the name of the Lord Jesus. As stated previously, Acts 5:14 also writes, "And more than ever believers were added to the Lord, multitudes of both men and women." Act 6:7 and 9:31 also tell us that the number of disciples multiplied greatly and the number of believers increased. In 14:1, we are told that a great number of both Jews and Greeks believed as the Gospel was preached throughout Asia Minor. As such, the Book of Acts utilizes numbers to demonstrate the expansion of the Kingdom of God.

Change

What is interesting to note in the Book of Acts is that wherever the Gospel was preached, change happened in individuals, families, cities, or the structure of society as a whole. In particular, this is referred to as "bewilderment" or "disturbance." In Chapter 2 when the Holy Spirit descended on the day of Pentecost, it is recorded that Jerusalem was "bewildered." And in Chapter 17 we are told that all of Thessalonica was "disturbed" after the Gospel was preached. The same is recorded for Ephesus in Chapter 19 and Jerusalem in Chapter 25.

Acts 17:6 records what others said regarding the Apostle Paul and his missionary team: "These men who have turned the world upside down have come here also." And in 24:5, people make accusations against Paul: "For we have found this man a plague, one who stirs up riots among all the Jews throughout the world."

Wherever the Gospel was preached, it did not remain silent. Individual lives were changed, and society as a whole was turned upside down. This is just like when you shine a light into a place that had remained in darkness for a long time: there will be a great disturbance. Insects will be disturbed and scatter, and plants that were dying due to the lack of light will cause huge disruption as they spring back to life.

Likewise, the place where the Word of God is preached cannot remain silent. The Word of God takes us from darkness to light, from despair to hope, from death to life, from a life of bondage to a life of freedom, from a city twisted in lies to an honest society, from a society in which every distrusted each other to a society of trust, from a place of hate and jealousy to a place filled with love. This is what it means to cause a "disturbance."

This is also what the Lord meant with the words He spoke when sending Paul. "I will deliver you from your people and from the Gentiles—to whom I am sending you to open their eyes, so that they may turn from darkness to light and from the power of Satan to God, that they may receive forgiveness of sins and a place among those who are sanctified by faith in me" (26:17-18).

The Book of Acts tells us that such disturbances will occur repeatedly when we preach the Gospel. The most fundamental cause of these disturbances is the Word of God. It is written in Acts 19:20: "So the word of the Lord continued to increase and prevail mightily." The verse speaks of the power of the Word that changed Ephesus. In 18:5, it is written, "Paul was occupied with the word," testifying the Gospel and shaking the city of Athens. In 17:11-13, it is written that "The people of Berea received the word with all eagerness, examining the Scriptures daily to see if these things were so," and in return, the Word moved the entire city.

The Book of Acts records that wherever the Word was preached, cities were shaken and disturbed, churches were established and the number of believers increased and grew. The Word of God has the amazing power to change and bring growth in individuals, churches, and cities. This is why it is so important to examine the Scriptures each and every day.

God's Masterplan for the Whole World

How will God fulfill His plan for the whole world? What is his strategy? God's plan and strategy are clearly explained throughout the Book of Acts.

First, God builds up people and works through them. The Book of Acts shows that from the beginning to the end, God works through the faithful and obedient (The twelve apostles, Peter and John, seven deacons, Stephen, Philip, Ananias, Paul and Barnabas, Silas and Timothy, and Apollos, to name a few).

Second, God pours out the power of the Holy Spirit on people to help them endure hardships. We repeatedly see how the Early Church was armed with the power of the Holy Spirit through the Church through Jerusalem at Pentecost (Chapter 2), through the church in Samaria (Chapter 8), through Paul (Chapter 9), through the events at Cornelius' home (Chapter 10), and through the church of Ephesus (Chapter 19).

Third, God always works through the prayers and petitions of His people. One hundred and twenty people pray in the upper room (1:14-15). Peter and John heal the cripples while on their way up to the temple to pray at 3 P.M. (that is, the ninth hour) (3:1-10). We also see Cornelius praying at 3 P.M. (10:3) and Peter praying on the roof while waiting for lunch (10:9).

Fourth, God wants His workers to work together to accomplish His plan. It is extremely rare to see the Apostles ministering alone in the Book of Acts; most of the time, they worked in teams of two or more. The Apostle Paul's missionary team comprised between 10 and 12 members.

Fifth, God called the church community His partner. The Church is not just a group of believers; it is God's partner in His plan for the whole world. God accomplishes His work through and with the Church.

Sixth, the Word of God is the most potent strategic weapon to accomplish His will. The revival of the Word brings change to individuals, communities, and societies.

Outline

Chapters 1-7	The formation and growth of the Church
Chapters 1-2	The descent of the Holy Spirit at Pentecost and forming of the Church
Chapters 3-6	The growth of the Church
Chapter 7	The blood of the martyr as the seed of the Church 1
Chapters 8-12	The Church's growth period
Chapter 8	Bridge (Samaria and the Ethiopian eunuch)
Chapter 9	Turning point (Paul's conversion)
Chapter 10	Removing barriers (Peter and Cornelius)
Chapter 11	First meeting (Overcoming barriers)
Chapter 12	The blood of the martyr as the seed of the Church 2
Chapters 13-28	The expansion of the Church
Chapters 13-14	Paul's first missionary journey
Chapter 15	Second Meeting (Overcoming barriers)
Chapters 16-18	Paul's second missionary journey
Chapters 19-21	Paul's third missionary journey
Chapters 22-28	Paul's fourth missionary journey

Voice Outline

ACTS

100-Day Bible Reading Plan

		CHECK
Day 89	Acts 1-10	
Day 90	Acts 11-20	
Day 91	Acts 21-28	

ROMANS

THE REVELATION OF GOD'S RIGHTEOUSNESS

The entire Book of Romans is an explanatory text on God's righteousness. It tells us that we can be justified only by faith. Paul's epistles generally addressed the issues of the churches that he himself planted, but the Book of Romans is a letter to a church in Rome, a church he did not plant.

Romans is the most organized and logical of Paul's epistles. Galatians, Romans, and Ephesians fundamentally deal with the Gospel, but each has its own way of explaining it.

If you know Romans, you will know Christianity. Martin Luther wrote in the preface of his commentary on Romans, "This letter is truly the most important piece in the New Testament. It is the purest Gospel." Many were influenced by Romans: St. Augustine was greatly influenced by Romans 13:13-14 in 386, Martin Luther by Romans 1:17 in 1513, and John Wesley in 1738 while reading Martin Luther's Commentary on Romans.

The Apostle Paul wrote the letter to the Romans while he ministered in Corinth during his third missionary journey. He had planned to go to Rome after Jerusalem and sent this letter to the church in Rome before his journey. It was written to settle the conflict between Jewish Christians and Gentile Christians within the Roman Church. It is thought that he learned more about the situation of the church in Rome through Priscilla and Aquila, whom he worked with while in Corinth.

Structure

The Book of Romans can be divided into two sections: Chapters 1-8 and Chapters 12-16. Chapters 1-8 explain how God resolves our sins so that we may become justified and sanctified. Then, from Chapter 12 on, we are taught how to live a righteous life once we have been justified by faith. In that sense, the first section speaks of the "way to salvation" and the second section speaks of "the practice of salvation" in our lives.

However, Chapters 9-11 appear to be more of an appendix or supplement to the first section, Chapter 1-8. These three chapters fundamentally explain the process of being justified by God's sovereignty. Chapter 9 talks about the past of Israel and the Gentiles; Chapter 10 speaks of contemporary Israel and the Gentiles; Chapter 11 reveals the future of Israel and the Gentiles.

Chapter 9 shows that Israel in the past was home to a chosen people by God's mercy, and the Gentiles were excluded from God for living in disobedience. However, Chapter 10 shows the present in which Israel has forsaken the wonderful grace of God and rejected Him by way of their disobedience. On the other hand, it explains that the Gentiles are seeking God's grace and in their obedience have been chosen by God through His mercy. In Chapter 11, Paul concludes with the words that God will first restore the Gentiles completely and then will go on to restore Israel. These three chapters represent God's sovereign wisdom, insight, and providence over all the earth.

The Revelation of God's Righteousness: First Section (1:1-8:39)

This section explains how God deals with our sins and what the consequences are.

In Romans 1:1-16, we see how the power of the Gospel brings the believer to salvation. Romans begins with the Gospel (God's Gospel) (1:1) and ends with the Gospel (my Gospel) (16:25).

In Romans 1:17-3:20, we see that both the Jews who have the Law and Gentiles who do not have the Law are sinners. Sin breaks all relationships. It breaks and severs the relationship between myself and I, you and I, and God and I. Furthermore, it breaks the relationship between me and creation.

That is why everyone needs God's righteousness. Righteousness is having the right relationship, and through it all broken relationships are restored. It means the right relationship between myself and I, you and I, and God and I. But to achieve this, we must believe in the Word of God as it is, and commit ourselves to His mercy and love.

What we need to consider is not what we can do to clear our sins, but what God has done to resolve our sins. We can try as much as we want to get rid of our sins, but all our efforts will be in vain. The more we try to do something about our sinfulness, the more apparent our sins and helplessness will become, leading us into despair. But it is when we are in that place of despair and in desperate need of help that God's righteousness will be revealed.

Sin and Sinfulness

God's righteousness is revealed in Romans 3:21-8. It is Jesus Christ. He is God's amazing solution to our sins. God resolves our sins with the blood, the cross, and the Holy Spirit of Jesus Christ. That is where the foundation of our faith lies.

Our sins are largely divided into two categories: sin and sinfulness. Sin refers to the specific act of sinning, and sinfulness refers to our sinful nature that is ever ready to manifest into action even if we have not taken action yet. Put simply, this is the question of "Are we sinners because we sin, or do we sin because we are sinners?" The world tells us that it is our sins that make us sinners, but the Bible tells us that we sin because we are sinful by nature.

Because the world only punishes acts of sin, the problem of sin cannot be fundamentally solved in this world. To try to remove sin in this way is like merely removing weeds that are visible to the eye. At first, it may appear that we have gotten rid of everything, but soon the weeds will grow back. To get rid of weeds once and for all, we must remove them from their roots. Likewise, we cannot simply deal with the action of sin; we need to address our sinful nature which causes us to sin. So, when God addresses our sins, He deals not only with our sinful actions but also our sinful nature.

Romans 3:21-5:11 talks about how our sins are dealt with through the blood of Christ. The blood of Jesus has the power to cleanse our sins. "Whom God put forward as a propitiation by his blood, to be received by faith. This was to show God's righteousness, because in his divine forbearance he had passed over former sins" (3:25). "Since, therefore, we have now been justified by his blood, much more shall we be saved by him from the wrath of God" (5:9).

Romans Chapter 5:12 through Chapter 7 talks about how our sinful nature is dealt with through the cross of Jesus Christ. The cross of Jesus has the power to completely heal our sinful nature. "We know that our old self was crucified with him in order that the body of sin might be brought to nothing, so that we would no longer be enslaved to sin" (6:6). "I have been crucified with Christ. It is no longer I who live, but Christ who lives in me. And the life I now live in the flesh I live by faith in the Son of God, who loved me and gave himself for me" (Gal. 2:20).

New Life, New Living

Through the death and resurrection of Jesus and our faith in these, we become new people. With the new life we have received, we then live a brand new life guided by the Holy

Spirit. Chapter 8 tells us that God is able to guide us to live this new life through the Holy Spirit. "If the Spirit of him who raised Jesus from the dead dwells in you, he who raised Christ Jesus from the dead will also give life to your mortal bodies through his Spirit who dwells in you" (8:11). "For if you live according to the flesh you will die, but if by the Spirit you put to death the deeds of the body, you will live" (8:13).

With the blood of Jesus, God has forgiven our sins and cleansed us of them; with the cross of Jesus, He has dealt with our sinful nature and justified us. That means that we now must live a righteous life. Even so, we do this not by our own strength, but only by the Holy Spirit who is able to let us live such a life.

Practicing God's Righteousness: Second Section (*12:1-15:13*)

The second half of the book explains how we have been gifted with the grace of the blood and cross of Jesus Christ and must therefore live by the Holy Spirit.

Chapter 12 is almost identical to the Sermon on the Mount. We must serve the church with the power of the Holy Spirit. We must build a community of service, a community of prayer, a community of the Word and worship, a community of inclusion, and a community of hope. It also points to three duties we have in our lives as Christians. It is our duty to God to devote ourselves to the Lord (12:1-2); it is our duty to our brothers and sisters in Christ to serve them with our gifts and love as a part of the body of Christ (12:3-16); it is our duty to all of mankind to live in harmony with everyone (12:17-21).

Chapter 13 explains our duty as Christians in the world. It is our duty to submit to authority when it comes to government-related matters. We must live as the light and salt of the world. We must not rebel against or criticize the government but fulfill our duty as Christians. We must live in justice, love, and prosperity.

Romans 14:1-15:13 speaks of our duty as members of the Church. In the Early Church, there was a group of narrow-minded people who refrained from certain foods and valued certain days and rituals. Paul considered them more vulnerable because they relied on external ordinances and rules. But there were those who were free from such formalities. Paul says that the latter is the more resilient group. Paul also belonged to this group.

However, he says that we should not injure the conscience of those who are weaker in faith or put a stumbling block before them. Paul exhorts, "So then let us pursue what makes for peace and for mutual upbuilding" (14:19) and "Let each of us please his neighbor for his good, to build him up" (15:2). Because "For the kingdom of God is not a matter of eating and drinking but of righteousness and peace and joy in the Holy Spirit" (14:17).

Our freedom should not be used to damage the faith and conscience of others. Paul says in 1 Corinthians 10:23-24, "'All things are lawful,' but not all things are helpful. 'All things are lawful,' but not all things build up. Let no one seek his own good, but the good of his neighbor."

Just as Christ tolerates us as we are, He asks us not to make demands or judge each other. Instead we should accept and embrace each other as we are. When we do this, we will all share in the same purpose and give glory to God as a unified heart.

Romans 15:14-33 informs us of Paul's ministry and his plans. Paul wanted to do his job as a priest of the Gospel justice. He explains that if by preaching to the Gentiles they come worshipping before the Lord, then as a priest, he is offering them as a sacrifice to the Lord. His greatest mandate in life was to preach the Gospel, so he worked hard to go to places and preach where the Gospel had never reached. So, he worked as an apostle for the Gentiles through the power of the Holy Spirit, passed through Jerusalem, visited Rome, and planned to spread the Gospel in Serbia (Spain).

In Chapter 16, Paul sends his greetings to his brothers and sisters in the church in Rome who he will meet in the future. Paul greets all twenty-six of them one by one. Reading Paul's list of greetings, we understand that the Lord takes a particular and personal interest in us and that He remembers all our hard work. We can also see that by mentioning the names of as many as seven women in his greetings, Paul sought to build respect for women and women's leadership. And the names of 13 high-ranking officials on that list show that the Gospel brings salvation to people from all walks of life.

Outline

Chapter 1:1-17	Introduction (Greeting)
Chapters 1:18-3:20	All men are in need of God's righteousness
Chapter 1:18-32	God gave them up to their unrighteous hearts by their lust, by their greeds
Chapters 2:1-16	God's judgment will be carried out according to the truth, one's stubbornness, impenitence and acts, and the Law
	Judgment on those without the Law will be carried out according to their nature and conscience
Chapter 2:17-3:8	God's judgment (Jews and the Law)
Chapter 3:9-20	God's declaration ("All have sinned, all have fallen short")
Chapters 3:21-8	The revelation of God's righteousness (Jesus Christ)
Chapters 3:21-5:11	Resolving sin with the blood of Jesus Christ
Chapters 5:12-8	Resolving sinfulness with the cross of Jesus Christ
Chapter 5:12-21	Sinfulness (the DNA of sin)
Chapter 6	Freedom from sin
Chapter 7	Freedom from the Law
Chapter 8	Triumph with the Holy Spirit
Chapters 9-11	God's sovereignty
Chapter 9	Israel's past
	The Gentiles' past (chosen and abandoned)
Chapter 10	Obedience, the present of Israel
	The Gentiles' present (disobedience and obedience)
Chapter 11	Restoration, Israel's future
	The Gentiles' future (restoration)
Chapters 12-15:13	The outcomes of God's gift of righteousness (service)
Chapters 12-13	The responsibilities and duties of the Christian
Chapters 14-15:13	The Christian's freedom
Chapters 15:14-16	Conclusion (Greeting)

Voice Outline

ROMANS

100-Day Bible Reading Plan

		CHECK
Day 92	Romans 1-16	☐

1 CORINTHIANS

DO EVERYTHING IN LOVE

The books of 1 Corinthians and 2 Corinthians jointly address issues related to the Church, the church ministry, and ministers at length. First Corinthians generally explains how to deal with real problems within the Church, and 2 Corinthians deals with issues that have to do with church leadership. In other words, 2 Corinthians addresses the topics of ministry and ministers. First Corinthians rebukes spiritual children by pointing out faults and mistakes and 2 Corinthians does so while encouraging the Church as well.

So, the leaders of the Early Church cited 1 and 2 Corinthians more than any of Paul's other epistles. That is how important and useful these books are. Both books are practical textbooks to guide us through issues in the Church as well as in church leadership.

Corinth was a central city in the province of Agaya in southern Greece. At the time, Corinth was a large city with a population of about six to seven million. It was an important city for commerce and was also considered important by the Greeks. The passage from northern Greece to the south went through Corinth; the city was also a hub for east to west trade. Just like other large cities in the Roman Empire, sports were a big part of Corinthian life. In those days the city often held big games, equivalent to today's Olympics (1 Cor. 9:24-27).

However, the city was a hotbed for immorality. It had the temple of Aphrodite, the goddess of beauty in Greek mythology. The temple had more than 1,000 priestesses working in relation to this temple. These priestesses were, at best, extremely morally disturbed. The city was so corrupt, that the word "Corinth" became synonymous with extravagance, drunkenness, debauchery, and even impurity.

Paul and the Church in Corinth

Paul spent a year and a half at the Church in Corinth to plant, grow, and nurture during his second missionary journey that took him through Macedonia, then Aden, until he reached Corinth (Act. 18:1-18). There were between 25,000 and 30,000 Christians in this church at its prime.

While in Corinth, Paul stayed at the home of Aquila and Priscilla from Rome, preaching in the Jewish synagogue with much success. Later, He moved to the house of Justus, who lived near the synagogue. He also converted Crispus, a ruler of the synagogue in Corinth. When Gallio takes over as governor of Corinth, the Jews bring charges against the Apostle Paul. However, Gallio dismisses the charges.

Paul stayed in Corinth for a while longer after the incident without any significant problems. Paul then left Corinth to go back to Antioch and complete his second missionary journey.

On the way, Paul made a brief stop by Ephesus. Priscilla and Aquila, who were accompanying Paul, remained there in Ephesus.

However, as the Corinthian Church grew in size, so did the problems that it faced. Members of the church wrote a letter to Paul to help them with these problems. At the time of writing 1 Corinthians, Paul was staying and ministering in Ephesus for a long time as part of his third missionary journey. After sending his first letter to the Corinthians, Paul briefly visits the Corinthian church in distress (2 Cor. 2:1). His second letter to the Corinthians was written shortly after he visited them and when he was staying in Macedonia after having left Ephesus. That was why he sent his second letter to the Corinthians via Titus. Paul visits Corinth again after his second letter and stays there for another three months. That was his last visit with the church in Corinth (Act. 20:1-2; 1 Cor. 16:5-7; 2 Cor. 13:1).

Answers to Questions

The Corinthian Church is truly an amazing church (1:4-9). It was abundant in all speech and knowledge. It was a powerful witness to Christ and it was not lacking in the gifts of the Holy Spirit. Still, it was a church with many problems (1:10-17). Its biggest problem was the division within the church. The church was divided into four groups: the "followers of Paul," "followers of Apollos," "followers of Cephas," and "followers of Christ." This caused conflict within the church and threatened to tear the heart and purpose of the Corinthian church.

Therefore, the first thing that the Corinthian church needed to restore was Christ's love to each other. First Corinthians places a huge emphasis on love. However, this does not mean that the book discards or disregards gifts of the Holy Spirit. The beautiful Christian reveals the gifts of the Holy Spirit through the love in his or her life.

First Corinthians is written in the form of answers to the questions of the members of the Corinthian church, beginning the answer to each of their questions with "concerning the matters about."

Between Verses 1-10 in Chapter 1, the name "Jesus Christ" is mentioned ten times. Solving difficult problems within the church is not easy; however, this book shows us that when dealing with such issues, it is important to go to Jesus and solve them with the wisdom of the Holy Spirit, not our thoughts, feelings, or methods. Led by the Holy Spirit, Paul writes his letter to the Corinthians with the heart of a father answering his children's questions.

The Content of the Answers

In Chapters 1-4, Paul rebukes them for the things happening in their church. He tells them not to boast that they are rich in knowledge and gifts. The spiritually immature walk in the flesh, but the spiritually mature walk in the Holy Spirit. No matter how much of the power and gifts of the Holy Spirit they receive, if believers quarrel among themselves, they are still children in a spiritual sense.

Divisiveness, strife, and pride are their characteristics. Paul invites them to abandon the path they are on and walk in humility with the Holy Spirit.

Chapter 5 deals with Christian self-indulgence and directs that such people be expelled from the Church. Paul also recommends throwing away the old leaven to maintain the purity of the Church. Although we must be strict in how we deal with our brothers who have sinned against Jesus, we should not completely sever ties with those who do not believe in Jesus. The sins and errors of those in the church must be dealt with firmly. Leaving people who do evil in the church as they are is like leaving old leaven: the evil will take effect on the whole Church. But to those outside the Church, we must be a holy influence.

Chapter 6 rebukes the believers for going to court to settle disputes. Paul says this because it is a grave disgrace to Christianity if believers are not able to solve their problems within the Church and have to resort to worldly courts. The Church should be the one to point out the wrong in the world; nothing is a greater embarrassment than the world having to rebuke the Church. All problems can be resolved with the Word of God. The world must look at the church and see love. To do this, we must resolve our internal issues with love and wisdom.

Chapter 7 touches on the subjects of whether to marry, live alone, divorce, or stay together. Paul says that celibacy is better than marriage. But he also tells the Corinthians to get married to avoid all kinds of sexual immorality. Marriage is not a subject to be ignored or avoided. Most important of all is love, devotion, and holiness before the Lord. Since marriage is such an important matter, it must be treated with care, appropriate consideration, careful judgment, and solid reasoning.

Chapter 8 answers the question about whether or not to eat the sacrifices offered to idols. Paul's faith has no reservations against eating the offering made to an idol, but he confesses that he would restrain himself in case he comes across a brother of weaker faith. More important than the knowledge about food offered to idols is love for one's brother. The great principle is that "This 'knowledge' puffs up, but love builds up" (8:1).

Chapter 9 refers to the rights of the Apostles. Quoting the words of Deuteronomy 25:4, "You shall not muzzle an ox to keep it from eating as it treads out the grain."

Chapter 10:1-11:1 speak about idol worship. Idolatry is the most heinous of sins. We must, therefore, avoid partaking in the practices of idol worshippers and sharing in the food they eat. Although we may eat the food that was offered to idols, we must not take part in any practices of idol worship. Chapter 8 tells us to act according to the principle of love. In other words, it tells us, "Let no one seek his own good, but the good of his neighbor" (10:24). Paul boldly proclaims, "Be imitators of me, as I am of Christ" (11:1).

Chapter 11:2-16 deals with the order of men and women. Verses 17-34 describe the correct attitude toward communion.

Chapters 12-14 illustrate the order of worship and the

correct use of gifts of the Holy Spirit. Chapter 12 covers the gifts of the Holy Spirit as a whole; Chapter 13 is the "love chapter" that covers love. Chapter 14 specifically deals with the gifts of tongues and prophecy among the gifts of the Holy Spirit. Paul tells the believers to use their gifts correctly and actively. But he tells them that there must be order and that love and gifts must move in unison.

Chapter 15 is the "resurrection chapter," covering the resurrection in detail.

Chapter 16 answers the question about how to handle collections for Christians in Jerusalem.

In conclusion, Paul tells the Church that all problems within the Church must be resolved through love, not by the Law. As he wrote in 8:1, "this 'knowledge' puffs up, but love builds up." Thus he says that it is in the spirit of Christianity not to unconditionally resolve problems based on the Law, but rather to resolve them through love that is based in the Law.

The Approach

When dealing with the problems of the Corinthian church, Paul has a three-pronged approach.

First, he treats the issue as a shepherd. A shepherd must own a positive heart and have hope for his sheep. He bears their shortcomings and weaknesses and lowers himself to be among them.

Second, he treats the issue as a brother. Paul says in 1:10, "I appeal to you, brothers, by the name of our Lord Jesus

Christ." He speaks as a brother who urges, not commands. He positioned himself to be a brother who walks alongside others.

Third, he treats the issue as a father. "I do not write these things to make you ashamed, but to admonish you as my beloved children" (4:14). He embraced the Corinthian church as a father would his children and treated them with love.

Outline

Chapter 1:1-9	Introduction (Greeting and thanksgiving)
Chapters 1:10-4:16	Regarding division in the Church
Chapters 4:17-6	Regarding inequity in the Church
Chapter 7	Regarding marriage
Chapters 8-11	Regarding the freedoms of the Christian
Chapters 12-14	Regarding spiritual gifts and love
Chapter 15	Regarding the resurrection
Chapter 16	Real plans and greeting

Voice Outline

1 AND 2 CORINTHIANS

100-Day Bible Reading Plan

		CHECK
Day 93	1 Corinthians 1-16	☐

2 CORINTHIANS

THE MINISTRY AND THE MINISTER

The content of 2 Corinthians is completely different from that of 1 Corinthians. The main reason Paul wrote 2 Corinthians was to refute misunderstandings about, difficulties with, and attacks made against him. Some accused Paul of not being a rightful apostle. Their greatest grievance was that the other apostles were people who had actually been with Jesus during His public ministry whereas Paul did not have any direct experience ministering with Him, which should disqualify him from being called an apostle.

However, Paul boldly proves that he was called directly by the Lord as an apostle when he met the risen Jesus on the road to Damascus. He tells them that he has performed the signs of a true apostle which are patience, signs, wonders, and mighty works (12:12). Paul's words are similar to those of Jesus' words in John 5:36: "But the testimony that I have is greater than that of John. For the works that the Father has given me to accomplish, the very works that I am doing bear witness about me that the Father has sent me."

The book also shows how Paul deals with the members

of the Church who slander and rebel against him in various ways, and how he goes about correcting their mistakes.

Second Corinthians describes the relationship between Paul and the Corinthian church as a relationship between a father and a rebellious son. As Paul writes his letter, his words express the pain of a father. He also expresses his joy over hearing that the Corinthian church has repented and turned itself back around. Second Corinthians is filled with Paul's rich sensibility, his shepherd's heart, and his love for the Church.

Another remarkable feature of 2 Corinthians is Chapters 8 and 9, the so-called "collection chapters." Throughout the two chapters, Paul thoroughly explains the biblical principles for giving and finances. Nowhere else does the bible provide such a detailed and rich description of offerings.

Main Content

Paul faces great danger in Ephesus. He goes to Troas and expects to meet Titus. However, unable to do so there, he crosses over to Macedonia to meet with Titus. There Titus reports that the Corinthian church received Paul's letter and was somewhat comforted by it. Paul writes a few additional things in his second letter to the Corinthians.

First, he gives further instructions to prepare collections for the poor Christians in Jerusalem. Second, he provides further basis for his apostolate and authority.

A Ministry of Reconciliation (Chapters 1-7)

Paul thanks the Lord who has given him comfort in his time of tribulation in 1:3-11. The word "comfort" appears 10 times throughout this passage, and the words "affliction" and "suffering" each appear 4 times. God is the God of comfort and the Father of mercy. These verses teach us that God intends for us to comfort those suffering affliction with the comfort with which we ourselves are comforted by God.

We are able to remain grateful during tribulations because we receive comfort from God. Paul tells us that where there is abundant suffering, there is abundant comfort. Another reason to be thankful is that we can comfort those who are afflicted. The third reason to be thankful is that it causes us to become more dependent on God. It is when we are weak that we are able to trust in and depend on Him more. Our faithful God is ever with us. The fourth reason to be thankful is that our brothers and sisters share in our suffering through prayer. We need to learn to ask our brothers and sister for their prayers if we are afflicted.

In 1:12-2:4, we read that Paul postpones the planned visit to Corinth because he does not wish to embarrass them. Paul's adversaries use it as an opportunity to reproach and criticize him. Paul, however, says that his own conscience is clean. He says boldly, "We are not trying to control your faith, but to be helpers of your joy" (1:24). He explains that the reason for postponing the visitation plan was not to be the organizer of their faith, but to be a helper. Paul writes his letter full of the tears and abundant love that he has for the church of Corinth (2:4)

Chapter 2:5-13 asks the church to forgive and embrace any brother who has sinned against the church community so that he may not be overcome with overwhelming grief. He also tells them not to be fooled by Satan. An unforgiving heart is easy for Satan to deceive.

In Verses 14-17, Paul says that God is One to always make us walk in triumph. We are the "aroma of Christ." We must not be peddlers of God's Word but must accept and preach it in its purest form. A "peddler" is someone "who makes unfair gains by tricking people into buying, or sells cheap goods at a high price." God's Word is more valuable than gold and silver. David states that the Word of the Lord is "More to be desired are they than gold, even much fine gold" (Psa. 19:10).

Chapter 3 is like a recommendation letter Paul wrote for himself. However, it is not a display of pride but instead intends to bring glory to God. We are "letters from Christ." Our sufficiency is only from God. We are the ministers of a new covenant. It is a glorious assignment that we hold.

In Chapter 4, Paul encourages ministers not to be discouraged. Despite the hardships of ministry, Paul says that we do not lose heart (Verse 1). What has protected us in our moments of affliction is our faith (Verse 13), our hope for resurrection (Verse 14), and the coming glory of God (Verse 15).

In Chapter 5, we learn that the old has passed away and the new has come: we are new creations. What is more, we are "ambassadors for Christ." We have been sent by God with the mission to reconcile people to God.

Chapter 6:1-10 is a deeply moving passage that lists all

the signs of a minister of God. Together with 11:21-33, these verses do a very good job of depicting the life of Paul as a worker in the Gospel. Let us study the signs and apply these in our lives.

In 6:11-7:1, Paul tells the Corinthians to "Widen your hearts. And keep ourselves pure in both our relationships and in our daily lives."

In 7:2-16, Paul encourages the Church to show due interest to ministers of the Gospel. "I am filled with comfort. In all our affliction, I am overflowing with joy" (7:4). He confesses that although it pained him greatly not to be able to meet with Titus, he was comforted after hearing about what was happening in the church in Corinth. What brought him greater joy was the church's repentance and fruits.

Offerings and Financial Principles of the Bible (Chapters 8-9)

In 8:1-6, Paul praises the believers in Macedonia: namely, the churches in Philippi, Thessalonica, and Berea for their offerings. Though they struggled with dire poverty, they made sure that their offerings were abundant. He uses these churches as examples to challenge and encourage the churches in Achaia. However, the greatest example is our Lord Jesus Christ.

"For you know the grace of our Lord Jesus Christ, that though he was rich, yet for your sake he became poor, so that you by his poverty might become rich" (8:9). Jesus took on the burden of our poverty so that he could give His riches to us.

This is the principle of "divine substitution."

In 8:16-24, Paul recommends three people to serve in the delivery of the offerings. They were to be responsible for delivering the donations from the churches in the Achaia to Jerusalem. This was an important matter for Paul. He handled it with great care so that he would not be blamed for having mishandled the offerings, and so that good may be done with the donations. It was quite a large sum, so Paul gives his seal of approval that the three he recommended were trustworthy men.

Titus was the first one to be recommended. He was ready to be a part of a ministry of service and earnestly sought the good of the believers in Jerusalem. Titus gladly volunteered himself for the work.

Paul recommended a second brother who he sent with Titus. This individual was praised by many of the churches in Achaia. He was to work with Paul on this ministry. Scholars agree that this individual is most likely Luke.

The third brother recommended by Paul was a brother who ministered with the previous two brothers. It is most likely that this brother was Apollos. He proved his earnestness in many ways.

Paul draws a common conclusion about these three men. He tells the church, "They are my co-ministers; they are messengers to the churches; they are the glory of Christ."

We must be extremely careful with how we handle offerings. We must be careful not to act in a way that is deserving of criticism. We must entrust them to those who are trustworthy. It is also best to have three people, not one, manage church finances.

In 9:6-15, Paul explains how to handle wealth by using the rules of farming. Using our wealth to give to those in need is like planting seeds in the ground. When sowing, expect to reap. This means that we must first learn the rules of sowing and reaping. If we wish to reap plenty, we must sow plenty. Furthermore, we must not be stingy or be compelled to do so when we make offerings. Instead we should be generous and do so willingly with joy in our hearts.

God gives us abundantly for our needs and more, so that we may abound in every good work. God especially wants to take care of the poor. It is written in Proverbs 19:17: "Whoever is generous to the poor lends to the Lord, and he will repay him for his deed."

The Ministry of the Apostle **(Chapters 10-13)**

In no other place was Paul attacked by false apostles more than he was in Corinth. Paul was humble and upstanding in every way, without fault. However, there remained those ill-willed few who were envious of him. They criticized Paul and tried to dishonor him. The church in Corinth was under the influence of such people. Paul wrote his letter to protect the Corinthian church from them.

In 11:5-6, Paul gently and humbly, yet with boldness, introduces himself as an apostle of Jesus Christ. He also humbly explains that he is equal to the other apostles. He does, however, say that he is not able to speak with the clarity of the other apostles. Referring to these words of Paul, some say that he was short or very small framed and had a small voice. Others say that he may have had a bit of a stutter when he spoke.

In 11:22-33, Paul comprehensively describes his qualifications, his work, and the suffering he endured. How stunning his hard work and dedication is!

Second Corinthians 12:1-10 is a testimony of the vision and revelation he received. He presents his suffering, honest life, sacrificial love, visions, and revelations as a sign of his authority as an apostle. He writes, "The signs of a true apostle were performed among you with utmost patience, with signs and wonders and mighty works" (12:12). This is because God confirms that we are His workers by accompanying signs (Mark 16:20).

Second Corinthians 12:11-21 shows us Paul's nature as a faithful servant of the Gospel. He showed no interest in wealth and was only interested in the work of saving souls. He willingly used his own time, talents, strengths, and rights toward this purpose. And despite the Corinthians' ingratitude, Paul did not diminish his love for them in any way. He used all that he had to build them up. He built them up so they may stand strong on their own two feet.

In 13:1-6, Paul states that he has sent two letters of advice and warning to correct the mistakes of the Corinthian church. He warns that when he visits in person, he will deal with the sinners among them harshly.

Second Corinthians 13:7-13 contains Paul's prayer to God

for the Corinthians. He prays for them to have integrity, to be completely freed from sin. The Book of 2 Corinthians ends with Paul's benediction for the church in Corinth in Chapter 13.

Outline

Chapters 1-7	The ministry of reconciliation, the principles of ministry
Chapters 8-9	The principles of donations and collections
Chapters 10-13	The ministry of the apostle

Voice Outline

1 AND 2 CORINTHIANS

100-Day Bible Reading Plan

		CHECK
Day 94	2 Corinthians 1-13	

GALATIANS

NOT MY SERVANT, BUT MY SON

The theme of this book is "the Gospel of Freedom." That is why the book is sometimes referred to as the "Christians' Declaration of Freedom" or the "Great Charter of Christian liberty (Magna Carta)." This book later became the driving force behind the Reformation. Some say the Book of Galatians "is like a shining sword in the hands of a mighty swordsman."

Romans and Galatians explain the New Covenant and how salvation comes only through faith in Jesus Christ. The Torah loyalists (the group mentioned in Acts 15:1) wanted to continue to influence the regions in Paul's first missionary journey. They tried to combine the Law with faith, and argued that deeds should go hand in hand with faith. In particular, this group taught that faith can only be perfected by abidance to the Mosaic Law. Paul writes his letter to the Galatians, still under the influence of the Torah loyalists, to reiterate that salvation only comes by faith.

The Book of Galatians can be divided into three parts. Chapters 1 and 2 contain Paul's testimony, Chapters 3 and 4 deal with the relationship between the Law and the Gospel, and Chapters 5 and 6 talk about growing in grace through the Holy Spirit.

***Paul's Testimony* (Chapters 1-2)**

Paul introduces himself as "Paul, an apostle not from men nor through man, but through Jesus Christ and God the Father, who raised him from the dead" (1:1). This verse tells us that Paul's apostolate was not granted by any man or organization, but by God.

Paul was deeply passionate about the Gospel. He unequivocally proclaims that there is no other Gospel than the Gospel in Jesus Christ. He says even angels shall be cursed if they preach another Gospel (1:6-9). He states that if even ever Peter acted in a way contrary to the Gospel, he would not hesitate for a moment to fearlessly and directly oppose him (2:11-14). Paul declares, "For am I now seeking the approval of man, or of God? Or am I trying to please man? If I were still trying to please man, I would not be a servant of Christ" (1:10) and says that, as a servant of Jesus Christ, he does not seek to please man but only to please Jesus Christ.

He was educated in the "School of Christ" (1:11,12,16,17). After meeting Jesus Christ on the road to Damascus and experiencing the Holy Spirit, he learned directly from Jesus Christ in the Arabian wilderness for three years. The Holy Spirit prepared him to fulfill his calling as a minister. Paul is a man with a testimony. His testimony to the people is that he is a former persecutor of Christians who turned into an apostle of God (1:21-24).

Paul was also a man who knew how to recognize the order and authority of the body of Christ (2:1-2). Having received a revelation directly from Jesus, he was called by the Lord to be an apostle and received revelations directly before Jesus Christ. However, he was not a lone wolf. He knew how to respect the authority of the body of Christ, to acknowledge order, to be fellowship within it, and work within the bounds of authority. He was a man who boasted only of the cross of Jesus Christ, and believed only in Christ, the crucified Son of God (2:20; 6:14).

In his testimony, Paul refers to the places of Arabia, Damascus, Jerusalem, Syria, and Tarsus Cilicia. Each of these places had a special connection with the Apostle Paul. Arabia was where Paul stood in solitude before the Lord and received revelations about the Gospel as he prepared for his future ministry. Damascus was where he was transformed from persecutor to evangelist, was baptized in the Holy Spirit, and began preaching the Gospel. Jerusalem was where he acknowledged the order and authority of the church, fellowshipped with them, and had his ministry recognized by them. Syria and Tarsus Cilicia are where Paul waited for God and trained to become a minister.

Law and Grace *(Chapters 3-4)*

God made a covenant with Abraham and Moses. The covenant that God made with Moses is called "the Law" and the covenant that God made with Abraham is called "the Gospel of grace." God's covenant with Moses proves to us that all men are sinners. The Law is not in conflict with God's grace; rather, it shows to us that we are indeed sinners. It proves to us that we cannot attain salvation on our own. The Law, by drawing us to Jesus, reveals to us that we can only reach salvation through Him. The Law's ultimate purpose is to bring us to salvation through the death and resurrection of Jesus.

The role of God's grace is to transform our lives. It is the equivalent of a convict serving life in prison and then suddenly being released as a free man. We no longer need to be punished because someone else has paid for all our sins. The Gospel and God's grace free us like a child who was under the custody of a guardian or steward and is then freed once he or she reaches adulthood. The grace provided to us with Jesus' arrival on earth is like the transformation from child to adult, from slave to free man.

Paul speaks of two special types of grace. One is the amazing grace that transforms us from slave to free man. The other grace takes this transition a step further and changes our status to God's son. The movie *Ben-Hur* covers the story of its protagonist Judah Ben-Hur, born a slave but then freed from slavery after being adopted by a Roman nobleman. The protagonist of the movie *The Count of Monte Cristo* was wrongfully sentenced to life imprisonment and death on a secluded island but was able to escape and become a free man. These two movies depict how the cross of Jesus Christ has transformed us from being slaves of sin and death to free men who are servants of the Son of God.

Chapters 3 and 4 tell us that this fundamental change in status and identity is made possible through Jesus Christ. This change takes place only through grace, and that grace is the Gospel.

***Growth in Grace* (Chapters 5-6)**

Having received this wonderful grace, we must seize it and prove it with the lives that we live. Although it is only through faith that we have received grace, that faith must be reflected in the works that we do.

Chapter 5:1 is the "Christians' Declaration of Freedom." It is written, "For freedom Christ has set us free; stand firm therefore, and do not submit again to the yoke of slavery."

This verse tells us that our freedom has been declared and that we should not continue on to live as slaves. Jesus Christ has freed us from the curse of the Law. Jesus has made us children of the promise; we are no longer slaves. Therefore, as free men and as children of God, we must no longer live by the Law or our own strength, but only by the Holy Spirit.

It is written that the works of the flesh are evident (5:19-21). And trying to do things by our own strength will only emphasize the works of our flesh. However, when we walk by the Holy Spirit, we will release "the fruits of the Holy Spirit." When Paul tells us to "walk by the Spirit" and "be led by the Spirit" in 5:16,18, he is telling us to walk in the teachings of the Holy Spirit, to act with the power of the Holy Spirit, and to be guided by the Holy Spirit.

Chapter 6:1-10 affirms that if we are saved only by our

faith in Jesus Christ, we must live our lives by the power and guidance of the Holy Spirit and not by our own strength, even after we have received salvation.

Chapter 6:1-10 is a practical guide to living by the Holy Spirit. We must hold our brothers who have sinned accountable in meekness. "Bear one another's burdens, and so fulfill the law of Christ" (6:2). We must treat our weak brothers with tolerance and acceptance. This does not mean that we should turn a blind eye to their mistakes, but that we should not be harsh in dealing with his sins and encourage, help, and support each other instead. We must give our brothers a chance. Yet, we should also reflect upon ourselves, using our brothers as our mirror. We must also make sure to examine ourselves.

"Let the one who is taught the word share all good things with the one who teaches" (6:6). This verse tells those who are taught the Word to make sure that the needs of those who teach the Word are met, and to share with them so that they may teach without being bound by material struggles. Furthermore, 6:10 tells us to do good to all people at every opportunity. Paul tells us to do good for those who teach the Word, then for our brothers and sisters in faith, and then for all people. We must seize every opportunity to help others and then the rewards will surely follow. We must do good but not become discouraged or lose hope. We will reap when the right time comes.

Outline

Chapters 1-2	The sincerity of the Gospel
Chapters 1:1-5	Prologue (Greeting)
Chapters 1:6-2	Paul's apostolic authority
Chapters 3-4	The Gospel's preeminence
Chapter 3	The bondage of the Law
Chapter 4	The freedom of grace
Chapters 5-6	The freedom seized with the Gospel
Chapters 5-6:10	Growing in Spirit through grace
Chapter 6:11-18	Epilogue (Review)

Voice Outline

GALATIANS

100-Day Bible Reading Plan

		CHECK
Day 95	Galatians, Ephesians	☐

EPHESIANS

THE FULLNESS OF THE CHURCH OF JESUS CHRIST

Ephesians is known as the most outstanding epistle. That is why it is sometimes referred to as "the queen of the epistles." Philosopher and poet Samuel Taylor Coleridge praised the book, calling it "the divinest composition of man." Furthermore, with over 55 verses similar to those in the Book of Colossians, Ephesians and Colossians are sometimes called the "twin epistles." Colossians is said to be like an overflow of Ephesians and Ephesians is likened to a second and improved version of Colossians.

Circular Letter

The Book of Ephesians was not addressed to a certain church, but rather to all the churches of Asia Minor that Paul had planted. It is also called a "circular letter" because it was intended for wide use across these churches. In Colossians 4:16, Paul wrote, "And when this letter has been read among you, have it also read in the church of the Laodiceans; and see that you also read the letter from Laodicea." "The letter from Laodicea" in the verse is referring to the Book of Ephesians.

"So that you also may know how I am and what I am doing, Tychicus the beloved brother and faithful minister in the Lord will tell you everything" (6:21) and "Tychicus will tell you all about my activities. He is a beloved brother and faithful minister and fellow servant in the Lord" (Col. 4:7) tell us that Tychicus served as Paul's messenger when Paul sent letters to the churches in Ephesus and Asia Minor while in prison in Rome. Tychicus comforted the churches by being the messenger of Paul's letters and news.

Ephesians tells us that all things are unified in Jesus Christ and that Jesus Christ is fullness itself. The epistle also tells us that the Church is the body of Christ and shares in His fullness. "The fullness of Jesus Christ" and "the Church as the body of Christ" comprise the entire content of this letter.

The Church

The book of Ephesians describes the church in several ways.

First, it explains that the Church is the body of Jesus Christ. Using the human anatomy as a metaphor, Jesus is the head of the Church and the Church is the body. Just as a person's head and body are connected as one, the fullness of Jesus Christ, the head of the Church, flows into the Church which is His body (1:22-23; 2:4-7).

Second, the Church is likened to a building. Jesus Christ is the cornerstone, the center of the building, and the Church is the building built upon that center. Just as the components of a building are connected to each other, Christians are being joined together to become the Church (2:21-22).

Just as a building consists of a foundation, pillars, a roof, and walls, the Church is made up of apostles and prophets who act as the foundation, teachers who act as the pillars, shepherds who act as the roof, and evangelists who fill the building with people (2:20; 4:11-12). This is the mandate of the Holy Spirit that is given to the Church leadership who builds up the Church through the Holy Spirit rather than any particular organization, name, or title.

Third, the Church is likened to a bride. Drawing comparisons to the relationship between a bridegroom and his bride, Jesus Christ becomes the bridegroom and the church becomes the bride (5:22-33). Paul explains the relationship between the Church and Jesus Christ using the way the bridegroom loves the bride with all his life and the way the bride obeys the bridegroom as an analogy.

Fourth, the church is called a soldier of spiritual warfare (6:10-17). The Christian life does not entail salvation and enjoying the things of this world, but the life of a soldier who fights against the spirits of darkness to expand the Kingdom of God. Hence, we must be fully aware of who our enemy is, and how we must arm ourselves as soldiers of the Lord.

Sit, Walk, Stand

The Book of Ephesians, just like the Book of Romans, is written in a very logical and structural manner. The first three of the six chapters in the book talk about the position of Christ and the position of Christians. Chapters 4-6 explain the kind of life Christians should live. The first three chapters deal with Christian privileges, and the remaining three refer to Christian responsibilities.

Watchman Nee wrote an excellent book titled *Sit, Walk, and Stand,* a study on the Book of Ephesians. The first word of the title is "sit." God sat Jesus Christ, who died on the cross and rose from the dead, on His right hand. The right hand of God is the seat of the one who rules over everything. God gave us life, raised us, and sat us with Christ in heaven when we were dead due to our sins and transgressions, living under the power of darkness. Therefore, the Church now sits with Christ at the right hand of God in heaven. That is the position of the Church and where we belong spiritually. With Christ, we are in a position from which to rule over everything. We rule, not in the future, but here in the now.

He gave us spiritual authority to bind and command even Satan. It is written in Luke 10:19, "Behold, I have given you authority to tread on serpents and scorpions, and over all the power of the enemy, and nothing shall hurt you." Our place is "in Christ." The Book of Ephesians repeats the words "in Christ" 22 times from Chapters 1 to 3 (12 times in Chapter 1, 6 times in Chapter 2, 4 times in Chapter 3).

The second word of Nee's book is "walk." Ephesians 4:1-6:9 describes the walk Christians need to walk in the following five areas:

First, we must "walk in a way that is befitting His call" (4:1-16). This means, "In oneness, in unity." We Christians must strive to keep whole that which the Holy Spirit has already united as one. There are seven elements to this unity: one body, one Spirit, one hope for His calling, one Lord, one faith, one baptism, and one God.

Even if there are different denominations and each emphasizes a different aspect of Christianity, it does not pose a problem to the unity of Christianity as long as they are built on the same seven foundations. We have to look at the picture as a whole. This is not, however, suggesting pluralism in the sense that it is inclusive of all religions. Only the above seven foundations are what keep us united.

Second, we must "walk in truth" (4:17-32). This means to put off the old self and to put on the new self. The key to doing this is to renew our way of thinking.

Third, we must "walk in love" (5:1-7). We are to live according to the new commandment: just as Jesus has loved us, we also are to love one another (John 13:34-35).

Fourth, we must "walk as the children of light" (5:8-14). The fruit of light is found in all that is good and right and true (5:9).

Fifth, we must "walk with wisdom in all our relationships" (5:15-6:9). This refers to saving time, spending time wisely, living according to the will of the Lord, and acting with wisdom in our relationships. Christians should conduct their relationships wisely: between husband and wife, between parents and children in the home, and between employers and employees in society.

The third and final word of the title of the book is "stand." In 6:10-20, God tells us that in order to establish the Kingdom of God in this world we must fight against the forces that try to interfere. As the Israelites who inherited Canaan followed Joshua's lead in war with the Canaanite tribes and seized the land, we must also seize our inheritance. It is written in Psalm 2:8, "Ask of me, and I will make the nations your heritage, and the ends of the earth your possession." And Jesus tells us in Matthew 28:19, "Go therefore and make disciples of all nations."

It is our mission to change this world. Our mission is not only to bring lost souls back to the Lord, but to change the structure of society so that the Kingdom of God may come. However, this may only be done through war.

Our fight is not against the flesh, but against the forces of Satan. The opponents of our fight are "the rulers, the authorities, the cosmic powers over this present darkness, and the spiritual forces of evil in the heavenly places" (6:12). These are invisible forces, no seen by the naked eye. That is why we call this "spiritual warfare." In order to achieve victory in this spiritual war, Paul tells us to take on the whole armor of God: the belt of truth, the breastplate of righteousness, the shoes of the Gospel of peace, the shield of faith, the helmet of salvation, and the sword of the Spirit. But above all, we must pray after we have taken on the whole armor of God. Paul tells us to keep alert and make supplications to the Lord (6:14-17).

What to Pray for

The Book of Ephesians presents us with two exemplary prayers. These prayers show us exactly for what we should pray. They are prayers for our family, friends, peers, and ministers. The "that we may know" in these verses may be substituted with "that we may experience."

Prayer 1 **(1:17-19)**

"Our Father, give _____ the Spirit of wisdom and of revelation in the knowledge of him."

The knowledge of God is essential to our lives. It is written in Jeremiah 9:23-24: "Thus says the Lord: 'Let not the wise man boast in his wisdom, let not the mighty man boast in his might, let not the rich man boast in his riches, but let him who boasts boast in this, that he understands and knows me, that I am the Lord who practices steadfast love, justice, and righteousness in the earth. For in these things I delight, declares the Lord.'"

"Please enlighten the eyes of _____ 's heart that they may come to know the following:"

We first pray, "Let _____ the hope to which You have called them."

It is important that we understand our calling. Each of us was sent to this earth by God for a mission. It is therefore crucial that we understand what it is that we need to do. Knowing our purpose can add momentum and dynamism to our lives.

Second, we pray, "Make it known to _____ what are the riches of Your glorious inheritance in the saints." It is important to understand that God's inheritance is not in this life but in the Kingdom that is eternal. Our life on this earth is not the final destination but a mere layover. When we fully grasp what our inheritance is and where we will live eternally, we will also understand how it is that we need to live on this earth.

And thirdly, we pray, "Make ____ know how immeasurably great Your power is toward those who believe."

Our God is Almighty. God's power is unleashed and revealed through His believers.

Prayer 2 **(3:16-19)**

This is the first part of this prayer: "Grant _____ to be strengthened through the Holy Spirit in their inner being."

The health of the outer being (body) is also important, but the health of the inner being is more important. As written in 3 John 1:2, "I pray that all may go well with you and that you may be in good health, as it goes well with your soul." If the inner being is strong first, everything will go well and the body will be strong as well.

The second part goes like this: "Let Christ dwell in _____'s hearts through faith."

Walking with Christ and remaining in His presence is of utmost importance. If we are able to do this, then we will be able to maintain peace and joy in our hearts."

In the third and last part of the prayer, we pray: "Let _____ know the love of Christ that surpasses knowledge."

Jesus' love is love from another dimension. How precious is it to experience the breadth, length, height, and depth of His love!

Outline

Chapters 1-3	The position of the Christian
Chapter 1	The Father's will
Chapter 2	The Son's salvation
Verses 1-10	The B.C. and A.D. of the individual
Verses 11-22	The B.C. and A.D. of the Church community
Chapter 3	The works of the Holy Spirit
Chapters 4-6	The Christian walk
Chapters 4-6:9	Our calling in Christ
Chapter 4:1-16	Keeping the unity
Chapter 4:17-32	Walking in truth
Chapter 5:1-7	Walking in love
Chapter 5:8-14	Walking as children of light
Chapters 5:15-6:9	Walking in wisdom
Chapter 6:10-20	Spiritual warfare (putting on the whole armor of God)

Voice Outline

EPHESIANS

100-Day Bible Reading Plan

		CHECK
Day 95	Galatians, Ephesians	☐

PHILIPPIANS

REJOICE IN THE LORD

Philippians is referred to as the "epistle of joy." It is also called "the most beautiful book." The recipient of this epistle is the Philippian church in the city of Philippi. This city was built by the father of Alexander, Philip II of Macedonia, and was also named after him.

The Church in Philippi

Although Paul's initial plan was to go to Asia, he changes his plans after hearing about the vision of a Macedonian man and crosses over to Europe. When he arrived in Europe, his first destination was Philippi. Paul and his team began spreading the Gospel there, eventually forming a church. Philippi was also the city in which Paul and his team were imprisoned and underwent tremendous suffering.

The church in Philippi was truly diverse. One of its believers, Lydia, was an Asian merchant who was a dealer of purple textiles. Back then, dealing in purple cloth was a very lucrative and popular business. Lydia was not a small trader but a very successful businesswoman belonging to the upper class.

Others who came to believe in Jesus Christ included a prison guard and his family. This man used to be a guard in the Roman prison where Paul and Silas were held and had beat them quite severely while there. He was a Roman soldier who belonged to the middle class. There was also a slave girl who used to be a fortune-teller but was eventually freed by Paul and came to believe in Jesus and became a member of the church. She was a Greek slave girl who belonged to the lower class. As described, the church in Philippi was formed by the coming together of people of different nationalities and social classes.

Rejoice

The Book of Philippians repeats the word, "rejoice." This was the message that Paul sent from prison to his brothers in Philippi outside the prison. Although it seems like the Philippian church should have written to Paul who was imprisoned while preaching the Gospel, "Rejoice, do not be discouraged, be patient," it was instead Paul who wrote from prison telling his brothers and sister outside to rejoice.

This is because joy is not derived from one's environment. Although Paul was in prison, his spirit was always free. He was a man who lived on this earth but was not influenced by the things of this earth and always maintained the joy of heaven. That is the specific kind of joy Paul wishes to express in his epistle to the Philippians.

The words of Habakkuk 3:17-19 in the Old Testament

illustrate the kind of life that the Apostle Paul led. "Though the fig tree should not blossom, nor fruit be on the vines, the produce of the olive fail and the fields yield no food, the flock be cut off from the fold and there be no herd in the stalls, yet I will rejoice in the Lord; I will take joy in the God of my salvation. God, the Lord, is my strength; he makes my feet like the deer's; he makes me tread on my high places."

The joy of the Prophet Habakkuk lay not in the environment, in matters, or in humans, but in God. Nehemiah said, "For the joy of the Lord is your strength" (Neh. 8:10). Paul was not affected by his environment because Jesus Christ was his joy.

The Book of Philippians speaks of this joy in many different ways. It is joyful when we pray for our brothers and sisters before the throne of grace (1:4) because we love our brothers with the heart of Christ. Christians should live with shining joy in all circumstances and environments, not with sadness, depression, or sunken faces (1:25). There is also the joy of fellowship as all the saints become one with each other (2:2) because such fellowship is to be with the Father and Jesus Christ (1 John 1:3-4). It is also a joy to suffer in the name of Jesus Christ (2:17).

Polycarp, the bishop of the church in Smyrna and a man of faith, cried out as he was being burned by Roman soldiers, "Father, I bless you for considering me worthy of this day and hour of sharing with the martyrs in the cup of your Christ!" Thus he confessed the joy of martyrdom. That is the kind of joy that is talked about in the Book of Philippians.

In 2:28, Paul speaks of the joy of hearing the good news from loved ones. This is the joy that is meant by Proverbs 25:25, "Like cold water to a thirsty soul, so is good news from a far country." In 2:29, Paul speaks of the joy of always keeping the doors of one's house open to entertain guests and travelers.

Philippians 3:1 and 4:1 refer to the joy of fellowship among believers in Jesus Christ. In 4:10-12, Paul tells us that by learning to be self-sufficient in any and every circumstance, he learned the secret of facing plenty and hunger, abundance, and need. Therefore he tells us that he rejoices no matter his circumstances.

As such, the Book of Philippians tells us that "joy" is the sign of Christianity. We cannot say that our lives reveal Jesus Christ if we live with depression, sullen faces, and anguish. We are people who have a heavenly job that transcends any environment belonging to this world.

The Amazing Jesus, Our Role Model

Philippians contains some of the best and most touching verses that show the true divinity and humanity of Jesus Christ. "Have this mind among yourselves, which is yours in Christ Jesus, who, though he was in the form of God, did not count equality with God a thing to be grasped, but emptied himself, by taking the form of a servant, being born in the likeness of men. And being found in human form, he humbled himself by becoming obedient to the point of death, even death on a cross" (2:5-8).

Paul urged the Philippian brothers to become one. They were told to abandon the disagreement and discord, personal ambitions and pride between them, and not to dispute or serve out of vanity but to serve each other with humility (2:1-4).

Then, Paul introduces us to different aspects of Jesus.

First, Jesus Christ is fundamentally the body of God. The nature of Jesus is God, and His nature does not change. Here, Paul is referring to the divinity of Jesus. However, Jesus did not count equality with God as a thing to be grasped. To grasp means to "seize and hold firmly." Since He is by nature God, He did not need to grasp equality with God.

Second, Jesus, by taking the form of a servant, emptied himself. Jesus emptied himself of his divinity and became a servant to be born in the likeness of men. Although He is by nature God, Jesus fully took on the likeness of man for a short while. Externally, he became everything that would identify Him as man. He was bound by the limitations of time and space, emotions, fatigue, and hunger. For Jesus, who is God, taking on the likeness of man was itself an immense sacrifice. This is the wonderful mystery of God's love that transcends all our understanding.

Third, Jesus humbled himself, becoming obedient to the point of death, even death on a cross. His life can be described by the three simple words of "humility," "obedience," and "sacrifice." He did not wish to be served, but rather served. He chose God's way and not His own. He gave up all His glory for the sake of mankind. Jesus is our role model even to this day. Egotism, self-assertion, self-flaunting, and self-glory only serve to destroy Christian fellowship. The Christian sign lies in being like Jesus Christ.

Two Letters of Recommendation

There are two letters of recommendation in Philippians. In Chapter 2, Paul recommends Timothy and Epaphroditus (2:19-25). Paul first introduces Timothy. "Brother Timothy is the man who will join your purpose and who will truly think about your situation. Everyone else may seek after his own work and not the work of Christ Jesus, but Brother Timothy is the first to seek the work of Christ Jesus. He is also a man of training. He has weathered hardship after hardship by faith. He is also a man with whom I have worked to spread the Gospel."

Next, he recommends Epaphroditus. "Brother Epaphroditus is my brother, the one who has labored with me for the Lord. He is, just as I am, a soldier of Jesus Christ. Brother Epaphroditus is your messenger to help me with my needs. He is a man who puts the work of Christ before himself, even risking his life to complete the work."

If someone wrote a letter of recommendation for us, what would you like for it to say? Moreover, what do you think that it would say? The Lord wants us to be like Timothy and Epaphroditus who were deserving of such an introduction.

Paul says, "Honor such men" (2:29). Here, Paul is telling us to respect such men. They are deserving of respect. Look around. Do you have men around you that are deserving of your admiration? If so, respect them and pray for them: "Lord, raise more people like them in the Church!"

Paul also writes a letter of recommendation for himself (3:4-8).

"If anyone else thinks he has reason for confidence in the flesh, I have more: circumcised on the eighth day, of the people of Israel, of the tribe of Benjamin, a Hebrew of Hebrews; as to the law, a Pharisee; as to zeal, a persecutor of the church; as to righteousness under the law, blameless. But whatever gain I had, I counted as loss for the sake of Christ. Indeed, I count everything as loss because of the surpassing worth of knowing Christ Jesus my Lord. For his sake I have suffered the loss of all things and count them as rubbish, in order that I may gain Christ."

This is the most amazing confession of faith in the Book of Philippians. It is also an exemplary description of the lives we should live on this earth.

Philippians 3:13-14 is Paul's mission statement: "Brothers, I do not consider that I have made it my own. But one thing I do: forgetting what lies behind and straining forward to what lies ahead, I press on toward the goal for the prize of the upward call of God in Christ Jesus."

We must make this our mission statement and hold on firmly to the following Scripture of promise as our own to fulfill our mission. "And I am sure of this, that he who began a good work in you will bring it to completion at the day of Jesus Christ" (1:6).

Then, we proclaim the following words as our own confession, "I can do all things through him who strengthens me," (4:13) "And my God will supply every need of yours according to his riches in glory in Christ Jesus" (4:19).

The Secret to Joy and Peace

Paul goes on to tell us that he has "learned to be self-sufficient in any and every circumstance." He says in 4:12, "I know how to be brought low, and I know how to abound. In any and every circumstance, I have learned the secret of facing plenty and hunger, abundance and need." It is important to be self-sufficient in relation to material things: it is how we lead truly satisfying lives free from the weight of debt.

In 4:6-9, Paul tells us the importance of maintaining God's peace in order to fulfill our mission. It is when we maintain our inner balance that we can employ our discernment, judgment, understanding, and insight to do what is right in practice.

The secret to maintaining this joy and peace is first to fill our minds with Christ. "Finally, brothers, whatever is true, whatever is honorable, whatever is just, whatever is pure, whatever is lovely, whatever is commendable, if there is any excellence, if there is anything worthy of praise, think about these things" (4:8).

The verse says, "Think about these things." In other words, it is telling us to keep these things on our minds. It is to control our minds so that only thoughts that contain the eight elements mentioned in the above verse remain on our minds. Whatever it is that we see or hear, we must not accept everything without a filter. We must filter everything that enters our minds to only think of these things as though we are filtering our thoughts through a sheet of filter paper. We can attain joy and peace when we only allow these things to come in and remain on our minds.

The second secret to maintaining joy and peace is the prayer of thanksgiving. It is written in 4:6, “Do not be anxious about anything, but in everything by prayer and supplication with thanksgiving let your requests be made known to God.” The words, “anything” and “everything” in this verse urge us to make a list of things that we should not be anxious about and all the things for which we have to be thankful and to pray.

Outline

Chapter 1	Walking with Christ Experience (suffering)
Chapter 2	The heart of Christ The people of Christ (obedience)
Chapter 3	The knowledge of Christ Following Christ (salvation)
Chapter 4	The peace of Christ The power of Christ (sanctification)

Voice Outline

PHILIPPIANS

100-Day Bible Reading Plan

		CHECK
Day 96	Philippians, Colossians, 1 Thessalonians, 2 Thessalonians	☐

COLOSSIANS

RESERVE THE BEST SEAT FOR JESUS

As already explained in the chapter on Ephesians, Ephesians and Colossians are "twin epistles" which share more than 55 verses in common.

Colossae was a central city of Phrygia, not far from Laodicea and Hierapolis. One of the many churches in Asia Minor, the Colossian church, was experiencing a revival at the time of this epistle's writing. Epaphras founded the church, and Philemon ministered in this church. There are no records indicating that Paul visited this particular church.

The Best Seat That He Deserves

The theme of the Book of Colossians is "the fullness of Jesus Christ." Paul explains the importance and wonder of the fullness of Jesus Christ in reference to the particular situation and the emergence of heretical sects at the time.

A heretical sect called the "Gnostics" had appeared. They maintained dualist thoughts about the spirit and body. They believed that the spirit is good, and all matter is imperfect and evil; the body, because it belonged to matter, was also evil. They held that the universe was not created out of nothing, but rather that matter was the raw material from which the world was created.

Such beliefs corrupted their views on the fact of creation and the humanity of Jesus Christ. They denied that Jesus came to earth in the flesh as well as the resurrection of the flesh. Moreover, they harmed Christian ethics. They argued that "because matter is evil, the body is also evil. Therefore, it is okay to treat the body in any way we please." Holding onto such ideologies, the Gnostics either fell into asceticism, physically whipping their bodies as though to control a slave, or into hedonism, living their life as they please because the body is evil. Paul's epistle to the Colossians gives them a stern warning about such beliefs. Such false teachings emphasize the wisdom and institutions of man and cause us to become obsessed with myths and legends.

In addition to the Gnostics, there were false teachers who valued and emphasized the Jewish tradition and who had close ties with the legalists. These people argued that in order to reach God, it was necessary to live a strict ascetic life, like climbing a ladder. As a result, they demanded that Christians obey the laws of Judaism, observe certain dates, and eat or forbid certain foods.

The Book of Colossians teaches that the Christian faith transcends all of this. The content of Paul's epistle can be summarized as follows: "Beware of Gnosticism. Beware of Jewish legalism. Be wary of angel worship and false mysticism. Be wary of human philosophy. And only to Jesus

Christ give the best seat that He deserves."

Structure

Chapters 1 and 2 describe the preeminence of Jesus Christ, and Chapters 3 and 4 describe how Christians should reveal this wonderful Christ through their lives on earth. The first part tells us what Christ has done for us, and the second part tells us how Christians should live on this earth.

In 1:3-8, Paul confesses his thankfulness to God for his brothers in Colossae. He gives particular thanks for their faith in Jesus Christ, their love for all the saints, and their hope in heaven. He gives thanksgiving to God, the Father of our Lord Jesus Christ, for the church's faith, hope, and love.

Verses 9-12 contain Paul's prayer for the Colossae Church. This is an exemplary prayer that can serve as a model for how we pray for others. The prayer consists of five petitions.

1. "We ask that they be filled with the knowledge of His will in all spiritual wisdom and understanding." - We pray so that our brothers may come to know God's will.
2. "We ask that they walk in a manner worthy of the Lord fully pleasing to Him." - We pray for them to lead a life that pleases God.
3. "We ask that they bear fruit in every good work." - We pray that they work hard for what is good.
4. "We ask that they increase in the knowledge of God." - We pray that they will come to know Him.
5. "We ask that they are strengthened with all power, according to his glorious might, for all endurance and

patience with joy." - We pray that they will endure through any circumstance and live in joy.

In verses 13 and 14, we read about the mighty redemption of Christ. "He has delivered us from the domain of darkness and transferred us to the kingdom of his beloved Son, in whom we have redemption, the forgiveness of sins."

In verses 15-18, Paul explains who Jesus is using eight descriptions.

1. Jesus Christ is the image of the invisible God.
2. Jesus Christ is the firstborn of all creation.
3. Jesus Christ is the Creator. All things were created by Jesus Christ, through Him, and for Him.
4. Jesus Christ is before all things, and in Him all things hold together. He was even before eternity. All things maintain their existence through him. He upholds the universe by the word of his power (Heb. 1:3).
5. Jesus Christ is the head of the body, the church.
6. Jesus Christ is the source of everything.
7. Jesus Christ the firstborn from the dead. He is the firstfruits of the resurrection (1 Cor. 15:20).
8. Jesus Christ is the chief of all things. He has all power whether on earth or in heaven, and surpasses all angels.

With a sound understanding of these eight aspects, we can strengthen our faith and nothing can cause our faith to falter.

Verses 19-23 tell us what God has done through Jesus Christ. God has allowed all fullness to dwell in Jesus Christ and through Him reconciled Himself to all things. God has made peace with the blood of Jesus' cross, reconciling all things whether on earth or in heaven in Christ. And us, who once were alienated and enemies of Christ, He has now reconciled in His body of flesh by His death on the cross. God has presented us holy and blameless and above reproach before Him through Jesus Christ. Paul goes on to confess that he became a minister of the Gospel in order to preach this wonderful Gospel of salvation to all creation under heaven.

Chapter 2 tells us how we should live. In this chapter, Paul tells us to live in Jesus Christ, to be rooted and established in him, to strengthen our faith, and to live a life full of gratitude. Jesus Christ makes it possible for us to live such a life.

Christ, the source and foundation of our lives, is the mystery of God. Hidden in Him are all the treasures of wisdom and knowledge. In him, dwells all the fullness of divinity. He has allowed us, who are knit together in Him, to reach fullness. God has removed the three obstacles of sin, the Law, and the power of darkness to allow us to live such a life. He forgave our sins by the cross of Christ, settled the Law on the cross, and with the cross, rendered the enemy completely powerless and triumphed over it.

Chapters 3-4 tell us not to think about the things of this earth, but to instead think of the things of heaven and to change our way of thinking so that we think, speak, and act as the people of God's Kingdom.

The Importance of Our Way of Thinking

The books of Romans, Ephesians, Philippians, and

Colossians particularly emphasize the importance of changing our way of thinking. These books then list the characteristics of the old and the new. The characteristics of the old self are sexual immorality, impurity, passion, evil desire, and covetousness, anger, wrath, malice, slander, and obscene talk from our mouths. The characteristics of the new self are compassionate hearts, kindness, humility, meekness, patience, tolerance, forgiveness, and love. Ephesians tells us to put off our old selves and put on our new selves (Eph. 4:22-24); Romans tell us to be transformed (Rom. 12:2); and Colossians tells us to put to death the old self and his ways and put on the new self (Col. 3:5-14).

But how do we live such a life? What is the key to changing our lives? We are mostly interested in living a changed life and where that change needs to begin. The above Scriptures consistently tell us that such change occurs when we transform our way of thinking. They tell us that once our thinking becomes new, so does everything else with it.

Romans tells us, "renew your mind." Ephesians tells us, "renew the spirit of your mind." And Colossians tells us, "renew the thoughts of your mind." All these verses, although expressed differently, contain the same meaning. In short, they tell us to renew our way of thinking.

Philippians 4:8 lists the 8 thoughts that should be on our minds: "Finally, brothers, whatever is true, whatever is honorable, whatever is just, whatever is pure, whatever is lovely, whatever is commendable, if there is any excellence, if there is anything worthy of praise, think about these things."

Paul tells us to filter our thoughts so that no other thoughts than those in these eight areas may enter our minds. As in Ralph Waldo Emerson's famous quote, "Sow a thought, reap an action; sow an action, reap a habit; sow a habit, reap a character," our lives begin in our thoughts.

Furthermore, Paul always emphasizes the relationship between Christians because this was an area in which he personally experienced the power of the Gospel. He speaks of the relationships between husband and wife, parent and child, and bondservant and master (3:18-4:1). "Whatever you do, work heartily, as for the Lord and not for men" (3:23). This is coram Deo, meaning in the presence of God, and is the principle by which we must live. Paul also talks about the importance of prayer in 4:2, "Continue steadfastly in prayer, being watchful in it with thanksgiving." Prayer is the lifeline that connects us to the power of God that enables us to live such a life.

Paul sent this epistle to the brothers in Colossae in the care of Tychicus while in prison in Rome.

Outline

Chapters 1-2	The absolute priority of Christ Christ's works for us
Chapter 1:1-14	Thanksgiving and prayer
Chapters 1:15-2:3	The preeminence of Christ
Chapter 2:4-23	The freedom that is in Christ Warnings against false teachings outside the Gospel
Chapters 3-4	Obedience to Christ Revealing Christ through us
Chapter 3:1-4	The place of the Christian
Chapters 3:5- 4:6	The practice of Christianity
Chapter 4:7-18	Greetings

Voice Outline

COLOSSIANS

100-Day Bible Reading Plan

		CHECK
Day 96	Philippians, Colossians, 1 Thessalonians, 2 Thessalonians	☐

1 THESSALONIANS

THE SECOND COMING OF CHRIST

First and Second Thessalonians deal with the Second Coming of Jesus Christ. They outline how we must live until Jesus' return and how His return will take place. These books were written in the form of two letters, the second of which was sent within weeks of the first letter.

Thessalonica

Thessalonica, the destination of the letters, was an important location both geographically and strategically. This region, which includes Philippi, Thessalonica, and Berea, is called "Macedonia," the home town of Alexander the Great.

Thessalonica is located in a strategic location with Istanbul, the gateway to Asia on one side, and Rome on the other. Rome and Istanbul were cities considered capitals of the world at the time. Hence, Thessalonica played an important role in the spread of the Gospel. Of course, it also was a culturally rich and economically prosperous city.

During his second missionary journey, Paul and his

missions team changed their plans to go to Asia and went to Europe after hearing the vision of a Macedonian man. When they arrived in Philippi, the gateway city of Macedonia, they started their ministry. Later, they moved on to Thessalonica to preach the Gospel.

When great many of the devout Greeks and not a few of the leading women accepted the Gospel, the Jews in the city grew jealous and formed a mob, setting the city in an uproar. In the city of Thessalonica, Paul and his missions team were known as "men who have turned the world upside down" (Acts 17:1-9).

Solid Faith and Misunderstanding of the Second Coming

Paul and Silas make their way to Berea to escape the uproar. Even there, many Greeks and noble ladies accepted the Gospel, but Jews from Thessalonica followed them and caused yet another uproar.

At this time, Paul leaves Silas and Timothy there so that they may continue their work and goes to the Achaia region alone. Silas and Timothy, who were ministering in Macedonia, come and join Paul after he begins his ministry down in Corinth after ministering in Athens. When they meet, Silas and Timothy deliver both good and bad news about the church in Thessalonia.

The good news was that their faith had grown stronger. Paul writes, "You became an example to all the believers in Macedonia and in Achaia... Your faith in God has gone forth everywhere" (1:7-8), and "We have been comforted about you through your faith" (3:7). Paul is greatly comforted seeing the Thessalonian Church's faith, love, and hope, even in the midst of many tribulations.

On the other hand, the bad news was that there was some confusion in the church due to a misunderstanding about the Second Coming of Jesus Christ. Paul sends two short letters to help them gain a proper understanding of the Second Coming.

Paul speaks of the Second Coming from two different angles. First, he talks about those uninformed about what the Second Coming is and subsequently live on without working or a purpose. Some Christians at the time refused to work because they believed that Jesus was coming soon and therefore they didn't need to plan for the future or work hard. Paul explains the importance of labor and planning by telling them sternly not to eat unless they have worked for it.

We must live on earth as if Jesus will return tomorrow. Every day, we must be vigilant, alert, and awake for His return. But when it comes to the work of the Lord that is entrusted to us, we must carefully plan and execute for the long-term, as if Jesus will come after 500 years. We must make a detailed plan and work diligently to do what has been entrusted to us without bringing things to a rush.

Another misconception about the Second Coming had to do with "what was to happen to those who die before Jesus' Second Coming." The Bible tells us that those who believe in Jesus and die will equally partake in the glory of the Second

Coming of Jesus. They will be raised from the dead and will be caught up together with those who are still alive in the clouds to meet the Lord in the air.

Therefore, Paul tells us not to be saddened like those who do not have the hope of Jesus' Second Coming and Resurrection, but to instead remember the Second Coming of Jesus every day and to comfort and encourage each other with this hope.

Similarities and Differences

First and Second Thessalonians share many things in common, but also have some big differences. An example of this is the first chapter of the two letters. First Thessalonians 1 speaks of the three elements that comprise the Christian life: the work of faith, the work of love, and patience of hope. And although 2 Thessalonians 1 also speaks about faith and love, the chapter speaks of them in terms of them being the indicators of a Church. Second Thessalonians tells us that the church must grow in faith, abound in love, and grow stronger in patience to overcome any persecution and affliction. In summary, 1 Thessalonians shows us the need for faith, hope, and love in our personal lives, and 2 Thessalonians points out the need for faith, hope, and love in the church community.

Moreover, the first epistle describes what a leader and shepherd is. Leaders must live a life that is pleasing only to God, that is not driven by money, and be a caretaker and father to other Christians. The life of a leader should both be marked by the gentleness of a nursing mother taking care of her children, and by the guidance, comfort, and discipline a father would provide for his children. Paul emphasizes the shepherd's duty to approach believers with love and care to help them with joy, and to serve them through prayer and encouragement.

The second epistle specifically refers to the rise of the man of lawlessness before the Second Coming. Paul tells us that there is an evil force on this earth, but that God will rule over all this and that ultimately Christians will be victorious and meet Jesus when He returns. That is why he tells us to be patient in our lives here and to turn away from lawlessness and instead to a lawful life of faith.

***Seven Characteristics of the Life of a True Minister* (2:1-12)**

1. A true minister must set an example (2:10-12). This is the most basic characteristic of a minister. Jesus set an example (Acts 1:1), as did Ezra (Ezra 7:10). To set an example means to walk in a way that is worthy of God. Paul boldly states that God and the church in Thessalonica are witnesses that he has led by example.
2. A true minister must be recognized by God (2:4). We must constantly be tested and confirmed to be acknowledged by God. This is not a one-time test that God conducts, but is a process that must be repeated time and time again. Only after we have undergone these tests, God will freely entrust His work.
3. A true minister does not give up or make excuses to serve the Lord faithfully with a steadfast heart even amid

difficult conditions and circumstances (2:2).

4. A true minister does not work for financial gain but is only motivated to do what is pleasing to God (2:3-5). We must know how to properly handle our finances and be blameless with money. Paul, for example, worked day and night so as not to be a financial burden to anyone (2:9).
5. A true leader does not claim authority, but rather refrains from exercising his power (2:7). Peter said, "Do not domineer over those in your charge" (1 Pet. 5:3).
6. A true leader treats his brothers with the heart of a mother raising her children (2:7-8). A true leader must live a gentle life and not be afraid to sacrifice their life for the sake of their children. "A gentle life" means to be affectionate, kind, and meek.
7. A true leader treats their brothers like a father with his children (2:11-12). The father reprimands, comforts, and sometimes sternly charges his children to walk in a manner that is worthy of God.

A Guide for the Christian Waiting on the Second Coming (5:12-22)

- With love, respect those who labor among you and are over you in the Lord and admonish you.
- Be at peace among yourselves.
- Admonish the idle and warn the disorderly or undisciplined.
- Encourage the fainthearted - this refers to the spiritually immature (Rom. 14:1-15:13; 1 Cor. 8:10).

- Help the weak - this refers to those who are weak in body and mind (Rom. 14:1-15:13).
- Be patient with them all.
- Overcome evil with good.
- Rejoice always.
- Pray without ceasing.
- Give thanks in all circumstances.
- Do not quench the Spirit.
- Do not despise prophecies.
- Test everything and hold fast what is good - This refers to testing for what is good in all things, holding firmly to things that have been verified, and possessing it as our own.
- Abstain from every form of evil - Do not go near, do not imitate, and shun evil.

Outline

Chapters 1-3	Paul's past and present Problems in the church in Thessalonica
Chapter 1	Thanksgiving for their faith
Chapter 2	The apostle's ministry
Chapter 3:1-10	Timothy's report on the faith of the brothers in Thessalonica
Chapter 3:11-13	Benediction
Chapters 4-5	Real problems in the church in Thessalonica
Chapter 4:1-12	The life of the Christian waiting on Jesus' return
Chapter 4:13-18	The rapture
Chapter 5:1-11	The Second Coming of Christ
Chapter 5:12-27	Final instructions and greetings
Chapter 5:28	Benediction

Voice Outline

1 AND 2 THESSALONIANS

100-Day Bible Reading Plan

		CHECK
Day 96	Philippians, Colossians, 1 Thessalonians, 2 Thessalonians	☐

2 THESSALONIANS

THE DAY OF THE LORD

Second Thessalonians was sent to the Thessalonians shortly after the first epistle. Paul wrote things not mentioned in his first letter to address some misunderstandings about the Second Coming. He also comforted Christians in their distress and outlined the duties of a Christian. In particular, he tried to instruct and correct Christians who were using the Lord's Second Coming as an excuse not to work hard and live in disorder.

There was a need to teach about "the coming of the Lord Jesus Christ" (2:1) and "the day of the Lord" (2:2). In his first epistle, Paul addressed the concern that those who died before the Second Coming might be missing at the Second Coming of the Lord. In his second epistle, Paul addresses the concerns that the Thessalonians had about the great tribulation and affliction that would come before the Lord's Second Coming. They also knew and were concerned that their present afflictions at the time were only just the beginning. Paul comforts the believers in Thessalonica. He lets them know that the Lord will repay with affliction those who afflict, and grant relief to those who are afflicted (1:3-10).

Paul tells them that the faithful Lord will strengthen their hearts, and that with the love of God and the steadfastness of Christ in their hearts, they will be able to endure and overcome any affliction, and that the Lord Himself will guard them from the evil one (3:3,5).

In Chapter 2, Paul tells believers not to be quickly shaken in mind or alarmed by what others have to say about the day of the Lord's Second Coming. We must not be deceived by words or writings other than those given to us through the Bible.

Paul then goes on to explain some events that will occur before the Lord's return. First, the great rebellion (the Apostasy) will come. Then, the Antichrist will appear. He will oppose everything that people serve and worship. And he will try to exalt himself and try to take his seat in the temple of God. And by the activity of Satan, he will perform false miracles, false signs, and wonders. He will try to draw people in with wicked deception.

But Paul tells the church not to be anxious or worry because the Lord loves us and He will strengthen those who believe with the Holy Spirit and the Word of truth. The God of comfort will provide even greater strength to the words and all good works of those who believe in Him. The Lord is faithful and He will establish us and guard us against the evil one (3:3).

In 3:6-15, Paul instructs the Church to work hard and not to be idle as believers in the Second Coming of Christ.

He says, "Do not take food for free from anyone. In other words, do not eat for free but earn it by working hard day and night. If anyone is not willing to work, let him not eat. Work quietly and earn what you need to eat yourself. Do not associate with those who lack self-control or busybodies that do not actually work. Nevertheless, do not treat them as your enemies but instruct them. I hope you imitate the example that we have set for you."

Paul's Prayer

At the end of each of the three short chapters of 2 Thessalonians, Paul concludes with a gracious prayer for them. "To this end we always pray for you, that our God may make you worthy of his calling and may fulfill every resolve for good and every work of faith by his power, so that the name of our Lord Jesus may be glorified in you, and you in him, according to the grace of our God and the Lord Jesus Christ" (1:11-12).

God will consider us worthy of His calling. Our faith in God will enable us to experience His power and He will allow us to fulfill His good will. Then, Jesus's name will be glorified further through us. And in turn, we will also seize that glory in Christ; we will be glorified in Christ. Paul prays, "Now may our Lord Jesus Christ himself, and God our Father, who loved us and gave us eternal comfort and good hope through grace, comfort your hearts and establish them in every good work and word" (2:16-17).

Our Heavenly Father loves us, gives us hope, and brings

comfort to our hearts. He will empower us in all that we say and all the good works that we do so we may do His work. Paul closes his letter with this beautiful benediction. "Now may the Lord of peace himself give you peace at all times in every way. The Lord be with you all" (3:16). Our Lord is the Lord of peace that transcends all circumstances. The Lord is with us and gives us such peace every moment in all that we do.

The Apostle Paul not only prays for his brothers in Thessalonica, but he also makes prayer requests to them. "The word of the Lord may speed ahead and be honored, as happened among you, and that we may be delivered from wicked and evil men" (3:1-2). Paul requested prayer not only from Thessalonica, but also from the Corinthians and Ephesians, the Philippians and Colossians, as well as the Roman Church (Rom. 15:30-32; 2 Cor. 1:11; Eph. 6:19; Phil. 1:19, Col. 4:3-4). It is a beautiful thing to ask for prayer. It is humble and biblical. Paul understood the power of intercession.

Outline

Chapter 1	Encouraging Brothers in Suffering
Chapter 2	Admonition on the day of the Lord
Chapter 3	Counsel for Christians Awaiting the Second Coming

Voice Outline

1 AND 2 THESSALONIANS

100-Day Bible Reading Plan

		CHECK
Day 96	Philippians, Colossians, 1 Thessalonians, 2 Thessalonians	

1 TIMOTHY

THE SECRET TO GODLINESS

First Timothy, Second Timothy, Titus, and Philemon are structured slightly differently from the rest of Paul's epistles. While the other Pauline epistles are public in nature, these four epistles were addressed to individuals. As a result, these epistles contain a personal feel and sentiment. But the content itself transcends the personal. They contain words on how the Church, the House of God, should conduct itself. That is why the books of 1 and 2 Timothy and Titus are referred to as "the Pastoral Epistles."

The Times During Which the Pastoral Epistle was Written

The Book of Acts ends with Paul, who had been under house arrest, with relative freedom, preaching the Gospel unhindered in Rome for two years (Acts 28:30-31). There is no mention of how his arrest ended, whether he was released, convicted, or executed. It is the general consensus that he was eventually convicted and died as a martyr, but there are differing views on what may have happened. Most agree that

Paul was released two years later, freely preached the Gospel in Rome for two or three years, then was captured again and martyred in A.D. 67.

Because these pastoral epistles were likely written near the end of Paul's life, the geographical names mentioned in the Pastoral Epistles do not match the dates recorded in Acts or the other Pauline Epistles, as can be seen from "As I urged you when I was going to Macedonia, remain at Ephesus" (1:3). During his third missionary journey, Paul did not leave Timothy when he left Ephesus for Macedonia, but went together with his team. He later visited Ephesus again, which is most likely when Timothy was no longer with him.

As we can see in this verse "When you come, bring the cloak that I left with Carpus at Troas," Paul visited Troas and Miletus (2 Tim. 4:13). When Trophimus got ill in Miletus, he left him there (2 Tim. 4:20). He also parted ways with Titus after their visit to Crete (Titus 1:5). We can see Paul's route through Troas, Miletus, and Crete is different from the route that Paul took on his second and third missionary journeys.

We can also see that Paul expected to be released from house arrest from the other epistles he wrote while imprisoned in Rome. "And I trust in the Lord that shortly I myself will come also" (Phil. 2:24). Also, in the letter that he wrote to Philemon for Onesimus, Paul says, "At the same time, prepare a guest room for me, for I am hoping that through your prayers I will be graciously given to you" (Phlm. 1:22). He was clearly expecting his release.

The original plan of the Apostle Paul was to stop in Rome

then and go to Spain. Paul's plan is recorded in the Book of Romans, which was written before he was captured in Jerusalem during the third missionary journey (Rom. 15:23,28). We are left to wonder if Paul's plans ever came to realization.

Clement of Rome says in a letter sent from Rome dated A.D. 90 to the Corinthian church that, "Paul went to the farthest bounds of the West before martyrdom." Here, "the farthest bounds of the West" refers to Spain. The historian Josephus writes that Paul spent two years as a prisoner in Rome, was released, went on a missionary journey, and was caught and martyred when he returned to Rome. John Chrysostom, the great Church father from the 5th century, says, "Paul went from Rome to Spain," and Jerome, a Church father from the same period, also mentions that "Paul was released by Nero and preached the gospel in the West."

Putting all these together, it seems that Paul's Prison Epistles were written while he was imprisoned in Rome for the first time, and his Pastoral Epistles were written during his second arrest before the end of his life.

"For I am already being poured out as a drink offering, and the time of my departure has come. I have fought the good fight, I have finished the race, I have kept the faith" (2 Tim. 4:6-7).

First Timothy: A Pastoral Handbook

In his first epistle to Timothy, who is both Paul's spiritual son and a minister, Paul tells Timothy about the order of the Church and tells him how to be a leader of the Church community. In his second epistle to Timothy, Paul teaches Timothy how to take care of sheep and the Church as a shepherd. His letter mainly deals with the criteria and standards for selecting leaders in the Church and the Church organization. The criteria and standards for Church leadership are only found in the Pastoral Epistles. At that time, the organization of the church consisted of three structures: elders, overseers, and deacons. But the peculiar thing is that the treatment of widows is laid out in such detail that the care of widows almost becomes an institution of its own.

The purpose of 1 and 2 Timothy is to explain how a minister should conduct themselves in the House of God, how to protect the Church from heresy, and how to deal with problems that may arise within a growing church. First Timothy deals with the subject of pastoral rules about the church order, and Second Timothy deals with the pastor's duty to bring up his congregation. As such, the Pastoral Epistles are like a "pastoral handbook" or "leadership manual" for spiritual leaders who serve the Church.

Sound Doctrine within the Church

In 1:5, Paul tells us that a leader must have love that stems from a pure heart, a good conscience, and sincere faith.

Verses 3-7 explain the difference between the Christian spirit and heresy.

- Heresy is indifferent to the truth and is interested only in new and novel things. Christianity emphasizes faith that is based on the Word of God.

- Heresy promotes speculations rather than stewardship. In Christianity, love is the motive. Love is what keeps us from destructive thought and speech.
- Heresy does not learn, it only tries to teach and belittles others. It is rooted in pride. But Christianity is rooted in humility, a pure heart, and a good conscience.
- Heresy falls into doctrinarism and legalism. The Christian faith gives us a sincere desire to know the truth without hypocrisy and gives us faith without deceit.

In Verses 8-11 Paul speaks on the seriousness of sin. Sin is like a cancerous cell, breaking not only God's Law and heart, but also our relationships. We must be driven by God's love, not God's Law. God's love is the law that guides our actions.

In Verses 12-17, Paul reveals his B.C. and A.D. Paul introduces himself as having been a blasphemer, persecutor, insolent opponent, and the foremost among sinners before he met Jesus. He confesses that it is entirely God's grace that Jesus has appointed him to His service of preaching and the Gospel and serving the Church.

Paul always remembered his life before he believed in Jesus. He did this because it was the surest way to keep him from becoming prideful. Also, it was a way for Paul to keep the grateful mind for God's calling and the grace that allowed him to serve the Lord. Moreover, reminding himself of his past helped him keep striving and also encouraged those who listened. Reminding ourselves of our B.C. and A.D. also leads us to gratitude and dedication.

In particular, Verse 12 contains a principle that should be deeply engraved in the hearts of everyone who wishes to serve the Lord. As a minister, Paul says three things about himself. First, Jesus Christ appointed him to his office as pastor; his office did not come from man. Second, the only criterion that Jesus judged before giving Paul his office was faithfulness. The word "judge" here means that Jesus, like a bookkeeper, first evaluates our lives as a whole then tests us in various areas before reaching the final judgment as to whether we are faithful. Third, it is Jesus Christ who gives Paul the power to fulfill the duties of his office.

When Jesus appoints a person to an office, it is not because of that specific individual's ability, education, or appearance. Faithfulness is His only criterion. It is written in 1 Corinthians 4:2, "It is required in stewards, that a man be found faithful." Faithfulness is the area in which we must perform. It is not our place to worry about what position we will be appointed to or whether we have the ability to perform. Doing our best in any circumstance is faithfulness.

In verses 18-20, Paul likens the life of a Christian to a battling soldier enlisted in a holy army. We are called to fight the good fight. Our weapon is faith and good conscience. Hymenaeus and Alexander, who rejected this, set an example as to what we need to avoid.

Public Worship in the Church

First Timothy 2:1-7 teaches us about prayer. In particular, Paul emphasizes the importance of intercession. Interceding with prayer is the single best way for a Christian to influence the world, and it is an act that pleases God. The Lord wants us to influence not just one individual, but cities, regions, nations, and people in high offices. Intercession is the best tool for us to exert this kind of influence.

Verses 8-15 tell us that there are barriers to prayer which must be removed. We must not hold anger or doubt in our hearts. This means that we must first set our relationships straight then pray with the faith that God will answer. Paul also talks about the role of women in the Church and describes what Christ-like behavior looks like. However, rather than looking at each sentence in a literal sense, we need to understand these verses taking into account the Jewish and Greek influences on the culture at the time. Considering these verses only under the context of our understanding of Jewish culture could cause us to misinterpret their meaning because of the high regard in which women were held in Jewish culture compared to other cultures.

Nevertheless, women were in a disadvantaged position in public matters. Men went to the synagogue to learn whereas women were only allowed to listen. Women were not allowed to read the Law or teach it publicly. Greek women were confined to their homes. Meanwhile, expensive garments and long braided hair were popular among Greek women.

These verses were written as the Church's provisional rules for responding to these immediate problems as Christians. Therefore, when trying to understand this passage, we need to keep in mind the context in which the verses were written. "There is neither Jew nor Greek, there is neither slave nor free, there is no male and female, for you are all one in Christ Jesus" (Gal. 3:28). As we already discussed previously, the Gospel of Luke gives a special place to the position and ministries of women. Priscilla, along with her husband, Aquila, was a competent teacher and minister in the Early Church. Romans 16 also lists the names of women who did amazing work in the Church.

A Good Shepherd

Chapter 3 lists in detail the qualifications of overseers and deacons who hold an office in the Church (3:2-13). In Chapter 4, Paul writes that good servants of Christ must train for godliness in order to reach godliness. In particular, Paul tells these people that they must set an example through their words and actions, their love and faith, and be pure and blameless. As such, Chapters 3 and 4 are the leadership manuals given to today's church.

First Timothy 5:1-6:2 contains instructions for the Church in its attitude toward members of the Church, including old men, old women, widows, young men, elders, bondservants, and masters.

First Timothy 6:3-21 tells us how Christians should conduct themselves in the world. In particular, it gives detailed instructions on how to use money correctly. Verses 6-10 and 17-19 are guidelines on the correct use of money.

- Be self-sufficient.

- Do not be haughty.
- The love of money is the root of all evil.
- Do not be proud, but be humble. Do not claim to have gained your riches on your own.
- Do not place hope in wealth, but hope only in God.
- Do good, be rich in good works, love to share, and be generous and ready to share.

Outline

Chapter 1	Sound doctrine within the Church
Chapter 2	Public worship in the Church
Chapter 3	Servants of the Church
Chapters 4-5	A good shepherd within the Church
Chapter 6	Final Instructions

Voice Outline

1 AND 2 TIMOTHY

100-Day Bible Reading Plan

		CHECK
Day 97	1 Timothy, 2 Timothy, Titus, Philemon	☐

2 TIMOTHY

SUFFER WITH THE GOSPEL

As he sat in Roman prison, Paul knew that his time was nearing the end. This is his last letter. Naturally, it carries a slightly different tone compared to the first epistle. While his first letter to Timothy was about Timothy's office as a minister, the second book places greater focus on Timothy's personal life. This letter counsels Timothy on how to live as a servant of Christ. Paul's first epistle to Timothy covers the ministry of a minister, and the second epistle deals closely with the personal life of a minister.

Timothy *(1:3-7)*

Timothy is Paul's spiritual son. Paul calls him "my beloved son." He encourages Timothy. Timothy came from a family with a long spiritual tradition: he inherited his sincere faith from his grandmother Lois and his mother Eunice. Furthermore, he was entrusted with a ministry by Jesus and was endowed with the gifts of the Holy Spirit.

Paul reminds him of four qualities that are attributed to a Christian. The first of these is "boldness." God has not given us a heart to fear. Instead, He has provided us with the courage to be bold in any situation. The second is "power." The Lord has given Christians the ability to endure any hardship. The third is "love." This is a love that accepts and embraces all people. Fourth is "self-control." It is the power to control ourselves in any given situation. We must have self-discipline.

The Power of the Gospel (1:8-14)

Paul boasted of the Gospel. He boasts that it is the power of the Gospel that allows us to endure any hardship. It is also the power of the Gospel that allows us to willingly devote ourselves to the path of service after hearing the amazing Gospel of salvation. It was by receiving the wonderful grace of God that Paul was able to readily respond to Jesus' calling as a messenger of the Gospel, an ambassador of Christ, and a teacher of the Word.

The Gospel reveals only Jesus Christ. The messenger of the Gospel may suffer along with the Gospel. And Paul is not ashamed of suffering. Paul commands Timothy, a servant of the same Gospel, to share in this suffering (2:3; 4:5).

In Chapter 2 Verses 1 and 2, Paul tells us that we should not stop at merely hearing the Word of God, but that we must be the link that connects the Word to obedience, action, and sharing. The torch of heaven must be passed from generation to generation without being extinguished. This wonderful Gospel should be entrusted to those who are faithful and those who know how to multiply it.

In Verses 3-13, Paul speaks of our three identities in Christ. First, we are soldiers of Jesus Christ. Second, we are athletes. And third, we are hard-working farmers. A soldier does not become entangled in civilian pursuits, but makes "sacrifices" to please the one who enlisted him. The athlete trains without engaging in self-indulgence; he obeys the rules of the race, and practices self-control every day to receive the final crown. The farmer constantly labors for fruit and waits patiently until harvest. We must learn to work and wait with patience. We must never be impatient and desire quick results.

Verses 14-26 list the characteristics of the life of a worker approved by God. A minister needs to remind his or her peers about the things which they already know. Paul tells us to stop quarreling and to abandon irreverent babble. Ministers must be careful of things that can harm the ministry. God's Church stands on a firm foundation and cannot be shaken. God uses the prepared. Paul tells us to flee from youthful passions. The pursuit of righteousness, faith, love, and peace is the antidote to youthful lust. Paul tells us to have nothing to do with foolish, ignorant controversies. Controversies benefit no one.

Prepare for the Last Days with the Word

In 3:1-14, Paul speaks of the Last Days and tells us to prepare. The best preparation is to know the Bible. Verses 15-17 tell us the six values of the Bible.

First, the Bible provides the wisdom that leads to salvation.

Secondly, it benefits us in the following four areas:

1) It teaches us. In other words, the Bible gives us the direction we should go.
2) It is a source of reproof. It warns us when we get on the wrong path and returns us to the right path.
3) It tells us what is right. Not only does it warn us and point out our mistakes, it teaches us how to turn from the wrong path to the right path.
4) It educates us in righteousness. It leads us to our destination.

Third, the Bible gives us the power to do all good things. It does not merely tell us to do what is good; it equips us to do good. Therefore, it is of great benefit to us to yearn for the Word and step into the Word each day.

Proclaim the Gospel

In 4:1-5, Paul lists the characteristics of the ministers of Christ. Above all, a minister must have zeal. It is written in Romans 12:11, "Do not be slothful in zeal, be fervent in spirit, and serve the Lord." Zeal in this verse refers to zeal and passion like that of boiling water. "Be ready in season and out of season" in 4:2 refers to persistence. A minister must not fear people but know how to rebuke. A minister must know how to persuade people, give them confidence, and instill courage and hope. A minister must not grow impatient or become distressed, but only act with patience. To do this, we need a resilient spirit that is not easily disappointed.

Paul's confession in 4:7-8 is as below:

"Amen! Come, Lord Jesus, come! I have fought the good fight, I have finished the race, and I have kept the faith. Henceforth there is laid up for me the crown of righteousness, which the Lord, the righteous judge, will award to me on that day, and not only to me but also to all who have loved his appearing."

Verses 17 and 18 contain Paul's words of encouragement for Timothy as Paul concludes his ministry. "But the Lord stood by me and strengthened me, so that through me the message might be fully proclaimed and all the Gentiles might hear it. So I was rescued from the lion's mouth. The Lord will rescue me from every evil deed and bring me safely into his heavenly kingdom. To him be the glory forever and ever. Amen."

Outline

Chapter 1	The power of the Gospel The responsibilities of a spiritual leader
Chapter 2	Characteristics of a faithful minister
Chapter 3	Prepare for the Last Days with the Word
Chapter 4	Proclaim the Gospel

Voice Outline

1 AND 2 TIMOTHY

100-Day Bible Reading Plan

		CHECK
Day 97	1 Timothy, 2 Timothy, Titus, Philemon	☐

TITUS

STRENGTHEN THE CHURCH

Titus is categorized as a Pastoral Epistle along with 1 and 2 Timothy. As Paul writes to Titus with the Holy Spirit, he tells Titus how he should build and strengthen the church. In many ways, this letter has the same character as 1 and 2 Timothy.

Timothy and Titus received their calling to minister through Paul. As peers who partook in Paul's ministry and suffering, they helped to fill in the shortcomings of the Church established by the Apostles so that the Churches could grow strong. Titus was Greek (Gal. 2:3). Paul referred to Titus as a man who shared in his heart and calling for the ministry, calling him, my son (Titus 1:4), my brother (2 Cor. 2:13), and my partner (2 Cor. 8:23). Titus was the person who Paul asked to deliver his epistle to the church in Corinth.

Crete is a large island at the mouth of the Aegean Sea where Paul and Titus sowed the seeds of the Gospel. Paul let Titus continue his ministry there. He wrote his epistle to Titus to support Titus in his ministry.

Handbook for Spiritual Leaders

Paul begins by introducing himself in 1:1-4. He explains the basis of his authority as an apostle as well as the message that he has been mandated to deliver.

In Verses 5-9, Paul talks about the qualifications for elders and overseers. Paul lists three qualifications that an elder must possess: an elder must be above reproach, the husband of one wife, and his children must be believers and not open to charges of debauchery or insubordination.

For overseers, Paul lists as many as thirteen qualifications: an overseer must be above reproach, not be arrogant or quick-tempered or a drunkard or violent or greedy for gain, but hospitable, a lover of good, self-controlled, upright, holy, and disciplined, and must be able to give sound instruction in the Word.

The terms used in the book of Titus for elders and overseers should not be confused with the terms used in the Church today. Today's church uses various terms depending on the denomination.

One thing is clear, however, that no matter what the term is used, all of the elders and overseers mentioned in Titus as qualifications of a leader still remain true today. The Book of Titus is also used as a "leader's handbook" along with 1 and 2 Timothy.

Warning against False Teachers

Titus 1:10-11 lists the characteristics of false Cretan teachers. They are undisciplined, like disloyal soldiers. They do not recognize the leadership of the church and speak nonsense. It is written in Colossians 4:6, "Let your speech always be gracious, seasoned with salt."

They are a deceitful people. They do not lead to the truth but instead cause people to turn away from the truth. They seek only their own gain and are more concerned with money than the souls of men.

Verses 12-16 record the Cretans' bad reputation. At the time, the Cretans had quite a reputation in society. They were known as "liars, evil beasts, and lazy gluttons." When Paul writes to Titus, he does not say, "They are detestable. There is no hope for them. Just let them be." Rather, he writes to Titus, "Go and preach the Gospel to these people." As written in 3:4-7, God loves even the Cretans and wants to show them grace. The Holy Spirit transforms and gives them new life.

The Character of a Christian

In Chapter 2, Paul discusses how to lead members of the Church, separating them into six demographic groups. It serves as guidelines for the character of a Christian.

First, Paul addresses older men. They are to be sober-minded, rejecting indulgence and worldly pleasures. They must lead reverent lives. They must be dignified and act out of sincerity. This means that they practice self-control. They must also be sound in faith, in love, and in patience.

Second, he addresses older women. They must be reverent in behavior, not engage in useless gossip, and not be slanderers or slaves to alcohol. They are to teach what is good and know how to instruct young women in the Church.

Third, Paul addresses young women. They must love their husbands and their children, be self-controlled, pure, work at home, kind, and be submissive to their own husbands.

Fourth, Paul addresses younger men. In their youth, the power of temptation is strong, making it easy for them to go astray. Due to their lack of experience, they can also become excessively confident. Therefore, young men must lead a life of prudence and self-restraint.

Fifth, Paul addresses ministers. Their motives must be absolutely pure. They must maintain dignity befitting the important responsibility of being the "ambassadors of Christ." Also, with sound teaching, they must set an example through the life they live, not the words they speak.

Sixth, Paul addresses bondservants. He speaks about how bondservants in the society of the time should act as believers in Christ. He tells them that there is no other way to testify for Christianity than through the lives that they lead. He tells them to spread the Gospel by putting the love of our Lord Jesus Christ into practice. They must reveal Christ by submitting to their masters, being dedicated to their work, and by being honest, loyal, and faithful. And although today we no longer have the bondservant-master system in society, Paul's words show us how we can be the salt and light of the world.

A Christian's Social Obligations

In Chapter 3, Paul tells all Christians to be faithful as

members of society on this earth. No other book in the Bible other than Titus presents this as a mandate. Christians must obey the law while living on this earth. They must be actively involved with volunteer work and take initiative for every good work. Christians must also be careful not to speak words of slander and judgment.

Christians must be tolerant. We as Christians must know when to let go of our stubbornness and when to give in during an argument. We must be kind, compassionate, and meek in how we treat everyone. We must know how to manage our anger and exercise self-control (3:1-2). Paul's epistle to Titus demonstrates how people from all classes, both inside and outside the church, must conduct their lives as Christians.

There are two facts that breathe momentum into the lives of Christians. The first of these is that we have nothing of which we can be proud from the time before we became Christians. Having this awareness, we are able to be understanding, compassionate, modest, humble, and above all grateful attitude toward society instead of approaching it with a critical, condescending, and condemning attitude.

Second is the fact that we are able to live as the salt and light of this world not because of our own strength or efforts, but purely because of what our Lord Jesus Christ has accomplished. By the cross of Christ and the power of the Holy Spirit, we have been renewed and have been given the power to live anew (3:3-7).

Therefore, we must devote ourselves to doing good work.

Here, “to devote” ourselves means to try to reflect Christ through our lives, like a merchant trying hard to sell his goods.

We must also make sure to avoid foolish controversies. We should try to avoid engaging in debates about theological matters, but instead spend our time with more important matters, such as treating people with love every day and being efficient, diligent, and honest with the work that has been assigned to us (3:8-11). Engaging in endless discussions that do not carry over into action can only be a waste of time and energy.

Christians must devote themselves to doing good work, know how to take responsibility for their lives, and help those in need. A true Christian lives not only for his or herself but lives so that others in need may be helped also (3:14).

Outline

Chapter 1:1-4	Greeting
Chapter 1:5-9	Handbook for spiritual leaders - elders and overseers
Chapter 1:10-16	Warning against false teachers
Chapters 2-3:11	A guideline for six demographic groups in the Church
Chapter 2:1-10	Older men, older women, young women, young men, ministers, and bondservants
Chapter 2:11-15	The foundation upon which a believer's life is built
Chapter 3:1-11	The social obligation of all Christians
Chapter 3:12-15	Final instruction and greetings

Voice Outline

TITUS

100-Day Bible Reading Plan

		CHECK
Day 97	1 Timothy, 2 Timothy, Titus, Philemon	☐

PHILEMON

A PLEA OF LOVE

Philemon is the shortest epistle among Paul's Prison Epistles which include Ephesians, Philippians, and Colossians. Given its date and the nature of the letter, it might seem more appropriate that the book is placed after the Book of Colossians in the New Testament. However because it is a privately written letter like the Pastoral Epistles and unlike the other Prison Epistles that were addressed to the Church, it is placed behind the Book of Titus with the Pastoral Epistles.

A Message of Forgiveness and Love

The Book of Philemon provides a good example of forgiveness and love. It contains the story of the runaway bondservant named Onesimus. Onesimus flees to Rome, inflicting severe financial harm to his master Philemon. That is where Onesimus meets Paul, who warmly accepts the runaway bondservant while he himself is in prison in Rome. Paul nurtures Onesimus as his spiritual son. And as Onesimus continues to grow in faith by Paul, a great change takes place within him and he becomes a Christian. It is not known whether Onesimus himself revealed his past to Paul or if it was Epaphras who visited Paul that told him about Onesimus' past.

But one thing is clear; Onesimus became indispensable to Paul. Paul wanted to keep him by his side, but he would not do so without the permission of Onesimus' master, Philemon. Paul writes in his letter, "I would have been glad to keep him with me, in order that he might serve me" (1:13). But for this to happen, there first had to be reconciliation between Onesimus and Philemon. So Paul sent Onesimus back to his master. In those days, the master had absolute power over his bondservant, including control over whether his bondservant was to live or die. When runaway bondservants were caught, they would be branded with the letter "F" on their forehead. The "F" stood for the Greek word fugitivus, meaning fugitive.

A Plea of Love

Paul outlines a path for Onesimus to reconcile with his master Philemon. He writes to Philemon asking him to forgive Onesimus and tells Onesimus to deliver the letter directly. Paul did this because he wanted Onesimus to meet Philemon and ask for forgiveness in person.

Paul writes, "For love's sake I prefer to appeal to you. Please forgive Onesimus." What is stunning about this is that Paul did not assert his position as a leader and unilaterally demand that Philemon free Onesimus, but appealed to him instead with love.

Paul is very humble as he makes his request; he writes, "I, Paul, an old man, appeal to you, Philemon." He adds, "If he has wronged you at all, or owes you anything, charge that to my account," demonstrating his stunning willingness and love to help his brother in need.

From Bondservant to Brother

Paul asks Philemon further to treat Onesimus "no longer as a bondservant but more than a bondservant, as a beloved brother." Paul shows us that Christians are first and foremost our brothers and sisters with whom we share in Christ's love and that whether they are our employers, employees, bosses, or clerks in the workplace, their position in this world is only secondary. Paul also writes this about Onesimus: "Formerly he was useless to you, but now he is indeed useful to you and to me." Onesimus means useful in Greek. Onesimus, who harmed another before, changed and became a useful man, thus living up to his name.

When we are changed in Christ, we are transformed from a useless person to a useful person who does good and gives love to all people. Onesimus, who began as a bondslave, later became a respected overseer in the church in Ephesus. Ignatius of Antioch, a martyr who wrote to the church in Ephesus while staying in Smyrna, highly praised the overseer of the Ephesus church in his letter. That overseer was Onesimus! This moving story of a fugitive bondservant who inflicted a lot of both financial and mental harm to others, was transformed by the Gospel, and became one of the most famed overseers in the church in his time is a story that should challenge all of our hearts.

This short letter touches our hearts in many ways. It shows us that if we are able to reconcile, forgive, and treat everyone as our brother, we can change and leave our past behind us. This letter moves us to take a step back, look behind us and see that we are very much like Onesimus. By God's grace, he was forgiven of his sins and by grace, he became His child. He was transformed by the Holy Spirit who turned him into a servant of the Lord. The useless one became the useful one. We can also see our own reflection in Philemon because we also find ourselves in the position to forgive those who have greatly wronged us.

We can also see that we are like Paul as well. We, too, are called to care for those who are rejected, bitter, fearful, and in pain and despair with love and bring them to the Lord as His children and servants. That is why we must always accept, forgive, give hope to, and stand with "our own Onesimus" and intercede for him or her.

True Freedom

Although Paul knew how wicked the institution of slavery was at the time, he never mentions it. Nor does he ever criticize the institution of slavery. Paul does not even tell Philemon to free Onesimus in the spirit of Christianity. Paul does not mention slavery because he believed that true freedom will be brought by the Christian faith. He also knew that the times were not yet ready to accept that message.

He knew that inciting people to free slaves would do more harm than good. A change like this cannot take place overnight. It is like yeast in dough: just as it takes time for the yeast to ferment and cause the dough to rise, the world has to wait for change. However, this does not mean that we should not take any action and just sit still; it means that we actively and diligently preach the Gospel so that the spirit of Christ and the spirit of the Kingdom of God may spread into and permeate each realm of society.

If a modern Rahab walks into our church, let us not demand to change the way she dresses, speaks, or lives; instead, let us share the Gospel with her because it is the Gospel that will fundamentally transform her from the inside. This is the kind of active waiting we need to engage in with hope in our hearts. Just as we would add yeast into the flour to make the dough rise when making bread, we must make a difference in society as a whole by living in the spirit of Christianity. Rahab will not only be transformed herself but become a person who influences society, just as the once useless Onesimus, the fugitive bondservant, became a respected church overseer and transformed into a useful Onesimus.

Outline

Chapter 1:1-7	Paul the encourager's prayer of thanks-giving Praises for Philemon
Verses 8-21	Paul the intercessor's heartfelt appeal Plea for Onesimus
Verses 22-25	Paul's promise as a partner Paul's promise to Philemon

Voice Outline

PHILEMON

100-Day Bible Reading Plan

		CHECK
Day 97	1 Timothy, 2 Timothy, Titus, Philemon	

HEBREWS

JESUS WHO IS PREEMINENT

The Book of Hebrews is the "Leviticus of the New Testament." No other book explains the preeminence of Jesus Christ better than this book. This book presents a wonderful and brilliant portrayal of the beautiful humanity and holy divinity of Jesus Christ. The message of this book was addressed to people of Greek and Hebrew backgrounds alike.

The book speaks to the Greeks, "You are seeking reality. Unfortunately, however, you are looking for reality only in the shadows. Reality can only be found in Jesus Christ. Jesus Christ is the reality you are looking for." Similarly, it says to the Hebrews, "You are seeking a perfect sacrifice that will open the way to a God closed off by your sins, but what you are looking for can only be found in Jesus Christ. Only Jesus Christ is the perfect priest and perfect sacrifice that will restore the relationship between God and man."

The Supremacy of Christ

The Book of Hebrews describes the supremacy of Jesus in many ways. Chapter 1 describes a Jesus who is greater than all angels; Chapter 3, a Jesus who is greater than Moses; and Chapter 5, a Jesus who is greater than Aaron.

Hebrews 1:2-3 describes six amazing aspects of Jesus.

1. Jesus is the radiance of the glory of God. He is not a reflector of God's glory, but is God Himself. Looking at Jesus, we can see the essence of God. Jesus is not a partial and fragmentary introduction to God, but is God Himself.
2. Jesus is the King and Master of the coming kingdom.
3. All the works of creation are through Jesus Christ.
4. Everything on the earth is upheld by Jesus Christ and His Word.
5. Jesus is the One who atones.
6. Jesus Christ is in heaven, interceding between God and man for mankind

Consider Jesus

The Book of Hebrews tells us to consider Jesus. The book introduces Jesus as a mighty apostle and the greatest ambassador God has appointed to this world. An ambassador represents the power and authority of the nation that has sent him. His message is the message of the nation that has appointed him. Jesus Christ is the ambassador of the heavens and He Himself is the Word of God.

Jesus is the greatest of all high priests. He lives eternally and will never die. And because He is without sin, He does not need to offer sacrifices for His sins. Jesus offered Himself as the perfect sacrifice so that we no longer need to offer sacrifices for our sins. That is why the Book of Hebrews repeatedly refers to the amazing "Great High Priest."

Jesus understands all our struggles; He is merciful and compassionate toward us; He provides practical help for all our needs. This is why the Book of Hebrews tells us to come before the Lord Jesus and to consider Jesus.

What is the New Testament?

One of the most wonderful messages of the Book of Hebrews is its explanation on "what the New Testament is." It answers the question, "what is the new covenant?" Hebrews 8 repeats the message of the New Testament in Jeremiah 31:31-34 and Ezekiel 36:24-28 once again.

It summarizes the message of the New Testament in three points.

First, "I will put my laws into their minds, and write them on their hearts, and I will be their God, and they shall be my people" (8:10). By writing His Word on our hearts and not on stone tablets, God has given us the strength to act upon and live according to His Word.

Although the old covenant reveals that we are incapable of living according to God's Word, the new covenant empowers us to live according to the Word of God through the Holy Spirit who is within us. "And I will put my Spirit within you, and cause you to walk in my statutes and be careful to obey my rules" (Eze. 36:27).

Second, "They shall all know me, from the least of them to the greatest" (8:11). This states God's call for us to enter into an intimate relationship with Him. In the Old Testament, only the priests were allowed into the sanctuary; into the Most Holy Place where God resided, only the high priest was able to enter once a year. People had to remain at a far distance. However, with the New Testament, anyone, at any time can come before the throne of God and live in close communion with Him because of Jesus Christ's death on the cross.

When Jesus died on the cross, the veil of the temple was torn in two, removing the last obstacle between God and us. Now, everyone can enter into the Holy of Holies where God resides and live in intimacy with God.

Third, "I will be merciful toward their iniquities, and I will remember their sins no more" (8:12). God promises a fundamental solution to sin. If the Old Testament made us face our sins, the New Testament is a promise that our sins have been forgiven, that they will not be remembered again, and that we will be able to stand as righteous before God. This amazing new covenant allows us to truly shine, be holy, have power, and live in fullness on this earth. Jesus Christ is "a much more excellent ministry, a better promise, and a better mediator of the covenant" (8:6).

Spiritual Existence

Chapters 9 and 10 speak of a life that leads us to a wonderful spiritual existence. We compare the tabernacle that Moses built on Mount Sinai with the heavenly tabernacle that guides us in Jesus Christ. The tabernacle of Moses was built by man, but the tabernacle of heaven brings us to Jesus Christ.

When Moses' tabernacle is a model or shadow, the tabernacle of heaven is the real existence and true thing. In the tabernacle of Moses, we needed offerings and sacrifices to step before the Lord, but in the tabernacle of heaven, Jesus took away all our sins once and for all through His death on the cross.

The surprising fact is that when God told Moses to build the tabernacle on Mount Sinai, He showed him the tabernacle of heaven and told him to model the tabernacle after it. The tabernacle of heaven is like a model house that we preview before moving into a new apartment. Moses saw the tabernacle in heaven and built it accordingly. Therefore, Moses' tabernacle is a model and a shadow, and the heavenly tabernacle is the real existence.

Jesus is not the priest of the tabernacle made by man, but the priest of the tabernacle of heaven. He also became the ultimate sacrifice and died in the flesh for us once and for all. As the High Priest, he brings us before the throne of God and takes us from this earth to the Lord who sits on the throne forever. Jesus also enables us to remain in the presence of God, to see His glory, to taste His amazing love, and to be in a wonderful spiritual fellowship with God.

Hebrews 10:19-25 describes a brand new life. It is a life that comes before and stays before the throne of God, a life of fellowship with God; it is a life that goes into the world with hope and lives in strength, a life that serves our brothers and sisters in Christ with love.

Chapter 11 lists the amazing people of faith whose names

are listed in the "Hall of Fame of the Faith." Abel, Enoch, Noah, Abraham, Sarah, Isaac, Jacob, Joseph, Moses, and Rahab the prostitute are introduced as "people the world could not handle."

Chapter 12 introduces a hero of faith far greater than those listed in Chapter 11. It is our Lord Jesus Christ. He is the Perfecter of our Faith. Jesus goes before us as an apostle of faith, and is the role model, Founder, and Pioneer whose footsteps we must follow in and imitate. He is also the One who equips us to be victorious. He encourages, cheers, supports, and stands by us as we run the race set before us.

If the predecessors of our faith have done their part running the race, it is now our turn to continue this race. We must look to them, look to the greatest predecessor of our faith, Jesus, as we run this race with endurance. The principles of faith they have laid out for us act as the handbook as we course through our race of faith.

Hebrews 13:20-21 presents the principles of spiritual life. God reveals His will among us and gives us the passion and strength to live according to His will so that we may fulfill His will in abundance.

Five Counsels, Cautions, and Warnings

The Book of Hebrews offers five things to be wary of as we continue in our journey of faith and serves to encourage, guard, and warn us so that we may win the race of faith.

1. Pay careful attention not to drift away from the Word by neglect (2:1-4).

2. Be united in faith by the Word that you have heard; do not harden your heart in rebellion (3:7-4:13).
3. Do not become sluggish or become dulled to hearing the Word of God (5:11-6:20).
4. Do not despise the Word in stubbornness (10:26-39).
5. Avoid disobedience that comes from refusing to hear the Word (12:14-29).

Outline

Chapters 1-4:13	The beauty of the humanity of the Son of God
Chapter 1:1-4	Jesus who is greater than the prophets
Chapters 1:5-2	Jesus who is greater than the angels
Chapters 3-4:13	Jesus who is greater than Moses
Chapters 4:14-10:18	The preeminent glory of the Son of God as the High Priest
Chapters 4:14-7	Jesus who is greater than Aaron
Chapter 8	Jesus who is a much more excellent ministry, a better promise, and a better mediator of the covenant
Chapters 9-10:18	Jesus who is a greater and more perfect tabernacle, a better offering, the one eternal sacrifice
Chapters 10:19-13	The faithful Christian life which is beautiful
Chapters 10:19-11	The work of faith
Chapter 12	The patience of hope
Chapter 13	The work of love

Voice Outline

HEBREWS

100-Day Bible Reading Plan

		CHECK
Day 98	Hebrews, James	☐

JAMES

FAITH THROUGH ACTION

The Book of James speaks of a faith as evidenced by works. This book is also referred to as the "Proverbs of the New Testament." The Book of James faced many difficulties until and even after it was recognized as part of the canonical Scripture. This struggle continued even after its adoption. In particular, Martin Luther refused to include James in the New Testament because its content seemed to contradict that of the Book of Romans.

The name of Jesus is mentioned twice in the Book of James. And even those instances could be considered to be accidental (1:1; 2:1). There is also no mention of Jesus' resurrection or of Jesus as the Messiah. However, it quotes the Sermon on the Mount, which is Jesus' words, 23 times. Considering the contents of the book, it appears that the person who wrote the Book of James was a person who was well versed in the Old Testament as well as the literature of wisdom.

Authorship

This book was written by James, as stated in 1:1. Five people appear in the Bible with the name of "James."

- James, the father of Judas (not Judas Iscariot) of the twelve disciples of Jesus (Luke 6:16), about who nothing is known.
- Of the twelve disciples, James the son of Alphaeus (Matt. 10:3; Mark 3:18; Luke 6:15; Acts 1:13). "As Jesus passed on from there, he saw a man called Matthew sitting at the tax booth, and he said to him, 'Follow me.' And he rose and followed him." (Matt. 9:9). "And as he passed by, he saw Levi the son of Alphaeus sitting at the tax booth, and he said to him, 'Follow me.' And he rose and followed him" (Mark 2:14). Matthew and Levi are the same person in these verses. Since Levi is also Alphaeo's son, Matthew and James are brothers.
- James the younger (Matt. 27:56; Mark 15:40), about whom nothing is known.
- Of the twelve disciples, James the son of Zebedee and the brother of John (Matt. 10:2; Mark 3:17; Luke 6:14; Acts 1:13) who was the first martyr. He cannot be the author of this book since he was martyred in A.D. 44 by Agrippa I.
- James, the brother of Jesus, was the leader of the Jerusalem Church and the chairman of the Jerusalem Council. He is not one of the twelve apostles, but he, along with Peter and John, are considered pillars of the church in Jerusalem (Gal. 1:19; 2:9). He was famously known as "old camel knees" for the callouses he formed while in constant prayer.

Considering all the options, it was James the brother of Jesus who authored the Book of James. James was one of the first epistles to be written along with the Book of Galatians.

A Test of Faith

The word "trial" appears several times throughout 1:2-15. But in fact, these are three words with distinct meanings.

First, it is the "test" that makes us perfect through hardship and difficulty (1:2-4). This is also the test Abraham received (Gen. 22:1). Tests come from God. These tests strengthen "and enrich us."

Second, it is the "trial" that comes from our faith in Jesus (1:12). It is also called "affliction" or "tribulation." Those who endure these tests are given the crown of life. Though they come from the spirit of darkness, God turns them into good. When we are faced with trials, we must rejoice, welcome, and accept them. After all, we will be rewarded.

Third, it is "temptation" as an attempt to knock us down (1:13-15). Temptations are not from God, and therefore we must not accept temptations. They are of the devil, designed to make us fall. Temptations must be confronted and defeated immediately. Because when we fall into temptation and give birth to sin, it is purely because we have been driven by our own greed.

Verses 16-18 introduce two aspects of God. Every good gift and every perfect gift come from God, and He only gives the best. He is also a God who never changes. "There is no variation or shadow due to change" is a terminology used in astronomy. It is referring to the changing of celestial bodies. The length of day and night and the orbit of the sun are described using these words. All light changes, but God, the creator of light, never changes.

The Reality of Faith

Verses 19-25 tell us to be quick to hear, slow to speak, slow to anger. With two ears and one mouth, we are told to hear twice as much as we speak. It is a truly precious thing to practice listening intently. What should be our greatest worry is that perhaps we listen lackadaisically and rush to speak without even having heard everything.

The speed of speech these days is truly stunning. It is written, "When words are many, transgression is not lacking, but whoever restrains his lips is prudent" (Prov. 10:19), "If one gives an answer before he hears, it is his folly and shame." (Prov. 18:13). The wisdom of being slow to anger, speaking less, and listening more cannot be stressed enough.

The Book of James also speaks about the importance of action (1:22-25). It tells us that after having heard the Word, the Word must be directly reflected in our lives as action. If hearing and speaking have to do with how we relate to people, hearing and doing have to do with how we relate to God. True beauty lies in responding slowly after listening intently and carefully to the words of others, and in quickly doing and obeying after listening intently and carefully to the words of God.

The "religion" in "religion that is pure and undefiled" in

1:26-27 refers to "worship." So, instead of asking "What does it mean to be a religious man?" we should be asking the question, "What is true worship? And what does it mean to be a true worshiper?" True worship is not the carefully planned out performance of magnificent music, and religious dress as a religious ritual, but rather to bridle the tongue in speech, to visit orphans and widows in their affliction, and to keep oneself unstained from the world. This is the characteristic of a true worshiper and a religious person. It is this kind of worship where Christians who live such a life are gathered together to sing praises to Him with which God is pleased.

Chapter 2:1-13 states that "love is the royal law." If the purpose of the Law is to point out what is right and wrong, compassion, including love, is to forgive, tolerate, understand, wait, give, and trust. It is written: "For judgment is without mercy to one who has shown no mercy. Mercy triumphs over judgment" (2:13). This verse shows us just how important it is to show mercy. Compassion includes tolerance, forgiveness, understanding, and love. Compassion does not ignore or neglect justice; it encompasses it and offers a chance with love.

Faith with Works

Verses 14-26 seem to completely contradict the Book of Romans written by Paul. "Faith with works" is the central message of the Book of James. It is written, "You see that faith was active along with his works, and faith was completed by his works" (2:22). However, we are told through the

Book of Romans that we are not saved by works, but only through faith. The Book of James, on the other hand, says, "Show faith by works; faith without works is dead." As such, Romans emphasizes "faith" and James emphasizes "action." We, as Christians, must accept both messages, because the combination of faith and action brings balance to our faith.

Jesus said that whether a tree is a good tree or a bad tree can be known by its fruit. He tells us that because it is a good tree, it produces good fruit. However it is also true that a tree proves that it is a good tree by bearing good fruit. Likewise, if we are saved only by faith, we must produce fruit that is befitting our salvation. That is what is meant by "show faith by doing." Therefore, Romans refers to the "seeds of the Gospel" and James refers to the "fruits of the Gospel."

Belief in Jesus Christ is neither a religion nor ethics, nor is it a theory. Believing in Jesus brings us into the truth of life. It is about a real change in our lives. If we are saved by faith through Jesus, Jesus' amazing power of life works within us so that we bear fruit that transforms our lives.

The Book of James clearly states that if we are saved, we must show our salvation through works. In a balanced faith, "thought" and "action" are consistent, "prayer" and "effort" are accompanied, and "belief" and "action" walk together.

A Wise Tongue

James 3:1-12 demonstrates how important our tongue is. A large ship is guided by the movement of a small rudder, and a big forest fire is set ablaze with one small spark. The tongue, used incorrectly, stains the whole body, setting on fire the entire course of life. As such, though the tongue is small, it has much influence and great power to destroy.

Proverbs tell us the same: "There is one whose rash words are like sword thrusts, but the tongue of the wise brings healing" (Prov. 12:18), "Death and life are in the power of the tongue" (Prov. 18:21). Therefore, we must use our tongue with care, and just as we put bits into the mouths of horses so that they obey us, we must put bits into our own mouths. That is when we can bridle our whole body.

Verses 13-18 speak of wisdom from above. The words, "No human being can tame the tongue" in Verse 8, may cause us to despair. However, this verse offers us a way to control this tongue that cannot be tamed. It is through wisdom from above. Wisdom tames the tongue. Wisdom is the key to taming the tongue, as it is written, "The tongue of the wise brings healing."

There are two kinds of wisdom: earthly wisdom and wisdom from above. Their difference is the difference between false wisdom and true wisdom. False wisdom is worldly, unspiritual, and demonic. It is not all good to have a sharp and brilliant mind. If it divides people, causes strife, and destroys relationships, it is earthly wisdom, and pride is at its root.

But the true wisdom from above is pure, then peaceable, gentle, open to reason, full of mercy and good fruits, and free from prejudice and insincerity. It is always sown in peace and brings a harvest of the fruits of righteousness and builds sound relationships. Such wisdom from above heals, restores, and creates harmony in relationships. The tongue of a person with wisdom from above brings healing and life.

Victory of Faith

James 4:1-10 tells us that our goals in life should not be set on the pleasures of this world, but instead only on obeying and acting in accordance with the will of God. God gives grace to the humble. The secret to receiving answers to prayer is to pray according to God's will and not according to our own will. We receive answers to our prayers when we pray not for our benefit, but when we pray for the glory of God. Friendship with the world is enmity with God. James likens God to a jealous woman and even says that the Holy Spirit jealously yearns for us. Verses 11 and 12 tell us that speaking against and judging a neighbor is a grievous sin.

In 4:13-5:6, we are told that even if a person has acquired wealth by just means, it is a sin for him to use it only for himself. A rich man who has laid up money and lives selfishly but does not pay the wages of his laborers is an evil man. He will not be allowed to properly spend the wealth he has accumulated.

Jeremiah 17:11 says, "Like the partridge that gathers a brood that she did not hatch, so is he who gets riches but not by justice; in the midst of his days they will leave him, and at his end he will be a fool." In the New Revised Standard Version, this verse is translated as, "Like the partridge hatching what it did not lay, so are all who amass wealth unjustly; in midlife it will leave them, and at their end they will prove to be fools."

A truly rich person is a person who uses the wealth that he has accumulated through hard work minimally for himself and mostly to do good to the poor and to use it for the Kingdom of God.

James 5:7-20 tells us that a true Church patiently awaits the Second Coming of the Lord, prays, sings, heals, experiences the power of prayer while walking in the light, and leads lost souls to the Lord.

Outline

Chapter 1:1-18	A test of faith
Chapters 1:19-5:6	The reality of faith
Chapter 1:19-27	Obeying the Word
Chapter 2:1-13	Acting with love
Chapter 2:14-26	Faith of action
Chapter 3	Taming the tongue with wisdom
Chapters 4-5:6	The truly rich
Chapter 5:7-20	Victory of faith

Voice Outline

JAMES

100-Day Bible Reading Plan

		CHECK
Day 98	Hebrews, James	☐

1 PETER

BE HOLY IN ALL YOU DO

The books of 1 and 2 Peter, Hebrews, James, 1 and 2 John, and Jude are called the "General Epistles." Whereas Paul's epistles were usually addressed to a specific church, these General Epistles were not addressed to an individual church but to the Church as a whole. Paul's letters were named after the recipients of his epistles and the General Epistles are named after each of their authors (with the exception of Hebrews).

The Book of 1 Peter is the most famous, read, and beloved of the General Epistles, and is written in eloquent Greek. New Testament scholar F. W. Beare said, "This letter is certainly the work of a writer who has a wealth of rhetoric skills, and is both eloquent and erudite. He was a scribe of extraordinary force and wrote some of the finest Greek prose in the entire New Testament. His sentences were written with greater literary erudition than the highly trained Paul."

However, Peter was not fluent in Greek. Nevertheless, the reason we cannot rule out Peter as its author is the words written in the final greetings of 1 Peter in 5:12: "By Silvanus, a faithful brother as I regard him, I have written briefly to you."

This verse reveals that Silvanus is Peter's ghostwriter. But Silvanus was more than a mere ghostwriter. While the words of 1 Peter belong to Peter, the prose and style in which they are expressed belong to Silvanus.

Peter addressed his epistle "to those who are elect exiles of the Dispersion in Pontus, Galatia, Cappadocia, Asia, and Bithynia" (1:1). All of these regions are large, highly populated areas located in the northeastern part of Asia Minor, mostly inhabited by Gentiles.

The Book of 1 Peter records Peter's loving heart that wishes to encourage and help as a leader, father, and shepherd of the Christians who have endured and may continue to face painful and difficult spiritual wars.

The Christian Faith

The entire Book of 1 Peter is filled with hope for the Second Coming of Jesus Christ. Christians earnestly long for salvation that will be given in the last days. Those who keep the faith will be saved from the coming judgment. Christians will receive great favor when Jesus comes to this earth. They will live forever as they are taken up into the heavens with Jesus upon His return.

The book also contains messages of encouragement for Christians living in the last days.

- The end of everything is near.
- We, who participate in suffering on this earth, will share and rejoice in the great glory to come.
- We must be sober-minded and watchful for judgment

that will soon begin in the household of God.

- Finally, when the chief Shepherd appears, those who believe will receive the unfading crown of glory.

The book tells us how to live given these facts. Christians living in the last days are told to hope for the Lord's return and live a life of the Ten Commandments even amidst suffering. In particular, the Book of 1 Peter repeatedly mentions that the return of the Lord is near and that we must stay sober-minded because it will come at a time when we least expect it. Therefore, we must live as if the return of our Lord is at hand. At the same time, we must make a solid plan to fulfill the Lord's Great Commission.

In 1:1-2, Peter lists the characteristics of Christians.

- They are the elect, specifically chosen by God.
- They are exiles in the world. Though they live on this earth, they are not of the world. They are the light of the world.
- They are in God's foreknowledge.
- They have been chosen to live a holy life. The Holy Spirit helps us to be holy in all areas of our lives. It is the Holy Spirit who gives us the longing for a holy life, and it is also the Holy Spirit who gives us the strength to live a holy life.
- They are a people who obey the Lord Jesus Christ. They have been called to a new relationship with God through Jesus' sacrifice, and they have been chosen to obey and dedicate their lives to Him.

First Peter 1:3-5 summarizes the great Christian thought.

Jesus' death and resurrection are evidence of our rebirth. We are born again by the mercy and Word of God (1:23). In the future, we will inherit a great inheritance. It does not rot, spoil, or decay. While living as exiles in this world, we will be under the protection of His power until we go to the Kingdom of God.

First Peter 1:13-3:22 reveals how we are to live as a holy people in this world. This passage tells us how to live in holiness (1:13-21), with sincere brotherly love (1:22-25), and grow (2:1-10). And it teaches us how to live as exiles (2:11-12), as citizens (2:13-17), as employers (2:18-20), with Christ as our role model (2:21-25), as a wife and husband (3:1-7), and as a people who suffer for righteousness' sake (3:8-22) in this world.

First Peter 4:1-11 sets a contrast between our new lives and our old lives.

Chapter 5 contains special instructions. It is given to spiritual leaders who shepherd a flock (5:1-4), to young people (5:5-7), and to all Christians (5:8-9).

The Ten Commandments of Christians in the Last Days

First Peter is "The Ten Commandments of Christians in the Last Days."

1st Commandment: Girdle up your loins, be sober-minded, and stay awake bend your back, be prosperous and stay awake. Resist the devil by strengthening your faith (1:13; 5:8-9).

2nd Commandment: Live a holy life. Live in this land, but do not belong to it, and be set apart (1:14-16).
3rd Commandment: Be someone who worships the Lord. Live as a worshiper who always goes before the Lord in worship (2:4-10).
4th Commandment: Fulfill your duties as a Christian on this earth (2:13-25; 3:1-7).
5th Commandment: Be zealous in good works (3:11,13-14).
6th Commandment: Preach the Gospel with zeal (3:15-16). Always be prepared to answer the person who asks about the reason for hope.
7th Commandment: Pray with zeal (4:7). In the last days, be sober-minded and pray.
8th Commandment: Love one another passionately (1:22; 4:8). Love your brother with heart, passion, and without deceit.
9th Commandment: Serve one another (4:9-11). Treat one another and serve one another as good stewards of God's grace.
10th Commandment: Rejoice in partaking in suffering (2:18-25; 3:13-17; 4:12-19). We have been called to suffer. Imitate Christ who suffered first.

Outline

Chapters 1-2:10	The Christian's faith - salvation
Chapter 1:1-12	Living hope
Chapter 1:13-25	Holy behavior
Chapter 2:1-10	The holy priest
Chapters 2:11-3	The Christian's behavior - obedience
Chapters 2:11-3:7	Do as the servant of God
Chapter 3:8-22	Suffering for doing good
Chapters 4-5	The Christian's suffering
Chapter 4	The good steward
Chapter 5	Be a role model for the flock

Voice Outline

1 AND 2 PETER

100-Day Bible Reading Plan

		CHECK
Day 99	1 Peter, 2 Peter, 1 John, 2 John, 3 John, Jude	☐

2 PETER

GROW IN GRACE AND KNOWLEDGE

Unlike 1 Peter, 2 Peter is the most overlooked book. This book is also more difficult to read compared to other epistles. This letter is a top-secret document and was written for the victorious Christian amid the persecution by those who threatened the Church. It was used to protect the Christians who were confused by the wicked who denied the Second Coming and perverted the Bible at the time. This book kept them grounded in the truth.

In many ways, 1 Peter is similar to the books of Ephesians and Colossians. On the other hand, 2 Peter is similar to the Book of Jude in many ways. The first epistle deals with present suffering and encourages suffering Christians while the second epistle deals with the judgment at the end and warns false teachers who confuse the Church with their false teachings.

Second Peter is also similar to Second Timothy in some ways. They were both written at the end of the two authors' lives, Peter and Paul. Both also express the authors' deep trust in the Lord. They also comment on the apostasy and tribulation that will come in the "last days."

Peter adorns the beginning of this letter by emphasizing the importance of knowing God and our Lord Jesus, a thought Peter returns to at the end of his letter. When we know God, grace and peace will be multiplied (1:2), we will resemble God's character (1:4), and grow in spirit (3:17-18).

Ladder of Eight Rounds

Second Peter 1:5-7 is characterized by the ladder of virtue: the "Ladder of Eight Rounds."

1. **Faith**[pistis] allows us to have the right relationship with God. Faith comes from listening to the Word of God. The foundation of the ladder begins with knowing God and having the right relationship with Him.
2. **Virtue**[arete] refers to character. When we have the right relationship with God as our foundation, we can build the right relationship with people.
3. **Knowledge**[gnosis] refers to practical knowledge and wisdom that can be applied in our lives. This knowledge helps us to do the right thing in a given environment or situation. It gives us the power to influence the world.
4. **Temperance**[egkrateia] is the ability to control oneself. It is the power to know how to control ourselves without reacting rashly.
5. **Perseverance**[hupomone] refers to being proactive in responding to a given situation. Patience, including courage, is the queen of virtue.
6. **Godliness**[eusebeia] is the power to do our duty to God and

man.

7. **Brotherly Love**[philadelpia] is love for our brothers.

8. **Love**[agape] is love without conditions.

This ladder of virtue begins and grows with knowing Jesus. Our faith becomes stronger from our knowledge of God and Jesus Christ. Knowledge allows us to become intimate with God and become like Him. This will become evident in our relationships with people. And as we continue to grow, we will gain the ability to bring change to the world. Furthermore, we will not only love our brothers but our actions will be led by God's unconditional love. Therefore, we must diligently strive to know God and Jesus Christ. Without the knowledge of God, we will become nearsighted, unable to see very far.

Characteristics of the Word (1:12-21)

The Word reminds us of what we already know. It keeps us in check during times that we forget and reminds us so that we may continue to walk in the truth. Peter wanted Christians to always retain and act on the truth even after his death.

We must deliver a message that is confident and well-founded. Peter could speak with confidence about the Second Coming of Jesus because he was a direct witness. The experience on the Mount of Transfiguration was a preview of the Second Coming of Jesus. As a witness, Peter wanted to inspire confidence in those who had doubts about the Second Coming. This message is not one that simply conveys theoretical knowledge; it is a message that conveys Peter's knowledge gained through personal experience.

Since the author of the Word of God is the Holy Spirit, we must not rely on our own knowledge or understanding when trying to comprehend His Word. On our own, we cannot understand God's Word and it is only when we have the help of the Holy Spirit that we are able to understand (1 Cor. 2: 9-12).

The 12 Traits of False Prophets (*Chapters 2-3*)

1. They distort the Bible and interpret it arbitrarily to suit their agenda (1:20; 3:16).
2. Because of them, the way of truth will be blasphemed (2:2).
3. They are destined to perish just as those listed below. Peter uses three illustrations of sin and ruin.
   - The angels who sinned and were cast into hell until the judgment (2:4).
   - The ungodly upon whom the flood was brought (2:5).
   - The destruction of the ungodly in the cities of Sodom and Gomorrah (2:6).
4. They are governed by irrational instincts (2:12).
5. They are like beasts that are driven by lust (2:10,18).
6. Their eyes are full of sinful adultery (2:14).
7. They are boastful, selfish, and arrogant (2:10,18).
8. They revel even in broad daylight (2:13).
9. They speak of freedom, but because it is indulgence without temperance they are only slaves to lust (2:19).

10. They not only deceive themselves, but also deceive and trick those who are not strong in their faith, leading them to corruption (2:3,14-16). Their wickedness is like that of Balaam in Numbers 22-26. Balaam is a quintessential false and evil prophet who led Israel down a crooked path.
11. They are worse than those who do not know righteousness. They have fallen back into evil (2:20-22).
12. They deny the Second Coming of Jesus (3:3,4).

Be Like God's Servant

Second Peter 3:1-2 shows us that Peter understood the principle of preaching. He knew the value of repetition. To preach is to repeat again and again to help people put teachings into practice. It is like the process by which food is digested in our bodies. Peter also knew about the need to remind people of things. Preaching is not about talking about novel things, but about reminding Christians about what they already know. It is to remind the congregation of God's Word. A sermon is like tracing over what has been erased with an eraser.

Peter believed in the value of praise and encouragement. A sermon encourages believers and praises them for what is already being done. Peter also knew that the Lord Jesus is the essence of the Bible. Jesus Christ is at the heart of every sermon. The Old Testament speaks about the Christ who will come, and the New Testament speaks about the Christ who has already come. The message of the Bible is only Christ.

We also need to have an understanding of the things to come before the Second Coming.

- The man of lawlessness, the son of destruction, will emerge (Matt. 24:15; 2 Thess. 2:1-12; Rev. 13).
- There will be great tribulation (Matt. 24:21,24; Rev. 13).
- The Gospel will be proclaimed throughout the whole world as a testimony to all nations (Matt. 24:14; Mark 13:10; 1 Tim. 2:4,6).

Second Coming

Second Peter 3:5-13 says that while the world was deluged with water and destroyed in the days of Noah, the earth will now be destroyed by fire. Verse 14 is a message for those who have the hope of the Second Coming. "Therefore, beloved, since you are waiting for these, be diligent to be found by him without spot or blemish, and at peace."

Second Peter reiterates that the Lord's Second Coming will surely take place over and over again in case any future generations begin to doubt it or become discouraged.

The reason for the delay in the Second Coming is that God is giving all people an opportunity to be saved and because the Gospel must be preached and the Great Commandment must be fulfilled. Therefore, those who are waiting for the Second Coming are encouraged to live in holiness and make sound plans for the fulfillment of the Great Commission and strive to preach the Gospel.

Many may wonder, "How will so many put on the body of the resurrection at the time of Jesus' Second Coming?" Some say this body will be a restoration of our bodies at their prime in life. However, the Bible says that just as a seed falls to the ground and a beautiful flower blooms, our body is like a seed, and when we are resurrected, we will wear a body of unimaginable glory (1 Cor. 15:35-54; 1 Thess. 4:13-17).

Outline

Chapter 1	The development of a Christian nature - faith
Chapter 2	False prophets - destruction
Chapter 3	Assurance of the Lord's Second Coming - hope

Voice Outline

1 AND 2 PETER

100-Day Bible Reading Plan

		CHECK
Day 99	1 Peter, 2 Peter, 1 John, 2 John, 3 John, Jude	

1 JOHN

THE JOY OF FELLOWSHIP

The Book of 1 John is not written to a specific individual or church, but it is like a message from the headquarters to the entire organization. We could see it as a sermon containing the love a shepherd has for his flock. It is full of deep love and consideration for Christians.

A very peculiar trait of this book is that it does not mention the names of any individuals. In the New Testament, only the Book of Hebrews and the epistles of John do not state the name of the author. Although it is an epistle, this book does not contain the elements of a letter such as the identity of the sender, recipient, or a greeting. This epistle is dated at around A.D. 100, written to second and third-generation Christians that came after the members of Early Church. This epistle was written during a time when the passion for the Lord had dwindled and the Church was struggling with Gnostic teachings pushed by false teachers.

We can consider 1 John to be a powerful dissertation proclaiming, "Jesus Christ is fully man and fully God. Salvation comes only from faith in Jesus Christ." In the book, the word "know" appears 35 times, referencing the assurance of salvation through Jesus Christ.

The book also speaks on the Christian way of life, especially how a Christian should conduct his or her life in three areas: Christians are told to love their brothers, live a life of obedience, and strongly urged to refuse the worldly way of thinking.

The Book of 1 John complements the Gospel of John. If the Gospel of John introduces the Gospel and focuses on evangelism (John 3:16), then 1 John is a letter sent to those who believe (3:16). The Gospel of John says, "God is love. God so loved the world, He sent His only begotten Son, Jesus Christ, and whoever believes in Him will be saved." Whereas 1 John says, "God is love. Those of us who have received this amazing love must love each other."

The Gospel according to John focuses on the divinity of Jesus Christ, and 1 John focuses on the humanity of Jesus Christ. If the Gospel of John introduces Jesus who came from above from a vertical perspective, 1 John introduces Him from a horizontal perspective and tells us Christians to live a life of fellowship in Christ's love.

God Who is Light

The central message of 1 John is "God who is light." There is no darkness in God. Therefore, He tells us that we each must also walk in the light. To walk in the light means to live in fellowship: where we have fellowship in love, forgive, tolerate, and understand each other without resentment and hatred. First John also tells us that "God is love." He is not only the One who gives love, but He Himself is love. Therefore, John tells us, we who have become children of God must live in that love and serve each other with love.

First John corrects our faith by using the word "if" five times.

1. If we say that we have fellowship with God and walk in darkness, we deceive ourselves and do not practice the truth (1:6).
2. If we say we have no sin, we deceive ourselves, and the truth is not in us (1:8).
3. If we confess our sins, he is faithful and just to forgive us our sins and to cleanse us from all unrighteousness (1:9).
4. If we say we have not sinned, we make God a liar, and His word is not in us (1:10).
5. If we do sin, we have an advocate, Jesus Christ (2:1).

John also emphasizes three things to strengthen the foundation of the believer's faith.

First, do not separate Jesus' humanity and divinity.

Second, practice balanced spirituality. Spirituality must appear in everyday life. If we love God, we must love our brothers.

Third, the Christian life of faith is not an independent and isolated life from others, but it is a life of coexistence with others.

A Community of Fellowship

First John 1:1-2:2 lays out the "path of fellowship." This

passage is related to the words of John 1:1-18. The Gospel of John speaks of Jesus who came so that we may be in fellowship with God, and 1 John speaks of the fellowship among Christians who believe in Jesus Christ.

First John 1:1-3 is composed of a single sentence and its main verb is "proclaim." This is also the central message of 1 John. First John begins with fellowship between Jesus, the Word who came to earth, and Christians who believe in Jesus, and the joy of fellowship among Christians.

"The Church," where Christians gather together, is not a place where something is taught. It is a place where there is fellowship.

And if we are gathered together in Jesus Christ to share in the fellowship of joy, we must walk in the light (1:4-10). This is because God is light. To walk in the light means to confess our sins by forming a community of confession. There must be a confession of sins before God and a confession of sins among believers. Some sins are only to be confessed before the Lord, but that does not mean that we can say, "I have confessed my sins to God. That is enough." We must become a Church community that confesses to each other whenever there is need for forgiveness among believers. When we do this, as a community, we will experience the power of the blood of Jesus, the cleansing of sins, and joy in our relationships.

The Confession of Sin and Freedom

The passages of 1 John 1:8-2:2 and 1 John 3:6-9 appear to

oppose each other like the two sides of a coin. However, rather than being contradictory, they create balance and protect us from holding extreme views. One side takes a theological approach while the other takes an ethical approach.

The words of 1 John 1:8-2:2 correct our way of thinking about sin. John first speaks about those who claim to have no sin. What they are actually saying is that they have no moral obligation for their sins. We must not make excuses, try to justify, or avoid responsibility for our sins. The way to be freed from our sins is to humbly admit and confess our sins; it is up to God to forgive and cleanse us of our sins.

The second passage is about those who say that they have not sinned and, in fact, truly have not sinned. God tells us that "all men are sinners" (Rom. 3:9-18, 23). Men are not sinners because of the sins they have committed, but they sin because they are sinners. A sinner sins. This applies to the saved who believe in Jesus as well. However, we have our Helper (advocate, intercessor) Jesus Christ, who nullifies our sins so that we may have fellowship with God. Jesus is our legal counsel who defends us before God.

The phrase "No one who abides in him keeps on sinning" in 3:6-9 refers to an act of sin that is committed habitually and repeatedly. The verses here are referring to an attitude and behavior that is not willing to turn away from sin even after having sinned. A Christian cannot sin deliberately and habitually, and he cannot make sin a habit or a way of life. Even though a believer may sin, they cannot live their lives surrounded by an atmosphere of sin.

We are free from the punishment of sin in Jesus Christ. We are justified by God's grace, through the redemption that is in Christ Jesus (Rom. 3:24). Nevertheless, we are still fighting against sin and are still in the process of becoming sanctified. And one day, we will be completely freed from sin.

Salvation is a free gift, but in order to be sanctified, we have to continue to fight and pay the price with our lives every day. The outcome of this fight depends on whom it is that governs us. If we try to attain holiness by our own strength, we will be led by the flesh and only be left with the works of the flesh. However, if we are guided by the Holy Spirit, we will bear the fruit of the Holy Spirit (Gal. 5:15-24).

The passage of 1 John 3:6-9 does not tell us that those who abide in Jesus Christ can never sin, but that they cannot sin habitually and deliberately.

Stages of Spiritual Maturity

First John 2:12-14 reveals the characteristics of each of the stages of spiritual maturity. Spiritual children know about the forgiveness of sins and know God as their Father. Spiritual young adults have the Word of God dwelling in them, are strong, and will eventually triumph. The spiritual father knows the One who was from the beginning.

In 1:5-2:27, John lists seven characteristics that serve as evidence for a community of true Christians.

1. **A community of confession** (1:5-9) where the confession of sins takes place continually.

2. **A community of obedience to the Word** (2:3-6) where the Word is heard and obeyed.
3. **A community of love** (2:7-11) where everyone loves one another.
4. **A community of victory** (2:12-14) where everyone lives in triumph over sin.
5. **A community of holiness** (2:15-17) where there is no love for the things of this world.
6. **A community of Koinonia** (2:19) where everyone is in fellowship with one another.
7. **A community of the Holy Spirit** (2:20-27) where the truth is known with the Holy Spirit as its teacher.

In 4:10, John tells us that while other religions are man's pursuit of God, in Christianity, God is the One who searches for us. What should surprise us is that it was not due to our love for God but rather because of God's love for us that He sent His Son (Rom. 5:8). The glorious truth of Christianity is that God so loves the fallen man that He meets us so that we may be changed.

In 5:1-5, we are told that the evidence for a true Christian is his or her love for God. A true Christian loves Jesus Christ, the Son of God (5:1). A true Christian also loves God's children, Christians (5:2). Our love for God is manifested in the way we love our brothers (4:20-21). A true Christian obeys the Word (5:2-3), and with faith, overcomes this world (5:4-5).

In 5:6-8, John explains three aspects of Jesus' humanity. Water represents Jesus' coming as a man, blood represents

Jesus' death on the cross, and the Holy Spirit represents the Holy Spirit's descent like a dove upon Jesus.

In 5:13-20, believers are told to know and be assured of the following seven things because the Son of God came and gave us the ability to perceive.

1. Know that the believer has eternal life (Verse 13).
2. Know that God hears the prayers of believers (Verse 14).
3. Know that God has answered the prayers of believers (Verse 15).
4. Know that the believer is freed from the power of sin (Verse 18). Sin cannot defeat us because we are upheld by Jesus.
5. Know that the believer belongs to God (Verse 19). Therefore, we stand on the side of God with our backs turned to the world.
6. Know Him who is true, Jesus Christ. We know that he is the true God and that He is the Son of God (Verse 20).
7. Know that the believer is in Jesus Christ (Verse 20). Without guessing, we have confidence in the truth. Speculation disappears and there is only knowledge of which we are fully assured. We know who we are, where we are, where we are going, and for what we are in this world.

Outline

Chapters 1-2	Abide in God's light
Chapter 1:1-4	Introduction
Chapters 1:5-2:2	A community of fellowship
Chapter 2:3-29	A community of obedience
Chapters 3-5	Abide in God's love
Chapter 3	A community of love
Chapter 4	A community that abides in love
Chapter 5:1-12	A community of life in the Son
Chapter 5:13-21	A community of confident believers

Voice Outline

1 AND 2 AND 3 JOHN

100-Day Bible Reading Plan

		CHECK
Day 99	1 Peter, 2 Peter, 1 John, 2 John, 3 John, Jude	☐

2 AND 3 JOHN

2 JOHN - DO NOT RECEIVE INTO YOUR HOUSE
3 JOHN - RECEIVE INTO YOUR HOUSE

The author of the books of 2 John and 3 John introduces himself as an "elder." Both books were written by the same individual. "The elder to the elect lady and her children..." (2 John 1:1), "The elder to the beloved Gaius, whom I love in truth" (3 John 1:1).

Here, the word elder refers more to the author's age rather than the title that is used for an office in the Church. However, it is evident that the author was a man who was admired by a great number of churches for his character. The only surviving member of the disciples of Jesus at the time, John the Apostle, was such a man.

The two epistles have similar opening and closing remarks.

The opening remarks for 2 and 3 John are "I rejoiced greatly to find some of your children walking in the truth, just as we were commanded by the Father" (2 John 1:4) and "For I rejoiced greatly when the brothers came and testified to your truth, as indeed you are walking in the truth. I have no greater joy than to hear that my children are walking in the truth" (3 John 1:3-4). The closing remarks are "Though I have much to write to you, I would rather not use paper and ink. Instead I hope to come to you and talk face to face, so that our joy may be complete" (2 John 1:12), and "I had much to write to you, but I would rather not write with pen and ink. I hope to see you soon, and we will talk face to face." (3 John 1:13-14).

All three epistles of John share the common theme of "Christian fellowship," but each of the epistles approaches the topic from a different perspective.

Second John tells us, "Shut the door. Do not be in fellowship." In other words, John is telling Christians to keep false prophets and evildoers out of their homes and not to associate with them. On the other hand, 3 John tells us, "Open the door." In other words, John is telling us to always open our homes and be hospitable to all ministers who are working hard and striving for the Gospel. These two epistles together tell us exactly to whom we should have our doors closed and not associate, and to whom we should always have our doors open and be open to fellowship, entertain, and serve.

Second John	Third John
Close the Door	**Open the Door**
Do not receive into your home	Receive into your home and support
Walk in love	Imitate good
Keep the truth	Welcome brothers
Shun false teaching	Do good
Bad example: false teachers	Bad example: Diotrephes
Good example: the lady and her children	Good example: Demetrius
Joint message: refuse false teachers	Serve true teachers

There are many other similarities in the three epistles of John. 1 John 4:3 and 2 John 1:7 mention the antichrist, who denies the coming of Jesus in the flesh. There is no mention of this in 3 John, but these three letters address the same circumstances, dangers, and people.

"And every spirit that does not confess Jesus (Jesus' coming in the flesh) is not from God. This is the spirit of the antichrist" (1 John 4:3). "For many deceivers have gone out into the world, those who do not confess the coming of Jesus Christ in the flesh. Such a one is the deceiver and the antichrist" (2 John 1:7).

Traveling Evangelist

At the time the three epistles were written, there were people called traveling evangelists who did not settle in one place but traveled to teach the Word in different places. They were either teachers of the Word or prophets. Although many of them were true teachers, some among them were false teachers. In particular, the Gnostics were representative false teachers. They denied the coming of Jesus Christ in the flesh, and were preoccupied with theological knowledge rather than acting or doing, in truth.

This is the reason why the verb "do" appears in so many of the verses in all three epistles of John. The Book of 2 John tells Christians not to receive particularly the false teachers and prophets among the traveling evangelists into their homes. The Book of 3 John tells us to receive the true teachers and prophets among the traveling ministers, to welcome them into our homes, and to support them so that they can do the work well.

Demetrius is a leader of the traveling ministers. Therefore, John tells us to receive ministers like him and serve them well. He also gives the name, Diotrephes, as a bad example of someone who did not serve these ministers. Not only did Diotrephes refuse to accept traveling ministers, he also tried to expel from the church those who received them into their homes.

Hospitality was regarded as one of the virtues of a church leader. In 1 Timothy 3:2, it is stated, "Therefore an overseer must be... hospitable;" in Titus 1:7-8, it is written, "For an overseer, as God's steward, must be··· hospitable, a lover of good." Furthermore, Romans 12:13 says, "Contribute to the needs of the saints and seek to show hospitality." Here the word "seek" means to say that we must practice showing hospitality. We need to be active in our hospitality and not be reserved or have a passive attitude citing our environment or personal issues as reasons. We need to practice hospitality until it comes naturally to us.

The passage of Hebrews 13:1-2, "Let brotherly love continue. Do not neglect to show hospitality to strangers, for thereby some have entertained angels unawares" is a statement made with Abraham in mind. Abraham welcomed and served passing strangers with sincerity. It was the result of his hospitality that he was promised Isaac by God (Gen. 18:1-15).

Four figures appear in the Book of 3 John who represent people in the Church. John represents the apostle, Demetrius represents traveling evangelists, Diotrephes represents the local leader who refuses to serve and interferes with the work of ministers, and Gaius represents the local leader who welcomes and serves the traveling evangelists.

Spiritual Principles of the Life of Faith

Third John 1:2 speaks of the spiritual principle of the life of faith, "Beloved, I pray that all may go well with you and that you may be in good health, as it goes well with your soul." In order for our body to be strong, our soul must first do well. To live a successful life, our soul must first be well. This verse tells us that when we live in close intimacy with God, we will live a successful life in the world, and our bodies will also be strong. But the world has this backward. The world emphasizes the health of the physical body that is always visible to the eye. However, our priority should first be our soul, then everything else, and finally the body.

It is also written in 1 Timothy 4:7-8, "Train yourself for godliness; for while bodily training is of some value, godliness is of value in every way, as it holds promise for the present life and also for the life to come." As it is written in Ephesians 3:16, "That according to the riches of his glory he may grant you to be strengthened with power through his Spirit in your inner being," the strength of our inner being comes first.

We should set our priorities in life in the following order: first, the soul becomes well through a close relationship with God; second, everything becomes well with a successful and prosperous life; and lastly, the body becomes healthy through physical wellbeing. Therefore, in order for the soul to be well, we must prioritize fellowship with the Lord as our top priority in our daily lives.

Outline

2 John	
Chapter 1:1-4	Acting in truth brings joy
Verses 5-6	Love one another
Verses 7-11	Do not receive into your house
Verses 12-13	Let us share the joy face to face

3 John	
Chapter 1:1-4	Acting in truth brings joy - Gaius
Verses 5-8	Receive into your house
Verses 9-11	An example of evil: Diotrephes
Verse 12	A good example: Demetrius
Verses 13-15	Hope to soon meet

Voice Outline

1 AND 2 AND 3 JOHN

100-Day Bible Reading Plan

		CHECK
Day 99	1 Peter, 2 Peter, 1 John, 2 John, 3 John, Jude	☐

JUDE

FIGHT FOR FAITH

Jude is a short book comprising a single chapter. In terms of content, it is closely related to the Book of 2 Peter and contains similar teachings about false teachers. The examples it uses from the Old Testament are very similar to those that are used in 2 Peter 2:3-3:4. As a result, the Book of Jude with the Book of 2 Peter complement each other well when read together.

The author of Jude is the brother of James, as stated in Chapter 1 Verse 1. James is the brother of Christ and the author of the Book of James. Several Judes appear in the Bible, but the author of this particular book is Jude, the brother of Jesus. The recipients of this epistle are "those who are called, beloved in God the Father and kept for Jesus Christ."

Warning against Heretics

The Book of Jude contains some very harsh words. James Moffat refers to the book as "a sort of fiery cross sent through the churches."

The Book of Jude gives strict warnings against those who deny Jesus Christ and those who use God's grace as an excuse for indulgence. In particular, the book explains very clearly what heresy is and warns against heretics. Throughout the Church's history, there have always been heretics who can be identified by the following markers:

- They are antinomians.
- They abuse grace.
- Like Sodom, they indulge in sexual immorality.
- They do not regard sin as sin.
- They live by their instincts like animals.
- They are driven by lust.
- They deny God and Jesus Christ.
- They even deny the existence of angels
- They are Gnostics. The Book of Jude once again warns against Gnosticism.

Taking Israel's history as an example, Jude strongly warns against such people. Though the Israelites safely made it out of Egypt, they were not able to enter the Promised Land because of their lack of faith. The author also uses the example of Sodom and Gomorrah's destruction by fire. This book reminds us that we must take lessons from them and stay vigilant. In particular, Verse 11 uses three examples to give us a warning. It warns us to beware of the way of Cain, Balaam's error, and Korah's rebellion.

1. Beware the Way of Cain

Cain's way is explained in Genesis 4. The way of Cain

is laden with envy, jealousy, rivalry, hatred, and cynicism toward his brother. A life that is atheistic and unbelieving in all respects, behaves at will, and is not centered on God is called life in "the way of Cain."

2. Beware the Crooked Ways of Balaam

Balaam's actions are illustrated in Numbers 22-25. Balaam is a quintessential example of a person who did not follow God's will and ignored God's will for material's sake. Jude tells us not to easily give in to material things, not to compromise for it, and to live solely for the will of the Lord by submitting entirely to His will.

3. Beware of Korah's Rebellion

Korah's rebellious acts are illustrated in Numbers 16. He is an archetypal figure of one who disregarded authority. He was the one who mobilized several people to openly fight against his leaders, Moses and Aaron. They ignored their authority, did not know that there was a God, and acted in the ways of man. As a result, Korah and his followers were swallowed up into the ground.

We must have a deep understanding of authority, look to God who gave the authority, and act with a fear of the Lord. Moreover, those in authority must think of the will of God who gave them their authority, and exercise it with humility to give life and abundance to their subjects. Authority figures must also ensure that their authority is well used to set them free and restore them. When the authority given to us is disregarded by others, we must know how to leave everything to God in silence and meekness, and learn to go before the Lord.

Characteristics of Heresy

Jude 1:12-13 continues to list the indicators of heretics.

- Reefs. They are like the hidden reefs that have sunk many ships.
- Shepherds who only feed themselves. They destroy Christian fellowship by creating a sect. They do not know the meaning of the broader fellowship and the Church. They take care of themselves over the sheep for which they are responsible.
- Waterless clouds, swept along by winds. They deceive others with false oaths, like clouds that trick those who are longing for rain.
- Fruitless trees in late autumn, twice dead, uprooted. They are like trees that cannot be harvested because they do not have fruits or roots.
- Wild waves of the sea, casting up the foam of their own shame. They spew shameful behavior as the rough waves of the sea spew out bubbles and leave the wreck of a ship on the shore.
- Wandering stars, for whom the gloom of utter darkness has been reserved. They disobey God in their arrogance and will perish on the path they take like stars that deviate from orbit and eventually die.

Their destruction was foretold long ago by Enoch (1:14-15).

God will execute judgment on the ungodly to convict them of their ungodly deeds. Jude repeats the word "ungodly" four times just in Verse 15. "(The Lord comes) to execute judgment on all and to convict all the ungodly of all their deeds of ungodliness that they have committed in such an ungodly way, and of all the harsh things that ungodly sinners have spoken against him."

"Godly" and "ungodly" are very important words. Verse 16 lists the traits of the ungodly: they are grumblers, malcontents, following their own sinful desires; they are loud-mouthed boasters, and show favoritism to gain advantage.

To conclude, Jude gives a word of counsel to those who believe (1:17-23). "Remember the predictions of the apostles of our Lord Jesus Christ. They said to you, 'In the last time there will be scoffers, following their own ungodly passions.'"

These people will cause divisions and act according to the passions of their sin-stained flesh because they are devoid of the Holy Spirit. So, we as Christians must fulfill the following five godly duties:

1. Build our lives on holy faith.
2. Pray with the Holy Spirit.
3. Remain within the love of God
4. Wait for the mercy of our Lord Jesus Christ to reach eternal life.
5. Have mercy on some who doubt. Bring them out of the fire and save them. Hate even the garments that are stained with the flesh, but have mercy on them with fear.

The book of Jude closes with a marvelous doxology

praising God.

"Now to him who is able to keep you from stumbling and to present you blameless before the presence of his glory with great joy, to the only God, our Savior, through Jesus Christ our Lord, be glory, majesty, dominion, and authority, before all time and now and forever. Amen." (1:24-25)

Outline

Chapter 1:1-2	Greetings
Verses 3-4	Reason for writing
Verses 5-11	Previous acts that were punished by God Israel in the wilderness, fallen angels, Sodom and Gomorrah, lawlessness, Cain, Balaam, Korah
Verses 12-19	Traits of false teachers and the consequence of their actions
Verses 20-23	Comfort and encouragement for those who believe
Verses 24-25	Conclusion: doxology

Voice Outline

JUDE

100-Day Bible Reading Plan

Day 99	1 Peter, 2 Peter, 1 John, 2 John, 3 John, Jude	CHECK

REVELATION

THE DRAMA OF THE REVELATION OF JESUS CHRIST

The Book of Revelation is the most amazing book among all the wonderful books of the Bible. It is also the book that has attracted the most attention. When we think of the Book of Revelation, "666, Armageddon, the Mark of the Beast, the Dragon, the Millennial Kingdom, and the seven-year Great Tribulation" all immediately come to mind. It is considered a very scary and terrifying book and is referenced with negative connotations and imagery.

But these are not at all what the Book of Revelation is about. This book begins with the glory of Jesus Christ. It introduces the Victor, the Savior, and the radiantly dignified King of beautiful glory (1:9-20). Then, it continues with praises to the King of amazing glory. Revelation describes four living creatures and the twenty-four elders bowing down before God in worship, the song of many angels, and every creature in heaven, on earth, under the earth, on the sea, and everything in them singing praises to the Lord.

The content of the book of Revelation is factual. But it is just not a record of history. It is also not literal; the Book of

Revelation is symbolic, metaphorical, and figurative. It is like an elaborate cipher text. Its symbols are colors and animals, and sometimes people and animals. Numbers also carry a symbolic meaning. This kind of format was common at the time the Book of Revelation was written. Today, books such as *The Lord of the Rings* and *The Chronicles of Narnia* fall into this genre.

Jesus Stands among the Lampstands

The structure of the Book of Revelation is well illustrated in verses 1:1-3.

Chapter 1 describes "what John saw: events that will surely take place soon." The introduction (1:1-3), God of the Trinity (1:4-8), Jesus of Glory (1:9-20), are actually a prelude to chapters 2 and 3. Chapter 1, together with chapters 2 and 3, comprise a single storyline that ends only in 3:22.

Chapters 2 and 3 describe "what is happening now: the events that will take place in the seven churches." Chapters 2 and 3 are not standalone chapters but are organically linked to the entire Book of Revelation. The names of Jesus, praise and reproof, listening to the words of the Holy Spirit, and promises for those who overcome are listed in a set format. The message for the seven churches in these chapters is a message given to today's churches as well.

After Chapter 4, John describes "the things to come." These are future events not written in chronological order but recorded in the order necessary to write the book. This is the same as how the seven churches mentioned in chapters 2 and 3 do not represent the seven sequential stages of church history.

The Message of the Book of Revelation

What God has planned will surely be fulfilled through His wisdom, insight, and providence. Only God is in charge of history. God put Jesus Christ at the center of history and placed the Church as Jesus' partner.

Reading the Book of Revelation along with the books of Daniel and Ezekiel can be of great help in understanding this greater scheme. This book is one that provides hope and encouragement to Christians in difficult times. It is the message that the catacomb church received while under persecution by the Soviet Communist state: "My children, you may face hardship, but be bold. I have already won. I will soon reveal my salvation."

The Soviet Union disappeared into the pages of history after 70 years. Just as Christians in captivity in Babylon heard God's message through Ezekiel and Daniel, Christians under persecution in Rome heard God through the Book of Revelation. And God continues to speak through the Book of Revelation to all Christians who are suffering for their faith in all ages.

The Book of Revelation is not just about the time of Jesus' Second Coming. God's sovereignty over the world is the central message of the book. The time of Revelation is not Chronos, which is the human concept of time, but Kairos, the time of God. This records time by important moments or moments of change. The time of the end is not a matter of when or what time, but rather it is a time of God's sovereign providence, wisdom, and insight.

For example, when John the Baptist says in Mark 1:15, "The time is fulfilled, and the Kingdom of God is at hand," "time" refers to Kairos, not Chronos. He is talking about the "time" when everything is shaped into a new order and God's work is believed in and accepted. It is referring to the time when what God had planned even before the creation of the universe will come true.

A Book of Praise

The Book of Revelation contains many praises and psalms. Its praises are filled with shouts of victory. The Book of Revelation can be broadly divided into seven songs of praise.

1. The Song of Creation (4:10-11). It is praise to God who created all things.
2. The Song of Redemption (5:8-14). It is praise to Jesus Christ, the Lamb who was slain, who by His blood ransomed people for God from every tribe and language and people and nation, and made them a kingdom and priests to our God.
3. The Song of Salvation (7:9-12). It is the beautiful, brilliant, and magnificent praise that the crowd of people who were saved after the Gospel was spread to the ends of the earth sings to God. A great multitude that no one could number, from every nation, from all tribes and peoples and languages, standing before the throne and before

the Lamb, clothed in white robes, with palm branches in their hands cry out in praise for their salvation. This imagery shows us the ultimate goal of global missions.

4. The Song of Victory (12:10-12). It is praise that is sung to God as a song of victory, for through the cross of Jesus Christ and the Lamb, the war is won and the spirits of darkness have been forever defeated.
5. The Song of Moses or The Song of the Lamb (15:2-4). It is the song of worship and praise sung by all nations who have come to the Lord upon hearing the Gospel.
6. The Song about the End of History (19:1-5). It is the praise of those who fear the Lord singing of His salvation, glory, and power after the Babylonians, who represent the world, and all those against God have been destroyed.
7. The Song of the Marriage Supper of the Lamb (19:6-10). After the end of history and at the beginning of the eternal kingdom, God invites all people to the wedding banquet of the Lamb. It is the song of the great multitude rejoicing and worshipping the Almighty God.

Grand Opera

The book of Revelation is like a grand opera, composed entirely of seven acts and seven chapters. The opera has a dramatic parallel structure that reveals the eschatological point of view in between Jesus' coming and His return.

Chapters 4 and 5 are where the story really picks up and the stage is set with a scene that begins with the opening of the skies. The opera does not begin in darkness, judgment, tribulation, and suffering on earth, but with God who sits on His glorious throne. This scene also reveals the beauty and wonder of Jesus Christ the Lamb of God. The final act, chapters 21 and 22, depicts a scene of the saved basking in the glory, joy, beauty, and fullness of God who sits on the throne, and Jesus Christ the Lamb.

As indicated by these images, the Book of Revelation is filled with the singing of the victory, glory, and salvation of Jesus Christ, as well as the amazing salvation and restoration of believers on this earth. On the other hand, Revelation also tells us that the spirit of darkness will completely collapse and be utterly destroyed.

Seven Churches and Seven Blessings

Chapters 2 and 3 describe the seven churches of Asia Minor, and each of these churches represents the Church in the course of History. The church in Laodicea is never praised while the three churches in Smyrna, Philadephia, and Thyatira are never admonished.

- Church in Ephesus: Do the works you did at first (2:1-7).
- Church in Smyrna: Be faithful unto death (2:8-11).
- Church in Pergamum: Repent (2:12-17).
- Church in Thyatira: Hold fast what you have (2:18-29).
- Church in Sardis: Strengthen what remains (3:1-6).
- Church in Philadelphia: Hold fast what you have (3:7-13).
- Church in Laodicea: Buy from me gold, white garments, and salve for your eyes (3:14-22).

Revelation has seven blessings just like the Beatitudes in the Gospel of Matthew.

1. Blessed are those who hear the Word and keep it (1:3).
2. Blessed are those who die in the Lord (14:13).
3. Blessed is the one who stays awake (16:15).
4. Blessed are those who are invited to the marriage supper of the Lamb (19:9).
5. Blessed is the one who shares in the first resurrection (20:6).
6. Blessed is the one who keeps the words of the prophecy of this book (22:7).
7. Blessed are those who wash their robes (22:14).

We also see that numbers are important in the Book of Revelation.

- 3-Refers to the trinity: the number of unity
- 4-Refers to the four corners of the world: the number of universality
- 7-The number of accomplishment as the Lord rested on this day after creation
- 10-The number of completeness
- 12-Refers to the people of God: the twelve tribes and the twelve apostles
- 1,000- Refers to a multitude: the multitude of the saved that no one could number

Understanding the Four Perspectives

One's understanding of Revelation differs depending on how one views the seven-year Great Tribulation, the

Millennium Kingdom, the Second Coming of Christ, and the eternal life of salvation for all believers.

The first perspective is called the preterist view. It is a perspective that sees all the events of Revelation as having already been fulfilled during the time of the Roman Empire.

The second perspective is called the historicist view. This view holds that the Book of Revelation is a panoramic representation of the history of the Church from the time of the Early Church to the Second Coming of Jesus.

The third perspective is called the spiritual view. In this view, all events in the book of Revelation are expressions, not realities, and are thus an allegorical portrayal of the spiritual war between good and evil.

The fourth perspective is called the futuristic view. The entire Book of Revelation is viewed as a description of future events that will take place in the end times.

Depending on which view is taken, there are different interpretations of when the Millennium Kingdom will come and to what it refers.

- **The premillennial theory**: Teaches that the Millennium Kingdom will begin after the Second Coming of Jesus. This theory then diverges into the two separate theories of pre-tribulational premillennialism and post-tribulational premillennialism.
  - Pre-tribulational premillennialism

    It is a futurist view that there will be the seven-year Great Tribulation before the Lord's Second Coming, and Christians will rule for a thousand years after the

Second Coming. Then there will be a final judgment and eternal reign.

- Post-tribulational premillennialism

This is another futurist view that teaches that the Millennial Kingdom will be ruled by Christians after the Second Coming. After the millennium, there will be the seven-year Great Tribulation, and after that, the Lord's Last Judgment, and then the eternal rule of the Lord.

- **The postmillennialist theory**: This theory holds that Jesus will return after the Millennium Kingdom. It refers to a thousand years as a concept of time, where there will be a thousand years of peace and justice before the Second Coming and then there will be judgment and eternal reign after the Second Coming. This theory tends to look at the Millennial Kingdom from a preterist or historicist point of view.
- **Amillennialist theory**: This theory teaches that there is no other Millennium Kingdom, but that the time between Jesus' first and second coming is the Millennium Kingdom. They hold that the kingdom of a numerical thousand years has no meaning, and take a spiritual view of the Millennium Kingdom where the thousand years mentioned in Revelation is symbolic and spiritual in meaning referring to the span of time between Jesus' resurrection and the Second Coming, after which judgment and eternal reign will take place.

The End Times

The Book of Revelation gives us a good illustration of the end times. However, Revelation's focus when dealing with the end times is not on fear, judgment, or the Beast, but rather on a time of separation. While some will ascend to the highest of heavens, some will fall into the deepest abyss of Hell. The end times is the end of Satan. God is eternal. It is the beginning of eternity for the Church that believes in him, but the end for Satan.

Revelation gives us a glimpse of the glory and victory of God and Jesus in advance, allowing Christians living in this time to overcome all trials and suffering and wait for the glory of heaven with patience. Just as hell actually exists and will reveal itself, heaven, where the throne of God and Jesus Christ the Lamb are at the center, also exists.

Whenever we look at the Book of Revelation, what should leave the greatest imprint on our hearts is the opening of heaven, the God of glory, Jesus of glory, and Christians who are victorious in faith on earth. The spirit of darkness will surely be defeated and be subjected to eternal destruction and all believers will live with the Lord in glory forever.

Outline

Chapter 1	Things that you have seen - Jesus who stands among the lampstands
Chapters 2-3	Things that are - Messages for the seven churches
Chapters 4-22	Things that are to take place
Chapter 4	The throne of God
Chapter 5	Jesus Christ who is the Lamb
Chapters 6-19	God's anger and the Great Tribulation
Chapter 20	The Millennial Kingdom
Chapters 21-22	New heaven and new earth

Voice Outline

REVELATION

100-Day Bible Reading Plan

		CHECK
Day 100	Revelation	☐

NCMN
The Word: Cover to Cover in 100 Days Movement

The revival of the Early Church in Acts sets an example for us in many ways.

First, it is an example of change in the life of the individual. The revival of the Early Church is not just an increase in the number of believers, but in the number of changed Christians. There was marked change in the lives of individuals.

Second, it is an example of the formation of a church community. The Early Church is not just a gathering of believers, but a community of love and passion. They shared their material possessions and worshipped God with all their hearts. The beautiful life they shared has been praised by people around the world.

Third, it is an example of change in the social community. The Gospel did not simply stay with individuals and churches; instead it changed the very nature and structure of society. It created justice, honesty, truth, holiness, and love in society. Idols were removed and a Christ-centric culture was formed.

Fourth, it is an example of passion for lost souls. This passion opened the way for evangelism and missions, and the Gospel reached farther and farther.

The key to this revival comes from three things.

The first is "prayer." The Early Church devoted itself to prayer. They prayed in their free time and they prayed during fixed times. Peter and John set 3 pm as their time in prayer. After he preached, Peter went up to the attic and prayed while the others prepared lunch.

The second is "the Holy Spirit." The early church longed for the presence of the Holy Spirit. The fullness of the Holy Spirit that came to Jerusalem at Pentecost (Acts 2) caused the Holy Spirit to come upon Samaria (Acts 8) and Ephesus (Acts 19) and the home of Cornelius, a Roman officer (Acts 10). The Holy Spirit is the driving force of revivals.

The third is "the Word." The Word flourished. The church in Jerusalem had a great influence because the Word continued to increase (Acts 6:7). The Word became the foundation of the church in Antioch that led World Mission (Acts 12:24). In Ephesus, one of the most central cities in Asia Minor, the revival of the Word led those who practiced magic arts to bring their books together and burn them. Those magic books were extremely costly items. This caused a disturbance in the city of Ephesus (Acts 19:20) where the School of Tyrannus was located.

God's Word, the Bible, edifies our lives and renews the structure of our society. This is because the Bible sets the standard for what is right. God's Word is like a fire that melts and refines, like a chisel that breaks and defines, like a sharp surgical knife, and like a navigation compass that guides the way. It presents the way not just for individuals and churches, but for societies and nations.

Prominent kings who led the revival in the Jewish kingdoms were David, Asa, Jehoshaphat, Joash, Hezekiah, and Josiah. Their revivals were characterized by the change they brought not only to individuals and communities but also to society and the nation as a whole. And even then it was the Word of God that strengthened and expanded this revival. Now is the time we need the Word of God. We need the Bible at the level of the individual, the church community, the society, and the nation. If individuals and the church community first thrive and flourish with the Word, then the revival of society and the nation will soon follow.

To this end, NCMN is heading 'the Word: Cover to Cover in 100 Days Movement' and 'Shema Bible School.' It is beneficial to read through the whole Bible alongside *The Word: Cover to Cover in 100 Days*. Reading the Bible aloud has several benefits. We can see with our eyes, make sounds with our mouths, and hear with our ears to triple the effect of the Word because we can see, read, and hear all at the same time. That is how the Bible should be read, cover to cover and aloud.

And I hope that you will not only read the Word alone but that you will lead the people around you to do the same. It is written in Ecclesiastes 4:12, "A threefold cord is not quickly broken." Let us participate in the Cover to Cover movement in groups of three or four. As we encourage and pray for each other, let us pray for the Word to first touch us, then the Church, then society, and then, the entire nation. Let us read the Word, pray, and seek the power of the Holy Spirit. If you read the entire Bible every 100 days, you can read it more than three times a year.

Through *The Word: Cover to Cover in 100 Days*, you will experience the amazing power of God both in your personal and family life. With your passion for God's Word, the church community, and even society and the nation will see the glory of God.

100-DAY BIBLE
READING SCHEDULE

Day	Today's Scripture	Check	Prayer	Devotion
Day 1	Genesis 1 - 10			
Day 2	Genesis 11 - 20			
Day 3	Genesis 21 - 30			
Day 4	Genesis 31 - 40			
Day 5	Genesis 41 - 50			
Day 6	Exodus 1 - 10			
Day 7	Exodus 11 - 20			
Day 8	Exodus 21 - 30			
Day 9	Exodus 31 - 40			
Day 10	Leviticus 1 - 10			
Day 11	Leviticus 11 - 16			
Day 12	Leviticus 17 - 27			
Day 13	Numbers 1 - 10			
Day 14	Numbers 11 - 20			
Day 15	Numbers 21 - 36			
Day 16	Deuteronomy 1 - 11			
Day 17	Deuteronomy 12 - 26			
Day 18	Deuteronomy 27 - 34			
Day 19	Joshua 1 - 12			
Day 20	Joshua 13 - 24			
Day 21	Judges 1 - 11			
Day 22	Judges 12 - 21			
Day 23	Ruth 1 - 1 Samuel 7			
Day 24	1 Samuel 8 - 15			
Day 25	1 Samuel 16 - 31			

Day	Today's Scripture	Check	Prayer	Devotion
Day 26	2 Samuel 1 - 10			
Day 27	2 Samuel 11 - 20			
Day 28	2 Samuel 21 - 1 Kings 2			
Day 29	1 Kings 3 - 11			
Day 30	1 Kings 12 - 22			
Day 31	2 Kings 1 - 8			
Day 32	2 Kings 9 - 17			
Day 33	2 Kings 18 - 25			
Day 34	1 Chronicles 1 - 10			
Day 35	1 Chronicles 11 - 20			
Day 36	1 Chronicles 21 - 29			
Day 37	2 Chronicles 1 - 10			
Day 38	2 Chronicles 11 - 20			
Day 39	2 Chronicles 21 - 28			
Day 40	2 Chronicles 29 - 36			
Day 41	Ezra 1 - 10			
Day 42	Nehemiah 1 - 13			
Day 43	Esther 1 - 10			
Day 44	Job 1 - 10			
Day 45	Job 11 - 20			
Day 46	Job 21 - 30			
Day 47	Job 31 - 42			
Day 48	Psalms 1 - 20			
Day 49	Psalms 21 - 40			
Day 50	Psalms 41 - 60			
Day 51	Psalms 61 - 80			
Day 52	Psalms 81 - 100			

Day	Today's Scripture	Check	Prayer	Devotion
Day 53	Psalms 101 - 120			
Day 54	Psalms 121 - 150			
Day 55	Proverbs 1 - 10			
Day 56	Proverbs 11 - 20			
Day 57	Proverbs 21 - 31			
Day 58	Ecclesiastes 1 - 12			
Day 59	Song of Solomon 1 - 8			
Day 60	Isaiah 1 - 12			
Day 61	Isaiah 13 - 25			
Day 62	Isaiah 26 - 38			
Day 63	Isaiah 39 - 52			
Day 64	Isaiah 53 - 66			
Day 65	Jeremiah 1 - 13			
Day 66	Jeremiah 14 - 25			
Day 67	Jeremiah 26 - 33			
Day 68	Jeremiah 34 - 45			
Day 69	Jeremiah 46 - 52, Lamentations			
Day 70	Ezekiel 1 - 11			
Day 71	Ezekiel 12 - 24			
Day 72	Ezekiel 25 - 39			
Day 73	Ezekiel 40 - 48			
Day 74	Daniel 1 - 12			
Day 75	Hosea 1 - 14			
Day 76	Joel, Amos, Obadiah, Jonah			
Day 77	Micah, Nahum, Habakkuk, Zephaniah			

Day	Today's Scripture	Check	Prayer	Devotion
Day 78	Haggai, Zechariah, Malachi			
Day 79	Matthew 1 - 10			
Day 80	Matthew 11 - 18			
Day 81	Matthew 19 - 28			
Day 82	Mark 1 - 9			
Day 83	Mark 10 - 16			
Day 84	Luke 1 - 9			
Day 85	Luke 10 - 19			
Day 86	Luke 20 - 24			
Day 87	John 1 - 11			
Day 88	John 12 - 21			
Day 89	Acts 1 - 10			
Day 90	Acts 11 - 20			
Day 91	Acts 21 - 28			
Day 92	Romans 1 - 16			
Day 93	1 Corinthians 1 - 16			
Day 94	2 Corinthians 1 - 13			
Day 95	Galatians, Ephesians			
Day 96	Philippians, Colossians, 1 Thessalonians, 2 Thessalonians			
Day 97	1 Timothy, 2 Timothy, Titus, Philemon			
Day 98	Hebrews, James			
Day 99	1 Peter, 2 Peter, 1 John, 2 John, 3 John, Jude			
Day 100	Revelation			

"Let Us Read the Heart of God;
Let Us Hear the Word of the Lord!"